PERSONS

AND

PASSIONS

PERSONS
AND
PASSIONS

Essays in Honor of Annette Baier

EDITED BY

Joyce Jenkins, Jennifer Whiting,
and Christopher Williams

University of Notre Dame Press
Notre Dame Indiana

Library of Congress Cataloging-in-Publication Data

Persons and passions : essays in honor of Annette Baier / edited by Joyce Jenkins,
Jennifer Whiting, and Christopher Williams.
    p. cm.
  Includes index.
  ISBN 0-268-03263-7 (cloth : alk. paper)
    1. Philosophy—United states. 2. Hume, David, 1711–1776. 3. Descartes,
René, 1596–1650. 4. Ethics. 5. Baier, Annette. I. Baier, Annette. II. Jenkins,
Joyce, 1958–   III. Whiting, Jennifer. IV. Williams, Christopher, 1960–
  B893.P47 2005
  190—dc22

                                                              2005010254

CONTENTS

CONTRIBUTORS

DONALD AINSLIE
Associate Professor of Philosophy, University of Toronto

LILLI ALANEN
Professor of Philosophy, Uppsala University

WILLIAM BEARDSLEY
Professor of Philosophy, University of Puget Sound

JANET BROUGHTON
Professor of Philosophy, University of California, Berkeley

DAVID GAUTHIER
Distinguished Service Professor of Philosophy Emeritus,
University of Pittsburgh

JOYCE JENKINS
Associate Professor of Philosophy, University of Manitoba

KAREN JONES
Lecturer in Philosophy, University of Melbourne

ALASDAIR MACINTYRE
Senior Research Professor of Philosophy, University of Notre Dame

MICHELE MOODY-ADAMS
Professor of Philosophy and Hutchinson Professor of Ethics and
Public Life, Cornell University

AMY MORGAN SCHMITTER
Associate Professor of Philosophy, University of New Mexico

LISA SHAPIRO
Assistant Professor of Philosophy, Simon Fraser University

ROBERT SHAVER
Professor of Philosophy, University of Manitoba

SERGIO TENENBAUM
Associate Professor of Philosophy, University of Toronto

SAUL TRAIGER
Professor of Philosophy, Occidental College

CECILIA WEE
Assistant Professor of Philosophy, National University of Singapore

JENNIFER WHITING
Chancellor Jackman Professor of Philosophy, University of Toronto

CHRISTOPHER WILLIAMS
Associate Professor of Philosophy, University of Nevada, Reno

CHAPTER I

Persons and Passions

An Introduction

CHRISTOPHER WILLIAMS

The papers in this volume are intended to honor the career of Annette
Baier by presenting a body of philosophical work that has been inspired by
Baier's own. Some offer revisionist interpretations of Descartes and Hume,
the two historical figures that have most influenced Baier, and about whom
she herself has written extensively. The influence of these figures is evident
in Baier's nonhistorical work in ethics and the philosophy of mind, and
some of the papers here take as their point of departure the contemporary
discussions that Baier has helped to pioneer. It is no surprise that the papers
in this volume, like the thinking that inspired them, suggest novel connections between topics in both the history and the ongoing practice of philosophy. In each area, however, the concepts of *persons* and *passions* are especially
salient, and I shall devote most of this introduction to tracing the lines that
connect these key concepts, not only in the contributors' papers but also (no
less importantly) in Baier's work itself.

The person who provokes the various intellectual passions that are on
display here, Annette Baier, was born in 1929 in Queenstown, New Zealand.
After receiving her undergraduate degree from the University of Otago, she
went to Oxford where she earned her B. Phil. by writing a thesis under the

supervision of J. L. Austin, the thinker who, in Baier's words, showed her the virtue of "fidelity to complex facts."[1] Several teaching positions followed, in Australia, Scotland, and America, but the longest and by far the most important phase of Baier's professional activity was at the University of Pittsburgh, where she taught from 1973 until her retirement in 1995. (Some of the papers here were initially presented at a conference held in Pittsburgh in October 1995, on the eve of Baier's retirement.)

It was in Pittsburgh that Baier's signature views were articulated and refined for publication. Much of her work has consisted of articles, some of which have been republished in her two collections, *Postures of the Mind* and *Moral Prejudices*. She has written a book-length study of Hume's *Treatise* called *A Progress of Sentiments*, and she was the first woman to give the Carus Lectures, which have been published as *The Commons of the Mind*. In 1990 she was elected President of the Eastern Division of the American Philosophical Association, one of only a few women to be so honored in the first hundred years of the association's history.

Let us now take up Baier's themes more directly. At the usual risk of oversimplification, there is, first of all, Baier's *naturalism*, which we might regard as the master theme, albeit one that requires a certain amount of commentary if it is to be intelligible. Naturalism is a concept of variable and uncertain meaning when philosophers make use of it, and much of its unclarity arises because it is a reactive concept. A naturalist standpoint is most easily understood as contrasting with a supernaturalist standpoint, and so a philosopher who naturalizes is most easily seen, in the first instance, as denying something that the supernaturalist asserts (such as the existence of contra-causal freedom of the will). By itself, a merely negative characterization of naturalism is insufficiently informative, because there are different commitments that a self-conscious naturalist might put in place of those that she denies. Without going deeply into these issues, I think that it will be useful for the sake of locating Baier in philosophical space to consider two opposing pictures, each of which makes a claim to being naturalistic.

In accordance with the first picture, a philosopher will try to do not only without any concepts whose content is explicitly supernatural, but also without the residues, so to speak, of supernaturalism. By a "residue" I mean any concept that is not expressible as a concept that an idealized physical theory would deploy in its explanation of the world. Thus, the attempt to reduce evaluative discourse to the discourse of the natural sciences represents one effort to banish supernatural residues. Another consists in the attempt to reduce epistemological practices to reliable causal mechanisms. Such projects, if collectively successful, would give us one compelling conception of a natural order of things—a merely natural order in which scientific questions are the only questions worth asking.

In accordance with the second picture, a philosopher will try to retrieve something of value from the discarded supernaturalism, repositioning the retrievals in the natural world but not dispensing with them. The old supernaturalism posited a divine mind as its explanatory center of gravity, but it is possible to delineate a naturalism that preserves the mind-centered explanatory framework but substitutes a human mind—or (better) many human minds—for the divine. To reverse a biblical formula, this naturalism remakes divine actions and attributes in *our* image. Thus, in the case of evaluative discourse, one could try to show how moral judgments are both possible and make sense for beings such as we are—human animals who are shaped by their passions, history, and community no less than by evolutionary processes—rather than for beings whose minds conform to a divine prototype but are embedded (by unaccountable contingency) in human animals. In the case of epistemology, one could try to show how good beliefs acquire their goodness through our unavoidable reliance on the word of those fellow human animals whom we have reason to trust.

Different philosophers who think of themselves as naturalists will be attracted to one of these pictures more than the other, but perhaps neither picture can unequivocally lay claim to being the more thoroughgoing or consistent naturalism. Nevertheless, the second picture is a serious claimant, even though the appearances may be against it. Yet because Baier's work aligns itself with this second picture, and because that work is as original as it is, at least one respect in which the first picture is less ambitiously naturalistic than the second should be pointed out. If physical science is thought to provide the only hallmark of intelligibility, such a thought seems to reflect a preoccupation with a type of purity—in this case an intellectual type—that is arguably better suited to a supernatural outlook than to a naturalized successor. For if we are truly naturalistic in spirit, we might think that there is no special reason to hold that only one truth-gathering practice gets at the whole truth, inasmuch as human beings are creatures whose self-scrutinizing habits are as natural a set of facts as any other that a theorist might investigate. A more naturalized acquaintance with ourselves should therefore arguably heighten, rather than diminish, the tendency to be skeptical about any putative ability to obtain all the truths through a single-minded methodology or to make clean breaks with obviously criticizable (though persistently useful) concepts of the past. Philosophers have attributed such abilities to us, yet their confidence about our possession of them can make these philosophers seem—to some observers—as otherworldly as their theologian ancestors.

For Baier, naturalism is a philosophical approach that stresses the complex concrete situations in which people actually find themselves, and facts about these situations do not play accidental roles in the reflective practices in which animals of our sort participate. The interest that she takes in the distinctive details of human natural history is not simply the descriptive interest that a psychologist or sociologist has (and which, despite its undeniable importance for a Baier-style program, is all that the first type of naturalizing agenda is apt to leave us with). Rather, such details are relevant to the project of reconceiving the evaluative and prescriptive practices that we have inherited from supernaturalist traditions as reflectively endorsable, in ways consonant with the non-reductive naturalist standpoint.

Naturalism, so understood, can serve to make four other motifs in Baier's thought more explicit:

(1) Resistance to atomism. Philosophers often treat human thought and action as if it were possible for a person to think and to act in complete isolation from the nurturing activities of fellow thinkers and agents. This atomistic disposition can find expression in very disparate styles of thought, and its persistence is one of the less attractive legacies of supernaturalism (which atomists themselves may or may not welcome as a legacy). Contractarian and Kantian ethical theories that focus on exercises of dispassionate calculative rationality; the idea that risk and vulnerability are evils to be avoided at all costs; Cartesian-style epistemological programs that emphasize either the certainty of results or the intuitive orderliness of the method used to reach the results; and the view (in action theory) that there must be a class of "basic actions" that a person is able to perform, on pain of not being an agent at all: these all bear the impress of the atomistic disposition that Baier steadfastly resists.

(2) Trust and mutual dependence. In her writings on ethics, Baier has helped to make trust a concept that moral philosophers must take seriously. The circumstances in which one ought to trust (or distrust) another person,

and for what reasons, had been a neglected topic in moral philosophy prior to the appearance of Baier's articles. But the topic should not be ignored if we are mindful of our natural history: we are creatures who are born, and who undergo an extended period of dependence on more powerful adults before attaining an adulthood that, in the ordinary course of events, sometimes ends in a period of renewed dependence on other persons. Baier has shown a lively awareness of the morally significant circumstances of people who either must, or cannot, trust others. There are people whose autonomy, in one sense or other, is limited, such as children, the elderly, and the infirm, as well as socially marginalized constituencies, such as women and those minority groups who feel driven to violence to secure a hearing for their grievances. But no matter how self-empowered we are, or think we are, we are never in a position (according to Baier) that is not dependent on the concurring judgment or the enabling cooperation of our fellows.

(3) Emotions as positive influences on judgment. Trusting other people makes us vulnerable to them, but we often come to trust others because our emotional attachments to them make us willingly vulnerable. These attachments moreover help to make us part of a community of mutually dependent persons (rather than helping to keep us safe from it). Our emotions thus exert an influence over us that is congenial to an anti-atomistic outlook. Baier has argued that this influence is not to be removed or regretted, contrary to those philosophers—Kantians and contractarians again come to mind—who distrust feelings because they fear the potential that our emotional responses have for enslaving us to other people or to ourselves.

(4) Self-correction. If emotions, on a more hopeful view of their potential, do not necessarily distort our evaluative judgments, it is possible to ask how, or in virtue of what, we are able to correct our judgments by means of our emotions. In Baier's view, self-correction is a vital activity for us, whether it is done individually or collectively, insofar as these two types may be distinguished. But how do we (either individually or collectively) do it?

To answer this question on Baier's behalf, I want to direct the discussion toward the historical figures who have had the greatest impact on Baier. In one of his methodological remarks, Descartes announced his intention "to turn truths into procedures, and procedures into truths": to establish actions from insights, and to derive action-guiding rules from established actions. Even though Descartes applied this remark to his own highly intellectualist approach to inquiry, in relation to which it is most easily interpreted,

Descartes' remark does afford the naturalist a cautionary tale in its intended application at the same time that it affords an insight. Unless one is prepared to accept the results of Meditation Three, the dubious centerpiece of the Cartesian meditator's progress from doubt to assurance, the Cartesian attempt to obtain a secure foundation for belief must be reckoned a failure. In this attempt, self-correction depends on nothing other than the contradiction-avoiding rules that unaided intellects are able to formulate and follow, and the result is an impasse that cannot itself be avoided to the extent that the mind endorses only those procedures that are intellectually transparent.

So much for the cautionary tale. As for the insight: the idea that procedures and truths can reveal each other when we make them objects of thought does not require rationalist commitments in order to be acceptable, and the form of Descartes' proposal need not be wedded to its content. If we eschew appeals to allegedly divine guidance, corrections to our thought will have to come from our own thinking about our thinking; but if they come from us, we shall have to make them in such a way as to avoid the dead-ends of the Cartesian intellect. The procedures that generate truths need not, therefore, be intellectually transparent, nor need the truths that generate procedures be truths about, or for, a solitary intellect. The process of self-correction will involve appeals to feeling, and to the judgments of others; and our thinking about thinking will combine exercises of both reason and emotion, will acknowledge that your reasons may be ours without being mine (in contexts where "mine" is equivalent to "producible by me alone").

The fashionable put-down of Descartes has been a staple of philosophical life for many decades now. Yet it is harder—and more interesting—to show where Descartes has gone right than where he has gone wrong.[2] In the broadly construed version of self-correction that Baier derives from Descartes, Baier shows us how resilient a thinker Descartes is, and how much of a resource for contemporary philosophy he can be, even for—especially for—the contemporary naturalist. (And her overt indebtedness to Descartes also illustrates the ways in which a naturalist can help herself to materials obtained from those with suspect affiliations to supernaturalism.)

More needs to be said, however, about Baier's understanding of self-correction, which takes us in another historical direction. The liberally conceived activity that guides our judgments about the appropriate or inappropriate is what Baier often calls reflection, and the methods open to reflection are not infallible nor do they necessarily yield deliverances that reflect a single, undivided view of things, free of conflicts. Baier herself much more memorably presents this view of reflection in a few remarks on Shaftesbury:

> Since [Shaftesbury] valued all sorts of reflections, and reflective conversations, including those that were witty, irreverent, and miscellaneous in their topics and logical structure, Shaftesbury's "reason" comes to include all of this. No particular priority is given to arguments that force a conclusion on us, nor even to reflections that arrive without any coercion at some conclusion, over those that are more tentative and raise interesting questions. What is more, Descartes's preferred unity, the imprint of one thinker's logical mind, is replaced by a delight in variety, miscellany, crooked mental streets, and entertaining byways. The art of the agreeable diversion becomes an exercise of reason.[3]

This accolade to Shaftesbury, whose delight in the byways makes him a difficult writer for argument-reconstructing philosophers, is high indeed. Yet the real source of inspiration for Baier's reflections on reflection is not Shaftesbury, but Hume, a thinker who undeniably paid more respect to logical structures and who exercised reason in a more usual sense. Those who reconstruct arguments have therefore not found Hume as inaccessible as Shaftesbury. Nevertheless, Hume does not *merely* have arguments either, and there is a point in linking his approach to Shaftesbury's.

On Baier's view, Hume's *Treatise* should be read as revealing the progression of the mind from the unfruitful intellectualism of Book One through the passion-informed examination of the passions in Book Two to an account of the moral sense, in Book Three, that ultimately requires the approval of that sense. At the end of this progression we reach a stable, reflectively self-conscious perspective where the mind is finally "able to bear its own survey." The reading that this approach attempts to secure is a far cry from the more common one that is often conjured up when people think about Hume's place in history, according to which Hume is a merely skeptical thinker whose unwitting achievement lies in having reduced British empiricism to absurdity.[4] This backhanded appreciation owes much to the historiography of Hume's nineteenth-century Idealist critics, and much of the Hume scholarship in the twentieth century may be regarded as attempting to portray him as having a much more positive project. Baier's account fits into this pattern, but Baier's Hume bears a closer resemblance, as a thinker, to the critics who helped to enshrine the common reading than to the portrait of Hume those critics painted. It is no small ambition to invert, as it were, the older reading. Nevertheless, Baier's Hume is not simply an Idealist revival, for this Hume remains a committed naturalist, mindful of human history and the variety of customs, distrustful of otherworldly explanations of distinctively human capacities, and friendly to scientific findings but not necessarily scientistic.

Most of the papers in this volume are historical to a greater or lesser degree. And, unsurprisingly, in view of Baier's influence, their focus is often on Descartes and Hume.

Most of the Descartes contributors chart the various ways in which the emotions appear in Descartes' thought, not only in the *Passions of the Soul* (as we might expect) but also in the context of the Cartesian thinker's enacted movement from doubt to confidence in the *Meditations*. Lisa Shapiro specifically asks us to consider what role the emotions have in the *Meditations*, and to confront the issue of whether the meditator's assorted expressions of emotion are merely rhetorical flourishes in a text that could have made its points more perspicuously without them, or whether those expressions are ineliminable elements in the meditator's mental progress. Shapiro is attracted to the second view, which she thinks will require us to reconceive the goals of Descartes' epistemological program by making our affective life essential to our knowledge claims. William Beardsley investigates a single passion—love—and argues that it is an important component of the search for truth; he thereby helps us to understand how a "clear and distinct" idea is able to compel assent. Amy Schmitter proposes, too, that intellect and emotion are not opposed notions for Descartes, and in seeking to dismantle the dualism of reason and feeling that some of his readers (including some feminists) have complacently attributed to Descartes, Schmitter attempts to make him safe for contemporary feminist purposes. Finally, in a discussion of Meditation Three, Cecilia Wee argues (contrary to Margaret Wilson's influential interpretation) that Descartes' treatment of material falsity is integral to the proof of God's existence. Although Wee does not discuss the passions, one of her themes is the meditator's abruptly announced dependence on a God who can be trusted not to deceive, and she holds that Descartes' inclusion of the material-falsity topic helps to explain that otherwise puzzling result of the proof.

These papers in effect make plausible the idea that while Descartes officially maintains a mind-body dualism, his procedures assign emotion a greater role in our mental progress than his official commitments would have encouraged us to believe. And so, the historical Descartes may be found to offer more resources for advancing us beyond "Cartesian" dualism when the thinker himself is more completely understood.

Some of the contributors pursue a similar strategy for Hume, showing how he can be read as having more coherent, and more defensible, views about the lives of persons than he is sometimes credited with having. Interpreting Hume can be more like interpreting a literary text, or Descartes' *Meditations*, than like evaluating a self-contained argument in a professional philosophical journal; and discussions of Hume have sometimes been impoverished because his readers have tended to focus too exclusively on what he says in isolated passages.

For instance, Hume *says*, "When I am angry, I am actually possesst with that passion, and in that emotion have no more a reference to any other object, than when I am thirsty, or sick, or more than five foot high." This statement can suggest, to a susceptible ear, that thoughts and feelings are radically distinct elements within our mental life, and that they enter into our plans and our reflections in very different ways. On the textbook reading of Hume that takes wing from this sort of statement, thoughts are about the world and are assessable as fitting or failing to fit the world, and as rational or irrational, whereas feelings are (to borrow Hume's own term) "original existences" that lack intentional objects and are brutely given states of the person who has them, not susceptible to rational assessment (save derivatively when they involve their possessor in an instrumental error or a mistake about a matter of fact).

Yet Hume generally treats emotions as if they were quite unlike thirst, illness, or height. Saul Traiger's paper helps us to see how Hume has a more sophisticated understanding of the relationship between emotion and reason, one that allows affective mechanisms to make contributions to causal reasoning and not simply to raise impediments. In articulating this conception on Hume's behalf, Traiger presents a view of the feeling-intellect relation that has striking affinities with the type of view that Shapiro, Beardsley, and Schmitter attribute to Descartes. Lilli Alanen's paper also deals with Hume's account of the emotions, and in her examination of the reason-as-slave-of-passion passage in Hume, Alanen explores the conception of passion that lies behind that passage, arguing that the intentionality of emotion is not simply of a propositional kind.

Hume's language occasionally also poses difficulties for the interpreter who wants to make sense of Hume's remarks about the self. To someone who reads only the section of his work titled "Of personal identity," the impression of the self is the object of a famously unsuccessful search. But if the reader perseveres with Hume, in particular taking note of his account of the passions, it is obvious that there is a conception of the self on which Hume has no difficulty relying. Donald Ainslie takes up this crux, arguing that Hume has a unified conception of the self and that it unproblematically enters into his doctrine of sympathy (or sentiment-transfer between persons)—a matter of importance for Hume's moral theory. In making his case, Ainslie pays attention to the embodiment of passionate persons, which includes their affective relationships to one another, in a public setting, as objects of love or hatred, pride or humility. And it is here that we can begin looking for a way, intelligible in Hume's terms, of reflectively assessing feelings and feeling-based attachments. Offering an account of reflective assessment is crucial if we are to naturalize both the sense of self and the feeling-intellect relation.

But before turning to the issue of reflective assessment, we should emphasize that not everyone is as sanguine about the naturalizing implications of Hume's thought as Traiger and Ainslie. Janet Broughton thinks that, given the materials Hume works with, we are not entitled to cast the movement of thought we observe in Book One of the *Treatise* as a "progress of sentiments" (to revert to Baier's phrase), but that we should regard it simply as an "inquiry" that may not be genuinely progressive. Whether inquiry is less desirable than progress is perhaps yet to be determined; but, either way, Broughton's account should at least give Hume's enthusiast some pause, since the vocabulary that we unreflectively use to describe reflection may not itself withstand reflection. Alasdair MacIntyre, who is mindful of Hume the moralist (and not just Hume the moral philosopher), holds that Hume's condemnation of "artificial lives" (such as those led by Diogenes and Pascal) is in fact groundless, and that this reveals a weakness in Hume's views about the relationship of reason to feeling. If MacIntyre is right, then, it will be more difficult for Hume's naturalist to know whether she can moralize in the manner to which she had been accustomed.

We turn now to reflective assessment, and to the reasons why the naturalist should be concerned about it. Reflection has sometimes been conceived as a matter of pinpointing and avoiding formal contradictions (either those arising from our desires, as in the textbook version of Hume, or those arising from maxims of rationality, as in the textbook version of the anti-Humean). We would expect a naturalist of the more thoroughgoing stripe that we are sketching to have a standard of assessment that is not merely intellectualistic; still, it can be difficult to tell what naturalized reflection should look like. The problem is magnified by the uncertainties we sometimes have about whether a particular feeling-based attachment in fact enhances a person's life or whether it disguises a refined exploitation on the part of another person (such as a friend or lover), or on the part of an institution, to which the person is attached. If the naturalist is to make good on the proposal that assessment involves the exercise of feeling, then she will have to offer some picture of what it is to assess feeling by means of feeling—a picture that is able to address the worry that naturalized reflection, unhappily, merely confirms affective tendencies that a person is already disposed to have.

The remaining papers deal with problems connected with reflection, broadly construed. David Gauthier, taking his point of departure from Hume, is concerned about the relationship between moral approval and an agent's reflective endorsements, and queries Hume's claim that an adequate moral theory will recommend duties that coincide with a person's true interest. Although Gauthier proposes that we can amend Hume's claim if we suppose that our interest can be redirected from actions to dispositions, he thinks that problems remain with the connection between reflection and morality as it is envisaged by Hume. Robert Shaver takes up the issue of reflective success, and in particular what it should mean for a habit to be approved by reflection. He argues that reflection does not lead ineluctably (as Christine Korsgaard supposes) to a Kantian deontology, and that reflection instead can be anchored in a person's welfare, understood in terms of a person's natural, contingently occurring dispositions. By contrast, Michele Moody-Adams and Sergio Tenenbaum want to argue for more Kantian versions of reflection. Tenenbaum tries to show how his Kantian version enables us to make sense of an important sentiment-based tie to other persons, that of friendship, which the defender of Hume's sentimentalist approach has often been quick to adduce as a difficulty for the Kantian. And Moody-Adams argues that the role played in Humean reflection by character-centered evaluation makes it difficult for the Humean to find an appropriate reflective stance from which we can understand what is wrong with institutionalized forms of cruelty. Instead, she proposes that we need a more Kantian mode of reflection.

Moody-Adams' discussion of cruelty emphasizes both the disparities of power typically involved in exercises of cruelty and the sorts of vulnerability to cruelty afforded by intimate relationships (such as the relationship between parent and child). Both types of relationship raise issues of trust, which has recently been the focus of much discussion in ethics, partly, no doubt, because trust (as Baier has made evident) is a likely topic for naturalized reflection. The final two papers are expressly concerned with this topic. Whom, or what, or how, to trust will be pressing questions for us if we attempt to integrate emotion into our understanding of the rational. Karen Jones presents a basic account of interpersonal trust according to which trust involves an "attitude of optimism" toward another, and which explains why the trusting person is justified in maintaining the vulnerability that allows other persons to have access to, and power over, the objects that she cares about. This formulation points up the commonplace conviction that trust and friendship are internally related notions; it may be tempting, therefore, to think that a defense of friendship must also be a defense of trust. But it is possible for these two notions to come apart, as Jennifer Whiting explains, and it may be that we need to have friends whom we in some sense distrust. Whiting observes that if people are members of groups whose views have been distorted because of their dominance (or subservience), then they have reason to be distrustful not only of themselves but of their friends (their "second selves," in her Aristotelian parlance). Her call for a measure of distrust notwithstanding, Whiting writes from a perspective that both regards our sentiment-based ties to others as important sources of progress for our moral sentiments, and accepts the terms of the challenge that Baier makes regarding the neat separability of cognitive and affective states of mind. Her paper thus offers a critical and constructive approach to the sort of naturalized reflection we have been examining here.

I bring this introduction to a close on a more personal note. The editors—Joyce Jenkins, Jennifer Whiting, and I—hope that Annette Baier will be pleased to witness the diversity of reflections her work has produced;

and if those reflections stimulate others to study Baier's work with the care we think that it deserves, we shall have ample cause—not to mention reason, in the catholic sense attributable to Shaftesbury and his heirs—for pleasure, too. Annette has been a trusted teacher, mentor, confidante, and friend. Accordingly, we dedicate this volume to her in gratitude for all that she has taught us, not just by her formal instruction (if we have had it), but by her witty, irreverent, and ever-judicious fellowship. In philosophy, and even in some of those matters that a good Humean recognizes as lying deeper than philosophy, we have been sustained by her example as we strive to fashion a progress of our own.

NOTES

I am grateful to Jennifer Whiting and Joyce Jenkins for their help in preparing this introduction. I have also profited from Whiting's "One Is Not Born but Becomes a Person," delivered at the Eastern Division meeting of the American Philosophical Association in 2001, for its précis of Baier's characteristic themes.

1. Annette Baier, *Postures of the Mind* (Minneapolis: University of Minnesota Press, 1985), xi.

2. When I was her dissertation student, Baier once warned me about the type of historian of philosophy who "tries to show that he is just a bit smarter" than the historical thinker he is writing about. This warning offers one of the best lessons anyone who writes on the history of philosophy can learn.

3. Annette Baier, *The Commons of the Mind* (Chicago and LaSalle, IL: Open Court, 1997), 11.

4. In this spirit, Bertrand Russell began chapter 17 (on Hume) in *A History of Western Philosophy* with these inauspicious observations: "David Hume (1711–76) is one of the most important among philosophers, because he developed to its logical conclusion the empirical philosophy of Locke and Berkeley, and by making it self-consistent made it incredible. He represents, in a certain sense, a dead end: in his direction, it is impossible to go further. To refute him has been, ever since he wrote, a favourite pastime among metaphysicians."

CHAPTER 2

What Are the Passions Doing
in the *Meditations*?

LISA SHAPIRO

In this paper I want to draw attention to an aspect of Descartes' *Meditations* which often gets neglected, or even goes unnoticed: the passionate life of the meditator. Let me clarify: If one reads the *Meditations* with a fresh eye, one may well be struck by the meditator's expressing his feelings about things, feelings of desire, fear, surprise, wonder, and the like, at certain pivotal moments of the work, as well as by a general tone, which imparts to the reader a sense of the meditator's affective engagement in the project at hand. I will review these expressions in some detail in section 1 of this paper, but first I should say a bit more about my aim here.

This paper is largely exploratory, for—I will be honest—I am not sure what to make of the meditator's expression of the passions he is feeling. Perhaps it is a mere rhetorical flourish and nothing more. Even on this weak reading, however, the presence of the passions is a bit surprising. This surprise brings to the surface a tacit assumption that readers tend to make about the meditator, namely, that all his philosophy is a matter of pure thinking and that his thinking in that way might as well be done by a disembodied substance. That the meditator feels passions, thus, challenges us to think about the nature of both pure thought and Descartes' dualism. I explore this line in section 2. But we can also read the presence of the passions in the *Meditations* more strongly, for these expressions might also be integral to the work. Certainly this sort of reading will challenge us in the ways the first sort of reading does. Taking the passions as integral to the *Meditations* might well also challenge certain conceptions of Descartes' philosophical program—about the project of the work and the goal of Cartesian epistemology. I sketch such a reading in section 3. So, it seems, the presence of the passions in the *Meditations* invites all sorts of questions.

My aim here is simply to begin to clarify those questions. Insofar as I raise questions about the standard readings of Descartes here, it might seem that I am implicitly concerned to undermine the received view of his thought. I thus want to be clear from the outset that I do not take these questions to imply that we should reject such readings wholesale. Rather, by considering the place of the passions in the *Meditations*, I want simply to press upon the way we tend to read Descartes, to bring to the surface just what we often take for granted, and to suggest that Descartes' own view might be more complex (and interesting in virtue of the tensions within it) than it initially appears.

I. THE MEDITATOR'S EXPRESSIONS OF HIS PASSIONS

It will be useful for us to have in view the meditator's expression of his passions, so in this section I provide a catalog of the occurrences of those expressions. I will return to consider just what we should make of these displays of emotion.[1]

If we look closely at the text of the *Meditations*, we will find that meditator not only feels passions but also does so quite overtly. The First Meditation—indeed the project of first philosophy itself—begins from the meditator's *desire* to "establish something firm and lasting in the sciences."[2] According to the *Passions of the Soul*, desire is a passion, and the definition Descartes gives of "desire" there fits quite nicely with the way it figures in the meditator's story. According to the *Passions*, "the passion of desire is an agitation of the soul, caused by the spirits, which disposes it to want for the future the things it represents to itself to be suitable" (PS a. 27; AT XI 349). What the meditator represents to himself as suitable is just certainty, and he sets about, at an appropriate time, seeking what he wants.

In trying to satisfy his desire, however, the meditator is propelled into the series of skeptical arguments which form the First Meditation. These arguments in turn lead to other passions, quite vividly displayed. The arguments not only leave the meditator "diffident" (L. *diffidentia*; Fr. *défiance*, AT VII 22; AT IX 17) toward his former beliefs, but they also urge him to persist "obstinately" (L. *obstinate*; Fr. *obstinément*, AT VII 23; AT IX 18) in his meditations. The effort this persistence requires exhausts the meditator, leaving him with a set of mixed emotions. His self-description at the conclusion of the First Meditation is striking in this regard:

> I am like a prisoner who has *enjoyed* [*fruebatur; jouissait*] an imaginary freedom while asleep; as he begins to suspect that he is asleep, he *fears* [*timet; craint*] being woken up and goes along with the pleasant illusion as long as he can. In the same way I spontaneously slide back into my old opinions and *am apprehensive about* [*vereor; appréhende*] being shaken out of them. . . . (AT VII 23; emphasis mine)[3]

The Second Meditation picks up where the meditator left off. He is "like one who has unexpectedly fallen into a deep whirlpool, so *confused* [*turbatus*] that I could neither fix a foot on the bottom nor swim to the top" [emphasis mine] (AT VII 24).[4] He does not know how to resolve his skeptical worries, and yet he cannot seem to go back to his old ways, to a time before those worries became explicit.

Later, in the Second Meditation, the passions come into play again. The meditator finds himself *amazed* (L. *miror*, AT VII 31; Fr. *étonné*, AT IX 25; CSM II 21) at how much he still wants to say that he understands the piece of wax through the eye and not through the mind, and so at just how prone to error his mind is. Moreover, this amazement seems to lead to other passions which then steer him back on course to perceiving the wax by the mind alone. He tells himself that "one *desiring* to know above and beyond the common people should feel *ashamed* of having doubts based on the forms of speech that the common people have invented" [emphasis mine] (AT VII 32),[5] and, in so doing, he brings himself back to the realization that he cannot "really and truly perceive" the wax "without a human mind."

The passions appear again in certain central passages in the Third Meditation. In the French edition, at the opening of the meditation, the meditator includes "loves and hates"—two of the six primitive passions Descartes sets out in the *Passions of the Soul*—in the list of things a thinking thing does (AT IX 27). Moreover, at the critical moment at the conclusion of the meditation—when he realizes not only that God exists as the all-perfect being but also that God is his creator and that he has "in some manner been made in his image and likeness"—the meditator pauses to *wonder* [L. *admirari*; Fr. *admirer*] and to *adore* [L. *adorare*; Fr. *adorer*] the beauty of God himself, "before examining this point more carefully and investigating other truths which may be derived from it":

> I should like to pause here and spend some time in the contemplation of God; to reflect on his attributes and to gaze with *wonder* and *adoration* on the beauty of this immense light, so far as the eye of my darkened intellect can bear it. (AT VII 52; AT IX 41; CSM II 36; emphasis mine)

Although one might not think of wonder as a passion, it is for Descartes—and a very important one. According to the account of the *Passions*, wonder is the "first of all the passions" (PS a. 53; AT XI 373). It is "a sudden surprise of the soul which carries it to consider attentively those objects which seem to it rare and extraordinary" (PS a. 70; AT XI 380), and Descartes claims that this surprise is useful insofar as it "makes us learn and retain in our memory things of which we have previously been ignorant" and that in so doing it "disposes us to the acquisition of the sciences" (PS a. 75; AT XI 384). Thus, that to which wonder disposes us is precisely the aim of the *Meditations* themselves: the meditator is engaged in these exercises just because he wants to achieve something firm and lasting in the sciences. Moreover, it is fitting that the meditator feels wonder *here*. For it is at this point in the *Meditations* that the meditator finds a crucial element of what he needs to meet his goal—a knowledge that God exists and is not a deceiver. Confident once again about his God-given faculty of reason, he proceeds to arrive at the method for avoiding error (in the Fourth Meditation). And from there, he makes swift progress to a knowledge of the nature of the material world, an understanding of his own place in the world as a whole as a union of mind and body, and ultimately to the scientific knowledge he seeks.

After the Third Meditation, the meditator expresses his passions several times, but less poignantly. All we see in the Fourth Meditation is the meditator proclaiming himself *confident* (L. *confidam;* Fr. *conclu si évidément,* AT VII 53; AT IX 42) that God exists and that his own existence depends on God. He also avers that he *should not be surprised*[6] that he cannot fathom the reasons God does what he does—in particular why God has made him vulnerable to error, both recalling the Second Meditation and bringing home just how much has changed. In the Fifth Meditation, the meditator suggests that he is constantly *suspicious* (L. *suspicio;* Fr. *soupçon,* AT VII 64; AT IX 51) of things that might have slipped in through the senses. Here there is little of the drama that informed the earlier expressions. It is perhaps worth remarking, however, that throughout these later meditations, the meditator urges himself to be ever diligent (L. *diligenter*). While diligence involves an act of will, and so might not be thought of as a passion properly speaking, there does seem to be a feeling of alertness or vigilance associated with it that might be considered a passion of sorts. Indeed, it might well be a passion akin to Cartesian generosity, the feeling we have upon knowing that we have a free will and resolving to use that will well.

However, there is a full-voiced expression of a passion again at the very end of the *Meditations,* when the meditator proclaims that "the exaggerated doubts of the last few days should be dismissed as *laughable*" [L. *risu dignae;* Fr. *ridicules;* emphasis mine] (AT VII 89; AT IX 71). Laughter for Descartes is a clear-cut expression of emotion, one he details in the *Passions* as occurring when we feel a moderate joy intermingled with some wonder or hatred. Certainly it makes sense that the meditator feels just this at the end of the *Meditations,* for he might well rejoice in his dissolution of the skeptical arguments he has set himself and, at the same time, hate all they represent: such doubts could be seen as unsuitable to one confident in his ability to reason, one who can wonder (and adore) a God whose mark he bears and to whom he bears a resemblance.

2. A MERE RHETORICAL FLOURISH?

While it is clear that the passions are present in the *Meditations,* it is not at all clear what we should make of this fact. Indeed, one might think we should make nothing much of it at all. In the survey of the previous section, I have suggested that the meditator's passions, as he expresses them, seem to be in keeping with what is going on in the work, at least according to the definitions of the passions that Descartes offers much later. But this consistency need not imply that they signify anything of particular philosophical interest. They might simply be rhetorical flourishes tacked on to help readers engage with the work, or to signal to them that they are following along. Indeed, they might not even be that intentional. The language of the passions might be a stylistic accident, a reflection of Descartes' personal predilections in writing.[7]

Either of these readings is possible. Since Descartes mentions nothing in either the Replies to Objections or in his correspondence about how the passions figure in the *Meditations*, one might well conclude that they are philosophically insignificant. Further, taking the meditator's passions as philosophically accidental is consistent with one way of understanding the *Meditations* as meditations. We might think of meditating as engaging in an interpretive exercise,[8] as looking within oneself and interpreting what one finds there. In doing so, one might well, and perhaps one should, arrive at a new self-understanding, but this understanding achieves only at the cognitive level. On this line, any insight one acquires through meditating has no practical consequences; one may have a changed understanding of the contents of one's mind, but this understanding does not affect one's actions—what one does and how one does it. Certainly, understanding the passions as an accidental feature of the *Meditations* is consistent with reading the work in this way. On this reading, the meditator will feel the passions he is disposed to feel, and that may well help him to understand himself better—as a being that has passions, or even as one that feels what he does upon entertaining certain thoughts. But that is all. At the end of his meditations, the meditator may no longer have thoughts he once had—he has managed to successfully overcome his habitual opinions—and so he may no longer have the passions that went with them. Instead, other thoughts may be at the fore of his mind, and hence also other passions. What is important, however, is that he has his thoughts in order, and the passions themselves have played no central role in achieving this result. Insofar as this is so, there is nothing very interesting to say about the passions: certain passions go with certain thoughts, and that is all there is to it. All the work of the *Meditations* is a matter of dispassionate reasoning, and the passions just follow along.

However, even this weak interpretation of the passions in the *Medita-tions* still leaves us with some real questions. Most readers of Descartes, it seems to me, do not think very carefully about the metaphysical status of this "I" which is doing the meditating, narrating as he goes along. Com-mentators do claim that the "I," and thus the meditator, is nothing but a thing that thinks, and of course there is good reason for them to do so—that does seem to be the lesson of the *cogito*, after all. But it also seems that many commentators do not reflect much on what that claim entails. If one pairs that claim with the substance dualism with which Descartes is usually associated, it can certainly seem that the meditator is—at least for the du-ration of his meditations—disembodied. My sense is that many readers do make this step, albeit unwittingly.[9]

However, the presence of the passions suggests that the narrator of the *Meditations* has a more complicated metaphysical status. For if the medita-tor were the disembodied thinking thing that Descartes' dualism seems to suggest is possible, then he should not be feeling any passions at all. The passions, for Descartes, while they are states of the soul and so proper to a thinking thing, are also brought on by a bodily state. As he defines them in a. 27 of the *Passions of the Soul*, they are "perceptions or sensations or exci-tations of the soul which are related to it [the soul] in particular and which are caused, maintained and strengthened by some movement of the spir-its" (AT XI 349). The "spirits" here are the animal spirits, the most rare-fied parts of the blood, and so are very much corporeal. Insofar as the pas-sions do take root in the body in this way, they are proper to the *union* of mind and body. Thus, the fact that the meditator *does* express passions at all, even if they serve only a rhetorical purpose, challenges us to think a little more carefully about what sort of thing the meditator is. For on standard readings of Descartes' dualism, it does not seem that the meditator could be *purely* a thinking thing *and* feel the passions he does.

There are two ways one might try to preserve the standard reading, but they are not without their interpretive challenges. On one hand, one can admit that feeling passions is antithetical to being purely an intellectual thing and remark that the meditator's expressions of passion do not come at a time when he is *supposed* to be separated from his body. Consider those which occur in the First Meditation: there, the meditator is still actively engaged in withdrawing from the senses, the material world and with them his body and his passions. Thus, the passions we find him expressing need not preclude our seeing the rest of the *Meditations* as the exercises of a purely in-tellectual being. And while those of the Second Meditation seem to occur at a time when the meditator *is* meant to be engaging in purely intellectual exercises—it is here that we get the *cogito*, and the study of the piece of wax that reveals to the meditator that he knows the wax by the mind alone and not by the senses directly—still, the presence of the passions here is explicable by those who would want to defend our prereflective intuitions about the meditator. While the passions expressed at the beginning of the meditation do indicate the meditator's equivocal position between his old ways and the new one he has committed himself to, in pressing forward, he is throwing himself wholeheartedly into the new way, and so giving himself over to his purely intellectual nature, and, at the same time, leaving off his confusion. Equally, in studying the piece of wax, the meditator has allowed himself to slide back to the position of the First Meditation; the meditator himself admits that he is giving his mind "free rein" to wander off to con-sider material things, though they be doubtful. And it is entirely in keep-ing with his re-entering the material world for the meditator to feel pas-sions just as he admits his sensations.

Yet as we have seen the passions persist *throughout* the *Meditations*, and one might think it a stretch to come up with similar accounts of the medi-tator's metaphysical entitlement to feel emotions again and again. Indeed, it might well be hard to do so in the case of the wonder at the end of the Third Meditation. But there is a greater difficulty. Such an interpretation must also provide an account of why the meditator slides in and out of his exis-tence as a purely intellectual being, and of how such slides are possible. It is not at all clear how such a story might go. Telling it would certainly seem to involve thinking in much more detail than most commentators have done about the nature of pure thought and about what it means for a human being (a *union* of soul and body) to engage in pure thought.

The other route one can go in defending the standard approach to read-ing the *Meditations* has similar consequences. One need not deny that a pure thinking thing can feel passions. One can get around the apparent prob-lem posed by the meditator's passions by leaning on a distinction Descartes draws between sensual or sensuous passions and intellectual or rational pas-sions in a letter to Chanut of 1 February 1647. He draws this distinction in the case of love. Sensual love "is nothing but a confused thought, aroused in the soul by some motion of the nerves" (AT IV 603; CSMK 306). It is the passion we feel as a result of the movements of the animal spirits. Rational love, on the other hand, "consists simply in the fact that when our soul perceives some present or absent good, which it judges to be fitting for itself, it joins itself to it willingly, that is to say, it considers itself and the good in question as forming two parts of a single whole" (AT IV 601; CSMK 306). What is rational about this sort of love is that we feel it *for a reason;* it is caused by a judgment on the part of the soul. And so, Descartes thinks that "[a]ll these movements of the will which constitute love, joy, sadness and desire in so far as they are rational thoughts and not passions, could exist in our soul even if it had no body" (AT IV 602; CSMK 306).[10] While the two kinds of passion often come together—the confused thought of sensual love, "makes it [the soul] disposed to have other, clearer, thought which constitutes rational love" (AT IV 603; CSMK 306)—they need not: we can feel the passion of love without finding a reason to love anything in particular, and similarly we can love something with good reason, yet not feel it in any bodily way. The passions the meditator articulates in the *Meditations* might just be instances of intellectual passions that are unaccompanied by their sensual counterparts.[11] The meditator could, after all, have felt them whether he had a body or not, and this seems to be just the status of the other more metaphysical claims the meditator makes; their being true is not at all contingent on whether he has a body or not.

While this suggestion does go a long way toward eliminating the problems posed by the meditator's passions, it is not as simple a solution as it initially seems. For these Cartesian intellectual passions are notoriously hard to make sense of. In what way are they different from the judgments from which they arise? And if they are not so different from them, then it is not at all clear why they should be called passions; judgments are paradigm cases of actions for Descartes. But even if we can get clear on this aspect of Cartesian mental life, it seems that we are only left with a further puzzle. If, for Descartes, we do have mental states which can be properly called intellectual passions, then it would seem that pure thought, the kind of thought in which we could engage even if we did not have a body, has an affective component. And if this is so, then we need to ask further questions: What is the structure of Cartesian pure thought? For Descartes, pure thought seems to be that through which we grasp a priori truths. How do we arrive at a priori knowledge? Does the affective aspect of pure thought figure in our attaining that knowledge? If so, how?

So the fact that the meditator feels passions raises important questions at the intersection of two elements of Descartes' philosophy—his dualism and the project of pure thought on the one hand, and his concern with *human* beings, and in particular *human* reason, on the other. Standard accounts of Descartes' dualism take as their starting point his claim that mind and body are really distinct, and this claim, by Descartes' own account, entails that mind and body are two independent entities. Many commentators take this claim of independence to be a claim about the *separability* of mind and body, relying on the discussion of the real distinction of mind and body in the Sixth Meditation: ". . . that I clearly and distinctly understand one thing apart from another is enough to make me certain that the two things are distinct, since they are capable of being separated, at least by God" (AT VII 78; CSM II 54).[12] Still, it remains to understand the nature of this separability, and most commentators seem to take it that whatever is proper to the mind alone could be attributed to it, even if the mind were never joined to the body at all. Thus, if the meditator feels passions, and passions have a bodily cause, then it seems that either he is not to be thought of as a purely thinking thing or we need to reconsider Descartes' notion of pure thought. Neither option is an easy course to take. Certainly, the difficulties of the first option should be clear: rethinking the metaphysical status of the Cartesian meditator would involve challenging a well-entrenched dogma of philosophy. The second option also poses difficulties, since the meditator takes himself to have found solid metaphysical ground in his investigation of thought alone. Any rethinking of the nature of pure thought should preserve the stability of this ground. In addition, if the meditator's passions are seen not as having bodily causes, but as intellectual in nature, we are faced with the challenge of further explicating the structure of pure thought such that it includes these passions. And doing this would involve getting clear on just what the relation of pure thought is to the rest of human thought—another large project.

Thus, even if we presuppose a very weak reading of the place of the passions in the *Meditations*, we are led to some rather daunting philosophical questions. Indeed, these questions are so philosophically central that one might begin to suspect that perhaps the passions are not such a philosophically neutral aspect of the *Meditations* after all. In the next section, I consider the consequences of a stronger reading, by asking just where we might be led if we initially presume that the meditator's passions are integral to his philosophical project.

3. THE PASSIONS AND THE MEDITATOR'S
SELF-TRANSFORMATION

In section 2, I noted that a weak reading of the place of the passions in the *Meditations* is consistent with understanding it as an interpretive meditative enterprise. There is, however, another way of understanding meditating: as a revolutionary enterprise. On this line, at the end of one's meditations, one is transformed; meditations are meant to change the meditator's *life*. Through one's new self-understanding, one's actions are affected. And insofar as our passions dispose us to action,[13] reading Descartes' *Meditations* along this line might well lead us to think that the presence of the passions could be philosophically relevant. At the end of his meditations, the meditator should feel differently—and so be inclined to act differently—upon having certain thoughts than he does at the beginning. Such a change in his passions might well be an integral part of the more general metaphysical and epistemological progress the meditator makes in the *Meditations*.

It does seem that the meditator changes how he feels about things over the course of the *Meditations*. That is, it does seem that the meditator does not think about different things. Rather, he thinks about the same things but feels differently about them. To see this, we need only look at the course his passions take. The meditator begins with a desire to establish something firm and lasting in the sciences. This desire seems to amount to nothing other than a desire for knowledge or certainty, for the meditator quickly moves from this desire to skepticism. And, as we have seen, the skepticism in turn leads to fear and apprehension. Since it seems he cannot ascertain any truth, the meditator seems left with a choice: either he can pursue his desire and risk the conclusion that he might well not be able to know anything, or he can forsake his desire and try to sustain the illusion of having the knowledge under which he has been operating. Either way, there is ground for trepidation. Yet by the end of the *Meditations*, his fear and apprehension have given way to laughter, though the meditator still presumably maintains his desire for knowledge. What has changed?

For one, the meditator has answered his own skeptical challenges.[14] At the end of the First Meditation, he worries whether he was given a nature such that he could ever have knowledge:

But what about when I was considering something very simple and straightforward in arithmetic or geometry, for example that two and three added together make five, and so on? Did I not see at least these things clearly enough to affirm their truth? Indeed, the only reason for my later judgement that they were open to doubt was that it occurred to me that perhaps some God could have given me a nature such that I was deceived even in matters which seemed most evident. (AT VII 35–36; CSM II 25)[15]

But by the Sixth Meditation, the meditator has achieved "a better knowledge of myself and the author of my being, [so that] although I do not think I should heedlessly accept everything I seem to have acquired from the senses, neither do I think that everything should be called into doubt" (AT VII 77–78; CSM II 54). Surely, the meditator's newfound confidence in his nature as a thinking thing goes a long way to making the earlier skeptical arguments laughable.

But is this enough? It can well seem that what he knows of his nature does not fully answer the skepticism of the First Meditation. At the end of the *Meditations* the meditator admits that he does go wrong about many things; indeed, he recognizes that he is susceptible to "true errors of nature" (AT VII 85; CSM II 59) and that "the nature of man as a combination of mind and body is such that it is bound to mislead him from time to time" (AT VII 88; CSM II 61). Surely, so long as he is prone to these sorts of errors, errors which are in principle unavoidable, he has not banished the specter of his skepticism. At the beginning of the *Meditations* it is just this possibility that he might go wrong unwittingly by his nature that leads him to despair.

Yet at the end of the work, the possibility of such mistakes no longer leaves the meditator in such a desperate state. One might say that his thoughts about the weakness of his own nature are no longer invested with the same passions. What once made him fearful now makes him laugh; he feels differently about things.

Here is a suggestion: the project of the *Meditations* involves the regulation of the passions just as much as it involves laying a metaphysical foundation which can answer the skeptical arguments of the First Meditation. In particular, the project involves a regulation of the desire for knowledge from which the project begins. At the beginning of the *Meditations*, the meditator seems to desire absolute certainty about everything. His hope appears to be to never make a mistake again. Thus, he does not find the distinction between opinions which are "patently false" and those which are "not completely certain and indubitable" significant in his quest for knowledge (AT VII 18; CSM II 12), for only if all his beliefs are true can he hope to go forward from them to further beliefs and ultimately to a body of knowledge. Yet by the end of the work, his desire seems to be for something subtly different. He still is seeking the truth, but he no longer demands to be assured that *all* his beliefs are true. In the last lines of the *Meditations*, the meditator is reconciled to the commonsensical notion that he will make mistakes. In dismissing his earlier doubts about whether he was sleeping or waking, he says:

> I ought not to have even the slightest doubt of their reality if, after calling upon all the senses as well as my memory and my intellect in order to check them, I receive no conflicting reports from any of these sources. For from the fact that God is not a deceiver it follows that in cases like these I am completely free from error. But since the pressure of things to be done does not always allow us to stop and make such a meticulous check, it must be admitted that in this human life we are often liable to make mistakes about particular things, and we must acknowledge the weakness of our nature. (AT VII 90; CSM II 62)

The meditator's desire for knowledge has been tempered. He now wants to know what he is capable of knowing, and he strives to know within those limits.

The conclusion of the *Meditations* follows the end of the Fourth Meditation. There the meditator has discovered the method for avoiding error: he will succeed in having only true beliefs if he affirms only those ideas he perceives clear and distinctly.[16] But this discovery is followed immediately by a recognition of the limits of what this method gets him. For he himself is limited: he has a finite intellect, and "it is in the nature of a finite intellect to lack understanding of many things" (AT VII 60; CSM II 42). It is not within his rights, however, to complain about his limitations—it is the nature God has given him.[17] With this recognition of his own nature, and the limitations that come along with it, the meditator clarifies his goals. The task can no longer be to be absolutely certain about everything, since some things will lie beyond his grasp. Rather, he is concerned to distinguish what he is capable of knowing from what he is not, and it seems that in drawing this distinction, he is able to temper his desire for knowledge: he now wants to know all he *can* know.[18]

Such a reading is consistent with the other passions expressed in the *Meditations*. In proceeding methodically to his first certainty—"'I am, I exist' is necessarily true whenever it is put forward by me or conceived in my mind" (AT VII 25; CSM II 17)—the meditator begins to temper himself. We see no pronounced expression of emotion in the rest of the first part of the Second Meditation. But this one truth is insufficient for the meditator's self-mastery. As he observes that his knowledge of material things seems more distinct than his knowledge of himself, it is as if the meditator is overcome once again by the desires that led him down the skeptical road:

> my mind enjoys wandering off and will not yet submit to being restrained within the bounds of truth. Very well then; just this once let us give it a completely free rein, so that after a while, when it is time to tighten the rein, it may more readily submit to being curbed. (AT VII 29–30; CSM II 20)

His strategy for overcoming his wanton ways seems to resemble that which might be imparted in a homily about raising children. And here, as he allows himself once again to desire "to know above and beyond the common people" (AT VII 32), we observe the meditator once again feeling a passion: he is ashamed at himself for slipping back into his old ways and taking them to be guiding him toward the truth. It is this shame that steers him back on course to thinking through just how it is that he understands the wax most clearly and distinctly. As the meditator proceeds, again we see no pronounced display of emotion—that is, until the end of the Third Meditation, where the meditator pauses to wonder and adore God. And, as noted earlier, once the meditator has come to understand himself in relation to God, we do not see any pronounced display of emotion from the meditator. Gone are his fear and despair, as well as his shame. We can take this reticence to reflect not so much the absence of passion as a newfound temperance.

This story about how the passions figure in the *Meditations* accords well with what Descartes says in the *Passions of the Soul* about the regulation of the passions. There, he suggests that the regulation of the passions is effected

primarily through generosity, and generosity, as Descartes explains it, involves the recognition on each of our parts that we have a free will, paired
with the resolution to use our will well. The meditator's diligence in following the method for avoiding error that he has discovered can be seen as
exemplifying this resolve. Furthermore, as I have argued elsewhere,[19] generosity in this sense requires that we understand that we have the power to
do otherwise—for this is what free will consists in—but also that we have
our limitations. We must figure out what we are capable of doing but also
come to terms with our limited ability to reach a definitive conclusion about
what the right thing to do is when we must take action. Now, one of the
principle functions of generosity is to remedy those "vain desires" which
we have for things which, in truth, lie outside of our proper domain. So, in
a. 144, Descartes writes:

> But because these passions can incline us to any action only through the
> mediation of the desire they excite, it is that desire in particular which
> we should be concerned to regulate; and the principal utility of moral
> philosophy consists in this. Now, as I have lately said that [desire] is al-
> ways good when it is follows true knowledge, it similarly cannot fail
> to be bad when it is founded on some error. *And it seems to me that the
> error most commonly committed in connection with desires is to fail to distin-
> guish sufficiently the things that depend entirely on us from those that do not
> depend on us.* (AT XI 436; emphasis mine)

The vain desires for which Descartes claims generosity is a remedy are just
those whose satisfaction we assume depends on us, even though it actually
does not. Generosity serves as a remedy for them just because it leads us
to draw the distinction which we are not prone to draw: a generous person
recognizes those things which depend only on herself as well as those things
which in no way depend on her, and she tailors her desires so that she wants
only that which is within her power. It is just such a recognition of his limitations that, I am claiming, leads to the transformation of the meditator's desire for knowledge.

  If we understand the meditator to be regulating his passions in this way,
then we are also afforded a richer understanding of the wonder he expresses
at the end of the Third Meditation. We can see it as not only particularly appropriate but also as a critical part of the argument of the *Meditations* them-

selves. I have already noted that it seems appropriate for the meditator to express wonder at this point in the work, for what follows it are precisely the effects proper to wonder as Descartes describes it in the passions—it leads the meditator to knowledge. Further, it seems to be a truism that God is wonderful in Descartes' sense: rare, insofar as God is the only thing which can be the cause of the meditator's own existence, and extraordinary, insofar as God is the perfect being capable of causing the existence of another being who has an idea of a perfect being. But I want to suggest that there is more to it as well.

Generosity, for Descartes, is a species of esteem, which itself is a species of wonder; we esteem something just when we wonder at its worth—its meanness or lowness. In the case of generosity, we esteem ourselves as highly as we legitimately can, and we do so just by recognizing our own freedom and then realizing that freedom in acting well. One might thus say that Cartesian generosity is a wonder at our own free will. There is a sense in which the meditator, in wondering at God at the end of the Third Meditation, is also beginning to wonder at himself, and in particular at his own free will. It is this wonder which leads him forward to further knowledge of his own nature, and ultimately to the method for avoiding error. And it is this method that holds the key to his resolution of his skeptical worries.

Let us consider the penultimate paragraph of the Third Meditation. It begins as follows:

> And indeed it is no surprise that God, in creating me, should have placed this idea in me to be as it were, the mark of the craftsman stamped on his work—not that the mark need be anything distinct from the work itself. But the mere fact that God created me is a very strong basis for believing that I am somehow made in his image and likeness, and that I perceive that likeness, which includes the idea of God, by the same faculty which enables me to perceive myself. (AT VII 51; CSM II 35)

The meditator here intimates that some identification between himself and God is in order—he is somehow made in God's image and likeness—and so it seems that in wondering at God, he also wonders at himself a bit. But there is more, for in the Fourth Meditation, the meditator goes on to claim that the similarity that he and God share lies just in the freedom of the will. Thus, the wonder at himself he feels through his wonder at God becomes precisely that wonder at one's own freedom that constitutes in part generosity. It is this generosity that allows him to see that he has no cause for complaint in how God has created him. And his coming to terms with his own nature as a finite thinking thing in this way ultimately leads him to remedy the excesses of his desire for knowledge. Once he understands himself properly, he cannot help but desire to know only that which he is capable of knowing.

So the laughter at the end of the *Meditations* is a laughter not only at the hyperbole of the skeptical arguments. It is also a laughter at himself and his own excesses. His earlier aspirations to absolute certainty amounted to wanting a superhuman degree of knowledge, and that desire was indeed ridiculous.

Reading the meditator's passions as integral to the project of the *Meditations* in this way does not take away from any of the epistemological or metaphysical claims of that work. Descartes is still to be understood as putting forward a view about what needs to be in place if we are to be able to claim to have knowledge about anything at all. But such metaphysical positions are not held in a realm of pure reason, divorced from our nature as human beings. Part of knowing, for Descartes, is knowing who one is, and this self-knowledge essentially involves feeling a certain way toward oneself. This feeling, the passion of generosity, in turn informs one's other thoughts. So, on this reading of the place of the passions in the *Meditations,* epistemology is not to be divorced from one's affective life. Knowledge involves self-knowledge, which is emotionally laden. Knowing involves not only having one's thoughts in order, but also having one's feelings in order. But if the passions are integral to the *Meditations,* there is still much to clarify. We are certainly left with the questions arising out of the weaker reading, questions about the affective dimension of pure thought, and about the relation between pure thought and full-fledged human reason. These questions also get a particular grip insofar as they are tied to questions about just how affect figures in self-understanding, and in our knowledge of the world.

My aim in this paper was to raise a slew of questions about the place of the passions in Descartes' *Meditations,* questions for which I have very few answers. For most readers of Descartes, the fact that the passions are mentioned there at all is surprising. I hope I have clarified just how it is surprising. On the one hand, even if we don not choose to make much of the meditator's expression of his passions, their presence challenges our assumptions about Descartes' dualism and, in particular, about the nature of pure thought, as well as our assumptions about the nature of Descartes' meditator. On the other hand, if we do choose to take the passions as integral to the work, we not only are faced with the same sorts of questions about Cartesian metaphysics, but also are presented with an epistemological program which takes our affective life to be an essential part of our claims to knowledge. Either course should move us to feel at least a bit of wonder, and lead us to set about exploring the new text we have found.

NOTES

An earlier version of this paper was developed in the National Endowment for the Humanities' Summer Institute on Mind, Self, and Psychopathology at Cornell University, 1998. I thank Shawn Gallagher, Tamar Szabo Gendler, Christian Perring, and Patricia Ross for their helpful discussions there.

1. In providing this catalog I hope to have been complete, but undoubtedly there are expressions I have missed. Clearly any interpretation of the significance of these expressions must be able to accommodate instances I overlooked.
I use the following standard abbreviations for Descartes' works:

AT	*Oeuvres de Descartes*, ed. C. Adam and P. Tannery (Paris: Vrin, 1996). Followed by volume and page numbers.
CSM	*The Philosophical Writings of Descartes*, vols. I and II, ed. and trans. J. Cottingham, R. Stoothoff, and D. Murdoch (Cambridge: Cambridge University Press, 1984–85). Followed by volume and page numbers.
CSMK	*The Philosophical Writings of Descartes*, vol. III, ed. and trans. J. Cottingham, R. Stoothoff, D. Murdoch, and A. Kenny (Cambridge: Cambridge University Press, 1991). Followed by page numbers.
PS	*The Passions of the Soul*, followed by article numbers. Translated from the edition in AT.

2. I provide the Latin: "aliquando firmum & mansarum *cupiam* in scientiis stabilire" (AT VII 17). The French points less conclusively to a passion here as it reads simply: " si je *voulais* établir quelque chose de ferme et de constant dans les sciences . . ." (AT IX 13). Emphasis mine in both cases.
3. I have here deviated slightly from CSM, which translates both *timet* and *vereor* as "dread" and what I have translated as "spontaneously"—from *sponte* in the

Latin and *insensiblement* in the French—as "happily," entirely misleading for my purposes here. See CSM II 15.

4. The CSM translation has *turbatus*, read "tumbles me around," but the Latin phrase is *ita turbatus sum*. Now, one might not think that confusion is a passion, but the meditator is here describing the way he is feeling. If doubts remain, one might consider two things. First, *turbatus* may alternatively be translated by "perturbed," which does seem closer to a passion. And second, this alternate translation is a least a little closer to the French, which straightforwardly refers to a passion, namely, surprise: "et comme si tout à coup j'étais tombé dans une eau tres profonde, je suis tellement *surpris*, que je ne puis ni assurer mes pieds dans le fond, ni nager pur me soutenir au-dessus" [emphasis mine] (AT IX 18).

5. The Latin text reads: "Sed *pudeat* supra vulgus sapere *cupientam*, ex formis loquendi quas vulgus invenit dubitationem quaesivisse. . . ." The French is comparable: "Une homme qui *tâche* d'élever sa connaissance au delà du commun, doit *avoir honte* de tirer des ocasions de douter des formes et des termes de parler du vulgaire" (AT IX 25). Emphasis mine in both cases.

6. The Latin reads "non mihi esse *mirandum*" (AT VII 55), while the French reads "Je ne me dois point *étonner*" [emphasis mine] (AT IX 44).

7. I tend to think not, given the tightness of the writing of the *Meditations*. Every word seems carefully chosen, the whole work very tightly scripted. Such consideration might well support reading the language of the passions as a rhetorical device.

8. In the discussion here and in that which follows in section 3, I am relying on the distinction Amélie Rorty draws between interpretive meditations and revolutionary meditations in her "The Structure of Descartes' *Meditations*," in *Essays on Descartes' "Meditations"*, ed. A. O. Rorty (Berkeley: University of California Press, 1986). Rorty suggests that Descartes is "thoroughly evasive" as to whether his *Meditations* are meant to be of the interpretive or the revolutionary kind. For two other perspectives on the *Meditations* as meditations, see L. Aryeh Kosman, "The Naïve Narrator: Meditation in Descartes' *Meditations*," and Gary Hatfield, "The Senses and the Fleshless Eye: The Meditations as Cognitive Exercises," both in *Essays on Descartes' "Meditations"*.

9. It is certainly hard to find anyone committing to the position in print. But then it is equally hard to find anyone taking up any position about the nature of the meditator in print.

10. Wonder does not appear here on Descartes' list. Certainly the wonder at and adoration of God of the Third Meditation seem like just the kind of intellectual passions we would need to preserve our assumptions about the meditator. But the absence of wonder from Descartes' list here is unsettling, especially since he does not refer to an intellectual wonder anywhere else (he does admit that the love

of God is an intellectual passion). Moreover, in the *Passions of the Soul*, Descartes makes clear that even though wonder is essential to our intellectual development, it has a bodily cause: it is "caused first by the impression *in one's brain* that represents the object as rare and consequently worthy of being accorded great consideration" [emphasis mine] (PS a. 70; AT XI 380 f.). The brain is, of course, for Descartes, not identical with the mind.

11. The French edition's inclusion of love and hate in the Third Meditation list of what a thinking thing does could help in this regard. Of course, one who wanted to take this line would need to demonstrate that each passion as expressed by the meditator is an intellectual passion. And as the point made in n. 10 above illustrates, this is not as straightforward as one might like it to be.

12. See for instance Paul Hoffman, "The Unity of Descartes's Man," *Philosophical Review* 95 (1986): 343, and Margaret Wilson, *Descartes* (Boston: Routledge and Kegan Paul, 1978), 190, 207. Marleen Rozemond interprets this argument differently. See her *Descartes's Dualism* (Cambridge, MA: Harvard University Press, 1998), ch. 1.

13. See PS a. 40: "the principal effect of all the passions in men is that they incite and dispose their souls to will the things for which they prepare their body" (AT XI 359).

14. Or at least he takes himself to have done so in good faith. There is, of course, a further question as to whether the arguments of the *Meditations* are successful.

15. Although this passage occurs in the Third Meditation, it brings out succinctly what the meditator has taken to be the point of the last skeptical move of the First Meditation (AT VII 21).

16. "If, however, I simply refrain from making a judgement in cases where I do not perceive the truth with sufficient clarity and distinctness, then it is clear that I am behaving correctly and avoiding error. But if in such cases I either affirm or deny, then I am not using my free will correctly" (AT VII 59; CSM II 41).

17. And though this nature is part of what makes it possible for him to err, the other part of the cause of his mistakes—an infinite will, one which can assent to confused ideas as well as clear ones—is what makes him like God. Moreover, since it is within his power to avoid making those mistakes, he has all he needs to avoid error.

18. The very end of the Fourth Meditation makes this clear: "For I shall undoubtedly reach the truth, if only I give sufficient attention to all the things which I perfectly understand, and separate these from all the other cases where my apprehension is more confused and obscure. And this is just what I shall take good care to do from now on" (AT VII 62; CSM II 43).

19. See my "Cartesian Generosity," *Norms and Modes of Thinking in Descartes*, ed. Tuomo Aho and Mikko Yrjönsuuri, *Acta Philosophica Fennica* 64 (1999): 249–75.

CHAPTER 3

Love in the Ruins

Passion in Descartes' Meditations

WILLIAM BEARDSLEY

> There is a single active power in things: love, charity, harmony.
> —*Cogitationes Privatae* (1619)[1]

In his *Meditations,* Descartes presents a drama of separation and renewed commitment. Struggling first to separate herself from falsehood, the solitary heroine of the *Meditations* resolves to set aside "anything which admits of the slightest doubt." Through the slow uncovering of matters "so much in harmony with [her] nature" that they seem to have been "long present within [her]," she finally is able to unite with Truth. [2] The pattern is repeated, in miniature, in many of the best-known moments of the *Meditations.* The central business of the Second Meditation concerns first her attempt to find all those things she had previously taken herself to be that can be "said to be separate from [herself]," followed by the discovery that thought alone is inseparable, followed by the early stages of a patient yet persistent clarification of her self-understanding as a thinking thing. This saga of setting aside and joining together is thus at the same time an account of an initial limiting and subsequent enlarging of a conception of self. A later stage of this process of self-clarification occurs in the Fifth Meditation, where the pattern of deliberate separation followed by re-union is repeated yet again. Here, our heroine notices what can and cannot be separated from her thinking and thereby discovers patterns of thought in harmony with her nature. The thought of existence, for example, can no more be separated from her thought of a supremely perfect being than her "idea of a mountain can be separated from an idea of a valley." Such links, isolated through attempted separation, become explicit features of her thinking, present to her attentive mind. The process is one of enlarging, through discovered unions, her understanding of herself as a thinker.

The struggles portrayed in this narrative presuppose a mind that is able to "will to be separated from the objects" that appear harmful or unsuitable to its nature as a thinking thing and, at the same time, able to "join itself in volition to objects that appear suitable to it." These twin abilities are discussed in some detail, if in a slightly different context, in the *Passions of the Soul*. The first of these abilities is associated by Descartes with the passion he terms hate, the second with the passion of love. Given the central role played by these patterns of separation and joining in the *Meditations*, it is worth asking whether and to what extent the account of the passions of love and hate illuminate Descartes' meditative strategies. Much could be said concerning this notion of separation and the relevance of Descartes' account of the psychology of hate to an appreciation of his strategy in the *Meditations*, particularly to that of the First Meditation, which aims to "demolish everything completely" and culminates in the image of a "malicious demon of utmost power and cunning." I shall focus here on the complementary notion of "joining" and the role of love in our heroine's attempt to establish something permanent in the ruins of her previous beliefs. I begin with a brief sketch of Descartes' account of love.

According to the elegant taxonomy at the heart of Part One of *The Passions of the Soul*, love and its twin, hate, are passions in the "restricted sense" (art. 25, AT XI 348; SV 32). As such they are thoughts, but they differ from those thoughts Descartes terms actions in that, unlike volitions, for example, their character as thoughts depends more on the body than on the soul (art. 17, AT XI 342; SV 28). While passions in the restricted sense count as perceptions, the fact that they have bodily causes distinguishes them from such perceptions as intentional imaginings, the perceptions of volitions, and the perceptions of those things "which are solely intelligible and not imaginable." The latter have the soul as cause, and are more properly termed actions (art. 20, AT XI 344; SV 29). Genuine passions, including love and hate, depend on the body, specifically on the nerves and animal spirits. Other thoughts have proximate bodily causes, of course, but unlike sense impressions, for example, which are "referred" to external objects, and such perceptions as hunger and thirst, which are "referred to the body," passions in the restricted sense are "referred to the soul." In short, passions like love and hate are "perceptions or sensations or excitations of the soul which are referred to it in particular and which are caused, maintained and strengthened by some movement of the spirits" (art. 27, AT XI 349; SV 33).

Descartes' official definitions of love and hate are as follows:

> Love is an excitation of the soul, caused by the motion of the spirits, which incites it to join itself in volition to the objects that appear to be suitable to it. And hatred is an excitation, caused by the spirits, which incites the soul to will to be separated from the objects that are presented to it as harmful. I say these excitations are caused by the spirits in order to distinguish Love and Hatred, which are passions and depend on the body, both from judgments which also incline the soul to join itself in volition with the things it deems good and to separate itself from those it deems bad, and from excitations which these judgments excite by themselves in the soul. (AT XI 381; SV 62)

Note that passionate love is not itself the "joining" of the soul to an apparently suitable object, but rather the perception that incites the soul to this subsequent act. Indeed, it is a central tenet of Descartes' moral psychology that the primary role of any genuine passion is to dispose the soul toward other thoughts. "The utility of all the passions consists only in their strengthening thoughts which it is good that the [soul] preserve and which could otherwise be easily effaced from it, and causing them to endure in the soul" (art. 74, AT XI 383; SV 59). Passions dispose the soul to think this thought rather than that, or induce in the soul a standing disposition or habit of thought.[3] Love serves to strengthen the original perception of the lovable object and "compels" the soul to "dwell upon" the perception of the object (art. 102, AT XI 404; SV 74). It also "incites" the soul to a subsequent act of union "in volition."

This distinction between the confused perception that is the passion and the subsequent act of volitional union is made clearer in a well-known letter to Chanut. There Descartes distinguishes between the passion of love and "love which is purely intellectual or rational"(1 February 1647, AT IV

602; CSMK 306). He goes on to claim that all passions have an intellectual counterpart, independent of the body. "All the movements of the will which constitute love, joy, sadness and desire, in so far as they are rational thoughts and not passions, could exist in our soul even if it had no body." These rational counterparts are "movements of will," and are actions rather than passions. Passionate, or sensual love "is nothing but a confused thought, aroused in the soul by some motion of the nerves, which makes it disposed to have the other, clearer thought which constitutes rational love." Passionate love is as different from rational love as the confused thought that is a sensation of dryness in the throat is from the desire to drink. "The thought by which the soul feels the heat [around the heart] is different from the thought which joins it to the object." The first is a passion, whose character is determined by the body. The second is an action, involving the will. Note that a judgment concerning the suitability of some object might also play the role of inclining or inciting the soul, according to Descartes' definitions. These judgments must be distinguished from the passion love. In such cases, it is an act of the will (the volitional component of the judging) that determines the soul.

In summary, then, when some lovable object is presented to the soul an impression is formed in the brain, which in turn leads to a complex set of changes in the animal spirit system involving the heart. These bodily changes are the cause of that thought which is the passion of love. This thought both strengthens the original perception and incites the soul to a subsequent movement of the will. Before we continue, however, I need to examine the volitional component of rational or intellectual love. What does Descartes mean when he describes the soul as "joining itself in volition" to some object?

This is a complicated issue, but because it is important to my argument I must advance an interpretive suggestion. Intellectual or rational love is described by Descartes in the letter to Chanut as consisting "simply in the fact that when our soul perceives some present or absent good, which it judges to be fitting for itself, it joins itself to it willingly, that is to say, it considers itself and the good in question as forming two parts of a single whole" (AT IV 601; CSMK 306). The "joining" simply is the "considering," and my suggestion is that this "considering itself and the good in question as forming two parts of a single whole," like affirming and denying, is an act of the will directed toward some representation, in this case, the complex of perception of the present or absent good and perception of the soul it-self. For the soul to "join itself in volition" to a suitable object is for it to "consider" itself in union with the object. In other words, my suggestion is that rational or intellectual love has a structure similar to that of a Cartesian judgment. It involves both a representation and a volitional attitude toward that representation. Rational love is an act of will. The intellectual counter-parts of passions in the strict sense are all of them "modes of willing"[4]

It should now be clear that this act of considering or joining is an act of self-constitution, self-definition, or perhaps even self-expression. For the soul to love something is for it to take an active, willful attitude first to itself and then to its object. In considering itself part of a whole together with the object in question, the soul is, in effect, expressing its nature or essence.[5]

We must return to the Fifth Meditation for some indication of the rele-vance of this examination of intellectual and passionate love to Descartes' strategies. At the heart of this Meditation is a sketch of an account of the "true and immutable natures" that inform our thought. This sketch, to-gether with various supporting discussions in the correspondence and Re-plies to Objections, seeks to ground the truths of mathematics, which describe "the essence of material things," or "corporeal nature taken in gen-eral," in the complex structure of our thinking. This discussion is also cru-cial to an understanding of the process through which perception becomes clear and distinct. In many ways, this discussion parallels the wax passage of the Second Meditation. There, through an imagined series of experiments, an attempt is made to "take away everything which does not belong to the wax, and see what is left." The process of successful separations eventually reveals the nature of the wax. The perception of the wax can be "imperfect and confused, as it was before, or clear and distinct as it is now," that is, at the conclusion of the process (AT VII 31; CSM II 21). The process is just a bit more complicated in the Fifth Meditation, where the primary task is to determine what is and what is not contained in a given nature, such as "triangle." These relations of containment constitute truth for Descartes. "When we say that something is *contained in the nature or concept* of a thing, this is the same as saying that it is true of that thing or that it can be asserted of that thing" (AT VII 162; CSM II 114). The search is for legitimate predi-cative inferences, movements of thought from some leading idea to some consequent. Inferences are identified and then, in effect, tested to isolate those where the antecedent or starting point contains the consequent. The solitary thinker discovers these truths through the fact that she cannot now fail to recognize the relationship whether or not she had previously noticed it, whether or not she now wants to, and even whether or not there is such an object in the world outside her thought.

Descartes makes this clearer in several important letters where he claims that the inability to separate in thought the consequent from the antecedent is the mark of this containment and hence of legitimate predicative inference. The antecedent and the consequent must be linked "in such a way that although one can think of the one without paying any attention to the other, it is impossible to deny one of the other where one thinks of both together" (to Gibeuf, 14 January 1642, AT III 474; CSMK 201). Descartes is careful to distinguish this way of holding things separately in thought from intellectual abstraction, which is nothing more than "my turning my thought away from one part of the contents of the richer idea the better to apply it to another part with greater attention" (AT III 475; CSMK 202). While genuine exclusion is based on recognizing the limits of thought, abstraction is a matter of focusing or restricting attention (to Mesland, 2 May 1644, AT IV 116; CSMK 234). Successive exclusions constitute a process whereby the implicit content of a perception, containment relations that had not been recognized previously, are "drawn out" from the perception and made part of its explicit, manifest content (Mersenne, 16 June 1641, AT III 38304; CSMK 183–84). It is these inferential patterns that, when discovered, seem "so open and so much in harmony" with our nature as thinkers.

According to the definitions of the *Principles*, a perception is clear when "it is present and accessible to the attentive mind" (AT VIIIA 22; CSM I 207). It becomes clearer "the more properties or qualities we perceive in that thing," that is, the more the implicit features of the conceived object are acknowledged and joined with the growing explicit or manifest content. A perception is more distinct the fewer qualities and features are mistakenly seen in it. "A concept is not any more distinct because we include less in it; its distinctness simply depends on our carefully distinguishing what we do include in it from everything else" (AT VIIIA 30; CSM II 215). Furthermore, a perception is made distinct by stripping away features that, while part of the original manifest or explicit content, are not in fact linked to the perception in the proper way. The perception of the wax is made distinct through thought experiments that are successful attempts at exclusion in that they remove features—the taste and smell of the honeycomb—that do not pertain to the essence of wax.

As I have described it, the movement toward clarity and distinctness has both a positive and a negative phase. Sustained success of the negative component, the moment of separation, exclusion, and denial, requires that those features which have been found by successful exclusion not to pertain to the nature represented by the idea remain excluded. It requires an act of separation or rejection, and this act must be strengthened and sustained. If exclusions are subsequently taken for mere abstractions, the excluded feature may creep back into the explicit content of the idea. This is likely to happen when there are other pressures to consider the excluded feature as part of the idea in question. These pressures include prior habits of assent that "capture the [meditator's] belief, which is, as it were, bound over to them as a result of long occupation and the law of custom." A judgment that the given feature is separable may be sufficient to incite the soul to separate it from the developing idea, but the soul is unable to sustain this separation in the face of long-standing contrary habits. This is why Descartes takes such great pains to construct the image of the malicious demon, to counterbalance the weight of preconceived opinion and to overcome the "distorting influence of habit." The thinker's inordinate attachment to the senses must be broken by the establishment of contrary habits as powerful as those that have been built up "from childhood." Descartes' deliberate strategy is to induce something very much like the passion of hate in order to instill counterbalancing habits and to dispose the soul to "separate itself willingly" from objects now perceived to be dangerous and unsuitable. The passion of hate is invoked through powerful imagery to dispose the soul to acts of intellectual hatred. The counterbalancing habits induced by the demon image prevent the soul, at least as long as it attends to the image, from backsliding and taking "the detachment from the senses" won by the skeptical reflections of the First Meditation to be something more like mere abstractions. The thinker must do more than not attend to the objects of her sense-based judgments; she must deny their very existence so as to "resolutely guard against assenting to any falsehood." A passion, not just its intellectual counterpart, is implicated here.[6]

The wax discussion might suggest that no further act of will is necessary in what I have been calling the positive phase of the process. ("[T]ake away everything . . . and see what is left.") This is because what is at stake here in the Second Meditation is the essence of the wax in the narrow sense captured later by the phrase "principal attribute."[7] There is a broader sense of "essence," however, that becomes increasingly important as the *Meditations* progresses. The essence of a substance in this latter sense includes everything "presupposed" by the principal attribute. The soul is a thinking thing, and its essence in this second sense includes everything stored away in the "treasure house of the mind," the entire range of possible acts of thought ordained by God when he created finite thinking substance. It is essence in this sense that is of concern when the meditatrix moves from the discovery that she is a thinking thing to begin to develop a "better understanding" of herself. The first self-understanding is gained through the *cogito* exercise — "what is left at the end" of the skeptical argumentation is the essence in this sense. The second, progressively richer self-understanding requires much more than this, namely, the incorporation of those inferential connections that have been found to be inseparable from one's nature as a thinker into one's developing self-conception. This positive part of the process does seem to require an act of will in addition to the attempted denials.

Commentators often recognize the involvement of the will and the role of passion in the negative phase of the process yet reject any parallel account of the positive phase, as if the process of ideas becoming distinct requires work while clarity is to be had for free. Descartes' obvious manipulation of the passions of his readers and fellow meditators is limited, on this view, to the establishment of the proper conditions for the acceptance of truth. Passions help to break bad habits of judging, detach the mind from the senses and prepare the ground on which innate ideas can "emerge" and "assert" themselves.[8] Remember, however, that clarity and distinctness are each a function of the content of perception and hence of the movements of thought one commonly or habitually makes. In other words, they are each a function of the inferences one is tempted to accept. Each is won through a process of willful restructuring of content-constituting inferential patterns. New habits of thought must be established willfully as old habits are discouraged. God has, of course, "ordained" the content of innate ideas, but this does not mean that acquiring and sustaining the related habits is not, in the relevant sense, up to us and a matter of meditative effort. The establishment of the "proper," divinely ordained habits requires passion and will every bit as much as does the destruction of bad old habits. The work of meditation does not end with the *cogitio*.

Intellectual love is the engine of clarity. When the intellect incorporates a candidate feature into an expanding and increasingly clear perception, it is, in effect, doing something very much like "joining itself to it willingly." First, there is the perception that a relation of containment between ideas is "in harmony" with the meditator's nature as thinker. We notice a failed attempt to exclude one feature from an idea, the failure to think one thing while denying another. This noticing is, in effect, a perception of an object as "suitable" to the soul, as a "good." It is this perception which then leads the soul to a further act, an action or movement of the will in which it incorporates the discovered inferential linkage into its developing self-understanding. Here, the soul is doing nothing other than considering itself (that is, its essence *qua* thinking thing as it has thus far been made explicit) and its object (the newly noticed inferential pattern) as forming "two parts of a single whole" (the complete and as yet only partially discovered essence — the totality of created thought). The harmonies are there in the soul all along, of course. I am suggesting that the positive phase of the task requires not just that they be noticed, perhaps only to be put aside, but that they be acknowledged, endorsed, and embraced. Clarity requires the appropriation of new idea content. This is the role of intellectual love.

Thus far I have argued that intellectual love, or something structurally similar to it, is implicated in the process of clarifying perceptions. Has the passion of love a role to play in this process? I suggest that it does. To make this clear, I must first examine the sorts of failures that are likely to occur as a real thinker seeks to clarify her intellectual perceptions.

The positive phase of this process, the moment of joining and incorporation, is susceptible to failure as serious as those plaguing the negative phase. There, new habits were needed to counterbalance the tendency to take exclusion for mere abstraction. In the positive phase, however, the thinker comes up against the finitude of created minds. Human attention has a limited focus. We cannot simultaneously attend to all of the features that we, through long and patient work in geometry, for example, have come to see pertain to the nature of a triangle. Perhaps only an angelic intellect can grasp in this way all the inferential links that, taken together, constitute a true and immutable nature. Yet these links have been made explicit and have been embraced through acts of intellectual love. These links, when not attended to, are easily broken or ignored. Any number of conditions, including the ongoing distraction of the senses, may cause them to degrade. Something like a passion is needed to condition a habit or standing disposition of the soul toward renewed acts of intellectual love. Passionate love disposes the soul toward continued acts of joining and strengthens and sustains volitional unions by causing the soul to dwell on perceptions of failed attempts at exclusion and conditioning habits of thought. Passion serves to unite perceptions across the inevitable periods of inattention and helps block the "distracting influence of false appearance." Only one trained in the discipline of love can progress beyond the limits of human attention.

Descartes explains the needs for meditative effort and the development of proper habits in the positive phase of the process in a letter to Princess Elisabeth, who, more than any other correspondent, pressed Descartes on the details of his meditative practice.

> Moreover, I said above that to be disposed to judge well always requires not only knowledge, but also habit. For, inasmuch as we are unable to be continually attentive to the same thing, however clear and evident might have been the reasons that formerly persuaded us of some truth, we can still afterward be turned away from believing it by false appearance— unless long and frequent meditation has so imprinted it upon our mind as to turn it into a habit. (AT IV 296; CSMK 267)

Meditation is more that just a means of securing the proper atmosphere for the magical emergence of truth; it is required to establish the habits of thought that enable finite, embodied thinkers to overcome their limited attentive capacities. Descartes is clear that meditation involves passion and the deliberate restructuring of mental dispositions.

I have suggested that rational or intellectual love has a role to play in the positive phase of the process of the clarification of perception. I have also suggested that passionate love may play a subsidiary role in this process. In my account of the role of intellectual love, however, I have taken its object to be a newly discovered inferential pattern or linkage. Now I must face the problem of how anything like that could possibly be the object of a passionate, sensuous love. Remember that the relation between passionate and intellectual love is understood by Descartes to be that between a confused thought and a clearer thought. What could be the object of the confused thought that would dispose the soul to consider itself part of a growing inferential web? What union could be the passionate analog of that between the thinker and those divinely ordained patterns of thought in harmony with her nature? My final, tentative suggestion is that the passionate love we are looking for here is the love of God.

Descartes considers the passionate love of God in a letter to Chanut. Interestingly, Descartes describes this love as possible only as the result of attentive meditation, using the very language in which he describes the task of the First Meditation. "The soul must be very detached from the traffic of the senses if it is to represent to itself the truths which arouse such a love" (AT IV 607–8; CSMK 308–9). The continuously distracting presence of other objects must be overcome if we are to enjoy "the most delightful and useful passion possible." It may be doubted, Descartes writes, that we can have such a love for God, as "nothing about God can be visualized by the imagination." Nevertheless, if we "consider that He is a mind, or thinking substance; and that our soul's nature resembles His sufficiently for us to believe that it is an emanation of His supreme intelligence" we make this love a genuine passion.

We still need something to imagine in order for our thinking to have an effect on the body and leave those traces in the brain that in turn cause the motions around the heart that produce the passion. Descartes' suggestion is that we can imagine "our love itself . . . that is, we can consider ourselves in relation to God as a minute part of all the immensity of the created universe." I take this to mean that if we are able to form a general idea of a union between our soul and an object and extend this idea to the "immensity of the created universe," then this idea is enough to cause the changes in the heart and animal spirit system that produce the passion. Attentive meditation, in other words, prepares the mind for thoughts of the relation of our finite natures to God's infinity and involves images of our own ability to love and join ourselves willingly to objects. The confused thought formed when these thinkings stir up the animal spirits is the passion for God.

If the Third Meditation is read in light of this discussion, it is tempting to see it as aimed at producing this passion for God-as-mind, through the deliberate use of images relating our nature as thinkers to His. There is clearly an effort on Descartes' part to get those who are meditating along with him to develop a conception of God in relation to their developing conception of themselves as thinkers. "I perceive that likeness [with God], which includes the idea of God, by the same faculty which enables me to perceive myself" (AT VII 52; CSM II 35). The conclusion of the Meditation also suggests that what been accomplished involves the passion of love. "I should like to pause here and spend some time in the contemplation of God; to reflect on his attributes and to gaze with wonder and adoration on the beauty of this immense light" (AT VII 53; CSM II 36). This contemplation "enables us to know the greatest joy of which we are capable in this life." Admiration and joy are the natural companions of passionate love. It might be argued that we are dealing only with rational joy, the intellectual counterpart of the passion, but I think that Descartes' discussion in the letter to Chanut gives us some reason to suppose that it is the passions of joy, wonder, and admiration, and hence the passion of love, that are evoked here.

Perhaps God plays a role in the subsequent positive phase of the *Meditations* similar to that played by his evil counterpart in the opening, destructive moments. Just as the demon is invoked as the cause of all deception and as related to the thinker in a personal way (all of his energies are employed to deceive and ensnare her judgment) in order to mobilize the passion of hate and dispose the soul toward sustained separation from the harmful objects of the senses, so the image of God—made concrete in the form of the thinker's relation to her own developing understanding—is perhaps invoked to produce the passion of love and hence to dispose the soul toward persisting acts of union and commitment. An image of God as the source of truth and light and as specially related to the thinker ("I understand that I am a thing which . . . aspires without limit to ever greater and better things. . . . he on whom I depend has within him all those greater things" [AT VII 51; CSM II 35]) agitates the spirits and causes a passionate love which incites acts of intellectual or rational love and sustains previous acts of union. This passionate love of God is useful because it focuses attention on our own development as thinkers and disposes the soul to other thoughts, including both new lines of intellectual inquiry and, especially, those acts of intellectual love central to our self-understanding as thinkers.

I have suggested in this essay that the passion of love is an important component of the search for truth. My focus has been on the account of the clarification of perception sketched in the Fifth Meditation. If I am on the right track here, this suggestion should help illuminate other episodes in the *Meditations.* It might, for example, help explain how clarity and distinctness of perception could compel assent. For those who limit the role of passion to the establishment of the context in which the power of clear and distinct ideas emerge, this compulsion remains a bit mysterious. But if, as

I have suggested, the very process of clarification involves acts of willful self-identification, then it becomes less mysterious how a perception that has been rendered clear and distinct could, "morally speaking" compel assent, even if it is "open to us to hold back from pursuing a clearly known good, or from admitting a clearly perceived truth, provided we consider it a good thing to demonstrate the freedom of our will by so doing" (to Mesland, 9 February 1645, AT IV 173; CSMK 245). If intellectual love is implicated in the process by which perception is clarified, insofar as it drives the incremental incorporation of features that is required for the full content of our ideas to be made "present and accessible to the attentive mind," then the will is so much involved, and the entire process is so much one of self-expression, that a subsequent act of denial would be all but impossible. The process by which a perception is made clear and distinct makes the resulting perception so much a part of who we take ourselves to be as thinkers that it cannot be denied. If the passion involved here is the love of God, then it becomes clearer how the patterns of inference He ordained when creating finite minds compel assent. The lover of God, Descartes writes to Chanut, unites herself "entirely to God in volition" and hence "loves Him so perfectly that [she] desires nothing at all except that His will should be done."

NOTES

I have been influenced here by Annette Baier's groundbreaking work on Descartes, published and unpublished, particularly "Descartes' Balancing Act with the True and the Good" (1987, unpublished). I am happy to acknowledge my indebtedness to Prof. Baier, whose example continues to inform my philosophical self-understanding. I am grateful to Andrew Youpa and Amy Schmitter for helpful comments on an early draft of this essay.

1. AT X 218; CSM I 5. I employ the following abbreviations:

AT   *Oeuvres de Descartes*, ed. C. Adam and F. Tannery (Paris: L. Cerf, 1897–1910).

CSM   *The Philosophical Writings of Descartes*, vols. I and II, ed. and trans. J. Cottingham, R. Stoothoff, and D. Murdoch (Cambridge: Cambridge University Press, 1985).

CSMK   *The Philosophical Writings of Descartes*, vol. III, *The Correspondence*, ed.
and trans. J. Cottingham, R. Stoothoff, D. Murdoch, and A. Kenny
(Cambridge: Cambridge University Press, 1991).

SV   *The Passions of the Soul*, ed. and trans. S. Voss (Indianapolis: Hackett
Press, 1989).

2. AT VII 64; CSM 45.

3. See Amélie Rorty, "Descartes on Thinking with the Body," in *The Cambridge Companion to Descartes*, ed. J. Cottingham (Cambridge: Cambridge University Press, 1992).

4. See *Principles* I 32 (AT VIIIA 17–18; CSM I 204). A similar account can be given of all the other passions. Joy, for example, has its purely intellectual counterpart "which comes into the soul by action of the soul alone" and is "the enjoyment it has of the good which its understanding represents to it as its own." That is, intellectual joy involves an attitude (enjoyment) toward a perception.

5. The idea that the passions, particularly that of love, are crucial to self-representations is explored by Amy Morgan Schmitter, "Representation, Self-representation and the Passions in Descartes," *Review of Metaphysics* 48 (December 1994): 331–57.

6. I agree with Zeno Vendler when, in a comparison of the *Meditations* to the *Spiritual Exercises* of Loyola, he writes: "The aim of the *Meditations* is not merely to convince the reader of the truth of certain propositions, but to *change the will of meditator* concerning the conduct of [her] intellectual life." Zeno Vendler, "Descartes' Exercises," *Canadian Journal of Philosophy* 19, no. 2 (1989): 193–224.

7. See *Principles* I 53 (AT VIIIA 25; CSM I 210).

8. See, for example, Thomas Wartenberg's perceptive account of Descartes' correspondence with Princess Elisabeth on the subject of meditation and its requirements. "Descartes's claim is that, in the proper sorts of circumstances, it is possible for the human being to get his or her consciousness to dampen the press of sensible ideas upon itself so that a set of rational ideas will emerge with a vigor and assertiveness that exceeds that of sensible ideas, at least within that specific context. Creating the proper context within oneself for the emergence of these rational ideas with all of their force is the key step in being a philosophic meditator. . . . " T. E. Wartenberg, "Descartes's Mood: The Question of Feminism in the Correspondence with Elisabeth," in *Feminist Interpretations of René Descartes*, ed. S. Bordo (University Park: Pennsylvania State University Press, 1999), 204.

The Passionate Intellect

*Reading the (Non-)Opposition of Reason and
Emotions in Descartes*

AMY MORGAN SCHMITTER

I

One of the many things for which her students can thank Annette Baier is
for showing us firsthand that a philosopher need not compromise her feminist commitments by falling in love with the works of a long-dead, quite
white and almost certainly male philosopher, even one who makes a habit
of wearing orientalizing turbans. Of course, the main object of her philosophical affections has been David Hume, but she has also shown us that
such primary attachments need not forbid strong affection for the works of
other (equally dead, white and male) philosophers. Quite a few of her students, indeed quite a few of her women students (as the contributions to this
volume will attest), have followed Baier to the study of a philosopher seemingly very different in temperament and views from Hume, namely, René
Descartes. Baier has speculated on why many women have been attracted to
Descartes' writings;[1] she has herself been an important contributing cause.
Because of her, many women (and men) have found themselves both interested in Descartes and equipped with the various skills that make reading his

works exciting and profitable. And because of her, we can pursue our commitments under circumstances of greater dignity and freedom than those in which Baier found herself for much of her career.[2]

Like a good caretaker of a new generation of philosophical persons, Annette Baier has done less to instill particular beliefs in her students than to equip them with the practices and techniques that make up an "ethic" of reading. I call it an "ethic of reading" because chief among its precepts is respect for the "reading instructions" of an author—be they Descartes' injunctions to respect the order of his meditations, or Hume's characterization of the *Treatise* as something that gains moral force as it proceeds. Hand in hand with this goes another precept seemingly at odds with the first: the injunction to read between the cracks. What constitutes reading between the cracks depends on where the cracks are; it particularly depends on what the history of reception, the tradition of reading has been. Reading between the cracks requires, at the very least, attention to what is *not* highlighted in current interpretations; even more, it involves a kind of contrariness directed not so much at the author as at what has been made of the works, especially if they have been treated reductively, or selectively, or anachronistically.[3] Both require the practice of what Baier has attributed to J. L. Austin, a "fidelity to complex fact," where the complex fact is the substance of the author's works and the fidelity in no way precludes flamboyance. Perhaps the Baierian ethic of reading is nothing more (or less) than "reading like a girl"—a discipline open to all and requiring neither slavish adherence nor dismissive rejection of the works of philosophical foremothers or forefathers.[4]

What follows will, I hope, exhibit some of the virtues of "reading like a girl." And I hope that it will seem merely a passing irony that this reading is directed at what is already a contrarian account. For my target is a critique of Descartes that takes his dualism to task on feminist grounds. I first started thinking about this critique a few years ago when I received a book sent by a publisher hopeful (in the way that academic publishers are hopeful) that it would be adopted for a course for which the texts were already long ordered. This book set out to provide a feminist reading of the history of western philosophy, aimed at the introductory student. The end is admirable, its execution difficult, but I must confess that I was rather taken aback when I turned to the section on Descartes and learned that his mind-body dualism also extends to a dualism about reason and the emotions. That is, it erects a sharp divide amounting to an opposition between the intellectual and the affective dimensions of human experience—one that easily takes on gender associations.[5]

This may be a crude way of putting the point, but it has the virtue of spotlighting what I think is a widespread (if often inchoate) view that "Cartesian" dualism endorses a sharp split between intellect and emotion, or cognition and affection, in which the prior term is privileged.[6] Familiar as these claims may be, it has mostly been left to feminist critics to articulate the thesis explicitly. Susan Bordo, for one, despite noting similarities between clear and distinct perceptions belonging to the intellect and the emotions, nonetheless claims that "the emotions may overtake us in ways that obscure our intellectual vision"—an innocuous enough claim until it is characterized as "the traditional picture that comes down to us from Descartes."[7] Even a sophisticated account such as Genevieve Lloyd's sees some sort of division between the two with the palm going to reason; as she describes "the drama of dominance between human traits" in Descartes' philosophy, whatever belongs to the body is seen as an encroachment from outside the soul; this includes sensation, imagination, and what she identifies as "non-intellectual passion."[8] Although Lloyd is careful to specify "non-intellectual" passions as what is to be dominated, she does not suggest that there is any other kind of emotion. And few others are as careful as Lloyd, with the result that it has become, as Amélie Rorty puts it,[9] "a familiar caricature" that Descartes has little use for the affective dimensions of thought. This assumption may have been perpetrated in part by the neglect, until recently, of Descartes' writings on the passions. It may also be largely attributed to the dominance of a certain kind of "conceptual map" associating dualisms between mind and body with dualisms between reason and emotion, between intellect and sensation, as well as between the theoretical and the practical (a distinction Lloyd points out).[10] This is not a *scholarly* view, but scholarly work on Descartes has done little to combat it.[11]

Although I think that this reading offers more of a caricature than a characterization of Descartes, I do want to emphasize my sympathy with the overall project. Feminist critiques in general have brought to light a bundle of issues that might not have been visible without them. And they have shown why they matter. It is because I am sympathetic to the ends of such critique that I hope to construct a view of Descartes that makes him much more congenial to the concerns current in feminist history of philosophy than he might otherwise have seemed. Presenting a Descartes who is not unsympathetic on the issues that matter may help to recover him for a feminist history of philosophy that goes beyond the strategy of "document and deplore," and to suggest that the familiar conceptual map is *not* Descartes' handiwork.

Nonetheless, the fact remains that many do deplore Descartes' views. Philosophers of widely varying stripes (not just feminists) unite in finding the source of current philosophical hobgoblins in Descartes' work, particularly in his dualism. That fact itself raises a number of questions: Why has Descartes received this sort of treatment? Why indeed has he been singled out for this treatment? On the other hand, if Descartes' views are as ripe for criticism as many intelligent people seem to think, what sense is there in saying that his "true" views are nevertheless quite different from what conventional wisdom holds? These are issues that are independent to some degree from decisions about how to interpret Descartes fairly. And when considering these issues, feminist critiques have a distinct advantage over most other forms of criticism. For they explicitly raise the questions about strategies of reading and the force of tradition that concern the history of reception. I hope to use some of the resources they provide when I return to such meta-historical considerations in the last section of this paper.

II

Critics of Cartesian dualism face a hurdle right from the start: an assertion about how many kinds of substance are to be found in the world does not seem *prima* (or even *secunda*) *facie* to involve a commitment to invidious and loaded oppositions between mind and body, reason and emotions, or theory and practice. True, the *Meditations on First Philosophy* does tell us that the mind is "better known" than the body, but that hardly amounts to asserting that the mind is *better* than the body. Descartes' claim here seems directed at the scholastic analysis of the order of concept-formation, particularly at the slogan that nothing is in the intellect unless first in the senses.

Still, many readers take Descartes' insistence on the epistemic priority of our access to the mental to be tantamount to claiming the greater value of the mind over the body. Something of this sort may be a familiar quasi-Platonic view, and as Susan James has shown, it enjoyed some currency among early modern thinkers. Descartes, however, does not make the intermediate moves required for reaching the conclusion. He neither associates epistemic accessibility with greater intelligibility, nor takes greater intelligibility to be tantamount to a higher degree of reality and proximity to the good. And since Descartes presents the view that the mind is better known than the body as an extraordinarily novel position designed to overturn reigning views about the genesis of our thinking,[12] he can hardly have held that our knowledge of the mind is always and necessarily incorrigible compared with our incorrigibly confused conception of body. Both require reformation and re-interpretation. Indeed, his physics is devoted to showing the thoroughgoing *intelligibility* of matter—in opposition to the low epistemic status traditionally accorded to matter by both Aristotelians and Platonists. In general, the distinction between mind and body looks like a straightforward metaphysical one—a distinction between two sorts of things in the world: one of which thinks, the other of which pushes out space. But the suspect brand of dualism requires the suppression of one term in order to secure the privilege of the other. Because it *recognizes* two sorts of things in the world, then, Descartes' dualism lacks the form of hierarchy and privilege.

So taking Cartesian dualism to be tantamount to valuing mind over matter rests on an association with a quasi-Platonic view that is otherwise quite foreign to Descartes' philosophical commitments. The next move made in the critique—identifying the distinction between mind and body with an opposition between reason and emotion—also rests on importing alien assumptions. Indeed, whatever sorts of distinctions Descartes may make between our intellectual and our affective characteristics fail to map neatly onto his mind/body dualism. What he calls "passions" are by strict definition bodily in origin, and thus distinct from what properly belongs to the soul (and especially to its active powers). But as we shall see, this notion of "passion" by no means exhausts the repertoire of affective states that Descartes recognizes, for not all emotions are bodily passions. At least some emotions derive from purely mental activities (although they may then have bodily effects), e.g., contemplating the true God produces joy and devotion. So any distinction between reason and "emotion" cannot be, as it were, even extensionally equivalent to the distinction Descartes makes between mind and body.

These may seem merely formalist quibbles, so let me now turn to my substantive argument: that Descartes grants a complex interdependence to reason and the emotions—that, in fact, he holds that the emotions can be rational and reason emotive. To be sure, Descartes does sometimes speak of "conquering" the passions, for he thinks our experience of certain passions under certain conditions can lead us astray. Nor does he dissolve all distinction between reason and emotion: having a reason for affirming (or denying) some claim is not the same thing as experiencing a passion that inclines (or disinclines) us toward something (although as we shall see, in some cases the latter will constitute the former). But even when he distinguishes most clearly between the two, Descartes never proposes that one should be the handmaid to the other, and he certainly never reduces all human goods to the goods of reason. Rather, he admits a diversity of goods relating to both emotions and reason, and many of the practices he recommends most strongly serve several ends. Disciplining the passions by making them rational is something Descartes values as much for the benefits it confers on our emotional life as for our ability to be reasonable: a well-ordered emotional life is an end in itself.

Of course, a happy and tranquil emotional life is not the only end recognized by Descartes: truth and the search for truth are also goods. But the emotions have an important role to play in even the most abstruse operations of our reason. The affective dimension of intellectual activity, dramatized perhaps most clearly in the *Meditations on First Philosophy*, has received too little attention in Descartes scholarship.[13] That is odd, for Descartes lavishes consideration on the passions attending our reasoning in some of his most interesting passages—and as I will argue, these passions may tell us a great deal about our cognitive successes and failures.[14]

Descartes chose both his French and Latin words with care, and care is due in treating the various terms he used: passion, emotion, affect, sentiment, and so forth. But his mature works show a fairly consistent conception of the main notion of passion.[15] The passions are to be classed with appetites and sensations as a kind of *internal* sensation, which, Descartes declares in *The Principles of Philosophy*, "must not be referred either to the mind alone or to the body alone,"[16] and in the *Passions of the Soul* are described as referred to the soul, but arising from changes in the body.[17] They count as emotions, because they are disturbances, literally movements, of the mind, distinguishable in part from other sensations by the specific changes in the body that are their causes. *What* those changes are remains a some-what unsettled question even in the later works,[18] but they always seem to be changes affecting large-scale bodily systems (e.g., the nerves, heart and circulatory system, and muscle groups). *The Passions of the Soul* declares that in all but the rather special case of wonder, the causes of the passions are those movements of the animal spirits that will cause changes in the heart and blood flow.[19] For this reason, the relevant changes can be understood functionally, in terms of the internal state of the body or events at the interface of body and environment (a feature of the passions that explains their value for medicine). As Amélie Rorty describes it, the passions are an important component of "the maintenance system"—those parts and operations of our bodies that are directed to their survival and maintenance.[20] Functionality[21] of this sort is not peculiar to the passions, and it seems unlikely that passions strictly understood can be distinguished from other sensations simply on the basis of their bodily causes (although Descartes seems to suggest this in the *Principles* IV §190);[22] rather, their distinctive feature is the "reference" they make to the soul. However, their bodily causes and the functional understanding of the changes they produce are quite important to the characterization of the passions.

We might expect the passions to have a special phenomenal character; indeed, the functions Descartes will attribute to the passions may seem to require that they have such a character. Since he admits that there are purely mental, or better intellectual, correlates to our passions, e.g., intellectual joy, we might also expect them to share some characteristic "feel," independent of their bodily or intellectual origins, which would qualify them both as "joy." Certainly, both bodily passions and their intellectual correlates count as perceptions; it is their causal antecedents that most concern Descartes when he makes the distinction. But he also sometimes suggests that the mind experiences them somewhat differently. Bodily passions, in particular, are taken to be confused thoughts, which the mind "*experiences* as a result of something happening to the body with which it is closely conjoined."[23] In both cases, however, he characterizes the nature of each passion almost exclusively in terms of its motivational force (for which the "reference to the soul" is important), paired with descriptions of how it "represents" the object that (at least under normal conditions) prompts the series of bodily changes resulting in the passion. He offers almost no description of any special phenomenal "feel" above and beyond the presentation of the object under some (evaluatively loaded) description and its effect on the will. And if our passions function properly, their phenomenal temper will correlate directly with the value (for the maintenance system) of the bodily changes that are their causes. So, it is not clear that bodily passions and intellectual emotions share a distinctive felt character isolable from their causes, or at least from what is perceived as their causes. Moreover, the antecedents of each sort of affective perception are importantly different. Thus, Descartes eventually suggests reserving "passion" to indicate "those perceptions, sensations or emotions of the soul which we refer particularly to it, and which are caused, maintained and strengthened by some movement of the spirits."[24] Bodily passions have bodily events as their proximate causes, the perception of which may well be confused (although clear), while their intellectual correlates always have *reasons* as their antecedents, and so qualify as distinct thoughts.[25]

On the other hand, by the time of the *Passions of the Soul*, Descartes most consistently groups both sorts of perceptions together as "'emotions' of the soul, . . . because the term may be applied to all the changes which occur in the soul . . . [and] more particularly, because, of all the kinds of thought which the soul may have, there are none that agitate and disturb it so strongly as the passions."[26] So although there may be no basic phenomenal "core," there does seem to be some ground shared between bodily passions and their correlated intellectual emotions, enough to justify applying the same categorizations to both. The passage just cited compares the two on the basis of their effects on the soul, effects that give them their particular motivational force: both a bodily passion and its intellectual correlate can prompt us to will the same sort of action. Then too, intellectual "passions" often stand in complex causal relationships to their counterpart bodily emotions (e.g., intellectual joy can cause the passion of joy and vice-versa).[27] Indeed, so intermingled can the two sorts of emotions become that we may be hard-pressed to tell what we are experiencing, or which came first.[28] Perhaps most importantly, the two kinds of emotions play similar roles in functional explanations: that is, the functions performed by the bodily passions for the compound substance constituting a full human being are analogous to those performed by the intellectual emotions for the soul *simpliciter*. So for all Descartes' insistence that "passion" should be reserved to indicate "those perceptions, sensations or emotions of the soul which we refer particularly to it, and which are caused, maintained and strengthened by some movement of the spirits,"[29] there is no atomistic core distinguishing the passions proper from other mental states. Descartes, in fact, offers us no way of describing or distinguishing the passions but by way of their causes, the evaluatively loaded representations of their objects, their motivational force and its functionality. The passions seem to come, if not already formed by judgments, at least tailor-made for articulation in judgment, and with natural (though not inescapable) relations to particular actions, to other emotions, and to various states of the soul.

This is a crucial point for understanding the susceptibility of the emotions to rational influence. On the one hand, Descartes emphasizes that he has no Cynical disdain for the passions, either as a whole or singly; indeed, he states in no uncertain terms that "the sweetest pleasures of this life" depend on the passions. On the other hand, as we have seen, he does sometimes talk about the conflict between reason and the impassioned body, and he does suggest that the "strongest souls" are those that "by nature can most easily *conquer* the passions."[30] The problem posed by the passions, however, is not that they oppose our rationally directed volition by their very nature. But they do have their origins elsewhere: namely, in the maintenance system of the body, which operates according to mechanical causes. Under standard conditions, this operation will indeed be functional for the maintenance system, but it can also misfunction. Now, the passions motivate action in two ways—their perception can sway our will, and the bodily events that are their causes may directly produce bodily movements (e.g., the movements of the animal spirits in the brain and through the pineal gland may produce both the perception of fear and running motions in the legs).[31] In both cases, the passions can direct our actions in ways contrary to the motivations springing from judgments of reason and the resulting application of the rational will to the pineal gland. Locating the first cause of a chain of bodily events in the pineal gland is particularly interesting, because there the possibility of conflict is most obvious and dramatic: the will may push the pineal gland in one direction, while the flow of animal spirits may push it in another. Thus, it is possible, though hardly inevitable, for the poor pineal gland to be literally caught in the middle, buffeted from both sides.

It is in the face of such conflicts that Descartes declares we need to "conquer" our passions. The question, then, is how a soul is to improve on untutored nature in its dealings with its passions. The most important thing, Descartes tells us, is for a soul to aid nature by equipping itself with proper weapons, that is, with "firm and determinate judgments bearing upon the knowledge of good and evil, which the soul has resolved to follow in guiding its conduct." But while such judgments allow us to form correct evaluations of our passions, by themselves they seem only to allow us to pick and choose among our passions in deciding a course of action. And that does not seem to be the sort of "conquest" Descartes has in mind. Instead, we should seek to alter the circumstances in which our passions arise. We do that by way of a kind of internal bodily training, whereby we gain new "habits."[32] These new habits seem to be either new and learned conjunctions of perceptions and movements in the pineal gland (as when we learn to respond to the meanings of spoken utterances), or actual changes in the conjunction of different sorts of bodily movements. The latter possibility arises when we form new "dispositions" of the parts of our brains, dispositions that can alter the coursing of the animal spirits (this is literally a change in the internal structure of our brains).[33] These new dispositions are akin to the changes sought by animal trainers, who train dogs not to run at each and every partridge they see. Now, the familiar, garden-variety techniques of rewards and punishments that modify animal behavior change only the "movements of the nerves and the muscles which usually accompany the passions." But we humans can gain new dispositions and habits that affect our experience of the passions themselves. Descartes compares these fully human dispositions and habits to those gained by learning spoken or written language: they are not merely mechanical, but meaningful. However, the trick to developing the appropriate sorts of habits is to alter the structure of our bodies, so that we can "stop the bodily movements which accompany" certain passions. The development of such habits is what constitutes our "conquest" of the passions, yet since we are merely altering the physiological basis and conditions under which we feel particular passions, Descartes can ultimately insist that our aim lies not in denying, but "in training and guiding" the passions.

Now the actual presence to the soul of some specific passion underdetermines its external, worldly causes. This is true of all sorts of sensations, as the first skeptical hypothesis in Meditation One shows, and as do Descartes' many examples of phantom pains. There are always alternate causal chains of bodily events that could produce the same mental perception. Still,

Descartes is perfectly comfortable talking about the "normal and natural" causes of various passions. And he does not mean "normal and natural" in a merely statistical sense. The normal causes of a passion will be those circumstances in which it is functional for the preservation of the mind-body union to experience the particular passion, with all its particular motivational force. One way in which a weak soul might fall prey to its passions is when it both feels them and *acts* on them in the *absence* of their normal and normative causal antecedents, as when I feel fear in the face of both grizzly and koala bears. But a soul that is weak and subject to bad habits is not simply giving up a struggle with its passions that a stronger soul would have no trouble winning. Descartes holds that there is no way to combat the actual presence to mind of a passion when its bodily antecedents (whatever they may be) are operating—any more than we can willfully stop perceiving sonic booms impacting our functioning ear drums. One can simply try to ignore the presence of the passion (if possible); one can resolutely decide not to act on it (if possible). However, these immediate measures are stop-gaps, at best. Success is most likely, and more commendable, if one resists those passions worth resisting *through* the body. We can, for instance, counteract the grip of an abnormal passion by actively *imagining* a new, different, and more probable state of affairs. Such imagining causes brain events, and therefore provides a voluntary, if indirect, means for changing the course of the animal spirits and eliminating the causes of the "abnormal" passion. And the long-term consequences of such voluntary action in concentrating on certain thoughts or imaginings is to reshape our internal bodily "dispositions" so that they produce specific passions under the appropriate circumstances. In such ways, we can work on our bodies in order that they *usually* cause passions only under *normal or standard* circumstances. Such efforts are the voluntary equivalent of the animal trainer's work to create new habits in a dog. In our case, however, the body mediates between the soul and its own passions.

The practice and effect of such voluntary alterations in the bodily causes of passions is what Descartes calls the discipline of virtue. Its aim and substance is the development of "normal and natural" dispositions and habits. But knowledge, the knowledge of good and evil, and of truth, both motivates this discipline and is a crucial part of it. Knowledge of any kind can play such a role not only because it gives us the end at which we aim, but even more because *entertaining certain thoughts simply carries an affective di-*

mension.[34] And, even if it starts as a purely intellectual emotion, that affective dimension can itself stimulate the bodily passions—a point that is important to Descartes for the promotion of health. Entertaining those thoughts frequently and on the appropriate occasions, that is, as our rational judgment recommends, is probably the most effective and rational way to develop bodily habits. So while Descartes certainly thinks that the passions can be quite unruly and can conflict with our own rationally considered interests, he also holds that they are susceptible to rational influence—indeed they can be educated so as to conform to rationally approved standards.

This does not mean that the passions should or can be made slaves to reason. Reason and passion are related in much more complicated ways than such a hoary truism would allow. True, a "weak soul," one that is prey to its passions, may well be subject to false opinions, e.g., to the incorrect belief that death is a great evil, since that is how it is represented in the passion of fear that has death as its object. But mere falsity is not the only problem affecting weak souls. It is certainly a problem, for Descartes holds that truth is something we seek for its own sake. But the equilibrium of a well-regulated emotional life is also a good in itself. Much of what is troublesome about false opinions is the way they affect the career of our passions: the evil of false opinion is measured as much by upset in our emotional life as by intellectual error. What Descartes seems to value most in the *Passions of the Soul* is tranquility, or a kind of consistency and constancy in our passions. When an opinion is shown to be false, the passions that are shaped by it share in its reversal of fortunes: the result is emotional turbulence, remorse, and repentance. The problem with those weak souls who experience the passions under abnormal circumstances and in accord with false opinions is that they are prey to a constantly changing parade of present passions. These present passions are often contradictory; they can literally push the pineal gland, and thereby the soul, in opposing directions at the same time, and they buffet the gland with the ever-changing winds of whim and frequent repentance. And this roller-coaster of passions is not restricted only to cases where we realize our error: when we love an unworthy object and attain or imagine joining ourselves to this object, we can experience sadness even if we do not realize its source.[35] Stubbornly cleaving to a false opinion is thus no protection against upset and repentance, but upset and repentance may be a good sign that we are saddled with false opinions. In contrast, those who practice virtue and maintain a true knowledge of good and evil are tranquil and constant. This state hardly marks an absence of passions, but the passions that are experienced are calm, long-lasting and move in an orderly and non-erratic course. And that is because their causes are—at a minimum—in conformity with reason, checked by reason, and strengthened by rational considerations.

III

I turn now to the second part of the story: the sense in which we can understand the operations of our reason through the passions. The passions have an obvious role to play in the practical reasoning of embodied humans, particularly in our attempts to preserve the union of mind and body—a union we hold dear. The value we place on that union is more than merely instrumental, although we may sometimes have other ends that override it. But it is this end that explains the very existence of the bodily-based passions, as in the defense Descartes offers in the Sixth Meditation of the functionality of our native make-up for figuring out what to do when maneuvering our bodies through the world. Of course, as we have seen, undisciplined passions can lead us astray even there. Again, we need knowledge of the truth to shape our characters properly, for we want the causes of passions to be reasons, or at least, to be in conformity with considerations of practical reason. But if we have practiced the discipline of virtue, are in good health, and so experience the passions under normal conditions, then the appearance of a passion "in" the body does constitute a genuine *reason* to will some action or another. To be sure, deciding when we can count our passions as reasons requires a diagnosis of what Amélie Rorty has called the "information system" of the body through its "maintenance system," an appeal that carries puzzles of its own.[36] But since Descartes did hold that it is possible to distinguish between normally functioning and abnormally functioning experiences of the passions—as well as to correct for certain kinds of abnormal, but law-governed experiences—then the appearance of a passion can count as a (defeasible) reason for acting. Indeed, our passions are the primary and natural institution whereby we gain knowledge of what is good for us as human beings in a rough-and-tumble world.[37]

We have now two senses in which our well-being as full human beings, as mind and body united, depends on the passions—first, because the normal and natural experiences of the passions are our best guide to what is good or bad for the union of mind and body, and second, because "the pleasures common to the [soul] and the body depend entirely on the passions, so that the persons whom the passions can move most deeply are capable of enjoying the sweetest pleasures of this life."[38] And I have not even touched on how Descartes thinks our emotional life can *produce* bodily health—an important topic in its own right, and one central to his medical aspirations. But as we have also seen, the passions can indeed be confused, produced by abnormal bodily causes involving false opinions. For this reason, they can sometimes mislead us with respect to our bodily well-being (although our errors "come home" to us later in regret). So too can undisciplined passions lead to emotional turbulence, however delightful isolated passions might be. But the function of the passions is not restricted to the roles they play for embodied human beings. Descartes also considers their effect on the soul alone. And he tells us that it is not directly vulnerable to the bodily harms whose causes we perceive only confusedly. For this reason, he states somewhat surprisingly, the pleasure afforded by such passions as joy is an unalloyed good for the soul: it cannot fail to be a good, with respect to the soul.

This last point deserves some elaboration. I do not think that Descartes takes the experience of pleasurable passions always to be incorrigibly good, even for the soul alone. But he does suggest that the well-being of the soul depends on intellectual joy and similar internal emotions.[39] Joy is a tonic for the soul, and the capacity for joy might well be a measure of the soul's "health." So I now turn to the role the passions—or more broadly, the emotions—may play in the activities proper to the soul alone. And the primary activity that is proper to the soul alone is thinking. The emotions, I will argue, have an indispensable role to play in promoting the ends of our *theoretical* reasoning, i.e., good reasoning, and the attaining of truth and avoidance of error. In short, Descartes gives us an enormous amount of material for understanding the operation of our theoretical reason affectively.[40]

A case in point is "the first of the passions"—wonder. Wonder has a special status among the passions: it has no opposite; and it involves no change in the heart or in the blood. That is because "its object is not good or evil, but only knowledge of the thing that we wonder at."[41] Wonder, however, is useful, as are the other passions, for they all "strengthen and prolong thoughts in the soul which it is good for the soul to preserve and which otherwise might easily be erased from it."[42] But whereas the other passions make us take note of those objects that appear good or evil for the mind-body union, wonder can be directed at things "which merely appear unusual." Indeed, wonder is useful particularly insofar as it "makes us learn and retain in our memory things of which we were previously ignorant."[43] The first function of wonder, then, is to drive us from ignorance and toward the search for truth. Nor is its motivational force restricted to knowledge that has instrumental value for our preservation as human beings.

But wonder, like any other passion, requires regulation and discipline if it is to be genuinely useful. Descartes often insists that excessive wonder is as dysfunctional as an absence of wonder, especially when it becomes a habit. Then it no longer motivates us to seek knowledge, but rather becomes "blind curiosity," and at worst, prompts us to "seek out rarities simply in order to wonder at them and not in order to know them."[44] Just as bad, excessive wonder can become insatiable, preventing us from enjoying the tranquil, even-keeled life Descartes values. Indeed, what we take to be wonderful and how wonderful we take it to be may well require correction by reasoning about the worth of the object and its place within an overall economy of our search for knowledge. But the *success* of our reasoning, as well as the success of the search for knowledge to which wonder can motivate us, may be measured by our emotional life just as well as by our judgments.

That seems to be the lesson of a peculiar and little-discussed work of Descartes: *The Search for Truth by Means of the Natural Light*.[45] A dialogue between three characters, the work examines how their passions operate to advance the search for truth. The intellect of "Epistemon" seems to have been corrupted by a surfeit of Scholasticism—a corruption displayed not only in the content of his beliefs, but even more by his emotional dispositions. Plagued by the desire for knowledge and by a curiosity[46] that only increases with study, Epistemon himself admits that his passions are a disease. Eudoxus goes one step further, comparing this disease to dropsy in the body—one of Descartes' favorite examples of how the mechanical workings of the body, which under normal conditions maintain health, can motivate self-destructive behavior. If the analogy holds, then the passions from which Epistemon suffers are destructive of the good of the inquiring mind, but properly regulated and disciplined, promote this good.

In contrast to Epistemon, Eudoxus has a well-ordered mind in a healthy condition. The value of his kind of knowledge over the bookish School-learning of Epistemon is supposed to be displayed in the satisfaction of his wonder and the secure contentment he enjoys in his knowledge. What Eudoxus particularly enjoys is a repose (*repos*), or contentment, that stems from his no longer having any passion to learn.[47] Eudoxus is not, of course, ignorant, nor did he always lack desire to learn. Rather, his current tranquility is the result of having satisfied a genuine curiosity with true knowledge of the most necessary things. That the *content* of his knowledge is true and important, however, seems measured mainly by the affective state it produces. This may seem to leave us with a problematic circularity, until we realize that Descartes holds that the nature and value of tranquility and contentment can command much wider recognition than does the content of what right reason tells us: Epistemon—despite his intellectual failings— has no trouble recognizing the character of Eudoxus's affective life, and takes it as evidence of the superiority and perfection of Eudoxus's knowledge over his own.[48]

Indeed, the dialogue suggests that, in some of the most crucial cases, our affective state in contemplating some truth simply cannot be distinguished from the reason for accepting it. That, I argue, is how we can understand the response given to Epistemon, when he challenges the right to claim knowledge of my own existence on the basis of awareness of my doubting, without first defining each of these terms.[49] Eudoxus denies that anyone can be so stupid[50] as to need to be told what these terms mean before drawing the conclusion. He then proceeds to explain why each of us ought to be in the position to acquire knowledge of these terms and of the truth in question without any additional help—and certainly without torturing our intellects.[51] But the real proof of this pudding is provided by the "common-sense" character Polyander, who agrees with Eudoxus by specifying why he is indeed in a position to know what doubt, existence, etc., are, once he attends to them. This admission forces even Epistemon to grant (albeit grudgingly) that Polyander has reason to claim that he knows all that can be known about these matters simply because he is satisfied (*contentus*) with his insight.[52]

Descartes does not maintain that mental satisfaction alone is always a guarantee of genuine knowledge: both Eudoxus and Polyander offer reasons why, in this special case, nobody could be content with her knowledge on inadequate grounds. Still, the satisfaction of a well-ordered intellect is here taken as evidence (defeasible evidence) for believing that all that can be known about the matter is known, and that our knowledge is both certain and complete. On the other hand, an intellect that never gained this sort of satisfaction, remaining in a state of intense curiosity and overcome with wonder, should count not only as ignorant of truths within its grasp, but as disordered.

It might be objected that the sort of contentment that *The Search for Truth* endorses as a sign of cognitive success could be the tranquility of the dispassionate (something like the *ataraxia* or *apatheia* of the Stoics), so that Descartes indeed contrasts right reason with the life of the passions. But Descartes does not present this state of contentment as one opposed to wonder or curiosity or disrupted by any appearance of these passions. Rather, proper contentment is the result of allowing these passions to run their course in their "natural" (that is, functional and uncorrupted) way. And the corrective for excessive wonder is not denial of the passion, but knowledge—and that can be, and usually is, motivated by curiosity.[53] Indeed, wonder itself can be sated by indulging the passion in the right way: thus Eudoxus says that he will cause the others to wonder, so that eventually they will have no reason for wonder.[54] We should remember also that not only can wonder stimulate curiosity, which can in turn motivate the search for truth, but that it serves to fix important pieces of knowledge firmly in our memories. Wonder provides a propaedeutic to our memory, the limits of which had been a source of worry to Descartes from the start of his career. On the other hand, too much wonder or wonder misdirected at mere novelties and unnecessary trivialities can overburden and weaken our memories. In short, wonder and curiosity can be either functional or dysfunctional, but the solution to the risk of the latter is the former. For these passions may be our best guide in our search for humanly accessible and genuinely important knowledge—knowledge available and efficiently available to finite, mortal beings who must spend the lion's share of their time in action. And what shows that we are succeeding in our mission is that these passions resolve in intellectual satisfaction—in other words, that they run their "natural" course.

The sort of intellectual satisfaction and content that are touted so heavily in *The Search for Truth* should not, however, be considered distinct passions in their own right. Rather, they mark the easy and tranquil succession of our passions—a constancy in their direction, as it were—which is the opposite of the sort of emotional turbulence and regret that Descartes held could result from false judgments about how to act. But a merely formal de-

scription of their overall progression may not capture what is characteristic
of cognitive success. For there may also be false or unwarranted intellectual "tranquility," the possibility of resting content with inadequate, false,
or even no knowledge.[55] Of course, such risks may be inescapable for any criterion; judging or believing that one has met some criterion is not the same
as meeting the criterion, however much that criterion may depend on the
judgment, belief, or other attitudes of the subject.[56]

But Descartes may also provide a more substantive piece of the puzzle
that will allow us to distinguish between false and unwarranted contentment
and the genuine article (although not incorrigibly). Whether from intellectual laziness or deep-seated ignorance, a person may remain satisfied simply
because he fails to realize that he lacks knowledge, even when that knowledge is easily had. That is the "contentment," not of passions that have run
their course, but of the absence of the relevant passion from the start.[57] The
key to distinguishing this sort of false satisfaction from real contentment
will lie in the presence of particular passions. We might, for instance, ask
whether the person in question has ever experienced wonder and curiosity,
or whether she has experienced the sort of despair and unease that arises
from doubt (and motivates us to resolve that doubt).

Perhaps most important, though, is the character of a person's current
satisfaction and whether it includes the sweet passions of love and joy. The
experience of these passions is no barrier to achieving sustained tranquility;
it neither need, nor should involve mood swings. Rather, if love and joy
are based on true judgments, then we love what truly brings (or will bring)
us joy, and receiving joy in return, love the object more. Thus, love is "extremely good because by joining real goods to us it makes us to that extent
more perfect," and joy is a mark of increasing perfection.[58] Since intellectual love and joy are not subject to any confusion about their causes and effects (unlike the bodily passions), it seems they will always motivate and
signal the increasing perfection of the thinking soul.[59] And since knowledge, the acquisition of truth, must count as the primary end of the activities proper to the thinking soul, we thinkers should love knowledge. If we
pursue knowledge through love and are rewarded by joy, then we have as
good evidence as we could want of our success at joining ourselves to real
knowledge, and thus of our increasing perfection. So, a constant joy in the
activity of thinking must be a sign of the truth achieved thereby. Certainly,
Descartes suggests time and again that clear and distinct perceivings bring

us joy in proportion to their clarity and distinctness. Perhaps the most dramatic avowal of this connection appears in the Third Meditation, where the narrator declares that the contemplation of God and of our dependence on God—*a contemplation both of the perfection of our soul and one that further perfects our soul*—constitutes "the greatest joy of which we are capable in this life."[60] By joining ourselves to God in loving, devoted contemplation, we experience a degree and constancy of joy that is a mark of the truth of our perceiving.

I do not want to argue that Descartes understands cognitive success solely in terms of our emotional states. But he does suggest that in many cases cognitive success may be best measured by the passions that accompany our thinking. And it is a rather fortunate fact that the acquisition of knowledge through our own intellectual activity normally induces a pleasing progression of passions. To be sure, cognitive success is a good to be valued in its own right. But the pleasures afforded by the passions are also goods. The successful exercise of our reason in the proper regulation and discipline of the passions, as guided by the uniform progression of pleasurable passions, seems to combine both goods; we can see why Descartes held it to be the good in this life, the good for the embodied person. Indeed, had we no body, we could hold our pleasant emotions (the intellectual ones, that is) to be indefeasibly good. It is true that our pleasant bodily passions may not be universally good in this way—that is, the good to be found in our experience of them may be overridden by the demands of some other end (e.g., the preservation of the mind-body union, or perhaps the search for truth itself). But the discipline of virtue is designed to so alter our dispositions to experience the passions that this sort of situation will not arise. Even were conflicts to arise, the goods found in the passions are and remain genuine goods, to be put alongside the achievements of our reason. Fortunately, the passions need pose no impediment to the search for truth; properly regulated and disciplined, they are extremely useful guides to the acquisition of knowledge—perhaps the best guides we humans have for how to position the search for truth within the overall economy of a life. For we are finite, mortal beings, who must negotiate decisions about what truths to pursue that will be accessible to us, chary of our time, and important to acquire, in the absence of anything like full knowledge and without having either world enough or time. It is the passions—perceptions arising from the impacts the world has on our bodies, and shaped as and by assessments of the meaning those impacts have for us—that can direct us about how much time and effort to invest in particular pursuits. Whether we value these pursuits of truth most for the knowledge we may acquire or for the pleasures of the passions they arouse and satisfy is, fortunately, not a question we need to decide.

I.V

If it is fair to understand Descartes as I have done, what becomes of those critiques of Cartesian dualism with which we began? Charging them with simple error seems beside the point. Critique, in general, aims to uncover what lies at the limits of consciousness, or is in the service of false consciousness, or is part of the structure of the unconscious.[61] Feminist critiques, in particular, seek to understand the way in which a philosophy can be put in the service of sexist ideology. For all these reasons, then, feminist critiques are perfectly justified in putting up for grabs the very notion of a "fair" reading, e.g., one that seeks to avoid error while respecting either the word of the text or authorial intention. It by no means follows, however, that feminist critique can afford to be "unfair." Feminist critique (like any such endeavor) seeks to do justice to its subject matter, even as it wants to see intellectual, social, and gender justice be done.[62]

I don't think it is mere equivocation to draw these two senses of justice together here. Although unjust practices do not arise solely from false beliefs, analyzing beliefs for consistency and correctness can be an effective way of attacking practices, especially since sexist practices often operate covertly. In any case, feminist philosophical critique is committed by its very nature to identifying and analyzing the unjust and unjustified gender practices perpetrated by a tradition of thought—to uncovering intellectual error. Doing so may require not only "reading between the cracks," but also "reading against the grain." The question we face, then, is to what extent the reading against the grain demanded by feminist critical goals might come into conflict with fairness to the work of a (long-dead) individual.

The possibility of such conflict should not be dismissed lightly. But neither should we expect a one-size-fits-all solution. Descartes' case presents various curious features that should give us pause. First is the near-universality among philosophers (and not just philosophers) with which

Cartesian influence is decried. Descartes has been accused of promoting an implausibly formalist, even mechanistic, view of scientific investigation,[63] of falling prey to a particularly egregious form of the "myth of the given,"[64] of committing grotesque category mistakes in his metaphysics,[65] of endorsing an unworkable foundationalism, and of course, of promoting a badly gendered view of reason. But here we encounter another peculiarity: the lack of agreement about the content of Descartes' influence. Consider, for instance, Richard Rorty's claim that Descartes "conflates thinking and feeling" on the grounds that each is characterized by givenness. On his view, the mind-body distinction developed by Descartes doesn't just demote the body, it moves the sort of corporeal and sensuous class of feelings formerly associated with the body into the realm of the inner, the realm governed by the mental.[66] But this view gives no comfort to those who think that Descartes privileges reason over affect. Reading Cartesian mind-body dualism as a dualism of inner and outer is simply inconsistent with the distinction between reason and emotion we have seen. Perhaps Descartes' thought is itself incoherent, but then it becomes difficult to attribute any determinate position to him at all. And it seems a bit sophistical to condemn Cartesian influence, if we cannot even decide what Cartesianism endorses.

More importantly, we may wonder *who* is supposed to be subject to this pernicious influence. Critics abound, but locating an advocate of Descartes is no easy task (at least among contemporary, secular Anglophone philosophers).[67] Yet the critics of Cartesianism seem to suppose that they are fighting views that dominate current patterns of thought. Perhaps Cartesianism spreads a bit like an infection, independently of our beliefs and intentions, desires and statements. But that is not the way the critics typically understand its operation; philosophic influence, they suppose, requires our more or less conscious acceptance of a set of beliefs, which may then serve to transmit various pernicious errors without our awareness. The result is a highly implausible picture of our own position vis-à-vis the history of philosophy: we are both conscious holders of propositional attitudes *and* passive recepients of a tradition we do not properly understand.[68] On this picture, only Descartes, or the tradition invoked by his name, seems really to exercise agency. And then, we face problems not only in identifying *who* accepts Descartes' influence uncritically, but also in explaining *how* and *why* that influence operates.

The problems only multiply if the readings that the critics present fail to be fair to the texts. We are then left only with a set of supposedly powerful views, which nonetheless float free of any vehicle by which they could be transmitted: they are anchored neither in the texts, nor in the belief systems of any individual. Yet this seems to be the posture adopted by some critics. It is hard to avoid the cynical conclusion that the culprit is a certain intellectual laziness: treating Descartes as the Ur-philosopher of a suspect modernism allows his name to serve as shorthand for views so familiar that they scarcely require identification, yet with a pedigree so illustrious that no case need be made for their die-hard influence.

Feminist critiques, however, have an advantage over other critical projects in their ability to take on issues of influence head-on. On the one hand, they can recognize that various philosophies or forms of philosophy are cultural *products*, which arose (and perhaps could only arise) under particular material and social conditions. Like any cultural product, a philosophy can play a role in masking, justifying, and perpetuating unjust conditions (social or intellectual). Philosophy can, in short, be a part of ideology. And that gives critique a target: diagnosing, demystifying, and (in some sense) deconstructing whatever role a philosophy might play in ideology, so as thereby to loosen its grip on us. Then too, since many philosophical works (unlike, say, looms or medieval armor) get taken up in the culture of societies in which they were *not* produced, it may be perfectly appropriate, even necessary, for critique to look at the changing history of reception of philosophical works. In short, feminist critique properly addresses the force of tradition, where that tradition cannot be located solely within a "fair" reading of some set of texts, which are in turn limited to their "proper" context.

On the other hand, we must still account for the "force" of a tradition. Whatever that may be, it is not something that can be wholly located in the views expressed by a single person or a single set of texts; this is not the sort of power that persons or texts could exercise all on their own. But neither can the "force" we assign a tradition be the force of mere inertia. Treating it as such seems like a way of refusing explanation of the intellectual and material conditions for a tradition to be a live tradition, and indeed looks rather like a category mistake, conflating *normative* force with physical force. And the normative force exercised by a tradition over time cannot be explained simply by reference to its initial impetus.

Now, when the tradition in question looks like a perfectly conscious preference for a foundationalist approach in epistemology, to which obvious alternatives exist, invoking the weight of tradition seems simply a way of avoiding the issue of transmission. But feminist critique is quite properly concerned with traditions and patterns of thought that may operate at a level *different* from that of conscious, individual choice; it is concerned (at least) with the norms and commitments shaping an individual's understanding of the nature and range of available alternatives. Unlike the intellectually lazy approach, feminist critique does not suppose that a tradition can operate in the absence of individual agency, but neither does it reduce the operation of tradition to individual agency, much less to *conscious* individual agency.

For this reason, feminist critique need not restrict itself to what might be considered authorial intent. There is, for instance, nothing inherently implausible in supposing that Descartes' mind/body dualism carries with it quite a bit of conceptual baggage—conceptual baggage of which Descartes was largely unaware—and that a contrarian reading will show the weight of that baggage. It is, in fact, quite plausible to hold that Descartes' express talk of "conquering" or "mastering" the passions hearkens back to metaphors of dominance found in Augustine and Plato. Those metaphors may then provide a foothold for introducing evaluations of the relative worth of mind and body into the formerly neutral territory of Cartesian dualism. Feminist critique performs a valuable service by showing how these sorts of divisions become gendered, how they map onto what we might call "concept-metaphors"[69] of maleness and femaleness—concept-metaphors that do not reduce to, but certainly influence the behavior and experience of individual men and women. All this may be admitted, while also acknowledging Descartes' own clearly marked tendencies toward a sexually egalitarian view of reason.[70] For egalitarian intentions are no guarantee against falling prey to traps of gender divisions. And so there is no contradiction in applauding Descartes' explicit and published insistence on respecting the intellect of women, while criticizing the influence of a Cartesian tradition that supports a suspiciously gendered view of reason.

However, acknowledging the special aims and devices of feminist critique does not mean that it or any critique of the history of philosophy can play harry with the *texts* that make up that history. Practicing historical critique may often require reading texts against the grain—looking, in other words, for what may not be explicit in those texts, but may operate ideologically out of them. On this basis, then, critique may well look at what can be made out of a philosopher's work, at what might have been a tradition stemming from that philosopher, even if it stems from a misreading. But even a misreading must somehow find a foothold *in* the text. It cannot be enough, for instance, to claim that so-and-so read Descartes, and so-and-so held sexist attitudes. Nor is it enough to claim that so-and-so read Descartes, and that event *caused* so-and-so to hold sexist attitudes. So too might a bump on the head cause susceptible individuals to develop irrational attitudes. Such a claim simply fails to establish the right kind of causality, for it goes no further than recording what might result from a mere quirk of individual psychology, and speaks not at all to the meaning of the text or to its *normative* influence. To get off the ground, a feminist critique needs to find in the texts themselves a possible reading, or misreading—one that supports, say, a conceptual mapping that privileges "the masculine" at the expense of the "feminine." This will not be sufficient to establish a tradition originating in those texts, but it is surely necessary.

Perhaps the importance of this requirement might be clarified by contrast with a somewhat different case from that of Descartes. The history of Nietzsche reception has been a checkered one. But it presents clear-cut hermeneutical problems, ones that repay philosophical examination, as has been shown in some detail by Jacques Derrida.[71] Now, on the one hand, it seems pretty obvious to any sympathetic reader that Nietzsche had no patience with either anti-Semitism or German nationalism—that as Derrida puts it, Nietzsche would have vomited at their politics. On the other hand, as Derrida also puts it, Nietzsche "died before his name," which does not mean simply that Nietzsche died young. Rather, it marks the fact that authorial intentions, even clearly marked ones, cannot control the possible readings of a text and their effects.[72] For it is equally obvious that Nietzsche's name figured as an authority for National Socialism, and that in fact, Nietzsche drew off the same concepts later invoked by the Nazis.[73] The Nazis undoubtedly misread Nietzsche. But if the result still counts as a misreading *of* Nietzsche, then there must be something in the text that enabled the Nazis to exploit his works as they did. Not every "misreading" is possible for every text, and even a tradition built on misreading must find some starting point in the founding texts.

But has the relation of *mis*reading between Descartes and the philosophic tradition assigned to him really been established? I have some doubts.

Consider just two kinds of claims made by several feminist critiques. The first presents a problematic choice of phrasing: "woman is frequently defined by qualities which directly contradict Descartes' requirements for rationality";[74] "women have been assigned responsibility for that realm of the sensuous which the Cartesian Man of Reason must transcend. . . ."[75] Both examples use the passive voice—which is, after all, a perfectly acceptable and often useful grammatical construction. But it can be dangerous if it is used to avoid specifying agency. And that is what seems to have happened in the passages cited here. The result is that the gendered distinction seems to float free, like some sort of atmospheric disturbance, as if it were not the product of human construction under particular, historical circumstances. Presumably, part of the point of using the passive voice in these cases is to allow that Descartes neither produced nor endorsed the gendered distinction. But then we deserve an account of how, through whom, and when the suspect distinction came into play. This does not mean that we must identify particular individuals who cooked up the distinction in their stereotype lab. But without some examination of its provenance, which when overlaid on Descartes' conceptual commitments shows the gendered effects of his tradition, we are left to wonder how the distinction establishes any specifically "Cartesian" tradition.[76]

Somewhat different problems arise with the use of translations. For instance, a number of critics cite a passage from the first part of the *Passions of the Soul* in which Descartes seems to talk about the opposition between soul and body.[77] But these citations refer to the rather questionable translation of Haldane and Ross, in which the verbs *être contraire* and *repugner* are both translated by cognates of "oppose." The difference between these verbs may seem slight, yet since the citation is supposed to support the claim that Descartes opposes the worth of mind and body, their exact meaning in context is pretty important.[78] Simply relying on the quirks of a relatively recent tradition is not merely a violation of scholarly procedure, it means that the critique fails to get a grip on what is *in* Descartes' texts.

Let me repeat yet again that the issue is *not* what will count as a fair reading of Descartes, but identifying a way of reading, or misreading, Descartes that might with some justice be considered traditional, or tradition-making. Of course, it is always possible to find (or force) the views attributed to Descartes in his texts; the mere existence of the critiques in question shows that. But that bare possibility is not enough to establish what these critiques of "Cartesianism" aim to establish: namely, that Descartes' works present us with various dualisms, which provide the norms instituting a tradition of gendered distinctions, a tradition that may with some justice be called "Cartesian." Still, although they fail to establish that the works bear any responsibility for such a tradition, these critiques may show something more modest: that Descartes' thought can be understood according to suspect, gendered distinctions. As James Winders puts it, "the text's reputation and claims upon our attention cannot be separated from powerful and persuasive (because usually undetected) processes of cultural hegemony that include the exercise of patriarchal bias."[79] And that is an important insight. But admitting that our reception of Descartes' texts is mediated through and through by such processes and practices is a far cry from claiming that his texts are themselves somehow responsible for those processes and practices. That these processes and practices affect our understanding of Cartesianism is not to say that they should be considered "Cartesian."

But even if no critique has yet succeeded in establishing a Cartesian tradition, it is by no means impossible that some future critique may do so. So let us suppose that there is a clear case to be made for the existence of such a tradition; imagine, if you like, that we discover that the World Council of Patriarchs has adopted Descartes as their patron saint. Even this hardly means that the jig is up. There are (at least) two responses we might make here. First, we could demand a critical history of reception. Susan Bordo tells us, "it is the dominant cultural and historical renderings of Cartesianism, not Descartes "himself," that are the object of [feminists'] criticisms."[80] The distinction between a philosopher's own views and their historical reception is an important one, and both are properly objects of concern for philosophy in general, and feminist critique in particular. But making the distinction, while maintaining the connection, is a difficult task indeed, and that is just where many critiques of the "Cartesian" tradition have foundered. What they have not offered, and what a critical history of reception should offer, is something that would take us from a "fair" reading of Descartes to those "dominant cultural and historical renderings of Cartesianism" that make it thoroughly at odds with that Descartes. To tell that story lies outside of the confines of this paper, and would, in fact, be an enormous undertaking. Yet for all my misgivings about the attempts that have been made, I remain confident that there must be some such story to be told: were one lone individual to offer a view of Cartesianism that seems belied by close readings of Descartes' texts, we might count it a mistake and an accident. When many intelligent people do—when the view seems recognizable, familiar, even part of a package of approaches to the texts—there is something that needs explanation.

But we should be clear about what the import of such a history of reception really is. As Derrida says about Nietzsche, even the fact that the only politics to call itself Nietzschean has been a Nazi one does not mean that the possibilities of Nietzsche's texts are closed. It is always possible to produce a "political rewriting of the text and its destination."[81] Such a "rewriting" and reorientation of Descartes' dualisms is, I think, not only possible, but desirable—both for the sake of fairness to Descartes and for the sake of undoing the gender privileging associated with those dualisms. Critique of a philosopher's work and of the history of its reception may indeed expose the ways in which conceptual divisions are set up, oppositions are associated, and one side is privileged over another according to gender divisions. Exposure is (at least) the start of dismantling a suspect conceptual map. But there may be other tools available for dismantling a map handed down to us by some tradition, such as appealing to some part of our traditions to reveal the questionable tradition in all its peculiarity, irrationality, and contingency. Indeed, it may be particularly effective to appeal to just those philosophical predecessors that seem most mired in a conceptual mapping (whether responsible for it or not), seeking resources within their works by which to pull apart what tradition has woven together. This discussion has been an attempt to intervene in the history of Descartes' reception to redirect it toward just that end.

Feminist critique of the last few decades has concentrated on unmasking dualisms that take the form of a One-Other opposition—that is, the form of a hierarchy in which one term is privileged against a contrasting "shadow" term, which must be devalued in order to maintain the privilege.[82] That such hierarchies can become gendered seems clear,[83] and that they can thus become a source of injustice should be obvious. But it would be a serious mistake then to assume that all such hierarchically ordered dualisms must have (roughly) the same content. (And it would be an even more egregious mistake to assume that all dualisms as such embody the same hierarchical ordering.) If the privilege of one term depends on repressing, denying, devaluing, or mystifying the other term, then we should expect the specific content of the privileged term to be shaped through and through by the nature of the opposition and devaluation in question. In short, we should understand the various suspect conceptual oppositions and hierarchies to be historically, perhaps even textually, specific ones. I do not think that this expectation has been extended to Descartes. But it should be, for it suggests that whatever sorts of oppositions and privileges we may find in Descartes' work (and I do not deny that they may be there) will fit only poorly with those familiar to us from more recent traditions, texts, and practices. And that sort of unfamiliarity may be an extremely effective tool in dismantling contemporary conceptual privilege.

NOTES

This essay is the product of many years' work in diverse venues. An earlier version of section II (and parts of I) was read at the Central Division Meetings of the American Philosophical Association, Chicago, Illinois, in April 1996. Thanks are due to the audience, and particularly my commentator, Kathleen Schmidt. Ancestors of section III were presented at the Northwest Philosophy Conference, Forest Grove, Oregon, in November 2000 and at the Pacific Division Meetings of the APA, San Francisco, California, in March 2001 (published in different form as "Descartes and the Primacy of Practice"). I was fortunate on those occasions in having particularly astute commentators, Julian Wuerth and Patricia Easton, and lively audiences (thanks in large part to David Owen and Roger Florka). Some of the issues of section IV were presented to the members of the graduate philosophy proseminar, University of New Mexico, spring 1998; I'd like to thank my attending (and attentive!) colleagues Rebecca Kukla, Jennifer Nagel, Fred Schueler, Sergio Tenenbaum, and Aladdin Yaqūb, as well as the students of the seminar, especially Amy Lund and Dan Gold. Penultimate versions of sections I–III were presented at Rice University, January 2001, and Reed College, April 2001. I'd like to thank the audiences at both institutions for their healthy and helpful skepticism. Last, I thank Barbara S. Schmitter, proofreader, versifier, and crossword-puzzler extraordinaire, for exceptional editing help—and a few other things.

    1. Annette Baier, "Ethics in Many Different Voices," in *Moral Prejudices* (Cambridge, MA: Harvard University Press, 1995), 310–11.
    2. See Annette Baier, "A Naturalist View of Persons," in ibid., 313–26, 358 n. 28.
    3. Baier's work itself shows both precepts in action: *A Progress of Sentiments: Reflections on Hume's* Treatise (Cambridge, MA: Harvard University Press, 1991) is a fine example of the first precept, and "Hume: The Reflective Woman's

Epistemologist?" in *Moral Prejudices*, 76–94, of the second—although both works embody both precepts.

4. The description "reading like a girl" is borrowed from Bill Beardsley, who attributed his own practice to Baier's influence, in a hilarious anecdote cited by Baier in *The Commons of the Mind*, the Paul Carus Lectures 19 (Chicago: Open Court Publishing, 1997), 16 n. 25.

5. For this view, see, e.g., Nancy Tuana, *Woman and the History of Philosophy* (New York: Paragon Press, 1992), 36–42.

6. See, e.g., Antonio Damasio, *Descartes' Error: Emotion, Reason and the Human Brain* (New York: Avon Books, 1994).

7. Susan Bordo, *The Flight to Objectivity: Essays on Cartesianism and Culture* (Albany: State University of New York Press, 1987), 85, see also 76.

8. Genevieve Lloyd, *The Man of Reason* (Minneapolis: University of Minnesota. Press, 1993), 46.

9. See "Descartes on Thinking with the Body," in *The Cambridge Companion to Descartes*, ed. J. Cottingham (Cambridge: Cambridge University Press, 1992), 371–72.

10. Although there have been few polls on this issue, I can provide some evidence that both stereotypes do indeed exist, often side by side, by citing one of my former students, Shawn McKenzie. When I asked students on the first day of my Descartes seminar in 1995 to bring up common, but unattractive views of Descartes, Shawn—without prompting—mentioned (though didn't use) just this stereotype. I hereby invoke Shawn as an independent and impartial witness.

11. Exceptions include Amélie Rorty; Susan James, *Passion and Action* (New York: Cambridge University Press, 1997); and Margaret Atherton, who addresses the "disturbing" gender distinction between "the man of reason" and "the woman of passion" in "Cartesian Reason and Gendered Reason," in *A Mind of One's Own*, ed. L. Antony and C. Witt (Boulder, CO: Westview Press, 1993), 19–34. Atherton argues against both Bordo and Lloyd that it is historically problematic to trace this distinction back to Descartes. Deborah Tollefsen also raises some doubts about the applicability of these distinctions in "Princess Elisabeth and the Problem of Mind-Body Interaction," *Hypatia* 14, no. 3 (1999): 59–77. None of these discussions, however, concentrates specifically on the supposed split between reason and emotion.

12. More properly, Descartes seeks to promote a novel view about the conditions, particularly the subjective conditions, for the possibility of our thinking, or at least so I argue in "The Wax and I: Perceptibility and Modality in the Second Meditation," *Archiv für Geschichte der Philosophie* 82, no. 2 (2000): 178–201.

13. Since I first wrote that sentence, several happy exceptions have appeared, including "Love among the Ruins" presented by Bill Beardsley at the Pacific Divi-

sion Meetings of the APA, April 2000, Albuquerque, New Mexico, and the last section of Susan James's *Passion and Action*.

14. It may also betray the largely practical bent of Descartes' work as a whole, as I have argued in "Descartes and the Primacy of Practice: the Role of the Passions in the Search for Truth," *Philosophical Studies* 108, nos. 1–2 (2002): 99–108.

15. In "Cartesian Passions and the Union of Mind and Body," Amélie Rorty distinguishes between such terms as "passion" and "emotion," but these distinctions are not crucial to this discussion. See *Essays on Descartes' Meditations* (Berkeley: University of California Press, 1986), 513–34, esp. 521.

16. *Principles of Philosophy* (PP) I §48, AT VIIIA 23, CSM I 209. All references to Descartes' works are to *Oeuvres de Descartes*, ed. C. Adam and P. Tannery (Paris: J. Vrin, 1996), cited as AT; all references to translations not my own are to *The Philosophical Writings of Descartes*, vols. I–II, ed. J. Cottingham, R. Stoothoff, and D. Murdoch (Cambridge, England: Cambridge University Press, 1984–1985), cited as CSM; and to *The Philosophical Writings of Descartes*, vol. III, ed. J. Cottingham, R. Stoothoff, D. Murdoch, and A. Kenney (Cambridge, England: Cambridge University Press, 1991), cited as CSMK.

17. *Passions of the Soul* (PS) I §25, AT XI 348, CSM I 337–38.

18. In the *Principles of Philosophy*, the causes of emotions are specified as changes in the small nerves around the heart (PP IV §190), while the later *Passions of the Soul* concentrates on the role of the animal spirits moving against the pineal gland in the cavities of the brain (PS I, §36–37).

19. PS I §37, AT XI 357, CSM I 342; PS II §70, AT XI 380, CSM I 353.

20. Rorty, "Descartes on Thinking with the Body," 378. Again, wonder is an exception.

21. I use the term "functionality" in preference to the more usual "teleology," because I think that Descartes' treatment of our passions, appetites, and sensations forms an important step on the way to understanding biological functions without built-in purposes. For a somewhat fuller explanation of this point, see my "Descartes and the Primacy of Practice," 107 n. 3. It is worth noting that at least part of the "discipline of virtue" endorsed by Descartes (and described below) seeks to change the *mechanical* structure of our bodies. Although Descartes treats "habits" as the preferred means of change, nothing he says rules out surgical interventions (ethico-surgery rather than psychosurgery perhaps?).

22. On the other hand, the inability to distinguish passions proper from other sorts of sensations on the basis of their causes alone may signal that most, perhaps all, sensations have an affective dimension, at least if they are part of the "maintenance system": it is quite plausible to think that appetites such as hunger are always accompanied by some sort of emotional disturbance.

23. PP IV §190 (emphasis mine), AT VIIIA 317, CSM I 281. The supposedly distinctive phenomenal character of the bodily passions is used in the Sixth Meditation, where the narrator comments (fairly uncritically) on his belief that he felt all his appetites and emotions "in, and on account of, this body"—one of the several considerations leading to the argument that material things must exist (and operate on my perception causally) on pain of calling God a deceiver.

24. PS I §27, AT XI 349; CSM I 338–39.

25. See PP IV §190, AT VIIIA 317, CSM I 280.

26. PS I §28, see also II §91, AT XI 350, CSM I 339. Strictly speaking, though, the classification Descartes gives of "functions" of the soul in Part I of the *Passions* §17–25 suggests that intellectual joy and other such "passions" caused by the action of the soul alone should be counted as volitions, and only secondarily as perceptions. This would not, however, seem to capture the affective character of these emotions.

27. For example, intellectual joy can cause the passion of joy and vice versa. See PP IV §190, and PS I §45–47. Further treatment can be found in my "Representation, Self-Representation and the Passions in Descartes," *The Review of Metaphysics* 48, no. 2 (1994): 331–57.

28. For a case in which it is particularly difficult to disentangle the two sorts of love, see Descartes' description of the love felt by our soul for "the blood, or some other juice entering the heart" as it "*began to be joined to our body*," PS II §107 (emphasis mine), AT XI 407, CSM I 365–66. On the one hand, this love is characterized as the first (and paradigmatic) of the bodily passions; on the other, it is used to explain why the soul would join with the body in the first place (although for the explanation to work, some sort of causal connection must be presupposed).

29. PS I §27, AT XI 349, CSM I 338–39.

30. PS I §47, 48 (emphasis mine), AT XI 364–67, CSM I 345–47.

31. The role of the pineal gland needs to be emphasized here, although only in its functional role. Descartes holds that events in the pineal gland are the proximate bodily cause of sensible perceptions, and the first cause of bodily actions that are directly perceived. Although processes of digestion may require brain events (perhaps), presumably such nonvoluntary, but still perceptible bodily actions as blinking in the face of an oncoming blow will involve pineal events.

32. PS I §50, AT XI 369, CSM I 348.

33. Lisa Shapiro has proposed a somewhat different view in "Descartes' *Passions of the Soul* and the Union of Mind and Body," in *Archiv für Geschichte der Philosophie* 85, no. 3 (2003): 211–48. There she argues that it is the causal connection between pineal gland and mind that changes, with the result that the same type of pineal event can produce a different passion. Although I agree that Descartes' language sometimes suggests this interpretation, my reading of this passage will produce the same results by simpler means. So, I'll stick with it.

34. This is the lesson of many of Descartes' letters to Elizabeth, and is dramatized in (at least) the first three of the *Meditations*.

35. Strictly speaking, the passion of love does not require joining ourselves with the loved object, but only "impels the soul to join itself willingly to objects that appear to be agreeable to it," or prompts that "assent by which we consider ourselves henceforth as joined with what we love in such a manner that we imagine a whole, of which we take ourselves to be only one part, and the thing loved to be the other" (PS II §79, 80, AT X 387, CSM I 356). My thanks to a previous, anonymous referee for emphasizing this point. But despite cases of unrequited love, Descartes thinks the normal course of love does involve such a joining, at least in imagination. Love is thus distinguished from desire, "which is a completely separate passion relating to the future," and "which disposes the soul to *wish*, in the *future*, for the things it represents to itself as agreeable," whether those things be absent or present (PS II §86, AT X 392, CSM I 358). So, we should be careful about what we love, for we may very well get it—if only in imagination.

36. See Rorty, "Descartes on Thinking with the Body," esp. 380–84.

37. My thanks to Gary Hatfield for reminding me of this function of the passions.

38. PS III §212, AT XI 488, CSM I 404.

39. See PS II §147, AT XI 440, CSM I 381.

40. Descartes draws frequent and robust analogies between our theoretical and practical reason, as Sergio Tenenbaum has pointed out. See especially his discussion of "theoretical weakness of will" in Descartes in "The Judgment of a Weak Will," *Philosophy and Phenomenological Research* 49, no. 4 (1999): 875–911. See also my "Descartes and the Primacy of Practice."

41. PS II §71, AT X 381, CSM I 353.

42. PS II §74, AT X 383, CSM I 354.

43. PS II §75, AT X 384, CSM I 354.

44. PS II 78, AT X 386, CSM I 356.

45. This is a piece that requires some delicate handling, since it was discovered only after Descartes' death and is of uncertain date. However, the themes and commitments that I treat in it are also present in other, more familiar works—albeit not as explicitly.

46. I do not identify wonder with curiosity, or the desire for knowledge, since there does seem to be a large component of desire in the latter, as well as a representation of the object as good (at least in the sense that it is worth knowing). However, curiosity and wonder would seem to be related in a natural progress of passions.

47. "ne . . . plus de passion pour apprendre aucune chose"; AT X 501, CSM II 402.

48. AT X 501, CSM II 403.

49. This sort of case is particularly important to Descartes: not only did this exact question come up in the Second Set of Objections to the *Meditations,* but the issue of whether it is necessary to produce definitions (by genus and specific difference) for particular, basic terms goes to the heart of Descartes' quarrel with Scholastic logic.

50. The word here is *stupidum,* which could also mean stunned or amazed.

51. AT X 523, CSM II 417.

52. AT X 525, CSM II 418.

53. See Epistemon's description at AT X 504, CSM II 404.

54. AT X 505, CSM II 405.

55. This is a spectre raised by Eudoxus: had his scholastic education maintained a greater veneer of plausibility, he might well have rested content with the "smattering of reason it contained." This undesirable kind of contentment would simply leave its sufferers in self-satisfied ignorance, rather than in the glow of knowledge achieved. See AT X 516, CSM II 411.

56. Even if intellectual satisfaction is the best or only criterion we have for cognitive success, we may remain uncertain whether it is warranted in any particular case. Indeed, Descartes could readily have held that most of humanity had suffered from an uncorrected, yet still unwarranted intellectual satisfaction for some two thousand years or so.

57. One can imagine a case where someone experiences genuine curiosity, yet somehow thinks it satisfied by false belief. On the basis of what was said above (and below), however, Descartes could easily argue that such satisfaction cannot be sustained over the long haul. What he thinks is a much more common result of false belief (including the belief in one's own ignorance) is dissatisfaction, of the sort Epistemon suffers, even when one lacks knowledge of its source.

58. Let us not forget that, in the long run, even bodily love and joy will be self-correcting, since a passion built on a false opinion is unstable.

59. Although hate may be more useful to the embodied person than are love and (its natural successor) joy—for it teaches us to avoid what does us real harm, and if false, merely deprives us of some good—love and joy can never fail to be a good for the soul alone. See PS II §141, 142, AT X 434–35, CSM I 378–79.

60. AT VII 52, CSM II 36.

61. Very roughly, the notions here are those of Kant, Marx, and Althusser (despite Althusser's sense of the inadequacy of critique).

62. I emphasize intellectual justice here. Worthy as philosophical critique may be, its project is a relatively modest one: it aims at enlightenment, not radical institutional change (although, of course, enlightenment may be both an impetus for and a result of such change). It is, however, a good way to make use of our philosophic skills.

63. See, e.g., Charles Taylor, *Philosophical Arguments* (Cambridge, MA: Harvard University Press, 1995).

64. See, e.g., Richard Rorty, *Philosophy and the Mirror of Nature* (Princeton: Princeton University Press, 1979).

65. This is a view famously put forth by Gilbert Ryle in chapter 1 of *The Concept of Mind* (Chicago: University of Chicago Press, 1984).

66. R. Rorty does, however, allow that Descartes may want to give the body responsibility for what we share with the brutes. But rather than being intrinsic to Cartesian dualism, Rorty considers this to be a sort of "backtracking to the standard position" of, e.g., Augustine; see *Philosophy and the Mirror of Nature*, 53n.

67. The case is far different in France, where Descartes (or at least Descartes' name) carries the weight of authoritative national identity, and where the history of philosophy exercises a hegemony that may well seem oppressive. Catholic institutions in the U.S. may also grant Descartes greater authority than is common among English-speaking philosophers.

68. Jennifer Hornsby raises a similar problem for Richard Rorty's claims (though in a wildly different context). On the one hand, she notes that R. Rorty thinks that it is pretty easy for contemporary philosophers to avoid the dualism of Descartes; on the other, he "also thinks that philosophy of mind has survived only because it is carried on in the Cartesian vein"; see *Simple Mindedness* (Cambridge, MA: Harvard University Press, 1997), 2.

69. I owe this term to Gayatri Spivak.

70. See Amélie Rorty, "Epistemological Egalitarianism in Descartes and Spinoza," *History of Philosophy Quarterly* 13, no. 1 (1996): 35–53.

71. I refer here particularly to the discussion of Nietzsche's lecture "On the Future of Our Educational Institutions," in *The Ear of the Other*, ed. C. McDonald, trans. P. Kamuf and A. Ronell (New York: Schocken Books, 1985).

72. The point here is not limited to explicit statements of authorial intent, which can be as deceptive and self-deceptive as any other human utterance or action, but also applies to the highly idealized notion of "intent" to which we appeal when we seek a sympathetic, fair reading of a text.

73. Notice that these claims remain agnostic about the direction of causality. What seems most plausible is that there are several overlapping directions in "der Fall Nietzsches": Nietzsche's language seems suspect because of its later use by the Nazis; yet the Nazis may have picked up on some of their language because Nietzsche used it, while Nietzsche's own language makes deliberate, but ironic reference to then-prevailing anti-Semitism. Of course, what makes such irony effective is also what opens it up to the risk of abuse.

74. Tuana, *Woman and the History of Philosophy*, 39.

75. Lloyd, *The Man of Reason*, 41.

76. Other forms of phrasing raise similar problems. For instance, Susan Bordo pairs the phrases "split between mind and body, reason and emotion" in describing the influence of Cartesian dualism: "Introduction," *Feminist Interpretations of René Descartes*, ed. S. Bordo (University Park: Pennsylvania State University Press, 1999), 1. But grammatical apposition does not entail conceptual equivalence, and she presents no argument for identifying the two. Tuana makes the same slide in *Woman and the History of Philosophy*, 42.

77. Lloyd, *The Man of Reason*, 45–46. See also Tuana, *Woman and the History of Philosophy*, 37–38. This passage, found in PS I §48, AT XI 364–65 provides their most damning evidence against Descartes.

78. It is, in fact, pretty clear that in this passage Descartes wants to contrast the explanatory apparatus of his views with that of scholastic faculty psychologies, *and* that he describes different actions in speaking of how those psychologies "contrast" the parts of the soul and how his views allow that the body can "repel" or "push against" the soul. What he seems to have in mind is how movements in the body can operate in a direction contrary to those movements given to the pineal gland by our willing. Amélie Rorty notes exactly the passage in question, but declares that "there is nothing in the body that in itself resists or opposes the guidance of the rational will," "Descartes on Thinking with the Body," 384.

79. James Winders, "Writing Like a Man (?): Descartes, Science and Madness," in *Feminist Interpretations of René Descartes*, 117.

80. Bordo, introduction to *Feminist Interpretations of René Descartes*, 2.

81. Derrida, *The Ear of the Other*, 32.

82. Perhaps the most widely acknowledged source of this technique for feminists lies in the introduction to Simone de Beauvoir's *The Second Sex*, although its roots surely go back at least to Hegel. The aim of unmasking conceptual hierarchy and privilege is not peculiar to feminist critique; Derrida gives an excellent account of how textual deconstruction can use the same technique in "Signature, Event, Context," in *Margins of Philosophy*, trans. A. Bass (Chicago: University of Chicago Press, 1982).

83. It must be a mistake, however, to think that feminist critique always requires a search-and-destroy mission for dualisms. Gender privilege need not be conceived of only in terms of a simple dichotomy; it does not require the assumption that there are exactly two sexes or genders (however powerfully that assumption may have operated in certain forms of sexism). Moreover, not all dualisms need involve hierarchy and privilege.

CHAPTER 5

Material Falsity and the Arguments for God's Existence in Descartes' *Meditations*

CECILIA WEE

In many recent interpretations of Descartes' *Meditations*, close attention has been paid to its "order of reasons," and commentators have traced the steps by which Descartes develops later arguments out of earlier findings. One such work is Annette Baier's "The Idea of the True God in Descartes,"[1] in which she traces the steps by which Descartes' proofs of God's existence in the Third Meditation develop out of his account of himself as a thinking thing in the Second Meditation.

While I do not agree with all of Baier's views, I adopt her method here. This paper, like Baier's, is concerned with the issue of how the Third Meditation proofs of God's existence develop from earlier findings. And, like Baier's, this paper explicates Descartes' views from within the "order of reasons" in the *Meditations*. That is, I will try to show here how the proofs of God's existence in the Third Meditation develop from "what has gone before"—in particular, from the discussion of material falsity that precedes these proofs.

Baier has also written extensively on trust and its important role in human relations. As I shall show, understanding the proofs of God's existence in the Third Meditation by reference to the earlier discussion of material falsity reveals why the meditator is able to claim plausibly at the end of the Third Meditation that God is not a deceiver, and is incapable of "fraud and deception." Having arrived at this knowledge, Descartes is able to place absolute trust in God. This trust in God is crucial, as the Sixth Meditation and the *Passions of the Soul* show, to Descartes' account of the role played by his God-endowed faculties in achieving the human good life.

I. MATERIAL FALSITY AND THE THIRD MEDITATION

In her influential book on Descartes,[2] Margaret Wilson maintains that the main role of the account of material falsity in the Third Meditation is to look forward to the Fifth and Sixth Meditations by developing on "the theme of knowledge of body."[3] She thinks, however, that the passage plays no obvious role within the Third Meditation. Indeed, it is not merely irrelevant to the subsequent proofs of God's existence, it actually impedes these proofs:

> the notion of material falsity provides the basis for an objection to Descartes' proof of God's existence, because it entails that the objective reality of an idea is not something the idea wears on its sleeve . . . With respect to the demonstration of God's existence, this complexity in determining the objective reality leads to the following problem. If our ideas can provide material for error concerning that which they represent, and can to the extent be misjudged with respect to whether they represent *res* or *nullas res*, what justifies our assurance that the idea of God possesses infinite objective reality (and therefore must have an infinitely real cause)?[4]

Contra Wilson, I argue that the passage on material falsity plays a crucial role in these proofs. In section 2 of this essay, I will examine how the passage on material falsity puts in place certain important concepts. In section 3, I trace how these concepts are applied in the proofs that God exists and that he is not a deceiver.

2. THE PASSAGE ON MATERIAL FALSITY AND WHAT IT ESTABLISHES

Having established with certainty in the Second Meditation that he is (at least) a "thinking thing," Descartes goes on to examine his thoughts in the Third. He classifies them as follows: ideas per se (which are simply "as-if images of things"), and ideas with an "additional form" of judgment or willing/emotion (AT VII 37, CSM II 25–26). He then goes on to examine his ideas per se, and in the course of this examination he introduces the notion of material falsity:

> [M]aterial falsity . . . occurs in ideas, when they represent no things as things. For example, the ideas which I have of cold and heat contain so little distinctness that they do not enable me to tell whether cold is merely the privation (*privatio*) of heat or vice versa, or whether both of them are real qualities or neither is. And since there can be no ideas which are not as it were of things, if it is true that cold is the privation (*privatio*) of heat, the idea which represents itself to me as real and positive deserves to be called false, and the same goes for other ideas of this kind. (AT VII, 44, CSM II, 30*)[5]

Descartes thus thinks that some ideas may be materially false. He had earlier mentioned that all ideas are "as-if images of things"; that is, all ideas purport to represent things. He now points out that some ideas, while purporting to represent things, actually represent no things at all. Such ideas are, therefore, materially false.

Descartes' account of material falsity has two interesting features. The first has to do with the example he uses to illustrate materially false ideas. The example involves an opposing pair of ideas—heat versus cold. Descartes points out that while both ideas purport to represent (positive) things, it may well be that one is the privation of the other. Cold, for example, may be the privation of heat, in which case the idea of cold that represents it as a (positive) thing is materially false.

Wilson has correctly observed that the notion of privation is "not as essential" to the actual argument for material falsity "as may first appear." Descartes, in fact, accepts that neither of the "qualities" mentioned (whether heat or cold) need be "real" at all: both may not actually be real things. Why, then, does he bring in the illustration of cold as a privation of heat (and vice versa)? Wilson suggests that the example was simply a convenient one, since the notion of privation vs. positive quality was familiar to Descartes' Scholastic audience. But in fact, Descartes had more important reasons.

As mentioned, after classifying his various thoughts, Descartes goes on in the Third Meditation to examine his ideas per se. Significantly, the ideas that Descartes examines—whether of noises, hippogriffs, God, or corporeal things—are all ideas as-if of positive things (AT VII 38–43, CSM II 26–29). Now, in bringing up the notion of heat as a privation of cold in the passage on material falsity, Descartes makes clear for the first time that there is another class of "idea," namely, "ideas" of privation, or "ideas" as-if of the *absence* of something.[6]

The example of heat and cold also highlights the relationship between the idea of an absence, and that of the thing it is an absence *of*. In mentioning that cold may be a privation *of* heat (or vice versa),[7] Descartes implies that one can only make sense of a privation if one knows what it is a privation of. Cold can only be seen as a privation if one sees it as a privation *of heat*. In other words, one can't have the concept of a privation without first having a concept of the positive thing whose absence constitutes a privation. If cold is seen as a privation of heat, then the concept of heat is logically prior to the concept of cold: one must recognize the positive quality heat in order to see cold as a deprivation of that quality. I shall try to show later that this contrast between the idea of a positive thing and its privation plays an important role in the Third Meditation proofs of God's existence.

Let us move on to the second interesting feature of the passage on material falsity. This involves Descartes' intriguing account of the origin of his materially false ideas:

> if such ideas are false, that is, represent no-things [*nullas res*], I know by the natural light that they proceed [*procedere*] from nothing [*nihilo*]—that is they are only within me because of a deficiency and lack of perfection in my nature. (AT VII 44, CSM II 30*)

The standard reading of Descartes sees his statement that his materially false ideas "proceed from nothing" as more or less a reemphasis of his previous assertion that such ideas "represent no things." If an idea represents no existent thing, then it fails to refer to a real thing: as such, it "proceed(s) from nothing," in the sense that it does not pick out anything real.

There are, however, a number of difficulties with this standard reading. First, the passage would provide an empty explanation. To say that materially false ideas proceed from nothing (if all that is meant is that such ideas do not pick out any real objects) is simply another way of saying that these ideas do not represent anything. To *explain* the latter in terms of the former does not seem to be very illuminating.

Second, it is odd that Descartes should have to appeal to his natural light to give an "explanation" which amounts to a trivial restatement of what has gone before. In the other contexts in the *Meditations* where the term "natural light" occurs, the conclusion or inference illuminated by this light is much less obvious. (For example, Descartes maintains in the Third Meditation that it is the natural light which shows him that a total and efficient cause must have equal or greater reality than its effect. [AT VII 40, CSM II 28])

A third difficulty with this reading is that it becomes hard to see why Descartes should then go on to further redescribe ideas which proceed from nothing as those which are in him "because of a deficiency or lack of perfection in me":

> For if such ideas are false, that is, represent no-things, I know by the natural light that they proceed from nothing—that is [*hoc est*], they are in me only because of a deficiency or lack of perfection in my nature. (AT VII 44, CSM II 30*)

Why should Descartes think that there is an obvious link between the fact that these ideas proceed from nothing, and their being in him because of some deficiency or lack of perfection in his nature?

All this suggests that this passage establishes something deeper than this straightforward reading allows. When Descartes states that a materially false idea proceeds from nothing, he does not merely mean that such an idea fails to pick out a real object. He is making a deeper point about the link between absence or nothing, and a defect such as his having materially false ideas.

We are apt to think of "nothing" (*nihilum*) as merely pure, neutral absence. Descartes' notion of "nothing," drawn from the Scholastic philosophers, is much richer. For Descartes, "nothing" is indeed understood as absence—but it is an absence *of* something, i.e., of some real thing. For Descartes, as for the Scholastics, blindness, deafness, and dumbness are all literally nothing—for they are the absence of the "real" qualities of sight, hearing, and speech. And while blindness, deafness, and dumbness are indeed nothing or absence, they are not neutral or harmless absence; rather, these absences constitute defects or deficiencies in their subject.[8]

Earlier in the Third Meditation, Descartes had (following the Scholastics) identified reality with perfection: "it follows from this that what is *more perfect—that is, contains in itself more reality*—cannot arise from what is less perfect" (AT VII 41, emphasis mine). "Nothing," then, is for Descartes an absence of perfection, where this absence is a defect or deficiency. Thus, when Descartes maintains that his materially false ideas "proceed from nothing," he does not mean that they don't pick out anything real. Rather, he is saying that his materially false ideas proceed from nothing *qua* absence of perfection. Furthermore, this absence is not neutral or harmless, but is (as he goes on to point out) "a deficiency and lack of perfection in [his] nature." In short, Descartes is stating here that the defect of having materially false ideas results from an absence of perfection (rather than anything positive) in his nature.

The passage on material falsity establishes two points. First, one cannot have the concept of a privation without first having a concept of the positive thing whose absence constitutes a privation. Second, defects (e.g., the having of materially false ideas) proceed from nothing, in the sense that they are the result of an absence of perfection.

These two points are especially significant in light of what has just gone before. As I have pointed out, prior to this discussion Descartes had examined only positive ideas, ideas which were as-if of *things*. Again, he had then established the relationship between the level of objective reality in an idea, and that of the formal reality required in the cause of such an idea. This entire discussion of the relative reality/perfection of cause and effect was couched in positive terms, or from a positive perspective. The effects of a cause were taken as possessing reality and perfection; their causes were established as having perhaps even greater perfection than their effects. Even the beginning of this latter discussion emphasized a positive perspective, as Descartes talked of ever-increasing levels of objective reality in ideas—beginning with modes, going on to finite substances, and finally to infinite substance (AT VII 41–42, CSM II 28–29).

The passage on material falsity, coming after this positive passage, shifts the perspective by emphasizing that there is a flip-side to the notion of perfection—namely, that an absence of such perfection implies deficiency and imperfection. Cold may be the privation of positive heat; materially false ideas may result from deficiency, that is, from lack of perfection in the thinker's nature. Thus, the passage establishes the twin "poles" of positivity and negativity; it shows that the possible presence of a perfection in a given subject implies that its absence may constitute deficiency and defect, and conversely, that deficiency and defect can only be understood as such if one first recognizes the corresponding perfection.

3. THE THIRD MEDITATION PROOFS OF GOD'S EXISTENCE

This interplay between positive and negative, perfection and imperfection, are crucial for developing the Third Meditation arguments for God's existence. These arguments have essentially one underlying theme: the constant comparison between the imperfection of Descartes *qua* thinker and the perfection of the idea of God he finds within him—with the subsequent conclusion that this situation would only be possible if God really does exist. In approaching this theme from its various perspectives, Descartes invokes notions that were put in place in the passage on material falsity. Consider first the opening salvo in Descartes' first argument for God's existence:

> I must not think that just as my conceptions of darkness and rest are arrived at by negating movement and light, so my perception of the infinite is arrived at not by means of a true idea but merely by negating the finite. On the contrary, I clearly understand that there is more reality in an infinite substance than in a finite one, and hence that my perception of the infinite, that is, God is in some way prior to the perception of the finite, that is, myself. For *how could I understand that I doubted and desired—that is, lacked something—and that I was not wholly perfect, unless there was some idea in me of a more perfect being which enabled me to recognize my own defects by comparison?* (AT VII 45–46, CSM II 31, emphasis mine)

Descartes begins by invoking a pair of opposing ideas like those brought into play in the material falsity passage—namely, the pairs of rest and movement, and of darkness and light. Just as he can have a perception of cold as the privation of heat, similarly, he can perceive rest as the absence of movement, or darkness as the absence of light.[9]

Descartes then asks whether his idea of infinitude is like his ideas of rest and darkness. That is, he asks whether he could conceive of infinitude as an absence of the perfection of finitude (just as he could conceive of cold as the absence of the perfection of heat). However, he had established earlier in the Third Meditation that the idea of infinite substance presents *greater* perfection (more objective reality) than the idea of finite substance (AT VII 41, CSM II 28), so how could he conceive of infinite substance as lacking the perfection of finite substance? He must therefore conceive of finite substance as lacking the perfection of infinite substance. Hence, he must first have the idea of infinitude before he can perceive finitude as a lack of infinitude (just as he must have the idea of heat before he can perceive cold as the privation of heat).

Descartes then reflects on himself as a thinking thing. He had mentioned in the Second Meditation that he was a thing which doubted and desired (AT VII 28, CSM II 19). But now he looks at these faculties in the light of what he had learned about perfection and the lack thereof in the material falsity passage. That he can doubt implies that he lacks full knowledge or omniscience (since the latter would be accompanied by certainty); that he desires implies that he lacks omnipotence (since one would only desire if one lacks some object, and wishes to attain it). That Descartes suffers these lacks indicates to him that he is finite; he lacks the perfection of infinitude.

But, as he had shown above, he must have an idea of infinitude *before* he can perceive himself as finite. Where does this idea of infinitude come from? Not from himself, since he can perceive himself as finite only if the idea of infinitude is already held up before him. Thus, the idea of infinitude comes from some source outside himself. And given the principle that a total and efficient cause must have a formal reality at least equal to the (formal or objective) reality of its effect, this cause of his idea of infinite substance can only be infinite substance itself. Thus, God or infinite substance must exist.

Clearly, in this first proof of God's existence, Descartes uses what he has learned in the material falsity passage to argue from his own recognized imperfection to the existence of a perfect, infinite God. And this theme—

that the thinker's own imperfections point to the existence of perfect God—
is played over again in the coda to the first argument for God's existence.
There, Descartes seeks reassurance that the idea of infinitude really cannot
have come from himself:

> perhaps I am something greater than I myself understand, and all the
> perfections which I attribute to God are somehow in me potentially,
> though not yet . . . actualized. For I am now experiencing a gradual in-
> crease in my knowledge, and I see nothing to prevent its increasing . . .
> to infinity. . . . finally, if the potentiality for these perfections is already
> within me, why should not this be enough to generate the idea of such
> perfections? (AT VII 47, CSM II 32)

He rejects the notion that he is the source of this idea of infinitude:

> But all this is impossible. First, though it is true that there is a gradual in-
> crease in my knowledge, and that I have many potentialities which are
> not yet actual, this is all quite irrelevant to the idea of God, which con-
> tains absolutely nothing that is potential; indeed this gradual increase in
> knowledge is itself the surest sign of imperfection. What is more, even
> if my knowledge always increases . . . , I recognize that it will never ac-
> tually be infinite . . . ; God, on the other hand, I take to be actually in-
> finite, so that nothing (*nihil*)[10] can be added to his perfection. And finally
> I perceive that the objective being of an idea cannot be produced merely
> by potential being, which is strictly speaking nothing (*nihil*), but only be
> actual or formal being. (AT VII 47, CSM II 32)

Here, Descartes tries to understand himself in the most positive light possible; he finds that though he is imperfect and suffers from a deficiency
of perfection, he is able to gradually improve himself, perhaps to infinity.
Could he not then be the cause of his idea of infinitude?

Once again, the capacity to improve oneself turns out to be a lack or
defect—the mere fact that one is striving to attain perfection presupposes
that one lacks it. Descartes finds himself back at this starting point: he recognizes himself as a being that lacks perfection, and this recognition of imperfection is contrasted with a prior idea of God as "actually infinite, so that
nothing can be added to His perfection." Such an idea of God as infinite

and completely perfect cannot, therefore, come from himself; it must come from somewhere else. The interplay here between complete perfection and the deficiencies which result from its absence draws on themes from the passage on material falsity.

These themes are also crucial for the second argument for God's existence. Here, Descartes considers himself once again as an imperfect, finite being, with an idea of a perfect, infinite God within him, and asks if he could have created himself with this idea in him. He answers:

> Yet if I derived my existence from myself, then I should neither doubt, nor want, nor lack anything at all; for I should have given myself all the perfections of which I have any idea, and thus I should myself be God. (AT VII 48, CSM II 33)

He points out that it would have been much harder for him as a substance, a thinking thing, to emerge from nothing than to acquire those perfections he now lacks. If he had indeed created himself, he could certainly have endowed himself with all the perfections contained in his idea of God, and which he now lacks—for the latter would be easier to achieve than the former. As he writes,

> I must not suppose that the items I lack would be more difficult to acquire than those I now have. On the contrary, it is clear that, since I am a thinking thing or substance, it would have been far more difficult for me to emerge from nothing than to acquire knowledge of the many things of which I am ignorant. . . . And indeed if I had derived my existence from myself, which is a greater achievement, I would certainly not have denied myself the knowledge in question, which is something easier to acquire, or indeed any of the attributes which I perceive to be contained in the idea of God; for none of them seem any harder to achieve. (AT VII 48, CSM II 33)

Once again, the key point for the above argument is Descartes' perception of himself as lacking in perfection, in contrast to the idea of God that is held up before him, and in virtue of which he knows himself to be lacking in many respects. In this second argument, Descartes finds that the very fact that he lacks many perfections implies an even deeper lack—that of omnipotence and creative power. For the fact that he lacks many perfections implies that he did not have the power to create himself: if he had had that power, he would also have had the lesser power of endowing himself with all the perfections found in his idea of God. Since he obviously lacks this lesser power, he must also lack the greater power of creation. And since he patently exists, the absence of creative power in him must in turn presuppose the presence of a being with such power:

> if there were such a power [to keep me in being] within me, I should undoubtedly be aware of it. But I experience no such power, and this very fact makes me recognize most clearly that I depend on some being distinct from myself. (AT VII 49, CSM II 33–34)

Once again, this argument builds on the relationship between perfection and its absence established in the passage on material falsity.

I have tried to show that Descartes' discovery that he fails, in his weakness and finitude, to measure up to the idea of infinitude and perfection within him eventually leads him (by various routes) to the conclusion that God exists. This form of argument would not have been possible without the passage on material falsity, which established the character of imperfection (as an absence or lack of perfection) and outlined the relationship between the conception of such an absence and its corresponding perfection.

One outcome of my reading of these arguments for God's existence is that it becomes clear why Descartes can assert at the end of these proofs, not merely that God exists, but that He cannot be a deceiver (AT VII 52, CSM II 35). One puzzle about the Third Meditation might have been this: Why does Descartes assert (out of the blue, as it were) that God cannot be a deceiver at the end of that Meditation? What chain of reasoning could have led to this abrupt assertion? However, if one sees the theme underlying the proofs of God's existence as that of a contrast between a weak, imperfect thinker and a God who is completely perfect, one can agree with Descartes when he concludes:

> By "God" I mean the very being the idea of whom is within me, that is, the *possessor of all the perfections* that I cannot grasp, but can somehow reach in my thought, who is *subject to no defects whatsoever.* (AT VII 52, CSM II 35, emphasis mine)

Having proved that such a God exists, one merely needs to show that a characteristic is a defect to conclude that it cannot belong to God. Since it is "manifest by the natural light that all fraud and deception depend on defect" (AT VII 52, CSM II 35), it is not surprising that Descartes then concludes that God cannot be a deceiver.

The passage on material falsity had shown that defect was an absence of perfection; Descartes, having proved that God, who is all-perfect, exists, is then able to assert that the defect of deception and fraud cannot be a characteristic of God. Thus, insofar as the passage on material falsity establishes defect as an absence of perfection, it constitutes an indispensable step toward Descartes' final conclusion in the Third Meditation, namely, that God cannot be a deceiver.

Once he knows that God is not a deceiver, Descartes is able to trust in God, and consequently to place confidence in his own various God-endowed faculties. It is, of course, a moot point (which will not be discussed here) whether Descartes' trust in his reason precedes his proofs of God's existence or vice versa. However, his trust in God clearly underpins his confidence in his other faculties. Because he knows God will not perpetrate fraud and deception, he can assert in the Sixth Meditation that he can generally rely on his God-endowed sensory perceptions and natural inclinations (e.g., hunger, thirst) in determining what is beneficial or harmful to himself (*qua* mind-body composite). Again, his trust in God assures him that his God-endowed passions "are all by nature good" (AT XI 486, CSM I 403) and are given to him for his preservation and betterment.

But what of the fact that such perceptions, urges, and passions may sometimes lead him to his own harm? For example, the urge to drink, if indulged by a man with dropsy, may lead him to harm; similarly, a man in the grip of the passion of anger may act to his own detriment rather than benefit. That such mistakes are possible does not shake Descartes' confidence in his God-endowed faculties. He points out in the Sixth Meditation that "the very fact that God is not a deceiver" makes it impossible that there is "any falsity in my opinions which cannot be corrected by some other faculty supplied by God" (AT VII 80, CSM II 55–56). That God can never perpetrate fraud and deception provides Descartes with the certainty that he has been endowed with means to avoid or correct such mistakes. Thus, occasional mistakes in perception or natural urges may be avoided or corrected by other faculties. Similarly, the unbridled passions may lead to harm, but when harnessed by faculty of reason they are able to contribute to human good.

In her well-known essay "Trust and Antitrust,"[11] Baier considers different kinds of trust—between articulate adults, between infants and their parents, between a theist and his God. Unlike the infant, whose objects of trust (her parents) are soon seen to be vulnerable, the theist's trust is placed in an object that is considered invulnerable. Descartes, too, sees his God as invulnerable (to deception), and it is this which gives him his unshakeable trust and his consequent conviction that his God-endowed faculties are put in him ultimately for his own good.[12] His aim, especially in later works like the *Passions of the Soul*, is to explore how he, as a weak, imperfect human, may gradually learn to best deploy these faculties to further such good.

At this point, I would like to return to Wilson's criticisms of the Third Meditation passage on material falsity. Wilson does not merely think that this discussion plays no useful role in the subsequent proofs of God's existence; she also holds that it actually impedes these proofs. Her arguments for the latter claim will be examined.

4. MATERIAL FALSITY AS AN IMPEDIMENT TO THE PROOFS OF GOD'S EXISTENCE

Wilson maintains that the problem with the notion of material falsity is that it entails that an idea does not "wear its objective reality on its sleeve." How then can one be assured that "the idea of God does possess infinite objective reality (and therefore must have an 'infinitely real' cause)?"[13] Wilson concedes that Descartes attempts to provide an answer to this problem in the following passage:

> Nor can it be said that this idea of God is perhaps materially false and so could have come from nothing, which is what I observed just a moment ago in the case of ideas of heat and cold, and so on. On the contrary, it is utterly clear and distinct, and contains in itself more objective reality than any other idea. Hence there is no idea which is in itself truer or less liable to be suspected of falsehood. The idea of a supremely perfect and infinite being is, I say, true in the highest degree; for although

one may imagine that such a being does not exist, it cannot be supposed that the idea of such a being represents something unreal, as I said with regard to the idea of cold. The idea is, moreover, utterly clear and distinct; for whatever I clearly and distinctly perceive as being real and true, and implying any perfection, is wholly contained in it. (AT VII 46, CSM II 31–32)

On Wilson's view, this passage offers two reasons why our idea of God cannot be materially false: first, because the idea contains more objective reality than any other, and second, because it is very clear and distinct.

With respect to Descartes' defense that the idea of God is not materially false because it contains more objective reality than any other, Wilson asks: "How can we be certain that our idea of God actually does contain or exhibit infinite reality, given that we make mistakes about the amount of reality exhibited by other ideas, such as that of cold?"[14] And with respect to his assertion that the idea of God is not materially false because it is very "clear and distinct," she states: "The problem with [this] is that we have been told the proof of God's existence is required to vindicate the clarity and distinctness of ideas as the criterion of truth."[15] Thus, Descartes' attempt to exempt the idea of God from possible material falsity is, in her view, unsatisfactory.

One can reply to Wilson's objections as follows. Wilson apparently treats the two adduced reasons for the idea of God not being materially false—namely, that the idea contains more reality than any other, and that it is very clear and distinct—as disjunctive or independent reasons, and accordingly responds separately to each. However, Descartes does not see them as separate reasons. Rather, what Descartes maintains is this: I have an idea of God which I perceive contains maximal objective reality, and because I *also* see that it is a clear and distinct idea, I am justified in maintaining that it does contain that level of objective reality—thus, this idea cannot be materially false. The two reasons adduced by Wilson are not independent: it is the clarity and distinctness in the idea which guarantees that it does actually have the maximal level of objective reality displayed, and is thus true. (If Descartes had had an idea of God as containing more reality than any other, but then found that his idea was both confused and obscure, he would not have been willing to say that it was not materially false.)

Thus, in answer to Wilson's first query, How do we know that the idea of God has infinite objective reality? Descartes would reply that we know it because we only make mistakes in the case of confused and obscure ideas, and the idea of God is not one of these. This would collapse the first objection into the second one: How can we guarantee that the idea of God is true because it is clear and distinct, when we need God's existence to guarantee that clear and distinct ideas are true?

There is, of course, no satisfactory short answer to this second objection (which after all involves the Cartesian circle, an issue on which the literature is enormous). So I will simply attempt a brief reply by pointing out that this objection presupposes that there *is* a Cartesian circle. A number of commentators have argued that there may not be such a circle. For instance, Anthony Kenny, Bernard Williams, and James van Cleve[16] have argued, quite persuasively, that God's existence is not required to guarantee the truth of clear and distinct perceptions (at least while the thinker is directly contemplating them). If one accepts some version of this view, then Wilson's second objection does not hold water.

Wilson has maintained that the introduction of the notion of material falsity impedes Descartes' argument for God's existence, but I hope I have shown above that this issue is at least open to question. I have also argued that if one follows the "order of reasons" in the *Meditations*, it becomes clear that the discussion of material falsity is by no means irrelevant to the proofs of God's existence in the Third Meditation, for this discussion introduces concepts that are crucial to these proofs. Moreover, by understanding the proofs of God's existence in the context of the earlier discussion of material falsity, we can see how Descartes can claim incontrovertibly that the God who exists suffers no defects and hence is not a deceiver. This in turn allows Descartes to trust God and the faculties with which God has endowed him.

NOTES

1. Annette Baier, "The Idea of the True God in Descartes," in *Essays on Descartes' Meditations*, ed. Amélie Oksenberg Rorty (Berkeley: University of California Press, 1986), 359–87.

2. Margaret Wilson, *Descartes* (London: Routledge and Kegan Paul, 1978).

3. Ibid., 113.

4. Ibid., 112.

5. Quotations of Descartes are from *The Philosophical Writings of Descartes*, vol. II, ed. J. Cottingham, R. Stoothoff, and D. Murdoch (Cambridge: Cambridge

University Press, 1984), cited as CSM II. Quotations in which I have in some way departed from the CSM translation are marked with an asterisk. References to *Oeuvres de Descartes*, ed. C. Adam and P. Tannery, vols. 1–12 (Paris: J. Vrin, 1983), are cited as AT, followed by the volume number.

6. Descartes wavers between calling these thoughts which represent absences of things "ideas" (in the Fourth Meditation) and merely calling them "perceptions" or "conceptions" (as in the Third Meditation), reserving the term "idea" for those which are "as-if images of things" (AT VII 44–46, CSM II 30–31). But whatever the terminology, the discussion of heat and cold establishes to Descartes that he can have perceptions of things as absent.

7. The term "privation," of course, carries a rather specific meaning when used by Scholastic philosophers like Aquinas or Suárez. A privation is thought to be an absence or deficiency of a quality which a substance should possess *according to its nature*. That is, a privation is an absence of a quality that a substance ought to have.

However, it should be noted that Descartes is not using the term in this sense, in this particular passage. To begin with, he seems, at this point, to use "privation" and "negation" quite interchangeably. Traditionally, a "privation" is an absence of a quality that a substance ought to have, and a "negation" is merely an absence of some quality (without any additional connotation). The ideas of heat and cold and of, say, rest and movement are similar in that they are of opposing pairs, yet in the Third Meditation Descartes describes cold as the privation of heat, and rest as the negation of movement (AT VII 44–46, CSM II 30–31). This suggests that Descartes is not yet making a clear distinction between negation and privation. (He does, however, go on to make this distinction in the Fourth Meditation. See, e.g., AT VII 55, CSM II 38.)

Again, at this point in the Third Meditation, he does not even know what substance heat and cold are features of (are they features of his embodied self? or of the physical world external to him?). Thus, when he says that cold is a privation of heat, he could not mean that heat is a quality that a substance *ought* to have, since he does not even know what substance it is which could have heat as a positive quality. Insofar as he does not know what sort of substance has heat as a quality, he has no clear idea of the nature of that substance. How then could he maintain that heat is a quality that belongs to that substance by virtue of its nature?

Thus, when Descartes says that cold may be a privation of heat, he means merely that cold may be an absence of the real quality heat—whatever substance the latter may turn out to inhere in.

8. Once again, Descartes departs from standard Scholastic usage in his use of the term "defect." For the Scholastics, blindness, for example, is not simply the absence of something positive: it is the absence of something positive in a subject *in which that positive thing should occur*. More generally, the Scholastics thought that a

defect is not simply an absence of something—rather, it is the absence of some-thing which should occur in a particular subject, but is absent in it.

This account of a defect may have been pervasive among the Scholastics, but it is not held by Descartes. He does not think that a defect is an absence of what a sub-ject ought to possess by nature: rather, a subject (in this case, himself) can suffer a defect or deficiency *because of* its nature (AT VII 44, CSM II 30). Since one may suf-fer a defect because one possesses a certain sort of nature, it follows for Descartes that defects are not confined to the absences of things which one ought to have by nature. Admittedly, the example of blindness, which is Descartes' own (see AT VII 191, CSM II 134), might be a bit misleading in this context, since blindness in a per-son seems to be an absence of a quality which he ought to have by nature.

9. See note 7 above for the claim that Descartes does not clearly distinguish between privations and negations in this meditation.

10. One objection to my view that nothing (*nihilum*) means to Descartes an ab-sence of perfection and carries a connotation of deficiency is that there are cases, this instance being a case in point, where Descartes' use of the term "nothing" does not carry such a connotation. Though I will not argue the point here, there is a strong case for maintaining that Descartes distinguishes between *nihil* and *nihilum*. Though they are often assumed to be synonymous, they are in fact separate words. Based on a check of Descartes' respective uses of *nihil* and *nihilum*, quite a strong case can be made that he uses *nihilum* primarily when he wants to convey the connotation of de-ficiency, and *nihil* when he means "nothing" in its more "ordinary" sense. (One im-portant exception to this claim is the use of *nihil* in his description of himself as be-tween God and nothingness in the Fourth Meditation [AT VII 54, CSM II 38].)

11. "Trust and Antitrust," in Annette C. Baier, *Moral Prejudices: Essays on Ethics* (Cambridge, MA: Harvard University Press 1994), 95–129.

12. Here I follow the standard view that the sense-perceptions, natural urges, and passions are put in the human to enable her *own* survival and betterment. How-ever, as I have argued in "Self, Other and Community in Cartesian Ethics," *History of Philosophy Quarterly* 19 (2002): 255–73, Descartes also accepts that the passions may appropriately serve to further the betterment of others.

13. Wilson, *Descartes*, 112.

14. Ibid., 113.

15. Ibid.

16. Anthony Kenny, "The Cartesian Circle and Eternal Truths," *Journal of Phi-losophy* 67 (1970): 685–700; Bernard Williams, *Descartes: The Project of Pure Enquiry* (Sussex: Harvester Press, 1978); James van Cleve, "Foundationalism, Epistemic Prin-ciples, and the Cartesian Circle," *Philosophical Review* 88 (1979): 55–91.

CHAPTER 6

Reason Unhinged

Passion and Precipice from Montaigne to Hume

SAUL TRAIGER

To illustrate a point about general rules in *A Treatise of Human Nature*, Hume instructs us to imagine what he calls "a familiar instance," the "case of a man, who being hung out from a high tower in a cage of iron cannot forbear trembling, when he surveys the precipice below him, tho' he knows himself to be perfectly secure from falling" (1.3.13.10; T 148).[1] Why does Hume characterize this case as a familiar instance, when it appears to be a rather unusual scenario? In what follows, I will show that precipice thought experiments were common fare in a philosophical debate about the relation between reason and the passions by Hume's predecessors. Hume's treatment of the precipice phenomenon is an important contribution to that debate.

I say that such thought experiments were common in a philosophical debate about the relation between reason and the passions to emphasize that this debate is one among many. Certainly, the most widely discussed of these debates today centers on the question of whether reason is merely instrumental in practical reasoning, and thus, as Hume famously put it, is, and ought only to be, the slave of the passions (2.3.3.4; T 414). Arguments from precipice phenomena by Hume and his predecessors do not broach this important issue. Rather, they concern a separate issue, one addressed today by cognitive psychologists and other cognitive scientists. The issue is as follows: is situated causal reasoning, understood as causal reasoning carried out in ordinary situations, independent of affect, where "independent" means that we can make judgments about causes and effects which judgments are not themselves influenced by our affective states? Montaigne and other philosophers with whom Hume was familiar deployed precipice examples to support one of the following claims: (1) Affective mechanisms can lead to beliefs which we must embrace, but which are incompatible with the beliefs we are led to by causal reasoning. (2) Affective mechanisms make it impossible to form beliefs that would be arrived at through reasoning in the absence of the affective response. Hume's predecessors argued for a form of epistemological skepticism based on endorsing both these claims. Hume does not draw the skeptical conclusion, because while he accepts (1), he rejects (2). Thus, Hume's treatment of precipice cases suggests that the passions can be integrated with, and even contribute to, proper cognitive processing.

If you place a sage "on the edge of a precipice," Montaigne wrote in his *Essays*, "he must shudder like a child."[2] Citing the Platonic and Stoic traditions, Montaigne offers this example as counterevidence to a view that took reason as a faculty wholly separate from and superior to the senses, imagination, and the passions. Even the philosopher, one who exercises reason and attempts to form beliefs through reason alone, Montaigne argues, is subject to the influence of the emotions. That influence is one that shuts down cognition, making reasoning impossible. Fear of falling prevents the philosopher from making the correct inference, namely that he is not in danger.

When he reintroduced Montaigne's example a century later, Pascal regarded reason and the imagination as separate faculties, each producing beliefs, but with the imagination often winning out and leaving the individual with false beliefs.

> Put the world's greatest philosopher on a plank that is wider than need be: if there is a precipice below, although his reason may convince him that he is safe, his imagination will prevail. Many could not even stand the thought of it without going pale and breaking into a sweat.[3]

Presumably, the "greatest philosopher in the world" is someone guided by reason, rather than by the irregular operations of the imagination and the passions. Place a philosopher on the precipice, and reason is unhinged. In such cases, we judge not by reason, but by the operation of our passions and imagination. Other experiences which can unhinge reason, according to Pascal, include "the sight of cats or rats, the crushing of a coal."

For both Pascal and Montaigne, the philosopher-on-the-precipice example supports a form of skepticism about reason. Reason is not all it's cracked up to be; its verdict is readily displaced by the imagination and the passions. Both philosophers assume that reason, undisturbed, would yield the appropriate belief. Reason correctly tells us that we are safe on the precipice, yet we tremble. Imagination and the passions give us the wrong answer. Our trembling on the precipice is inappropriate.

Montaigne and Pascal employed the precipice example to argue against a conception of reason as a faculty that operates in isolation from other aspects of the human mind and the human body. Montaigne adds an admonition from Terence to the Stoics: "Let him think nothing human foreign to him."[4] In short, we cannot transcend our bodily human nature, our nonrational responses to our physical environment. Neither Montaigne nor Pascal explains the nature of the interaction and the conflict, the possible benefits of the influences of the passions, or how reason reaches the right conclusions and how the imagination blocks the inferences that lead to them.

In *The Passions of the Soul* Descartes explicitly treats the passions and reason as separate faculties. Reason is wholly nonphysical, but, notoriously, Descartes held that reason still influences the body through the pineal gland.[5] The passions, in contrast to reason, are bodily, not mental; they can arise from sensory stimuli. When we see a lion, for example, the brain forms an image of it which is available both to the soul, which performs the cognitive processing of the image, and to the passions, which respond to the image based on past experience:

> If, in addition, this shape is very strange and terrifying—that is, if it has a close relation to things which have previously been harmful to the body—this arouses the passion of anxiety in the soul, and then that of courage or perhaps fear and terror, depending on the particular temperament of the body or the strength of the soul, and upon whether we have protected ourselves previously by defence or by flight against

the harmful things to which the present impression is related. Thus in certain persons these factors dispose their brain in such a way that some of the spirits reflected from the image formed on the gland proceed from there to the nerves which serve to turn the back and move the legs in order to flee.[6]

The account Descartes develops here is generalized to all the passions. Spirits in the brain affect the nerves and the blood, and the brain also receives feedback from both systems which, in turn, sustain or modify the passions. These bodily processes develop as habitual responses to stimuli, and require no cognitive intervention or support. Passions are a "mere disposition of the organs."[7]

Passions can direct human action, however. If reason is not directing the will and pushing on the pineal gland, then the passions move in and exert their influence at the gland, thus affecting the body. The passions, then, do not compete with reason; they simply take over when we are not exercising it. Fear, Descartes argues, is typically caused by surprise, and can be avoided by the exercise of forethought. So, reason and passion compete for control of the body at the pineal gland, but the integration of affective and cognitive functions is one-way. Reason can quell the passions, but not vice versa.

Although Descartes did not discuss the precipice phenomenon, we can see what he might have said about it by examining a related case he does discuss. Descartes offers the following argument for the claim that any passion can be controlled by reason. Consider the behavior of animals. Dogs typically run toward partridges and away from loud sounds. But one can train a setter not to run from a gun and not to run toward a partridge. If the passions of animals can be modified without the resources of reasoning, Descartes argues, human passions can be even more easily modified with the assistance of reason. As dispositions of the organs, our passions are plastic.[8]

Montaigne and Pascal held that the precipice phenomenon is compelling evidence that some passions will displace our best reasoning. In contrast, Descartes thought any passion would yield to reason properly exercised. The philosopher on the precipice might tremble initially, but like a good setter, he can be trained to not feel fear on subsequent trips to the summit. The disagreement is not about how ordinary persons react to heights. Descartes does not think that ordinary folk use reason to overcome their passions. Rather, it is the philosopher, or other careful users of reason, who can overcome the passions. In contrast, Montaigne and Pascal claim that *even the philosopher*, the individual well practiced in the use of reason, will find that his reason is unhinged in the precipice case and similar situations.

In spite of these differences, the three philosophers share the assumption that reason and the passions are separate and competing faculties, with reasoning occurring in the mind, emoting and imagining in the body. Further, in spite of their insistence that reason cannot be separated from the passions, Pascal and Montaigne have very little to say about the relation between mind and body, reason and passion. Descartes' account of the separation is problematic in a number of ways. How do the passions register the cognitively rich images to which they respond? How can reason train the passions? Does the setter example really support the claim that reason can *always* overcome the effects of the passions?

Nicolas Malebranche attempted to explain how passions interface with reason in terms of "brain traces"—changes in the fibers of the brain. Like Descartes, Malebranche takes the mind to be wholly separate from the body. Although there are brain traces "connected" to the mind's ideas, the mind can have its ideas without knowing that there are such traces, indeed without knowing that it has a brain. There are three kinds of connections between ideas and brain traces. First, there are what Malebranche calls "natural connections." The connection between the idea of a tree and the brain trace one has when seeing a tree is a connection of this kind. The second type is a connection involving "identity," which, for Malebranche, consists of brain traces that happen to occur, but need not occur, simultaneously with some occurrence of an idea. If I heard Frank Sinatra sing "My Way" when I first saw the Grand Canyon, for example, then the song will always lead me to some idea, perhaps confused, of the Grand Canyon. Finally, certain idea-brain trace connections are due to the will. Language-idea connections are willed. The fact that a certain sequence of sounds or characters which produces a particular brain trace or traces regularly corresponds to a particular idea is due to our desire to communicate and the employment of our will to achieve such communication.[9]

These three types of connections have different degrees of strength. The natural connections are the strongest; the willed connections, the weakest. Malebranche suggests that this is why it is sometimes easier to explain something through a visual demonstration than by offering a verbal account. A verbal account depends on a willed connection of brain traces of words and ideas; a visual demonstration exploits the natural connection of perceptual brain traces and ideas. Also, the more we abstract, using unfamiliar symbols to represent concepts, as we do in mathematics, the more difficult it is for the mind to grasp those ideas.

There are mutual connections among traces, as well as connections from traces to ideas and to emotions, and these connections can be either "identity" or "natural" connections. If two traces are "imprinted at the same time," then, when one of them recurs, so will the other. The natural connections among brain traces are hardwired into us because such an organization is necessary to the preservation of life. The precipice phenomenon is offered as an example of such a connection. Malebranche writes:

> For example, the trace of a great elevation one sees below oneself, and from which one is in danger of falling, or that of a large body, about to fall on us and crush us, is naturally tied to the one that represents death to us, and to an emotion of the spirit that disposes us to flight and to the desire to flee. This connection never changes, because it is necessary that it be always the same, and it consists in a disposition of the brain fibers that we have from birth.[10]

In Malebranche's hands, the precipice example has changed from one concerning the philosopher on the precipice to a claim about all human agents. In further contrast to Pascal and Montaigne, the threat of the precipice is real in Malebranche's example. It is clear, however, that Malebranche is providing grounds for Montaigne and Pascal's claim that the philosopher on the precipice cannot reason his way out of the fear of falling. The connection between perceiving the precipice and the emotion of fear "never changes," either for the ordinary person or for the careful reasoner. Malebranche is at odds with his strongest intellectual influence, Descartes.

In Malebranche's example, there is more going on than a connection of mutual brain traces; there are connections among brain traces, representations, and emotions. The visual stimulus of the precipice is connected with both the representation of the precipice in thought, and the affective response of the body. Unfortunately, Malebranche says little about how these different faculties are related and how they conspire to achieve the resultant fear. His main point is the surprisingly anti-Cartesian one that the affective response is hardwired and immune to change by reasoning. Still,

Malebranche's understanding of the precipice case, though confused, represents an advance over Montaigne and Pascal's treatment. Malebranche recognizes that the case involves not only the imagination or the passions, but both. Further, he seems to hold that there is some sort of belief or pattern recognition at work. One recognizes the precipice as a precipice, and this "represents death to us." But it also seems clear that for Malebranche, the belief or representation of the precipice is only an epiphenomenal link. It is the "*trace* of a great elevation," not the *idea* of it which gets things going, and the rest follows automatically and without further cognitive processing.[11] This fits with Malebranche's celebrated view that we see all things in God. There is no real connection from perceptions to ideas. God, rather than the external world, is the source of all of our ideas.

Immediately after the precipice example, Malebranche takes on Descartes' passion-plasticity example:

> All the connections that are not natural can be and should be broken, because different circumstances of time and place are bound to change them so that they can be useful to the preservation of life. It is good that partridges, for example, flee from men with guns in places and times they are being hunted, but it is not necessary that they flee at other times and places. Thus, it is necessary for the conservation of all animals that there be certain connections of traces that can easily be formed and destroyed, and that there be others that can be broken only with difficulty, and finally, still others that can never be broken.[12]

Malebranche concedes that some affective responses are plastic, but those necessary for survival are not. Interestingly, he anticipates Darwin's views on affective brittleness as well as subsequent speculation about the cognitive value of such hardwired affects.[13]

To summarize the historical discussion thus far, philosophers whose works were well known to Hume frequently discussed questions about the relation of cognition and affect.[14] They were particularly concerned about whether cognition can overcome inappropriate affective responses to our environment. The dominant view, with Descartes dissenting, was that cognition cannot always overcome the effects of the passions and the imagination. When we tremble on the precipice we simply cannot reason our way out of our fear. Further, this inability demonstrates the separation of mind and body. Our passions are bodily, and our mental states are powerless to redirect them.

By the time Hume takes his turn discussing fear on the precipice, the example is so well known that he refers to it as a "familiar instance." It is found in his "Of Unphilosophical Probability," in a discussion of the influence of general rules on belief. Although lengthy, the passage deserves quotation in full:

> To illustrate this by a familiar instance, let us consider the case of a man, who being hung out from a high tower in a cage of iron cannot forbear trembling, when he surveys the precipice below him, tho' he knows himself to be perfectly secure from falling, by his experience of the solidity of the iron, which supports him; and tho' the ideas of fall and descent, and harm and death, be deriv'd solely from custom and experience. The same custom goes beyond the instances, from which it is deriv'd, and to which it perfectly corresponds; and influences his ideas of such objects as are in some respect resembling, but fall not precisely under the same rule. The circumstances of depth and descent strike so strongly upon him, that their influence cannot be destroy'd by the contrary circumstances of support and solidity, which ought to give him a perfect security. His imagination runs away with its object, and excites a passion proportion'd to it. That passion returns back upon the imagination and enlivens the idea; which lively idea has a new influence on the passion, and in its turn augments its force and violence; and both his fancy and affections, thus mutually supporting each other, cause the whole to have a very great influence upon him. (1.3.13.10; T 148–49)

Reasoning from experience, that is, from the constant conjunction of being suspended from an iron cage (and of being on platforms "attached" to something "of the solidity of iron") and yet not falling, yields a vivid idea of safety, though not of "perfect security."[15] The imagining of "depth and descent" brings about the passion of fear, which increases the vivacity of the idea of depth and descent. One cognitive process, causal reasoning, yields a high-vivacity idea of our safety. Another process, involving imagination and the passions, yields a high-vivacity idea of our danger. The resulting doxastic instability is due to the incompatibility of our competing ideas of safety and danger. Which process should we follow? If beliefs are themselves sentiments or feelings, then why should we prefer causal reasoning to the influence of the passions?

Can reason, on Hume's conception of it, be set in opposition to our passions and sentiments when beliefs, the products of reason, are, as Hume famously held, themselves sentiments? In many passages Hume emphasizes the similarities of belief and passion, rather than their differences.[16] In the first *Enquiry* he says that beliefs, like other sentiments, "must arise from the particular situation, in which the mind is placed at any particular juncture."[17] At the very end of Book II of the *Treatise*, he notes that belief produces the same pleasure ("though in a lesser degree") as that which arises from moderate passions (2.3.10.12; T453). Not only is reasoning passion-like, but the passion's mechanisms are reason-like: the passions of admiration and surprise which the vulgar experience in commerce with "quacks and projectors" can so vivify their ideas that they come to resemble "the inferences we draw from experience" (1.3.10.4; T120). It is tempting to conclude that the conflict between reason and passion is really just a conflict among passions and that the contrast of distinct faculties vying for attention and control vanishes. Everything becomes a matter of affect.[18]

In my view, Hume is not in danger of merging reason and passion in this way. Beliefs are indeed feelings or sentiments; they are lively ideas. The key difference is the way our beliefs are formed, in contrast to the formation of our other sentiments. Beliefs can share phenomenological features with sentiments without being *mere* sentiments.[19] While beliefs and other sentiments arise from what Hume calls situations of the mind, his accounts differentiate these situations. The difference will occupy center stage in Hume's final explanation of the precipice phenomenon.

Hume faces another potential problem in attempting to account for the conflict evident in the precipice case. In the same passage where he calls reason the slave of the passions, he says that passions have no representative quality, and thus cannot be opposed to belief (2.3.3.5; T 415). Still, that does not prevent our passions from aiding and abetting the imagination in the formation of lively ideas that are opposed to the deliverances of reason. Hume says that the "passions can be contrary to reason only so far as they are accompany'd with some judgment or opinion" (2.3.3.6; T 416). This may seem a weak conflict, but, I will argue, it is a significant one. It appears that nonreasoning mechanisms play an important role in bringing about high-vivacity ideas that can be fully opposed to beliefs formed by causal reasoning. In reference to the precipice phenomenon Hume claims that fear "produces a species of belief."[20] So, the conflict which interests him is not a conflict of passions or a conflict between belief and passion, but rather a case of incompatible beliefs.

In dealing with the precipice phenomenon, Hume has an advantage over his predecessors, insofar as he has a unified account of belief and the passions. The passions, the imagination, and reason can all affect the vivacity of our ideas. But this very feature makes it difficult to see how Hume can, as he will, challenge the skeptical position of Montaigne, Pascal, and Malebranche that the passions unhinge reason in the precipice case.

The precipice example, in Hume's hands, is not merely a simple conflict of reason and passion. Hume does not think a direct opposition is possible. The passions do not work alone in opposition to reason; they are aided by the imagination. The idea of depth and descent originates in the imagination and is then stoked by the passions. The passion-enlivened idea "returns back upon the imagination," resulting in a new passion and thereby enlivening the idea. The process is cyclical, continually increasing the vivacity of the idea of depth and descent. There are two important insights here: (1) the conflict is between the union of passion and imagination against causal reasoning, and (2) the passion/imagination process reiterates. Reason seems to be no match for the imagination aided by passion. The idea of safety will be a less vivid idea than the continually passion-enriched idea of depth and descent.[21] The skeptical position seems to find support here.

The point of Hume's example might merely be that the imagination can gain temporary control of our judgment, which is a species of unphilosophical probability. Reason eventually steps in to make the necessary corrections. Instead, with Robert Fogelin, I read the section as setting up a genuine conflict of belief-forming mechanisms.[22] Fogelin, however, thinks that Hume's resolution is a skeptical one: there are no grounds for accepting the deliverances of reason over those of passion and imagination. I see the case as a difficult challenge for Hume's naturalism, but one he can meet. Just as superstitions, understood as the products of natural causes and the social interaction of epistemic agents, can be epistemically assessed by an analysis of those very origins, so, too, we can correct the influence of high-vivacity ideas based on passion and imagination. If all Hume has to offer is the claim that we attend to the deliverances of reason and ignore the passion-enriched imagination, then he hasn't advanced beyond Descartes.

Hume agrees with his predecessors that the influence of passion and imagination on a person on the precipice is great. There is no reason to think that the vivacity of the idea of falling is less than that of one's safety. Indeed, Hume's way of describing the situation suggests that the idea of depth and descent may be more lively than the idea of safety. Elsewhere he suggests that beliefs always have higher vivacity than ideas of the imagination, but he is in no position to make that claim here, and he does not.[23]

Before Hume can resolve the conflict between the understanding and the imagination, he needs to say something about the difference between the two faculties. Surprisingly, however, Hume only further emphasizes their similarities:

> According to my system, all reasonings are nothing but the effects of custom; and custom has no influence, but by inlivening the imagination, and giving us a strong conception of any object. It may, therefore, be concluded, that our judgment and imagination can never be contrary, and that custom cannot operate on the latter faculty after such a manner, as to render it opposite to the former. (1.3.13.11; T 149)

Here "all reasonings" includes both the understanding, which produces the idea of safety, and the imagination, which produces the idea of depth and descent. The latter idea is the result of custom. We have experience of precipices and of falling. The circumstance of being hung out over the precipice adds to the idea's vivacity, and thus we do a bit of causal reasoning and infer that we are in danger. The precipice example is Hume's illustration of the fact that "custom takes the start, and gives a biass [sic] to the imagination" (1.3.13.9; T 148).

To appreciate that the idea of depth and descent is the result of a custom, Hume suggests that we simply examine the relevant regularities and determine their relative strengths. This will enable us to resolve the conflict among the deliverances of these equally natural, but not equally efficacious, faculties. The practice of determining the relative strengths of the parallel customs requires reflection and general rules. When we have beliefs in the absence of competing high-vivacity ideas, we often simply embrace those beliefs without reflection. But when there is a conflict, reflection is forced on us. Either we are safe on the precipice, or we are going to plummet to our deaths. It becomes imperative to reflect on the circumstances under which the competing ideas are formed and, by seeing both ideas as the effects of causes, to distinguish the "accidental circumstances from the efficacious causes" (1.3.13.11; T149).

How are we to distinguish accidental circumstances from efficacious causes? Both the imagination and reason fall under general rules, and both generate lively ideas. Hume calls the effects of the regularity of the two faculties the "first influence of general rules." That is, there are general rules that govern the formation of the high-vivacity ideas of security on the precipice and general rules governing the formation of the high-vivacity ideas of depth and descent. Reflection on these two sets of rules is possible and, in case of a contest, necessary. The "second influence of general rules" involves our reflective judgments about the first rules. We discover that the imagination is accidental and irregular, (though still rule governed) while the understanding is "more general and authentic" (1.3.13.12; T 150).

Fogelin challenges Hume to provide grounds for the claim that the beliefs provided by the understanding are "general and authentic," while those of the imagination are merely "accidental and irregular." Hume classifies fear as a direct passion, a passion arising from the contemplation of possible evils. Fear contrasts with hope, which follows the contemplation of possible pleasures. The degree of fear or hope that we experience is a function of both the severity of the anticipated evil or pleasure and the judgment of the likelihood of the occurrence of evil or pleasure. The more likely an evil, the more our imagination will turn to it. The more severe the anticipated evil, the more lively our idea of it will be. This suggests that part of our reflection on, and correction of, our sentiments of fear and hope are the assessments of the initial judgments of probability that we make when we experience the direct passion in question. Consider the precipice example: the pit-of-the-stomach "I'm going to fall" feeling does not, thankfully, precede an actual incident of falling in most cases. It is not an a priori truth that the imagination provides an idea without a predictive punch; it is merely an empirical fact, discovered by causal reasoning .

Hume had already mentioned the interplay of passion and probability in Book I, "Of the Influence of Belief." There, while famously emphasizing that belief "is nothing but a more vivid and intense conception of any idea" (1.3.8.11; T 119–20, emphasis Hume's), he also introduces several examples in which one can distinguish the respective contributions of passion and probability. The coward "readily assents to every account of danger." This suggests that the coward on the precipice is one who would already have a high-vivacity idea of anticipated pain, which communicates vivacity to the idea of falling, raising it to the level of a belief that he will fall.[24]

Precipice phenomena are treated in closely related passages in the *Treatise*, the second *Enquiry*, and the *Dissertation on the Passions*. Surprisingly, Hume does not say that fear of falling is a combination of the low probability of falling compensated by the lively terror of falling. Rather, he says that we can fear the impossible as well as the improbable. In the *Treatise* Hume writes:

> But they are not only possible evils, that cause fear, but even some allow'd to be *impossible;* as when we tremble on the brink of a precipice, tho' we know ourselves to be in perfect security, and have it in our choice whether we will advance a step farther. This proceeds from the immediate presence of the evil, which influences the imagination in the same manner as the certainty of it wou'd do; but being encounter'd by the reflection on our security, is immediately retracted, and causes the same kind of passion, as when from a contrariety of chances contrary passions are produc'd. (2.3.9.23; T 445)

This precipice passage is very close to those of Montaigne, Pascal, and Malebranche, and by characterizing the evil as impossible, Hume seems to be agreeing with them that such fear is opposed to reason.[25] However, Hume means not strict logical impossibility, but very low probability, due to the fact that falling would require an act of the will that we are strongly inclined not to take, namely, to "advance a step farther." The so-called impossibility of falling is initially overcome by the strength of the imagination's idea of falling. Experience with precipices, however, leads to a correction. "Custom soon reconciles us to heights and precipices, and wears off these false and delusive terrors."[26] Reflection on the first influence of general rules leads to a second influence of general rules. Namely, we now possess rules that incorporate our understanding of the imaginative and passional mechanisms that generate the initial, unreflective fear and the associated high-vivacity idea of danger.

One might think that Hume has ruled out any role for the feeling of fear. The direct passion of fear turns out to have a reasoning component, namely, causal inference. The experience of terror or fear is itself corrected by custom. It is true that the direct passions have a causal reasoning component, but Hume says it goes both ways: "As belief is almost absolutely requisite to the exciting our passions so the passions in their turn are very favourable to belief" (1.3.10.4; T 120).

How can the passions help us form and regulate beliefs, if their deliverances, while regular in the first sense, do not provide us with correct causal beliefs? Hume appreciates the fact that passion and imagination have an important practical role in the way we report belief. We use "concealed strokes of satire" when criticizing others because we know that direct criticism will stir their passions. But utilizing our folk psychology of the passions, which we obtain by reflecting on them, is different from using our own passions in our pursuit of knowledge. The moral of Hume's example is negative; we are not going to fall, so we can use reflection to discount the fear of falling. It is difficult, however, to accept that the fear of falling has *no* epistemic value. Such fears may motivate us to use caution when on the precipice and refrain from taking that next step; in other cases, they may motivate us to revise our beliefs.

In the precipice case, reflection corrects the fear of falling. The belief that we are safe prevails. But in other fearful circumstances it could go another way. The example of cowardice mentioned above demonstrates this. The coward's feeling of fear makes him hypersensitive to the belief that he will fall. Such a predisposition is often useful. Imagine that you are at the top of a mountain on skis, looking down at the expert run below. You are confident that you can ski this run without getting hurt. But on this occasion, probability cannot overcome the fear of injury. The anticipation of pain calls your attention to your assessment of the likelihood of a fall, and prods a reassessment. Coward or no coward, your passions play an important role in the assessment of belief. The passions call attention to the salient features of the environment that may prompt a change of belief.[27]

In the iron cage example, we learn to overcome fear by reflecting on past experience. In the skiing example, we might reflect and discover that fearful feelings and painful spills on the slopes have a certain regularity. In neither case is reason unhinged. Thus, Hume can distinguish those cases in which we ought to take our fears seriously from those in which we ought to dislodge them, and in doing so, he offers a response to the skepticism first introduced by Montaigne.[28]

Both Descartes and Hume hold the nonskeptical position that we triumph over the passions on the precipice. But their routes to this conclusion are quite different. Hume's science of the mind places reason, passion, and imagination in a shared arena, where regularities can be investigated and appropriate conclusions drawn. Descartes' view depends on taking the intellect as dominating our passions, but he does not provide a framework in which that position can be elaborated and defended. As surprising as it might be that Hume's conclusion is nonskeptical, perhaps the greater surprise is that Hume's account depends less on the claim that beliefs are sentiments (Hume's purported noncognitivism) than it does on the claim that sentiments have a doxastic component.

NOTES

Annette Baier introduced me to the complexity and richness of Hume's texts. My intellectual debt to her is incalculable. I would like to thank David Fate Norton and John Biro for helpful comments on an earlier version of this paper, presented at the 22nd Hume Conference.

1. David Norton has emphasized the relevance of Pascal and Montaigne to the key passage in Hume discussed here, and subsequently documented it in the new critical edition of Hume's *Treatise of Human Nature*, ed. David F. Norton and Mary J. Norton (Oxford: Oxford University Press, 2000), 465. All references to the *Treatise* are to the critical edition. The text is cited by book, part, section, and paragraph. T (followed by the page number) refers to David Hume, *A Treatise of Human Nature*, ed. L. A. Selby Bigge and P. H. Nidditch (Oxford: Clarendon Press, 1978).

2. Michel de Montaigne, *Essays*, trans. Donald M. Frame (Stanford: Stanford University Press, 1958), 250.

3. Blaise Pascal, *Pensées*, trans. A. J. Krailsheimer (Baltimore: Penguin Books, 1966), section 44.

4. Montaigne, *Essays*, 250.

5. René Descartes, *The Passions of the Soul*, in *The Philosophical Writings of Descartes*, Volume I, ed. and trans. John Cottingham, Robert Stoothoff, and Dugald Murdoch (Cambridge: Cambridge University Press, 1985), 340.

6. Ibid., 342.

7. Ibid., 343.

8. Ibid., 348.

9. Nicolas Malebranche, *The Search after Truth*, trans. Thomas M. Lennon and Paul J. Olscamp (Columbus: Ohio State University Press, 1980), 102–3.

10. Ibid., 106.

11. John P. Wright, *The Sceptical Realism of David Hume* (Minneapolis: University of Minnesota Press, 1983), 205.

12. Malebranche, *Search*, 106.

13. Cf. Charles Darwin, *The Expression of the Emotions in Man and Animals* (Chicago: University of Chicago Press, 1965); Antonio Damasio, *Descartes' Error: Emotion, Reason and the Human Brain* (New York: Avon, 1994).

14. Cf. Peter Jones, *Hume's Sentiments: Their Ciceronian and French Context* (Edinburgh: University of Edinburgh Press, 1982), 18 ff.

15. We may be in an iron cage for the first time. Thus, Hume needs to explain how we can make the appropriate causal inferences when there are no past resembling constant conjunctions. See T 103 ff. and my "The Secret Operations of the Mind," *Minds and Machines* 4, no. 3 (August 1994): 303–16.

16. For a good discussion of this question and its connection to general rules, cf. Thomas K. Hearn, Jr., "'General Rules' in Hume's *Treatise*," *Journal of the History of Philosophy* 8 (1970): 405–22.

17. David Hume, *An Enquiry Concerning Human Understanding*, ed. Tom L. Beauchamp (Oxford: Oxford University Press, 1999), 48.

18. A. T. Nuyen, "The Role of Reason in Hume's Theory of Belief," *Hume Studies* 14, no. 2 (1988): 372–89.

19. J. A. Passmore, "Hume and the Ethics of Belief," in *David Hume: Bicentenary Papers*, ed. G. P. Morice (Austin: University of Texas Press, 1977), 77–92.

20. David Hume, "A Dissertation on the Passions," in *Essays and Treatises on Several Subjects*, vol. 2 (Edinburgh, 1825), 173.

21. Why reject the belief formed by the imagination? Clearly, we are not going to fall off and die, but were we to fall, we would die. It would seem that there are at least conditional beliefs formed by the imagination, beliefs worthy of our assent. This point, that the imagination and passions appear to generate beliefs, will figure more prominently later.

22. Robert J. Fogelin, *Hume's Skepticism in the Treatise of Human Nature* (London; Boston: Routledge & Kegan Paul, 1985), 61 ff.

23. Cf. 1.3.10.6; T 121 ff., 13.7.6; T 97–98.

24. 1.3.10.4; T 120. Note that a coward could also be one who is predisposed to believe that he will fall, which then could increase the vivacity of anticipation of pain. But, as Hume emphasizes at 2.3.3.3; T 414, the causal reasoning that leads to the belief cannot, by itself, induce the fear. See also 2.3.6.1; T 424 ff.

25. In correspondence, John Biro has suggested that the passage shows that Hume was concerned about the opposition between demonstrative reasoning and the passions, since the passions seem to hold sway even over things we know demonstratively to be impossible. However, we do not know demonstratively that we won't fall, since the proposition that we will fall is not demonstratively true, given the evidence, but only very likely. The use of "impossible" here must be read as hyperbole.

26. David Hume, *Enquiries Concerning Human Understanding and Concerning the Principles of Morals*, 3rd ed., ed. P. H. Nidditch (Oxford: Oxford University Press), 217.

27. This aspect of the influence of passions on belief has been suggested in Ronald de Sousa, *The Rationality of Emotion* (Cambridge, MA: MIT Press, 1987).

28. In *An Enquiry Concerning the Principles of Morals*, Hume writes, "Experience being chiefly what forms the associations of ideas, it is impossible that any association could establish and support itself, in direct opposition to that principle" (p. 218). The passions can still have their role. When the thing feared is impossible, experience will correct our initial fear-induced judgments. But where it is probable, our fear cannot and should not be so easily dismissed.

CHAPTER 7

Reflection and Ideas in
Hume's Account of the Passions

LILLI ALANEN

In presenting his provocative claim that reason is and "only ought to be the slave of passions," unfit for "any other office than to serve and obey them" (T 415), Hume relies on a new and narrow conception of reason as a power of judgment and inference-making without any direct influence on the will or the passions (T 414–15 and T 457).[1] This paper is concerned not with this thesis itself but with the conception of the passions that underlies it. Although Hume stresses that passions are "original existents" which "do not contain any representational quality," large portions of the *Treatise* are spent on analyzing the ideas which cause the passions and which they produce, and their central role for our self-understanding and morality. My aim here is to understand the nature and intentionality of Humean passions by looking more closely at the notion of reflection in terms of which Hume defines the passions.

The first section of this paper lays out the background by considering, more generally, Hume's many uses of the notion of reflection, his view of the regulation of passions, and the role of passions for our self-identity. The second section presents the problem interpreters confront because of Hume's denial of representational qualities in the emotions. The last four sections discuss Hume's account of the passions in terms of his distinction between impressions of sensation and impressions of reflection, and suggest an interpretation of the claim that passions are original existents which is not inconsistent with the claim that they are complex intentional states. The reading defended here takes its inspiration from Annette Baier—her work on Hume as well as on emotions—and advocates a conception of intentionality which is broader than one that construes intentionality in terms of propositional attitudes.

I. VARIETIES OF REFLECTION, THE ASSOCIATION OF IDEAS, AND THE PROBLEM OF THE SELF

Among the new ideas central to Hume's treatment of emotions are, first, the introduction of special psychological laws to explain the causes, associations, and effects of the passions governing our behavior; second, the bodily and behavioral expressions of passions through which they are communicated to and affect others, to be reflected back on us by their emotional reactions and behavior; and third, the idea of reflection which is constitutive for the passions themselves as impressions. The first two ideas are anticipated by Spinoza, though Hume develops them in his own way and perhaps independently of Spinoza. The third notion, that of reflection, is interesting both in itself and because it works at so many levels of his account of the passions and their regulation. Reflection is also central to Hume's general account of perception, for ideas are reflections of impressions, and passions are (secondary) impressions reflecting the ideas causing them. They are themselves reflected in the ideas that the mind immediately forms of them—in the copies it takes.

The sense in which ideas reflect impressions is not, however, the same in which passions, as impressions of reflection, reflect ideas. Part of the problem is to understand exactly how they differ. Ideas represent impressions—they are copies of them—but impressions, being original existents, do not represent ideas. Yet secondary impressions are impressions of reflection, and what they reflect are ideas. Do we have two different metaphors here? One is visual—the copy–relation—and illustrates how ideas reflect impressions. The other is musical and illustrates how the secondary impressions are resonant of primary impressions and their ideas, prolonging and enforcing their effects as if by vibration and echo in the person perceiving them, whose body and mind together serve as sounding-boards when the right chords or strings are plucked. For the souls perceiving sensory impressions and their idea-copies are embodied, and the reflections of the ideas conjoined with the passions are affections of the body as much of the mind: they are felt, resonated, and expressed in the whole body, in its gestures, postures, and behavior, and they are also reflected in the ideas copying them, through which they affect the mind, disrupting its train of thoughts.

The reverberations of passions do not end here, in how they affect our own minds, bodies, and actions. They are also reflected in yet another sense, through their bodily effects and expressions, onto our fellow human beings, and through their emotional responses back onto the subject experiencing them in the first place. Hume writes:

> In general we may remark, that the minds of men are mirrors to one another, not only because they reflect each others emotions, but also because those rays of passions, sentiments and opinions may often be reverberated, and may decay by insensible degrees. Thus the pleasure, which a rich man receives from his possessions, being thrown upon the beholder, causes a pleasure and esteem; which sentiments again, being perceiv'd and sympathiz'd with, encrease the pleasure of the possessor; and being once more reflected, become a new foundation for pleasure and esteem in the beholder. (T 365)

In perceiving the reactions of surprise, antipathy, disgust, pity, fear, or tension, that a person's own uncontrolled emotional reactions provoke in others, she may come to recognize these reactions as matters of moral judgment and conscious reflection—or reflexivity—through which they can be indirectly ruled and corrected. Likewise, one's reactive responses of pride, love, anger, benevolence, and so on, when justified by the circumstances, may be reinforced and sustained by the similar passions they provoke in the others whose approval one needs and whose judgment one cares about. At none of these levels is reflection a matter of deliberate, rule-governed, inferential reasoning or judgment according to independent intellectual standards. It is not driven by the actions of an allegedly rational mind commanding the thoughts of the individual thinker, but is the product of a lawful (mechanical) interplay of the ideas and passions of animals capable not only of articulating, expressing, and sharing their emotional responses with each other, but who can also reason about their causes, effects, and implications, and control and correct each other through their reactive responses to each others' passions and sentiments. For while driven by self-love like other animals, human beings are endowed with natural sentiments of sympathy, making them sensitive to the emotional reactions of their fellow human beings, and also with benevolence, giving them some concern for the interest and benefit of others. No matter how weak the latter sentiment may be, it is enough to move us to reflect on our actions and reactions from a more general, moral point of view, and to make distinctions between what we approve of or disapprove according to some shared moral standards.[2] Moral progress can only take place as a result of the cultivation of these sentiments through interaction between human beings who are affected by, and responsive to, the reactions of approval and disapproval of the others whose company and approbation they need to thrive and flourish.[3] This is a new picture in stark contrast to the reigning picture of the rationalist tradition that internalized our moral life as a personal drama, in which the main actors are parts or powers of the individual soul and where moral therapy, ultimately, aims at personal salvation.

In speaking of the lawful or mechanical interplay of passions, I do not mean to suggest that Humean passions are some kind of brute feelings or emotions without cognitive or intentional content. The regularities that govern them are psychological, or perhaps sociological and psychosocial. They are not mechanical laws of motion, even though, as part of Hume's ambitious project of creating a new science of human nature, the laws of the mind are supposed to be somehow analogous to the laws of Newtonian physics. It is not clear to me what to make of Hume's talk of attraction between ideas—as if ideas were acting on or repelling each other in the same way as do celestial bodies or material particles. It is not really a matter of attraction between ideas, but of the associations regulating the system of more or less loosely connected ideas that constitute the individual self.[4] For although Hume wants to deflate the idea of a continuous self and downplay the active role of the mind, explaining all its actions by the association of ideas, the very association of ideas to be explained takes place within individual minds with their particular dispositions and memory, which keep track of the resemblance between ideas and the relations of cause and effect that determine those associations. Hume's laws of association, as I understand them, do not explain how ideas behave in relation to each other, as much as how the mind moves from one idea to another—the transitions of attention of an individual subject. The principles of the association of ideas are, as we know, contiguity, resemblance, and causality, and in the case of impressions, they boil down to resemblance. Understanding how these principles work presupposes that we understand the self or the "we" whose transition of thoughts they are supposed to explain. But then the identity or continuity of a self, or of the memory which turns up the resemblances that count, is itself explained through those same principles. This does strike a reader unfamiliar with Hume's own transitions of thoughts in the *Treatise* as strangely circular. The mind or self is formed by a collection of replaceable ideas in the same way as a republic or commonwealth is constituted by its citizens. But what constitutes this collection of varying ideas as a whole? What marks it out from other systems of changing ideas? Hume helps himself out of this conundrum by distinguishing two senses of personal identity: "as it regards our thought or imagination," and "as it regards our passions or the concern we take in ourselves" (T 253). He uses the latter to corroborate the former, for the passions are what hold together the particular collection of ideas that are mine, and they do so "*by the making our distant perceptions influence each other, and by giving us a present concern for our past or future pains or pleasure.*"[5]

The pains and pleasures and the passions arising from them are the key to our self-understanding because our affectivity—the ways in which we are affected by things—explains not only our personalities and actions but our very trains of thought. Having mentioned this problem of self-identity and Hume's solution to it as a reminder of the important role Hume assigns to passions, for our moral lives as well as for our theoretical self-understanding, I will set it aside and turn to the question of the nature and intentionality of the passions themselves, which is the central topic of this paper.

2. INTENTIONALITY AND HUMEAN PASSIONS

To frame my discussion, I want to distinguish three kinds of philosophical accounts of emotion. Each comes with different evaluations of the emotions and different strategies for mastering them: the cognitivist, the emotivist, and (for want of a better term) the moral phenomenologist. The first approach treats emotions as essentially cognitive and tends to reduce them to purely mental states or propositional attitudes. The Stoic view that the passions are false evaluative beliefs is a classic representative of this approach and is probably the most powerful and uncompromising formulation of a cognitivist account. The second approach views emotions as subjective feelings of a particular kind, often reduced to nonintentional bodily sensations and physiological states. It is typically exemplified in the literature by William James' theory. Descartes' and Hume's theories have also, though in my view mistakenly, been classified as "feeling-centered" approaches, which assimilate emotions to nonintentional bodily sensations.[6]

In the contemporary literature, discussions of emotions are often based on a more or less explicit dichotomy between propositional (hence, cognitive) cultural attitudes and natural, nonpropositional (hence, blind or brute) feelings or sentiments. It is often thought that in order to be cognitive (or rational), emotions must be reducible to propositional attitudes; if they are not, they must be mere feelings or affective states, having no cognitive value or function at all. This unfortunate dichotomy perverts many discussions of emotions, and it also lies behind classifications of Hume's account among mere emotivist theories.[7] It is bridged by what I call the moral phenomenologist approach, which recognizes both the complex psychophysical and the sociocultural nature of the emotions, thus avoiding the reductionism of the first two approaches. Hume's theory, as I understand it, is an example of this third approach.[8]

The very order of disposition of the *Treatise* tells us something about the importance of representational ideas for Hume's account of the passions. The latter is preceded by his account of ideas and the laws that govern them (Book I) precisely because the passions, as impressions of reflection, depend on their antecedent ideas, of which they are reflections. And even if their intentionality is one of reflection and hence is "borrowed," as it were, from the ideas that cause them, it is nevertheless constitutive of them as passion. They have not only causes but objects, which make them identifiable and determine how they direct and move the mind. In making this claim, I am opposing both a fairly common recent understanding of intentionality and, it would seem, Hume himself, who in an often quoted passage declares:

A passion is an original existence, or if you will, modification of existence, and contains not any representative quality, which renders it a copy of any other existence or modification. When I am angry, I am actually possest with the passion, and in that emotion have no more a reference to any other object, than when I'm thirsty, or sick, or more than five foot high. (T 415)

Those who endorse the received view of intentionality have no problems with this passage. By the received view, I mean the one expressed by the usual roundabout references in discussions of cognitive science and philosophy of mind to Brentano and "aboutness."[9] Such characterizations go hand in hand with taking intentional states to be propositional, and holding that sensations, emotions, and the like are not about—that is, do not refer to or represent—anything. Given this common understanding of intentionality, which excludes sensations, emotions, and other nonpropositional states from the domain of the intentional, Hume's remarks above may not seem in the least surprising.[10] Yet Hume's denial of the intentionality of passions and desires has struck scholars as "wildly implausible."[11]

Hume makes this claim in the context of his equally famous (and controversial) argument that reason is and ought to be a slave of the passions. As a subspecies of impressions, the passions do not represent ideas but are instead what is represented in ideas. As such, they cannot be opposed by reason, for they contain no representations and hence no falsity for reason to oppose or correct. So far one can follow Hume. It is more difficult to agree with his claim that emotions have no reference to any other objects, in particular since, as Annette Baier points out, this very statement is preceded by over a hundred pages in which Hume explains his own intricate theory of the many relations to objects and causes and even ends of passions that his own phenomenology detects.[12] Baier has a hard time understanding how Hume could announce that "anger is an original existence" right after he has recognized "the complex intentionality of anger" in Sections VI and IX. She asks if Hume had, all of a sudden, forgotten his own account of the objects of passions, being perhaps himself "so 'possest with the passion' of anti-rationalist zeal, so 'carry'd away by the Heat of Youth & Invention' that he misrepresented his own views, the views he had been spelling out with such appreciative detail in the preceding parts of Book Two." She also suggests, as another "partial explanation of how Hume could have written that unfortunate paragraph at T 415 . . . that the claims made there are perfectly plausible for 'emotions,' though not for passions." As Hume and his contemporaries use the term "emotion," it is a bodily disturbance, which should be classified as an "impression of sensation" rather than an "impression of reflexion."[13] Baier reiterates this distinction later and quotes the O. E. D. definition of emotion as "a moving, stirring, agitation, perturbation" (in a physical sense), and she also quotes Locke who talks of the emotion left in the "Blood or Pulse" by exercise.[14]

It is, however, difficult to believe that the unfortunate passage employs such a distinction between the terms "passion" and "emotion" because it is a general claim made for all passions, repeated in several contexts where the passions are contrasted with reason without any mention of emotions.[15] Moreover, Hume seems to use "passion" and "emotion" interchangeably.[16] And even if he presupposed some distinction between the two, it would still be misleading to construe "emotions" as mere physical states. That would amount to driving precisely the kind of wedge between what happens on the level of the "mere" body and what happens on the mental or psychological level that Hume's phenomenology seems to exclude. Physiological disturbances and bodily stirrings are indeed part of what causes the particular feelings of the passions, and as bodily changes they may have independent neuro-physiological descriptions. However, *qua* the immediate, concomitant causes or effects of the passions, they cannot be dissociated from the impressions perceived. The passions can neither be reduced to physiological events, nor characterized as mere "raw feels." My own view is that the impressions which are essential to the passions are themselves intentional, although the kind of intentionality they display is neither that of propositional representation nor that of the Humean copy-variety of representation.

Neither Penelhum nor Baier ask what the intentionality that Hume (implausibly) denies to the passions might be. Davidson, who has reflected on this question in "Hume's Cognitive Theory of Pride," does not hesitate to spell it out as a cognitive account of the passion that Hume calls pride, where both the cause of pride (which also becomes its reason or rationalization) and the objects of pride are construed as propositions. The passion itself then turns into a pro-attitude to a proposition—in the case of pride, an attitude of approval of oneself as the possessor of some praiseworthy or estimable property. While this account has merit, it also has problems, and one of them, as Davidson himself admits, is that it does not, in the end, give any role to the affective element that it recognizes.[17] Interpreting Hume's talk of the causes and objects of passions merely in terms of propositional attitudes and syllogisms seems to leave out most of what is interesting and novel in his theory. To sort this out, a fuller account of Hume's view of impressions and ideas is required than can be given here. But even a brief glance at the text will show the complexity of Hume's theory of passions.

3. IMPRESSIONS OF SENSATION AND IMPRESSIONS
OF REFLECTION

Impressions are the immediate contents of our actual sensory and emotional experience. Whether they originate in the body, as sensory impressions, or in the mind, as reflections of sensory impressions or other ideas, they are always marked by "the force and liveliness, with which they strike upon the mind, and make their way into thought and consciousness." In contrast, the ideas which copy them are nothing but "faint images" of the impressions as they appear in our "thinking and reasoning." Hume assumes that everybody understands his distinction between impressions and ideas, because "everyone of himself will perceive the difference betwixt feeling and thinking" (T 1–2).

The clue this gives us is that impressions, hence passions, belong (like sensations) to feelings, but ideas belong to thinking. One might be tempted to conclude that the former are merely felt, and that only the latter have contents properly speaking. But this conclusion would be too quick. Feeling and thinking seem to be on the same continuum, and "in particular instances they may very nearly approach to each other" (T 1–2). One should not be misled by the talk of feeling here and come to think of Hume's impressions as brute impressions or "raw feels." Feeling and thinking must resemble each other just as much as impressions and ideas, which differ only in "their degree of force or vivacity" (T 2–3).

Of the two kinds of impressions—of sensations and of reflection—the first are said to arise "in the soul originally, from unknown causes." The second, which are also called secondary impressions and which "resolve themselves into our passions and emotions" (T 16), arise directly from fresh ideas of a certain kind of sensory impressions: heat or cold, thirst or

hunger, pleasure or pain. Such ideas follow immediately upon corresponding sense impressions and, in turn, immediately cause a secondary, reflective impression: a passion, a desire, an emotion (T 8). Reflection here, however, cannot be reflection in the same sense as before: the impression does
not reproduce everything that is in the idea it reflects. Indeed, according to
the quote above, it "contains not any representative quality" (T 415). Ideas,
in copying or reflecting impressions, resemble them, but secondary impressions do not resemble the ideas or impressions they are reflections of. They
reflect ideas in some other way, affectively: they are affective responses to
certain ideas, reflecting not the ideas causing them but how those same ideas
move us and matter to us. They do not represent or contain the idea they
"reflect," but they immediately relate it to some other idea by directing or
moving our mind to the latter. The connection here is neither effected according to the laws of reasoning, nor is it a matter merely of association of
ideas: as we will see, some further conditions or principles are presupposed.

For a passion to be experienced as a passion of some determinate kind,
ideas other than the corresponding antecedent idea that the passion reflects
are presupposed. This holds for sensory impressions as well, which are directly caused by some bodily affection. Ideas of thirst, hunger, pain, or pleasure never come to us in isolation; they occur in a context of other impressions and ideas. Thirst comes not only with a funny feeling in the throat or
a dry mouth, but with some idea of what quenches it. The sensation and the
idea of thirst reflecting it causes and is reflected in a desire for, say, a cool
drink; similarly, the impression/idea of pleasure, whenever its cause is related to myself or another person, is immediately reflected in another kind of
affective response, like pride or love or benevolence, depending on how the
qualities of the person or things causing it are immediately perceived.

Note that we are hard put even to pick out and describe the original
sense impression or its idea, since there is nothing in the idea which was
not in the impression—except in terms of some object to which it is correlated and which it brings to mind: the impression itself brings some specific kind of object to our attention. As for so-called indirect passions, such
as pride, humility, love, and hate, their very identification presupposes a
complicated set of other, interrelated ideas: of their causes, the qualities of
the causes, their relations to self, and the dispositions of the self or mind that
perceives them. How does all this square with the above claim that they are
original existents or modifications of existence and that they have no repre-

sentational quality nor any relations to other things? What does Hume mean by original existents in the first place? And what does he mean by representational quality?

4. PASSIONS AS ORIGINAL EXISTENTS

Hume has little to say about the original impressions which arise directly "from the constitution of the body, from the animal spirits, or from the application of objects to the external organs" (T 276). To these belong all the impressions of the senses and bodily pains and pleasures, which, whether "felt" or "consider'd by the mind," always *arise originally in the soul, or in the body, whichever you please to call it, without any preceding thought or perception.* A fit of gout produces a long train of passions, as grief, hope, fear; but is not deriv'd immediately from any affection or idea."[18] Reflective impressions— passions and emotions—"proceed from some of these original ones, either immediately or by the interposition of its idea" (T 276).

Hume emphasizes elsewhere that only if there is agreement or disagreement with either real relations of ideas or real existence or matter of fact can there be truth or falsehood. Passions, volitions, and action, as original facts or realities, bear no such relations: they are said to "be complete in themselves, and implying no reference to other passions, volitions or actions."[19] They are not, as I read this passage, representations or copies of other passions, and hence not derivable from ideas of other passions either. They are mere affective reflections of original impressions, and, like the original impressions whose ideas they reflect, they belong to the category of facts: they are direct modifications of existence. The existence they modify is thinking; that is, they are modes of thought caused directly by external things or events, whose action on our bodily organs affects us first with (perceptions of) pleasure or pain. (I return to this point in section 6 below.)

The impressions of pleasure and pain, good and evil, or their ideas cause passions in two ways, directly and indirectly.[20] What Hume calls indirect passions also require further qualities—impressions or ideas—but this seems to hold for the direct ones as well, since direct passions presuppose the indirect ones, and seem in the end to differ from the latter only by their lesser degree of complication.[21] By qualifying emotions as original existents, Hume means to say not that they do not have causes, but that they cannot be produced, caused, or modified by ideas alone. Our whole person must be affected by their idea-cause—the things or events perceived through our sensory organs as pleasurable or painful or their ideas. That a given idea or belief affects me thus or so cannot be deduced from its content alone but depends on other relations this particular idea or belief has to myself; that is, it depends on its connection with the contingent history of other causally related ideas that constitute the self of which I am intimately aware at all times.[22] As simple existents, passions are not themselves objects of reason: they cannot be operated on or modified by rational considerations or arguments. Though they depend causally on ideas, they do not themselves copy or represent anything and hence are in a category different from the ideas on which reason operates (cf. T 458). It does not follow that they are brute physical facts. "Bodily pains and pleasures are the source of many passions" says Hume in the passage quoted above, and adds in his careless manner that they "arise originally in the soul, or the body, whichever you prefer to call it, without any preceding thought or perception" (T 276). Body or soul, whichever: we are not worrying here about their metaphysical nature and status. Whatever we want to call it, there is a phenomenological distinction to be made between states of the body and those of the soul, and the latter cannot be described without the network of perceptions and the natural principles governing their associations, which constitute them as psychological as opposed to physical states. Amélie Oksenberg Rorty has emphasized that "the individuation and identification" of passions is cognitively charged, but I would go further and claim that passions themselves "are cognitively charged" and that it is because of their meaning or cognition ladenness that they are related to other ideas as they are. Rorty stresses that they are analytically distinct from ideas, that they are not "in and of themselves representational: taken simply as psychological facts, they are only contingently connected with representational ideas."[23] I agree that their particular motivational directions depend entirely on the ideas to which they are conjoined, but I take the same to hold for their individuation and identification as well. They would not be psychological facts at all without those ideas, since what makes these states psychological and accounts for our awareness of them as affective states of a kind is the whole network of ideas with which they are causally conjoined.

5. THE COMPLEX INTENTIONALITY OF INDIRECT PASSIONS AND THE DOUBLE ASSOCIATION PRINCIPLE

Hume says that passions cannot be "justly defined" because they are "simple and uniform impressions," and yet, as impressions of reflection, they are always inserted into a network of other ideas and impressions and can therefore be described "by an enumeration of such circumstances, as attend them" (T 277). Such enumeration is precisely what Hume, as a moral scientist, undertakes, and he shows, throughout Books II and III, that they have not only causes (or "subjects"), which are as it were their reasons, but objects at which they are directed, all of which are intentional. Consider the account of the causes and objects of the first two passions, namely, pride, and its opposite, humility, in the *Treatise* account: their object is the same— the Self—but their causes are different.

> According as our idea of ourself is more or less advantageous, we feel either of those opposite affections, and are elated by pride, or dejected with humility. . . . when self enters not into the consideration, there is no room either for pride or humility. (T 277)

An idea of ourself, advantageous or depreciative, is a necessary presupposition of the passions of pride or humility, but that, in turn, requires a whole set of other ideas about what it is that makes us deserve esteem or contempt. Moreover, we also need to have ideas of some admirers or critics to mirror our self-image (T 316). This awareness of self and of how others perceive us is an essential dimension of the passions in Hume's analysis, and it is no accident that pride is the first on the list, for pride (and its reverse, humility) is the immediate affective self-perception of how one's actions or circumstances may appear to others and affect their image of one-self.[24] If the object of pride and humility is always the self, it cannot also be their cause. This leads Hume to distinguish between the cause—the idea that excites the passion—and its object, "that to which they direct the view, when excited. Pride and humility, being once rais'd, immediately turn our attention to ourselves, and regard that as their ultimate and final object." The passion itself is in between these two ideas, one of which represents the cause, the other its object or, rather, the object to whose idea the passion turns our attention, in this case the self (T 278).

This may seem to be grist for the mill of those who take Humean passions to be nonintentional. The passion is an in-between impression, itself without content, hence a brute feeling, perhaps merely the conscious perception of a physiological change or agitation in the body. But why is it placed between these two ideas—that of its cause and that of its object? Nothing may connect those two ideas except the very impression the first causes, and the associated impression the other produces. To so connect them, to turn our attention in a particular direction, the passion, as an original existent, must have some informational content or cognitive quality directing it. For the idea of self to be produced, as Hume suggests, by the passion of pride, this passion must somehow already contain it; the idea of its object must be contained in the very feeling of it. Nature itself, Hume tells us, has assigned causes and objects to the passions through which they act on and motivate us. This type of content differs from the one of representation through a copy relation, but I claim that it is, nevertheless, an intentional content.

Consider Hume's example of the man who is proud of his house. There is no link between the mere idea of a house and its qualities on the one hand, and the favorable idea of its possessor on the other, without the live impressions of pleasure its beauty produces. These, when combined with the awareness of having crafted or acquired it himself, immediately produce another pleasant impression, in which the pride properly consists, and which reflects the man's favorable idea of his own craftsmanship or discernment in acquiring it. No matter how strongly the idea of the cause and that of the object of a passion were connected, no passion would arise without a further particular quality of the cause affecting us directly with impressions of pain or pleasure.[25]

To the question of what determines each of the two components of the cause (the subject and its quality) of pride or humility "to be what it is and assigns such a particular object, and quality, and subject to these affections," Hume really has no answer other than the appeal to the nature of passions themselves and the nature and original qualities of the mind. Passions have natural and original properties, and it is the property of pride and humility to have the self as an object.[26] The causes here are as natural as the object, and this holds universally "in all nations and all ages, the same objects still give rise to pride and humility." The objects to which, given human nature, no one can be indifferent are "their power, riches, beauty or personal merit," but their role and the qualities through which such general personal advantages, or the lack thereof, affect a person's pride and vanity are bound to cultural and historical variation, as Hume's examples suggest. [27]

Hume also notes that every cause of pride produces a separate pleasure, and of humility, a separate uneasiness, and these sensations of pleasure and uneasiness are always related to self. The passions themselves are said to contain something "correspondent to the suppos'd properties of their causes." Thus, "the peculiar object of pride and humility is detemin'd by an original and natural instinct," and it is necessarily such that it always looks to that individual self or person, "of whose actions or sentiments each of us is intimately conscious":

> Here at last the view always rests, when we are actuated by either of these passions; nor can we, in that situation of mind, ever lose sight of this object. For this I pretend not to give any reason; but consider such a peculiar direction of the thought as an original quality. (T 286)

"Original" here again seems to mean that no further reason can be given for it. The object to which pride and humility direct the thought, the self, is given by nature—these emotions always come with this object. The same holds for

> their sensations, or the peculiar emotions they excite in the soul, and which constitute their being or essence. Thus pride is a pleasant sensation, and humility a painful; and upon the removal of the pleasure and pain, there is in reality no pride nor humility. Of this our very feeling convinces us; and beyond our feeling, 'tis here in vain to reason or dispute. (T 286)

Thus the passions, whose very being or essence is in the "peculiar emotions they excite in the soul," are produced by a systematic relation between two pairs of ideas and impressions. The cause of pride (the idea of some prized thing related to the self) is related to its object (the idea of self) as the pleasure separately produced by the cause is related to the pleasant sensation of the passion of pride itself. The one idea easily converts into its correlative, and the same holds for the impressions, which thus reinforce and strengthen each other. This is what commentators call Hume's double association principle. Hume goes as far as to suggest that the human mind has, as it were, organs disposed so as "to produce a peculiar impression or emotion, which we call *pride*," to which nature has assigned an idea, "that of the *self*, which it never fails to produce," just as "the nerves of the nose or palate are so dispos'd" as to produce in certain circumstances "peculiar sensations," e.g., of lust and hunger, which "always produce in us the idea of those peculiar objects, which are suitable to each appetite." Our sensory organs are disposed by nature to produce specific sensations in given circumstances which always produce ideas of their specific objects, and similarly for our "mental organs" in the case of particular passions, for instance, pride:

> The organs are so dispos'd as to produce the passion; and the passion, after its production, naturally produces a certain idea. All this needs no proof. 'Tis evident we never shou'd be possest of that passion, were there not a disposition of mind proper for it; and 'tis as evident, that the passion always turns our view to ourselves, and makes us think of our own qualities and circumstances. (T 287)

In summary, "nature has bestow'd a kind of attraction on certain impressions and ideas, by which one of them, upon its appearance, naturally introduces its correlative." These two attractions of impressions and ideas, when "they concur on the same object" (the double-association principle), "mutually assist each other, and the transition of the affections and of the imagination is made with the greatest ease and facility," so that the two related impressions are "in a manner inseparable." This is compared to the mechanism by which our beliefs about causation are formed (T 289). One pair of ideas and impression is "transfused" into another in such a way that they strengthen each other's effect, and although the elements—the separate impressions and ideas—may be sorted out in analysis, their individuation and content depend on the complex phenomenon of which they are constitutive parts.

The same points are repeated in Hume's analysis of another pair of indirect passions, namely, love and hatred (discussed in Part II of Book II), though the object to which they direct attention is not the self but another person, and they are caused by some quality of that person.[28] Like pride and humility, love and hatred are always produced by a "transition arising from a double relation of impressions and ideas." An object without this double relation "never produces either of these passions; and 'tis found that the passion always varies in conformity to the relation" (T 347).

> Nothing is more evident, than that any person acquires our kindness, or is expos'd to our ill-will, in proportion to the pleasure or uneasiness we receive from him, and that the passions keep pace exactly with the sensations in all their changes and variations. Whoever can find the means either by his services, his beauty, or his flattery, to render himself useful or agreeable to us, is sure of our affections: As on the other hand, whoever harms or displeases us never fails to excite our anger or hatred. (T 348)

It is not merely the pain and pleasure caused by a person alone that determines our affective response, but the awareness that it has been caused intentionally, "with a particular design and intention." Somebody who harms us accidentally does not thereby become an object of hate. "By the intention we judge of the actions, and according as that is good or bad, they become causes of love and hatred" (T 348).[29] Here, a judgment of evaluation, the object of which is an intentional action, is presupposed in the production of the passions of love and hate. But passions themselves, as intentional acts (mental or physical) with bodily expressions, need not presuppose conceptually articulated propositions or judgments. The kind of intentionality displayed by Hume's passions can be detected in animals, too, in the "port and gait" of animals such as peacocks, turkeys, and swans, and not just any passions, but the complicated indirect passions of pride and humility.[30] Although passions in the case of humans involve intricate intentional relations including thoughts of the propositional kind that animals do not have, Hume still ascribes both thoughts and (intentional) passions to animals. Passions, I conclude, display a natural intentionality which escapes a straightforward account in terms of Humean impressions and ideas and the mere laws of their association—hence, Hume's appeal to relations, dispositions, and organs bestowed by nature.

6. MENTAL ORGANS, ACTS, AND OBJECTS

The metaphor of mental organs requires some attention. On Hume's view, there is nothing in the mind—or more precisely, there is nothing to the mind—except its perceptions, namely, impressions and ideas. As a bundle of perceptions, the mind can have no organs or dispositions that are not dispositions of its impressions and ideas to be connected in determinate ways. That Hume does not talk of bodily organs here seems clear: he compares the workings of the bundle of ideas and passions constituting the self to the workings of the sensory body through its bodily organs. The mental organs might be described as sub-bundles of perceptions, so disposed or connected that in the appropriate circumstances, when some are present, others are automatically produced. Thus they can bring certain features of the things perceived, more particularly, those that affect us with pleasure or pain, to our attention by relating the ideas of their causes to their natural ("peculiar") objects and ends. The affection by which these transitions are brought about makes us attentive to the value or importance things have for us. Through these natural, affective organs and associative mechanisms, our passions constitute us as enduring selves, in giving us, as Hume says, "a present concern for our past or future pains or pleasure" (T 262).

This suggests the following solution to the puzzle about passions as original and simple, nonrepresentational existents. Particular sensory organs, when properly affected, produce acts (or impressions) of sensing. The sensory act (seeing, smelling, touching) always comes with some idea of an object related to it by natural association, which it brings to our attention, and by which this particular act of smelling, say, of fresh coffee, is distinguished from that of fried bacon. As for sensations of the inner senses of thirst or lust, for instance, they are caused by physiological conditions of the body, but they unfailingly come with some ideas of objects satisfying them. The sensory organs have their own acts, and so, to elaborate on Hume's own metaphor, do the mental ones. The affective reaction or passion itself, as an original existent, would then, in the language of Hume's predecessors, be a manifestation of the act of perceiving itself, considered in abstraction from its correlated idea-object or content. Although the former, the act or the reflective impression, does not occur without its content (without the idea it reflects), it has its own characteristic qualities (feelings and bodily expressions) which do not depend on its objects.

Descartes, Arnauld, and Malebranche all recognized a general distinction of two senses of the terms "idea" or "perception." While Descartes treats the term as ambiguous between these two senses, he seems to agree with Arnauld, who construed the distinction between ideas as acts and ideas as objects as two different aspects of one representational act. If Hume's simple impressions of reflection were acts—the act-aspect of the ideas with which they are correlated—the idea-object to which they direct the mind would indeed be essential to their individuation as acts (passions) of a determinate kind.[31] While Hume may well have retained the Cartesian sense of idea as object (ideas in the strict sense of the word, in which ideas do have a reference to truth or falsehood), it is less obvious that what he calls impressions of reflection and qualifies as original existents could be that aspect of the idea that Descartes calls the idea taken materially or formally, namely, the idea considered in its aspect of an actual mode of the mind. Yet it is not far-fetched to suppose that is what they are—in fact, some passages strongly suggest it.[32] If the reflective impression—as argued earlier—is an impression of how the idea, which causes it, affects me, we could say that the way it affects me is precisely by causing a determinate act (of loving or hating or feeling humiliated) with a determinate kind of object. The passion it causes is a mode of thinking—hence a perception or a representational act—and as such it comes with a determinate content or object. It can also, upon reflection, be itself an object of thought. But since it is caused by mechanical association of ideas (for Descartes, by mechanical movements in the body), it is not grounded in reason. That is, neither its idea-object or content nor the way in which it is represented (as pleasing or fearful, lovable or hateful, for instance) is deducible from other thoughts on rational grounds or by way of mere relations between ideas.[33] Hume's insistence that passions—*qua* acts or impressions—are original existents may then be seen as his way of making a point similar to the one Spinoza makes in his own terms when characterizing affections (of which the passions are a subspecies) as conclusions without premises.[34]

But Hume's theory differs from those of the Cartesians in many ways, not least through his insistence on the principles of sympathy and comparison. These, in his view, are crucial in the production and sustaining of our passions. Sympathy is a force acting "thro' the whole animal creation." It makes the communication of sentiments from one thinking being to another easy and associates creatures that do not prey on one another together;

insofar as human beings are concerned, it makes us so dependent on each other's company that solitude is, for Hume, "the greatest punishment we can suffer."[35] Nothing can give pleasure to a person who has no one to share his happiness with, "whose esteem and friendship he may enjoy" (T 363). It is because the passions we feel in our own minds, and which are part of the train of ideas which make up our individual histories and self-image, are not only caused but also expressed in our bodies, that we, infused with natural sympathy with other thinking beings, react to each other's emotions and can so easily share and communicate them to each other. The idea of the joy or suffering of another is converted, through the sympathy that binds us, into a live impression of that same joy or suffering (T 320).

CONCLUDING REMARKS

In spite of their description as simple original existents, complete in themselves, passions for Hume come with a peculiar load of natural qualities, relations, and functions. It is hard not to conclude that they are, in themselves, intentional and cognitively charged, pregnant with spontaneous evaluations.

Did Hume then misrepresent his own view in the passage from T 415 quoted above in section 2? Annette Baier points out that no such claims are made in his later writings, so perhaps he did. But perhaps he did as well as he could, given his own distinctions and peculiarly narrow view of representation. Passions, as impressions of reflection, are clearly not copies of other passions: they have no antecedents to copy. So nothing is left but to classify them as simple existents. The kind of existents they exemplify are not all that simple, however, as the examples of Humean passions here discussed show. First of all, they are perceptions—thoughts—so they have natural objects: they are acts of perception or thinking which are about something. As acts of a specific kind, whose very essence is the emotion or stirring they cause in the mind (itself a naturally instituted reflection of the idea causing them), they turn the mind so moved to other objects assigned to them by nature or habit. We can, by analysis, separate the acts—in Hume's terminology, the impressions—from the ideas that cause them, as well as from their objects— the ideas to which they turn the mind. One kind of act or impression, e.g., anger, can have many kinds of objects; likewise, the idea of one object can affect one in different ways. The impression or passion itself, however, never occurs singly, without the ideas between which it is placed. One may argue that the passions, through a characteristic inertia, can continue to affect one when the idea of their cause and their object is long forgotten. But if a particular passion (say, of hate, pride, fear, desire) is to affect one, it must come with some other corresponding object. Hume, I suspect, was driven to his claim that passions have no representational quality because his own youthful, rough-and-ready distinction between matters of fact and relations of ideas left no room for more subtle distinctions or qualifications, to say nothing of his own frequent appeals to human nature, to bodily and mental organs with characteristic functions, and to passions with their "peculiar" qualities, feelings, and objects. All of these go beyond the purely causal and representational relations for which his new science of mind allows.

NOTES

Earlier versions of this paper have been presented at the 29th Annual Hume Society Conference at the University of Helsinki, August 6–10, 2002, and at the *Institut International de Philosophie Entretiens de Madrid*, September 17–21, 2002. I am grateful for helpful comments and suggestions by participants at both occasions, in particular, Donald Ainslie, Pascal Engel, and Simo Knuuttila. I owe special thanks to Annette Baier for valuable remarks and questions on an earlier draft, many of which I have not been able to address adequately here, and also to Fred Stoutland, who read and corrected the manuscript.

1. T (followed by the page number) refers to David Hume, *A Treatise of Human Nature*, ed. L. A. Selby Bigge and P. H. Nidditch (Oxford: Clarendon Press, 1978).

2. David Hume, *Enquiry Concerning the Principles of Morals*, IX. I am grateful to David Wiggins, who stresses the importance of benevolence as an irreducible component among the natural endowments essential to morality in Hume's picture, for allowing me to read chapter 2 of the manuscript of his forthcoming book on moral philosophy. See also David Wiggins, "Natural and Artificial Virtues: A Vindication of Hume's Scheme," in *How Should One Live? Essays on the Virtues*, ed. Roger Crisp (Oxford: Oxford University Press, 1996).

3. T 316. For an account of how such a process of moral correction and regulation could work, see Annette Baier, "Master Passions," in *Explaining Emotions*, ed. Amélie Oksenberg Rorty (Berkeley: University of California Press, 1980), 403–23, and Annette Baier, *A Progress of Sentiments* (Cambridge, MA: Harvard University Press, 1991).

4. See Terence Penelhum, "Hume's Moral Psychology," in *The Cambridge Companion to Hume*, ed. David F. Norton (Cambridge: Cambridge University Press, 1993), 117–47.

5. T 261. Emphasis mine.

6. See Cheshire Calhoun and Robert C. Solomon, *What Is an Emotion?* (Oxford: Oxford University Press, 1984), 8–11, and the more recent survey article by John Deigh, "Cognitivism in the Theory of Emotions," *Ethics* 104 (1994): 822–54.

7. The dichotomy between cognitivism and emotivism underlies much of the discussion in, e.g., Martha Nussbaum's *The Therapy of Emotions* (Princeton: Princeton University Press, 1994). It is also assumed in the literature mentioned in the previous note. Because of his commitment to this dichotomy, Deigh misconstrues the classic theories he discusses. Descartes' theory of emotions, notably, is described, together with Locke's and Hume's, as a representative of "feeling-centered" theories assimilating emotions to nonintentional bodily sensations (Deigh, "Cognitivism in the Theory of Emotions," 825–26). See my discussion of Descartes' theory in "The Intentionality of Cartesian Emotions," in *Passion and Virtue in Descartes*, ed. Byron Williston and André Gombay (Amherst, NY: Prometheus Books, 2003). See also my "What Are Emotions About?" *Philosophy and Phenomenological Research* 67 (2003): 311–334.

8. Annette Baier, in *A Progress of Sentiments*, has brought the originality and interest of Hume's phenomenology of passions and its moral significance to our attention. The view of emotions she develops in her own articles, which takes its inspiration from ideas she has found in Descartes, Spinoza, Hume, and Darwin, is an important representative on the contemporary scene of the third kind of approach. See Annette C. Baier, "What Emotions Are About," in *Action Theory and Philosophy of Mind, 1990*, ed. James E. Tomberlin, Philosophical Perspectives 4 (Atascadero, CA: Ridgeview, 1990), 1–29; "The Ambiguous Limits of Desire," in *The Ways of Desire*, ed. J. Marks (Chicago: Precedent Publishers 1986), 39–61; and "Master Passions." I discuss Baier's views in my "What Are Emotions About?"

9. It is exemplified in John Biro's paper, where perceptions of memory in Hume's account of causation are described as "intentional, in the sense of referring to, being about other things," including "other perceptions." J. Biro, "Hume's New Science of the Mind," in *The Cambridge Companion to Hume*, ed. Norton, 50, 53, and 62 n. 23.

10. Alasdair MacIntyre is quoted by Baier as seeing Hume's passions as "preconceptual and prelinguistic," in *A Progress of Sentiments*, 311 n. 9.

11. Penelhum, "Hume's Moral Psychology," 128. Annette Baier brushes off the whole passage as being "silly" and "unfortunate" (*A Progress of Sentiments*, 163).

12. Baier, *A Progress of Sentiments*, 159–61.

13. Ibid., 163. But this goes against Hume's own definition in VI: ". . . the impressions of reflexion resolve themselves into our passions and emotions" (T 16).

14. Baier, *A Progress of Sentiments*, 310 n. 9. Baier contrasts Reid's "thought-free feeling," which Hume would call "emotion" and contemporary authors have termed "raw feels," and which—contrary to the claims of those who (with Reid) charge Hume with emotivism—plays no role in his moral theory, to the "necessarily thought-caused" passions and sentiments from which our morality arises according to Hume (180).

15. Cf. T 458, quoted below, note 19.

16. Hume talks about "passions, and other emotions resembling them" at T 276. It is not very clear to me how his use of the terms differs between passions and emotion here. We read a little further on about esthetic emotions as belonging to the category of calm passions. But emotions too can be violent, and he starts his account with the violent "emotions or passions, their nature, origin, causes, and effects," and divides them first into *direct* and *indirect*.

17. Donald Davidson, "Hume's Cognitive Theory of Pride," in his *Essays on Actions and Events* (Oxford: Clarendon Press, 1980), 277–90. For some other difficulties with Davidson's account, see Annette Baier, "Hume's Analysis of Pride," *Journal of Philosophy* 75 (1978): 27–40.

18. T 276. Emphasis mine.

19. "Reason is the discovery of truth and falsehood. Truth and falsehood consists in an agreement or disagreement either to *real* relations of ideas, or to *real* existence and matter of fact. Whatever, therefore, is not susceptible of this agreement or disagreement, is incapable of being true or false, and can never be an object of our reason. Now 'tis evident our passions, volitions, and actions, are not susceptible of any such agreement or disagreement; being original facts and realities, compleat in themselves, and implying no reference to other passions, volitions and actions, 'Tis impossible, therefore, they can be pronounced either true or false, and be either contrary or conformable to reason" (T 458).

20. The passions which "arise immediately from good or evil, from pain or pleasure" are called direct. They comprehend desire, aversion, grief, joy, hope, fear, despair, and security. Indirect passions "proceed from the same principles, but by the conjunction of other qualities." They comprehend pride, humility, ambition, vanity, love, hatred, envy, pity, malice, and generosity, "with their dependants" (T 276–77).

21. Hume says he cannot justify this distinction between direct and indirect passions, and he abandons it later in his "Of Passions," where he describes the latter merely as "passions of a more complicated nature." Cf. Annette Baier, "David Hume," in *Routledge Encyclopedia of Philosophy*, ed. Edward Craig (London: Routledge, 1998).

But see also Jane McIntyre, who points out that Hume's categorization of the passions into the direct and indirect ones is distinctly original, and also argues that though Hume fails to make this explicit, his direct passions presuppose the indirect ones: ". . . our desires, direct passions, are always embedded in, and emerge from, the associative and sympathetic context of the indirect passions." Jane McIntyre, "Hume's Passions: Direct and Indirect," *Hume Studies* 26 (2000): 77–86, quotation from 82.

22. "Ourself is always intimately present to us" (T 320).

23. Amélie Oksenberg Rorty, "From Passions to Sentiments: the Structure of Hume's Treatise," *History of Philosophy Quarterly* 10, no. 2 (1993): 165–80, 172.

24. See Baier, "Master Passions," 403–23.

25. "A man, for instance, is vain of a beautiful house, which belongs to him, or which he has himself built and contriv'd. Here the object of the passion is himself, and the cause is the beautiful house: which cause is again sub-divided into two parts, viz., the quality, which operates upon the passion, and the subject, in which the quality inheres. The quality is the beauty, and the subject is the house, consider'd as his property or contrivance. . . . Beauty, consider'd merely as such, unless plac'd upon something related to us, never produces any pride or vanity; and the strongest relation alone without beauty, or something else in its place, has as little influence on that passion" (T 279).

26. "Unless nature had given some original qualities to the mind, it cou'd never have any secondary ones; because in that case it wou'd have no foundation for action, nor cou'd ever begin to exert itself. Now these qualities, which we must consider as original, are such as are most inseparable from the soul, and can be resolved into no other: And such is the quality, which determines the object of pride and humility" (T 280).

27. "Can we imagine it as possible [Hume asks rhetorically], that while human nature remains the same, men will ever become entirely indifferent to their power, riches, beauty or personal merit, and that their pride and vanity will not be affected by these advantages?" (T 281). Though the causes are natural, they are not original, since many of them are effects of art; ". . . each cause of pride and humility is not adapted to the passions by a distinct original quality; but that there are some one or more circumstances common to all of them, on which their efficacy depends" (T 281–82).

28. T 330. The object of love and hatred "is evidently some thinking person; and the sensation of the former is always agreeable, and of the latter uneasy." Hume further supposes "that the cause of both passions is always related to a thinking being, and that the cause of the former produces a separate pleasure, and of the latter a separate uneasiness" (T 331).

29. The passions of love and hatred differ from pride and humility, which are "pure emotions" unaccompanied by any desire, and do not immediately excite us to action, in that they are always conjoined with benevolence and anger (T 367). The desire produced depends, again, on "the original constitution of the mind." "As nature has given to the body certain appetites and inclinations, which she encreases, diminishes, or changes according to the situation of the fluids and solids; she has proceeded in the same manner with the mind" (T 368).

30. "'Tis plain, that almost in every species of creatures, but especially of the nobler kind, there are many evident marks of pride and humility. The very port and gait of a swan, or turkey, or peacock show the high idea he has entertain'd of himself, and his contempt of all others. This is the more remarkable, that in the two last species of animals, the pride always attends to the beauty, and is discovered in the male only" (T 326).

31. John P. Wright has drawn my attention to Hume's possible debt here to Descartes (who makes this distinction in the Third Meditation, and elsewhere), or to Malebranche, who uses it in his account of emotions in *De la Recherche de la Verité*, or to Arnauld's *Des Vrais et de Fausses Idées*, all of whom Hume says he consulted while working on the *Treatise*. In his Preface to the reader of the *Meditations*, Descartes distinguishes two senses of the term "idea," which can be taken materially, as an act or operation of the intellect, or taken objectively, as the thing represented by that operation (AT VII 8, CSM, II 7). References to Descartes' work are to *Oeuvres de Descartes*, ed. C. Adam and P. Tannery (Paris: J. Vrin, 1996), cited as AT; *The Philosophical Writings of Descartes*, vols. I-II, ed. and trans. J. Cottingham, R. Stoothoff, and D. Murdoch (Cambridge: Cambridge University Press, 1985), cited as CSM. Descartes stresses in the Third Meditation that it is only when taken in the latter sense that ideas can be said to have reference to the truth or falsity of their objects; when considered simply as acts, ideas involve no error (AT VII 232, CSM II 163). I do not wish to impute to Hume Descartes' account of representation in terms of objective reality. I merely point out that Hume may well have presupposed the distinction between perception as act and perception as content made by his predecessors. The ideas-as-acts are "original existences"—the ideas' contents alone have reference to the truth or falsity of their objects.

32. Compare the following passage, where Hume says, "[I]n thinking of our past thoughts we not only delineate out the objects, of which we were thinking, but also conceive the action of the mind in the meditation, that certain *je-ne-sais-quoi*, of which 'tis impossible to give any definition or description, but which everyone sufficiently understands" (T 106), and the remark "It has been observ'd, that nothing is ever present to the mind but its perceptions; ant that all the actions of seeing, hearing, judging, loving, hating and thinking, fall under this denomination"

(T 458). Annette Baier recognizes that Hume's account suggests this reading but does not pursue it, in a note in "Master Passions," 422.

33. For Descartes, passions are thoughts which are confused and obscure precisely because, although their first cause is always some perception or judgment, their last and most proximate cause is some bodily turmoil, disposing the soul to represent its object in this particular way, as lovable, fearful, or desirable, and hence as inclining the will one way or another. The connection between the initial perception and the passion is made through a series of physiological reactions and changes in the blood, designed by nature to incline the mind in determinate ways. How a particular perception comes to occasion this particular emotion—say, of anger or fear—in the soul and body of this particular person at this time, will depend on the constitution and history of the person. See Descartes, *The Passions of the Soul*, Part One, arts. 27–40, AT XI 349–59, CSM I 338–43. See also my "The Intentionality of Cartesian Emotions."

34. Spinoza, *Ethics*, 2P28Dem. That is, they are affections of the mind the occurrence of which is determined by laws of emotion governing the body rather than logical laws of inference.

35. "In all creatures, that prey not upon others, and are not agitated with violent passions, there appears a remarkable desire for company, which associates them together, without any advantages they can ever propose to reap from their union. This is still more conspicuous in man, as being the creature in universe, who has the most ardent desire of society, and is fitted for it by the most advantages. We can form no wish, which has not a reference to society. Every pleasure languishes when enjoy'd a-part from company, and every pain becomes more cruel and intolerable. Whatever other passions we may be actuated by; pride, ambition, avarice, curiosity, revenge or lust; the soul or animating principle of them all is sympathy; nor wou'd they have any force, were we to abstract entirely from the thoughts or sentiments of others" (T 363).

CHAPTER 8

Sympathy and the Unity of Hume's Idea of Self

DONALD AINSLIE

Annette Baier's *A Progress of Sentiments*[1] has changed the way we read Hume's *Treatise*[2] largely because of her recognition that there is thematic and structural unity in this classic text. She suggests that the *Treatise*, with its dramatic first-person narrative (notably in the "Conclusion" to Book 1), first *enacts* for us the crisis philosophy creates for itself when it restricts its interest in human nature merely to our cognitive capacities; the detailed account of the mechanisms lying behind our beliefs and feelings that supersedes this crisis then serves to *demonstrate* for us what the study of human nature should look like, namely, a careful, naturalistic investigation of the "social and passionate" (PS 278) ways we relate to one another in all the complexities of what Hume calls our "common life." In her many and multi-faceted interventions in contemporary ethics, Baier applies the lessons she has learned from her study of Hume to correct what she sees as a tendency among contemporary moral philosophers to overintellectualize our place in the world. She offers us instead an account of humans as animals who relate to one another (and to our environments) both emotionally and cognitively and who can reflectively correct these ways of relating to one another at an individual and social level.[3]

Both Baier's reading of Hume and her Hume-inspired offerings in moral philosophy might seem to be open to the same objection. The problem is that Hume's explanation of the central element in his social and moral philosophy—sympathy, or our instinctively taking on the feelings and sentiments of those around us—seems to be riddled with inconsistencies. If they are real, Baier's attempt to offer a unified reading of the *Treatise* must fail, in that there would be no real unity to be found in it. Norman Kemp Smith, for example, goes so far as to conclude from these inconsistencies that the three Books of the *Treatise* must have been written in reverse order, with Books 2 and 3 providing the inspiration for the kind of naturalistic project the ramifications of which he takes Hume to have fully understood only in Book 1.[4] Moreover, an incoherence in Hume's account of sympathy in the *Treatise* would also jeopardize Baier's neo-Humean project in moral philosophy, since she sees Hume's recognition of our fundamental emotional resonance with one another as one of the insights that sets his views apart from the dominant individualist and rationalist traditions in ethics.[5]

Baier herself indicates that she thinks that the seeming inconsistencies in Hume's treatment of sympathy can be reconciled (PS 130–31, 142, 145), but she does not provide the details of how this is to be done. In what follows, I take up this task. First, I outline the many roles sympathy plays in the *Treatise* and the mechanism that Hume provides as an explanation of it. I then point to six problems that seem to threaten this explanation, the most grave of which are brought about by Hume's reliance on an ever-present "idea, or rather impression of ourselves" (T 2.1.11.4, SBN 317), despite the fact that he previously denied the existence of an impression of self in his discussion of personal identity (T 1.4.6.2, SBN 251). In sections 3–4 of this paper, I show that these problems dissolve once we recognize that Hume gives two different accounts of the self. On the one hand, he investigates the self as the locus of experience—the self as *mind*. On the other hand, he has a notion of the self as *an embodied person with a distinctive place in the social sphere*. I argue in section 5 that through his treatment of sympathy Hume shows how these two seemingly quite distinct views of the self display a certain kind of unity.

I. SYMPATHY AND ITS MECHANISM

Humean sympathy is a process whereby one person's sentiments are trans-fused into another's mind so that she too comes to feel the same senti-ments as the first person. This is not an uncommon occurrence. When we are confronted with someone's anger or joy, for example, we are often car-ried into these same emotions ourselves; when we are surrounded by people who hold a certain opinion, it is easy to find ourselves doing the same. Hume himself takes the influence of sympathy to be much wider than these commonplace examples might suggest; indeed he appeals to it throughout Books 2 and 3 of the *Treatise* in his explanations of such things as the phe-nomenon of "national characters," that is, the common traits exhibited by people who share a nationality (T 2.1.11.2, SBN 317);⁶ the "love of rela-tions," the tendency among those who share a common feature to feel an affinity for one another (T 2.2.4); our "esteem for the rich and powerful," which turns out to be based on our sympathetically sharing in their plea-sure in their possessions (T 2.2.5); our feelings of compassion and pity (T 2.2.7); and our susceptibility to *Schadenfreude*, malice, and envy, each of which depends on our comparing the sentiments we receive sympathetically from someone else's suffering or good fortune with the sentiments arising from our own condition in life (T 2.2.8).⁷ Hume goes so far as to say that without the influence of sympathy, our mental conditions would start to deteriorate:

> We can form no wish, which has not a reference to society. A perfect solitude is, perhaps, the greatest punishment we can suffer. Every plea-sure languishes when enjoy'd a-part from company, and every pain be-comes more cruel and intolerable. Whatever other passions we may be actuated by; pride, ambition, avarice, curiosity, revenge or lust; the soul or animating principle of them all is sympathy; nor wou'd they have any force, were we to abstract entirely from the thoughts and senti-ments of others. Let all the powers and elements of nature conspire to serve and obey one man: Let the sun rise and set at his command: The sea and rivers roll as he pleases, and the earth furnish spontaneously whatever may be useful or agreeable to him: He will still be miserable, till you give him some one person at least, with whom he may share his

happiness, and whose esteem and friendship he may enjoy. (T 2.2.5.15, SBN 363; cf. T 2.1.11.2, SBN 316–17)

But sympathy plays its most important role for Hume in constituting "our sense of beauty, when we regard external objects, as well as when we judge of morals" (T 3.3.6.1, SBN 618). We take pleasure in objects by sharing sympathetically in the (primarily utilitarian) pleasures they give their owners (T 2.2.5.16–20, 3.3.1.8, 3.3.5.4–5; SBN 363–65, 576–77, 615–17). We approve of character traits by sharing sympathetically in the pleasures they give to their possessors or to those who surround them (T 3.3.1.30, SBN 591). We approve of the "artificial" virtues of justice, fidelity to promises, and allegiance to rulers out of a "a sympathy with public interest" (T 3.2.2.24, 3.2.8.7; SBN 499–500, 545–46).

Despite the fact that Hume makes multiple uses of the principle of sympathy, he attempts to account for all of them within a single explanatory schema. The explanation has two steps. In the first, we acquire an idea of another person's sentiment through a causal inference from "those external signs in the countenance and conversation" (T 2.1.11.3, SBN 317) she or he displays. As Hume points out, this inference depends on a generic resemblance among all humans (T 2.1.11.5, SBN 318). We all feel more or less the same kinds of sentiments and we express our feelings in more or less the same ways. Only with this base-line resemblance in place can we develop the customs through which we are able to infer one another's sentiments. Note, however, that an inferred sentiment is a mere idea, albeit as a belief, a somewhat vivacious one. To explain how we actually *feel* the sentiment *as our own*, Hume introduces the second step:

> 'Tis evident, that *the idea, or rather impression of ourselves* is always intimately present with us, and that our consciousness gives us so lively a conception of our own person, that 'tis not possible to imagine, that any thing can in this particular go beyond it. Whatever object, therefore, is related to ourselves must be conceived with a like vivacity of conception. . . . (T 2.1.11.4, SBN 317; emphasis mine)

In this step, the presence of a relation between ourselves and the sympathetic communicant allows the vivacity that Hume attributes to the "idea, or rather impression of ourselves" to be transferred to our idea of the communicant's sentiment, thus enlivening it into an impression. We ourselves come to feel the same sentiment as the other person feels.

Hume extends this basic explanation of sympathy by introducing variations in both steps of the mechanism. First, there are cases where we acquire a sentiment without even knowing that it has its source in sympathy (say, someone feels cheerful because of the influence of the good mood of a co-worker, without even being conscious of the co-worker's mood). Let us call such cases *pure contagion* (cf. T 3.3.3.5, SBN 605). Here the causal inference in the first step is so automatic that we are unaware of its occurrence; it is like the inference we make when we instinctively stop at a river's edge, to avoid falling in (T 1.3.8.13, SBN 103–4). The relation in the second step in this case is contiguity, since it is the physical presence of the co-worker that is responsible for the influence of her sentiments on the sympathizer. But in many other cases of sympathy, where the communicants are physically present to one another, the sympathizer *knows* the source of his feeling (someone's feeling embarrassed *for* another person is a clear example of this). In such cases, the causal inference in the first step occurs more consciously; we are aware that we have formed a belief about the communicant's sentiments. I will call these cases of contiguity-based, conscious sympathy *human sympathy*.[8]

In addition to these variations on the first step of the sympathy mechanism, Hume introduces two new types of sympathy involving the second step. For one thing, he allows the other natural relations—causation and resemblance—to take the place of contiguity as the medium for the transfer of vivacity (T 2.1.11.5–6, SBN 318). This makes room for the possibility of our sympathizing with people who are not physically present with us: When an absent person is a member of our family or is connected to us by a socially meaningful resemblance—Hume specifies a commonality in "manners, or character, or country, or language" (T 2.1.11.5, SBN 318)—we can sympathetically share his sentiments whenever we can infer their existence from our knowledge of that person's attitudes or from other indirect signs. Thus, when we are in a "poor condition," we continue to feel our family's scorn sympathetically, even when we move away from them in an attempt to lessen the influence their contempt has on us (T 2.1.11.17, SBN 323). Many of the uses to which Hume puts sympathy that I have noted above similarly involve noncontiguous partners: we sense beauty out of a sympathy with the owner of an object, even without being in his presence (T 2.2.5.16–20,

SBN 363–65); we esteem a rich man from afar; we sympathize with the public interest even though it is an abstract construction (T 2.2.5.14, 3.2.2.24; SBN 362, 499–500).[9] Let us call this kind of sympathy, based on relations of resemblance or causation in the second step of the mechanism, *social sympathy*.[10]

Note that the efficacy of this kind of sympathy will be proportional to the closeness and salience of the connection between ourselves and the communicant in the particular context (T 3.3.1.14, SBN 581). I will refer to this relativity of sympathy as the *differential nature* of sympathy. This differentiality is relevant not only when the communicants are physically absent from one another; Hume thinks that socially significant connections also tend to make a difference to whom we sympathize with when we are confronted with a number of possible, contiguous, sympathetic communicants.[11]

The other variation based on the second step has to do with the way in which the sympathetic communicant is conceived by the sympathizer. Consider two ways that we might respond when we encounter someone suffering, say, a street person. On the one hand, our sympathetic sharing of his distress might lead us to feel compassion for him and to take some steps toward helping him out, minimally, by giving him money. On the other hand, since Hume's account of hatred entails that we will hate any person who bears a displeasing quality (T 2.2.1.6, SBN 331), our receiving the street person's pain sympathetically might lead us to hate him for causing us discomfort (T 2.2.9.11–15, SBN 384–87); moreover, since hatred is generally accompanied by anger—the desire to harm the person we hate—sympathy in this case might lead us to want to hurt the street person (T 2.2.6.3, SBN 367). What explains the difference, then, between these two ways of sympathizing with someone? In the latter case, our hatred for the street person arises because our interaction with him is so limited that all we consider is this particular moment in his life. We fail to take any interest in him, to consider how he ended up where he is or what the future holds in store for him. But, in the former case, we come to care about the street person because we not only sympathize with his *present* plight but also sympathize with *future* pains or pleasures we imagine in his life (we might even think about how our own interventions might make a difference to his future). This "interest" in his fortune mimics the effects of benevolence and leads us to develop an active concern to help him (T 2.2.9.14–15, SBN 386–87). Hume calls this latter kind of sympathy *extensive* (also "double" [T 2.2.9.19,

SBN 388–89] or "compleat" [T 2.2.9.18, SBN 388]) sympathy, as opposed to the *limited* sympathy we feel when we resonate to someone's feelings only superficially (T 2.2.9.15, SBN 387). It is extensive sympathy that Hume invokes in his discussion of moral evaluation in Book III (T 3.3.1.23, 3.3.6.3; SBN 586, 619).

Whether our sympathy is limited or extensive, Hume says, will depend primarily on the force with which we feel the communicant's sentiment (T 2.2.9.15, SBN 387). When we are greatly moved by the street person's pain, the vivacity of our sympathetically felt pain will overflow into ideas relating to his future and past, thus leading to extensive sympathy. When the sympathetic pain is felt only weakly, we will not be inclined to take into account the conditions of his life unless we have some other reason to do so (a preexisting friendship, perhaps). But Hume here introduces one more qualification to his account: The extra vivacity necessary for conceiving the sympathetic communicant's past and future prospects need not be the result only of a strong affection; we can *intentionally* imagine ourselves into a concern for someone. That is, he allows that sympathy will also be extensive if the affection is "strongly sympathiz'd with" (T 2.2.9.15, SBN 387) because of the *effort* we put into our sympathetic reception of the other person's sentiments—because of our intentionally extending our attitude toward the communicant to encompass his life.[12]

This is a crucial qualification. Hitherto, sympathy has been viewed as an automatic process, the causal inference and the relation-mediated vivacity-transference being beyond our control. But just as more traditional forms of communication such as speech can be entered into intentionally, so too can the sympathetic communication of sentiments. It is possible for us to be active in promoting both steps of the sympathy mechanism. In the first step, we can engage in the sort of investigation Hume discusses in his treatment of causation (cf. T 1.3.15) in order to discover another person's sentiments. In the second step, we can, through attention and inquiry, come to recognize relations between the communicant and ourselves that we had not previously acknowledged. Or we can, at least in our imaginations, bring the communicant closer to us—say, by representing her situation to ourselves in "lively colours" (T 3.2.1.12, SBN 481)—so that contiguity can be the relation in the second step of the mechanism. Hume uses the automatic cases of sympathy to show the plausibility of his schema; once it is in place he is able to make room for our intentionally sympathizing with others. Indeed, most of Hume's uses of sympathy in Book 3, where he attempts to explain the possibility of our taking up a moral point of view in making judgments of one another, are of the intentional sort.

2. SIX PROBLEMS

We have seen that Hume's sympathy mechanism is remarkably flexible, encompassing everything from pure contagion to intentional extensive sympathy. But we must consider his account of this mechanism to be a failure if we cannot make sense of the "idea, or rather impression of ourselves" that plays such a crucial role in its second step. It is here that Kemp Smith finds the inconsistencies that lead him to reject a unified interpretation of the *Treatise*. Consider the following six problems.

(1) *What is the status of the "idea, or rather impression" of self in the sympathy mechanism? How does it cohere with Hume's earlier rejection of an "impression of self" (T 1.4.6.2, SBN 251)?* Kemp Smith's primary accusation against Hume is that he has contradicted himself in asserting that there could be an impression of self, let alone one always accompanying our thought.[13] For in the first few paragraphs of the section in Book 1 dealing with personal identity (T 1.4.6), Hume levels a devastating attack on the idea that we have an immediate awareness of a simple identical self (T 1.4.6.1–3, SBN 251–52). More recent critics have pointed out that Hume here rejects only an impression of a certain kind of self, and thus he can consistently argue for the existence of an ever-present "idea, or rather impression" of self if it is not viewed as the awareness of something persisting and simple.[14] Mere consistency does not guarantee plausibility, however, and there have been surprisingly few attempts to describe just why Hume thinks he can rely on an awareness of self in his sympathy mechanism. Any successful attempt would have to include an explanation of Hume's hesitancy about the status of this perception of self—what it means to say that it is an "idea, or rather impression"—as well as an account of the link that he draws between this perception and our consciousness or conception of ourselves, e.g., his description of it as an "impression or consciousness of our own person" (T 2.1.11.6, SBN 318; cf. T 2.1.11.4, 2.2.2.15, SBN 317, 339–40).

(2) *Why does Hume think that this perception of self is* always *present to us? Why is it always* intimately *present to us (T 2.1.11.6, 2.1.11.8, 2.2.2.15,*

2.2.4.7, 2.3.7.1; SBN 317, 320, 339, 354, 427)? There are three related problems here. The first is phenomenological: Why would Hume think that we
are always thinking of ourselves? On the face of it, this seems rather implausible. The second problem concerns how this supposedly ever-present perception of self can cohere with some of the other claims that Hume makes.
For example, he says that sympathy is a principle which "takes us . . . out of
ourselves" (T 3.3.1.11, SBN 579), with the result that if our attention is focused on our idea of self—say, as an effect of pride or humility—the sympathy mechanism would be blocked:

> [W]hen the affections are once directed to ourself, the fancy passes not
> with the same facility from that object to any other person, how closely
> so ever connected with us. . . . Some may perhaps find a contradiction
> betwixt this phænomenon and that of sympathy, where the mind passes
> easily from the idea of ourselves to that of any other object related to
> us. But this difficulty will vanish, if we consider that in sympathy our
> own person is not the object of any passion, nor is there any thing, that
> fixes our attention on ourselves. . . . (T 2.2.2.16–17, SBN 340)

The third problem concerns the mode of awareness we have of the "idea,
or rather impression." What does Hume mean with his repeated use of the
modifier "intimate?"[15]

(3) *Why is "the idea, or rather impression" of self the special repository of vivacity?* This question is connected with (2) above, for Hume says that vivacious perceptions "engage the attention, and keep it from wandering to other
objects, however strong may be their relation to our first object" (T 2.2.2.15,
SBN 339). This makes it sound as though one's awareness of self has "the
sort of highlighted consciousness . . . which one might achieve in moments
of meditation or introspection, self-examination, or acute embarrassment."[16]
But the passages I noted in connection with (2) suggest that if the vivacity of
the "idea, or rather impression" of self is understood in these terms, it would
block the operations of the sympathy mechanism entirely. Nonetheless, the
special liveliness of this perception of self is crucial in the second step of
Hume's explanation of sympathy, for it is what leads to the conversion of our
idea of someone's sentiment into an actually felt sentiment.

(4) *How is the "idea, or rather impression" of self able to account for pure contagion, human sympathy, and social sympathy? In particular, how can it explain*

sympathy's differential nature? An interpretation of this perception of self must show how it functions in both the relation of contiguity, so as to support human sympathy and pure contagion, and relations of resemblance and causation, so as to support social sympathy. The case of resemblance offers particular problems, for Hume says that

> [i]f we resemble a person in any of the valuable parts of his character, we must, in some degree, possess the quality, in which we resemble him; and this quality we always chuse to survey directly in ourselves rather than by reflexion in another person, when we wou'd found upon it any degree of vanity. So that tho' a likeness may occasionally produce that passion by suggesting a more advantageous idea of ourselves, 'tis there the view fixes at last, and the passion finds its ultimate and final cause. (T 2.1.9.2, SBN 304)

Here Hume says that a valued resemblance between ourselves and another person will often bring us to feel pride which, as we have seen, would block sympathy (T 2.2.2.17, SBN 340–41). How then can he also say that valued resemblances between ourselves and the sympathetic communicant can also serve as the relation in the second step of the sympathy mechanism?

(5) *How can the sympathy mechanism apply to animals, which, Hume says, also communicate sentiments sympathetically (T 2.2.12.6, SBN 398)?* It follows that the "idea, or rather impression" of self cannot be so abstruse that animals will lack the capacities to form it. (Presumably animals will not experience the same forms of sympathy as humans; usually, one expects, they will acquire sentiments sympathetically through pure contagion or the animal-analogue of human sympathy.)

(6) *Why does Hume seem to be unconcerned about his explanation of sympathy—especially its reliance on the "idea, or rather impression" of self—when, in the "Appendix" to the* Treatise, *he reconsiders much of the original account of the self that he offered in "Of personal identity?"* The second thoughts Hume expresses in the Appendix concern only Book 1. He gives no indication that the problems he diagnoses for his account of our belief in personal identity threaten his analysis of sympathy. Indeed, as we saw above, Book 3 of the *Treatise*, to which the Appendix was attached, makes considerable use of sympathy. It is true that Hume does not repeat his full account of the mechanics of sympathy in Book 3, omitting most notably an account of the source—in Book 2,

the "idea, or rather impression" of self—of the vivacity through which the idea of a sentiment is enlivened into the sentiment itself (T 3.3.1.7, SBN 575–76). But given that the focus of Book 3 is on morals, it is not clear that we should expect more than a cursory explanation of the operations of sympathy; the account of sympathy in Book 2 is available for those who are interested in the details of this psychological capacity.[17]

3. "THE IDEA, OR RATHER IMPRESSION OF OURSELVES"

How then are we to make sense of the "idea, or rather impression of ourselves" in the sympathy mechanism and the problems that come with it? Part of the difficulty in answering this question arises from the fact that, without being very clear about it, Hume seems to have provided two quite distinct accounts of the self in the *Treatise*. On the one hand, in his discussion of personal identity, he considers the self from the point of view of "thought or the imagination" (T 1.4.6.5, SBN 253). This introspective analysis of self ultimately yields an understanding of the *mind* as a "bundle or collection of distinct perceptions . . . in a perpetual flux and movement" (T 1.4.6.4, SBN 252). And, despite there being nothing tying these perceptions together into a single object, causal and resemblance relations between them can cause someone to form a "fictional" belief that they constitute an identically continuing mind (T 1.4.6.18–19, SBN 260–61). On the other hand, in Book 2, Hume considers persons from the point of view "of our passions or the concern we take in ourselves" (T 1.4.6.5, SBN 253). Although his exploration of this topic is not as explicit or as textually compact as the arguments in "Of personal identity," much of the analysis in Book 2 of the so-called indirect passions of pride, humility, love, and hatred can be read as an investigation of how only some of our many features come to define us as particular kinds of persons.[18] This, it turns out, is a product of the social coordination of the indirect passions brought about by sympathy and "general rules"—the expectations we come to have about people based on the customary ways that we make sense of one another (T 2.1.6.8–9, SBN 293–94). The upshot is an understanding of persons as being defined primarily by their bodily qualities (T 2.1.8), their virtues and vices (T 2.1.7), their socioeconomic status (T 2.1.10), and by any other feature or possession that has come to be invested with social significance (T 2.1.9). As Baier says, "The metaphysics of persons in Book Two are the socio-biophysics of human reality" (PS 139).

So, which of these two treatments of self is Hume relying on when he invokes the "idea, or rather impression of ourselves" in the sympathy mechanism?

Don Garrett takes the "idea, or rather impression" to be connected with the idea of the mind as a system of causally related and resembling perceptions, described in "Of personal identity." He suggests that this idea should be thought of as an abstraction, like our ideas of space and time, and, appealing to Hume's analysis of abstract ideas (T 1.1.7), he concludes that an idea of self is structured as a particular idea (the complex of occurrent perceptions we have at a given moment) accompanied by a willingness (indicated by the use of a general term) to consider other possible perceptions in place of these occurrent ones whenever such a replacement is required. This analysis leads Garrett to suggest that *all* of our impressions are impressions of ourselves, since any one of them could take its place as part of the particular complex perception standing in for the general term "self." And since there are always some impressions present to the mind,[19] there will always be an impression of self available to play its role in the sympathy mechanism.[20]

Garrett's interpretation faces five problems. First, it is not at all clear that Hume means for the "true idea of the human mind" (T 1.4.6.19, SBN 262), which is the outcome of his investigation of personal identity, to be taken as an abstract idea. For this idea is not the abstract idea of a collection of perceptions at a given moment, without regard to certain aspects of their content (as the idea of time is the abstract idea of perceptions in succession, without regard to their content); rather, it is the idea of a temporally extended "bundle" (T 1.4.6.4, SBN 252) or "system" (T 1.4.6.19, SBN 261) of a *particular* group of perceptions. The relation of our occurrent perceptions to the self of the "true idea" seems to be one of part to whole, rather than of particular to abstraction.[21]

A second problem for Garrett's supposition that the idea of self in the sympathy mechanism is an abstract idea is connected with question (5) above, namely, the question of the ability of animals to sympathize with one another. Given that animals lack the linguistic capacities required to form a Humean abstract idea (T 1.1.7.7, SBN 20),[22] how could they have the impression of themselves requisite for sympathy if this impression is derived from an abstract idea of themselves?

A third and more general issue, somewhat similar to this second problem, is that the idea of mind developed in "Of personal identity" is quite abstruse, not only for animals, but for most humans. Even though "bundle of perceptions" may be an accurate *description* of the minds of all of "mankind" (T 1.4.6.4, SBN 252), there is no reason to expect all of them to have *formulated* an idea of their minds in these terms. Such an idea is a product of a peculiar kind of philosophical reflection on our experiences, since we will see our minds as bundles of perceptions only if we "enter most intimately" into ourselves in the way that Hume suggests (T 1.4.6.3, SBN 252). As he acknowledges, this means that the "vulgar" will not have this kind of idea of mind: "[I]n common life 'tis evident these ["abstruse" and "metaphysical"] ideas of self and person are never very fix'd nor determinate" (T 1.4.2.6, SBN 189–90). Since Hume never suggests that his account of the sympathy mechanism is meant to apply only to philosophers and not to the vulgar, it seems hard to believe that he means for the "idea, or rather impression" of self in the sympathy mechanism to be based on ideas of ourselves that only philosophers will have formed determinately.

A fourth problem for interpretations such as Garrett's, which take the "idea or rather impression" of self to be the idea of the mind, is connected with question (4) above. Even if Garrett could successfully make out that the idea of self is an abstract idea, his analysis would still be unable to account for the differential nature of sympathy. As we have seen, relations between someone's idea of self and his idea of someone else will ease the sympathetic communication of sentiments between them. But how does the idea of mind as a bundle of perceptions capture the socially articulated features that the idea of self seems to display here? The bundle in question has a peculiarly *flattened* character, so that all of our perceptions are taken to be equivalent in, and potentially detachable from (T 1.4.2.39, SBN 207), the complex constituting our mind: The perception of a tree we happen to see counts for as much (or as little) as the perceptions of our bodies or our characters or our family members. It would seem that if the idea of self is to be understood in these terms, then any common perception shared by two persons would create a resemblance between them; and this resemblance, as a means for the transmission of vivacity, would promote sympathetic communication. How could Hume be justified, then, in privileging manners, character, country, and language (T 2.1.11.5, SBN 318) as the most significant resemblances for sympathy? Hume clearly recognizes that only socially meaningful resemblances promote sympathetic communication. The flatness of the "true idea" of self has no room for this sort of meaningfulness.

Fifth, taking the "idea, or rather impression" of self to be tightly linked with the idea of self as it is found in "Of personal identity" leaves an interpreter with no straightforward way of answering question (6) above, namely, how Hume both can reject the argument in "Of personal identity" in the Appendix and, at the same time, exhibit no worries about his use of a perception of self in his explanation of sympathy.[23]

The last three of the five problems that I have posed for Garrett's interpretation will also confront any reading which takes the "idea, or rather impression" of self to be the idea of the mind as a bundle of perceptions. This might lead one to conclude that a better interpretation would take the perception of self that is involved in sympathy to be the one occurring in the account of the passions in Book 2, namely, the sense of one's place as an embodied person living in a social world. Since these conceptions of ourselves register our social locations, the proposed reading would have no problem accounting for the differential nature of sympathy ([4] above). Since Hume thinks that we form such conceptions as a consequence of our experiences with the passions, especially the indirect ones, the problems with abstruseness plaguing accounts such as Garrett's would also easily be avoided. All of us—including animals (see [5] above)—feel pride and humility, with the result that we all have self-conceptions. And, since the discussion of personal identity deals primarily with the structure of minds and philosophers' beliefs about them, not the "vulgar" sense we have of our place in the social world, the proposed interpretation would also allow us to understand why Hume does not take the second thoughts in the Appendix to threaten the use of the "idea, or rather impression" of self in the sympathy mechanism ([6] above).

This does not mean that the above reading is entirely adequate. Consider Nicholas Capaldi's attempt to interpret the "idea, or rather impression" of self in terms of our idea of ourselves "as it regards our passions" (T 1.4.6.5, SBN 253), which I have been calling our conception of ourselves. He suggests that Hume relies on the implicit presence of pride or humility in his explanation of the sympathy mechanism. After we have acquired the idea of the communicant's sentiment, we feel what Capaldi calls an "independent impression of pleasure or pain"; this impression is associated with either pride or humility, which in turn directs our attention to our idea of self; the vivacity attached to the independent impression is transferred to the idea of self, which can then serve as the source of the vivacity that converts the original idea of the communicant's sentiment into our own version of that sentiment.[24]

Unfortunately for Capaldi's interpretation, though, Hume's detailed description of the operations of sympathy makes no such appeal to the indirect passions, nor to Capaldi's interpolated "independent impression." Indeed, as I noted when discussing (2) and (3) above, Hume even suggests that when we experience pride or humility, sympathetic communication is blocked, since our attention remains focused on ourselves (T 2.2.2.17, SBN 340–41). Capaldi does mention this phenomenon, but only to take it as a sign of the failure of Hume's account of sympathy; indeed, Capaldi appeals to it as part of an explanation for what he takes to be Hume's abandonment of sympathy in the second *Enquiry*.[25] I suggest, however, that rather than accusing Hume of contradicting himself, we should find an interpretation that makes sense of both the sympathy mechanism and his claim that pride and humility block the operations of the mechanism.[26]

A further problem with Capaldi's taking the "idea, or rather impression" of self to be one's self-conception is that he does not answer (2) above; he does not explain how Hume can repeatedly say that this perception is *always* present to us. Presumably, Capaldi takes this omission as a virtue, for it is hard to see how Hume could say that we are constantly aware of ourselves and our social affiliations. Capaldi seems to take Hume to mean that the idea of self is present not "always without qualification," but rather "always *when we are sympathizing* with someone," in which case pride or humility would guarantee the presence of the idea of self. But the textual evidence is quite clear: Hume means for the "idea, or rather impression" of self to be ever-present without qualification (T 2.1.11.6, 2.1.11.8, 2.2.2.15, 2.2.4.7, 2.3.7.1; SBN 317, 320, 339, 354, 427). It follows not only that Capaldi's interpretation must be rejected, but also that any interpretation which takes the "idea, or rather impression" of self to be simply one's self-conception will face difficulties similar to those Capaldi faces.

But what are we to do, given that the "idea, or rather impression" of self that Hume relies on in his account of sympathy cannot be understood in terms of either of the two accounts of the self that he offers us—the self as mind or the self as a socially-located person? My suggestion is that the problem with each of these two general interpretive approaches is that they focus on only *one* of Hume's two treatments of selfhood, whereas Hume seems to draw on *both* in his explanation of sympathy. The perceptions making up the mind as a bundle—if they are not understood too abstrusely—seem to be ever-present and to be able to act as the source of vivacity in sympathetic communication; however, the mind does not have the social dimension needed to explain the differential nature of sympathy. Self-conceptions can explain this differentiality, but it is hard to see how they are ever-present to us or especially vivacious. To solve these interpretive problems, we must explain how Hume manages to bring the two views of self together.

He does this explicitly only once.[27] Near the end of "Of personal identity," he says that "[o]ur identity with regard to the passions serves to corroborate that with regard to the imagination, by the making our distant perceptions influence each other, and by giving us a present concern for our past or future pains or pleasures" (T 1.4.6.19, SBN 261).[28] I take this to mean that because of our present sense of who we are, we act in such a way as to bring about future perceptions, thus creating causal connections among the perceptions constituting the mind-bundle; because of the memories and intentions in the mind-bundle, we count our future and past as relevant to who we take ourselves to be. Nonetheless, a "corroboration" between two objects' identities does not make them the same thing.[29] Accordingly, this passage does not offer us much help in understanding why Hume thinks that our embodied, socially articulated mode of being in the world and our minds are both properly viewed as the objects of something called the "idea of self"; nor does it shed much light on the "idea, or rather impression" of self involved in sympathy.

We need a connection between our minds and ourselves as socially-located persons that is stronger than a mere "corroboration" of their identities. To recognize such a connection, consider again the bundle of perceptions that is the object of the "true idea of the human mind" (T 1.4.6.19, SBN 261). As noted above, when we introspectively "enter most intimately" into ourselves, we observe perceptions appearing one after another. But why do we have just these perceptions and not some others? Why does the philosopher have so many perceptions of books, computer screens, and lectures, in addition to all the ideas connected with her philosophical thinking? Why is her passion of curiosity oriented toward things philosophical? Why does she desire time alone in her study rather than time on the tennis courts? Of course, these perceptions come with her commitment to being a philosopher: She reads, writes, attends lectures, and engages in philosophical inquiry. Part of being a philosopher involves having relevant perceptions. My point is that who she is—in this case, a philosopher—is reflected in the particular *patterns* her perceptions form, the *manner* in which they appear to her; perceptions would occur in a different manner were she a different kind of person. Indeed, all the perceptions we have at any given moment—our "peculiar points of view" on the world (T 3.3.1.15, SBN 581)—reflect who we are; our paths through the world result from our being the kinds of persons we happen to be. The generous person has perceptions reflecting the outlook of someone disposed to see opportunities to benefit others (cf. T 1.3.10.4, SBN 120); the Briton has perceptions conditioned by her national character, her historical sense, and her national customs; and so forth. As Hume says in connection with socioeconomic status: "The skin, pores, muscles, and nerves of a day-labourer are different from those of a man of quality: *So are his sentiments, actions, and manners.* The different stations of life influence the whole fabric, external *and internal*" (T 2.3.1.9, SBN 402; emphasis mine).[30]

This is not to deny that most of the perceptions we receive will be only loosely connected to the features that make us who we are. The philosopher must eat, sleep, play backgammon with friends, and so forth, and each of these activities will add perceptions to her mind-bundle. But when the passions cause her and others to focus on what defines her as who she is, they will focus on those aspects of her that exemplify her philosophical activities. The concreteness and specificity of our paths through the world yield many perceptions that are only negligibly connected to who we are; but these paths nonetheless reflect our concerns, even if at the same time they lead us to change or to rethink these concerns. I suggest that Hume is pointing to our recognition of these paths, that is, the manner in which our perceptions appear to us, when he refers to our "idea, or rather impression" of ourselves.[31]

Although I describe the "idea, or rather impression" in terms of our awareness of the manner in which perceptions appear, I am not suggesting that we usually recognize it in exactly these terms. In "common life," we do not think of our experience in terms of perceptions, and consequently we cannot be said to be aware of the manner in which they appear. But we do have a sense of our experiencing the world from a certain perspective, one conditioned by the kind of persons we are, not only as embodied beings but also in terms of our social positions. One might be tempted to call Hume's ever-present "idea, or rather impression of ourselves" our *subjectivity*, where this term is meant not merely in an epistemological sense, but in a sense that captures "the social and cultural dimension of mind."[32]

4. PROBLEMS SOLVED

Let me now show how my suggested interpretation of this perception of self helps to solve the six problems identified above.

(1) First, there is the question of the status of the "idea, or rather impression of ourselves." Hume's tentativeness in identifying the type of this perception seems to be connected with its unusual provenance; our sense of our particular situations in the world as they are manifested in the manner in which our perceptions appear is some distance from his paradigms of ideas as thoughts and of impressions as sensations or feelings (T 1.1.1.1, SBN 1). But there are a number of other places in the *Treatise* where Hume focuses on the manner in which perceptions appear, such as his discussion of space and time (T 1.2). There, he rejects the suggestion that we have distinguishable impressions which are the sources of our ideas of space and time; instead, these ideas are abstractions from the *manners* in which objects appear to us (either contiguously or in succession). This means that we recognize spatiotemporality only because of the cumulative effects of our perceptions as experienced in common life. There is no single experience in which we encounter space or time. Nonetheless, Hume does in one case refer to a temporal impression: "Five notes play'd on a flute give us the impression and idea of time" (T 1.2.3.10, SBN 36). Thus, in his discussion of space and time, Hume seems to be at least tempted to consider that the manner in which perceptions appear is an impression. It is possible, then, that in mentioning an impression of self in the discussion of the sympathy mechanism, Hume has once again allowed the cumulative effect of perceptions' appearances—in this case, the way in which they reflect who we are as socially-located persons—to qualify as an impression.[33]

Most of the time, Hume resists the temptation to speak of *impressions* of space and time, because he thinks that we only have access to the spatio-temporal manner of perceptions' appearance through the sort of comparisons that lead to an abstract idea. Indeed, although Garrett does not suggest that the impression of self is connected with the manner of our perceptions' appearances, he uses this discussion to motivate treating the idea of self as an abstract idea.[34] I argued against this treatment above, and thus I am left with the question of how, if we do not engage in some sort of abstraction, we can be aware of the manner in which our perceptions appear as a reflection of who we are as persons. The answer lies in recalling how we become aware of ourselves in the first place, namely, through our experiences with the passions, especially pride and humility. These passions make us explicitly aware of our social locations, causing us to form conceptions of ourselves; once we have this awareness (and Hume thinks that we all will have such conceptions, at least after early infancy), we can recognize that the manner in which our perceptions appear reflects who we are. This does not mean that I follow Capaldi in thinking that an episode of pride or humility is internal to the operations of sympathy; rather, my suggestion is that because we have had *previous* experiences with these passions and thus are aware of what makes us who we are, we recognize ourselves in our "peculiar point of view" on the world. On my reading, Hume's vacillation, indicated by his description of our self-awareness as an "idea, or rather impression," is a product of his seeing a role for both the idea of self as the object of pride and humility, and also the impression-like manner in which our perceptions appear as a reflection of the persons these passions reveal.

(2) It is useful to continue this comparison of the "idea, or rather impression" of self to the ideas and space and time in considering the second problem I outlined above, namely, the question of how the former perception is "always intimately present with us" (T 2.1.11.4, SBN 317). For Hume also says that since there is a "continual succession of perceptions in our mind . . . , the idea of time [is] for ever present with us" (T 1.2.5.29, SBN 65); furthermore,

'Tis obvious, that the imagination can never totally forget the points of space and time, in which we are existent; but receives such frequent advertisements of them from the passions and senses, that however it may turn its attention to foreign and remote objects, it is necessitated every moment to reflect on the present. (T 2.3.7.2, SBN 427–28)

Hume goes on to compare the ever-presence of our ideas of space and time to the ever-presence of our ideas of self, saying that we are "every moment recall'd to the consideration of ourselves and our present situation" (T 2.3.7.2, SBN 428). This is not to say that we become fixated on ourselves or our spatiotemporal locations; as we saw above in question (2), such a fixation would preclude the possibility of sympathy (T 2.2.2.17, SBN 340–41). Hume's point seems to be rather that some of the perceptions, both sensations and passions, that we receive are inescapable. As embodied, perceiving persons, we cannot escape the fact that we have particular points of view on the world. We may not need to attend to these points of view, but nonetheless they remain in the background of our minds. Hume's repeated use of the modifier "intimate" in his description of this mode of self-awareness seems particularly apt here. For "intimacy" conveys a kind of closeness that can be taken for granted, one for which we do not need a constant reminder. Thus, the "intimate" awareness of the idea of self seems to be linked to the fact that our awareness of traveling along particular paths in the world, while constant, rarely needs to be the focus of our attention.[35]

(3) The third problem is the most intractable. Why does the "idea, or rather impression" serve as a special repository of vivacity? In particular, it seems hard to see how Hume can think both that vivacity brings with it attention (T 2.2.2.15, SBN 339) and that attention to the idea of self precludes sympathy (T 2.2.2.17, SBN 340–41). My suggestion is that we focus on Hume's description of the "idea, or rather impression" of self as arising from our "consciousness of our own person" (T 2.1.11.6, SBN 318); he says that the vivacity in question is that of the "conception, with which we always form the idea of our own person" (T 2.1.11.5, SBN 318). These phrases are reminiscent of his description of the vivacity constituting belief: "it . . . lies in the *manner*, in which we conceive" an object (T 1.3.7.2, SBN 95; emphasis in original). If we accept the suggestion that the "idea, or rather impression" of self is connected with the *manner* in which our perceptions appear to us, we might be able to connect this manner to the vivacity-defining manner of conception that is belief. After all, Hume does eventually acknowledge dissatisfaction with his characterization of belief and vivacity (T 1.3.7.7, SBN 629). Perhaps the concreteness of a "peculiar

point of view" on the world brings with it a special kind of vivacity connected with our belief in our being in the world (surely a background condition for all of our beliefs).[36]

On this account, why does this high-vivacity perception not consume our attention, preventing us from opening ourselves up to the affections of others? Recall that, on my interpretation, the "idea, or rather impression" of self is not a discrete perception in the mental economy; it is a feature arising from certain general features of the economy itself. Perhaps we can conclude that the vivacity of this self-awareness will not distract us, since it will not draw our attention to a single perception.

(4) Fourth, we must consider how my suggested interpretation of the "idea, or rather impression" of self serves to anchor relations of contiguity and of resemblance and causation. How does it allow for pure contagion, human sympathy, and social sympathy? The dimension of the "idea, or rather impression" connected with the "true idea" of the mind as a bundle of perceptions serves to explain the force of contiguity. When we are physically in the presence of someone, she enters into our "point of view"; she has a relation to us insofar as she is perceived by us. The fact that the "idea, or rather impression" reflects who we are as persons accounts for the influence of relations of resemblance and other social relations. And since our self-conceptions link us with others differentially, my interpretation can also account for the differential nature of sympathy.

There remains the question of why resemblance relations do not, by eliciting pride, preclude sympathetic communication (T 2.1.9.2, SBN 304). But when we notice how Hume is careful to qualify his claim in the relevant passage—it applies only "when we wou'd found" the indirect passions "upon" the resemblance in question—we can see that Hume is making a useful qualification to his account. Part of the reason we do not sympathize with everyone indiscriminately is that sympathy only has significant effects when we resemble the communicant *and* when we do not happen (because of our disposition or our circumstances) to take that resemblance as meriting our turning inward to dwell on our own qualities. Recall that Hume is very aware that our sympathetic nature is often derailed by self-obsession; the principle of comparison leads us to experience the opposite affection to that which we receive sympathetically (T 2.2.8.8–9, SBN 375).

(5) The fifth question I posed above concerned Hume's commitment to animal sympathy. Does my interpretation of the "idea, or rather impression"

of self allow us to see how the sympathy mechanism can apply to animals? Hume argues that they feel pride and humility in the same way that we do (T 2.1.12). It follows that they must have an idea of self, a conception of themselves, as the object of these passions (T 2.1.12.4, SBN 326). Since their self-conceptions are based almost entirely on bodily qualities (T 2.1.12.5, SBN 326), and since they will constantly be receiving impressions of their bodies, we can surmise that there is a sense in which animals, too, can be taken to have a (perhaps rather primitive) awareness of how their perceptions reflect who they are.

(6) Lastly, we must consider whether my interpretation can make sense of the Appendix, where Hume rejects his explanation of our belief in personal identity but does not reconsider his invocation of an "idea, or rather impression" of self in the sympathy mechanism. Whatever the problems in the Appendix may be,[37] Hume's concern there seems to be primarily with his account of why we believe in the mind's identity when we reflectively observe its contents; he does not withdraw his claim that the mind is a "bundle or collection of different perceptions" (T 1.4.6.4, SBN 252).[38] But on my interpretation, Hume relies only on the fact that the mind is a bundle (consisting of perceptions with contents that reflect its possessor's place in the world) in his use of the "idea, or rather impression" of self; there is no expectation that the person with this kind of self-awareness even knows of the perceptual constitution of her mind. (This avoids the problems with abstruseness that I noted earlier in connection with Garrett's interpretation.) Nor is the aspect of the "idea, or rather impression" that captures our social location threatened by the Appendix retractions. For this aspect is a product of our experiences with the passions, and Hume is quite clear that "Of personal identity" and the Appendix concern only persons "as it regards our thought or imagination," not "as it regards our passions or the concern we take in ourselves" (T 1.4.6.5, SBN 253).

5. TWO IDEAS OF SELF?

I have suggested that Hume's account of sympathy can be rescued if the "idea, or rather impression" of self he invokes is understood to combine his analyses of selves as minds and as socially-located embodied persons. But this way of understanding the "idea, or rather impression" of self can also help us to understand what has always been a puzzling feature of Hume's account of the self in the *Treatise*, namely, why he takes these two analyses to concern the same thing—the self or person. It is true that these analyses investigate the self from two different perspectives—"as it regards our thought" and "as it regards our passions" (T 1.4.6.4, SBN 253)—but in each case he offers a definition of the idea of self as if he is defining the *same thing* in two different ways.[39] On his official view, two ideas of the same thing can differ only in the degree of vivacity with which they present their common object (T 1.3.7.5, App.22; SBN 96, 636). But the idea of mind and the idea of a socially-located embodied person seem to present quite different things. How can he call them both "ideas of self?"

It is easy to see why he calls the passionally produced idea of a socially-located embodied person an "idea of self." This notion of selfhood speaks directly to the way we understand what it is to be a person in everyday life. If someone asked me to describe who I am, I would appeal to exactly the sorts of qualities that are included in this passional idea of self. The more difficult question is why Hume also calls the idea of mind an "idea of self." In what sense to do we take ourselves to be equivalent to our minds, even if we consider ourselves only "as it regards our thought or imagination" (T 1.4.6.5, SBN 253)?

Hume seems to think that restricting our consideration of the self in this manner means that we are to turn our minds inwards introspectively and see what we find there. He tells us:

> For my part, when I enter most intimately into what I call *myself*, I always stumble on some particular perception or other, of heat or cold, light or shade, love or hatred, pain or pleasure. I never can catch *myself* at any time without a perception, and never can observe anything but the perception. (T 1.4.6.3, SBN 252; emphasis in original)

But if "what I call *myself*" is taken in any ordinary sense—in the sense of the passionally produced idea discussed above—it is not clear that I would "observe" all of my (occurrent) perceptions when I "enter most intimately" into myself. Why do I not observe only those perceptions that make me into the person I am? On the interpretation of the sympathy mechanism that I offered above, there is a way to answer this question. We saw that the ever-present "idea, or rather impression of ourselves" is a product of the fact that *all* of our perceptions, taken as a whole, manifest to us our place in the world as embodied, socially-located persons. The idea of mind counts as the idea of self "as it regards our thought or imagination" because the whole mind plays a role in producing the "idea, or rather impression" of self, that is, the sense we have of our "peculiar points of view" (T 3.3.1.15, SBN 581) on the world.

Thus, Hume's treatment of sympathy—especially its reliance on the "idea, or rather impression of ourselves"—shows the connection between his accounts of personal identity and of social and moral persons. Moreover, we can now understand how, for Hume, the fact of our being persons in this latter sense is *prior* to an understanding of personal identity.[40] Why, we might ask, should we extend our mind-bundles to include all the perceptions—remembered and unremembered—since sometime near our births?[41] Hume's answer seems to be that we count all of these perceptions as constituting our minds because who we are as embodied persons stretches back to sometime near our births. There is a "corroboration" (T 1.4.6.19, SBN 261) between the two ways Hume has of understanding the identities of persons because part of what defines the temporal limits of our minds is our passionally produced conception of ourselves.

6. SYMPATHETIC ETHICS?

I have argued that Baier's thesis that the *Treatise* must be read as a unified work can surmount the problems arising from Hume's treatment of sympathy. Indeed, my discussion shows how Hume's account of sympathy involves the same sort of reflexivity that Baier has suggested is at the heart of the overall argument of the *Treatise* (PS 277–88). Just as our causal propensities allow us to correct the prejudices our causal propensities cause (PS 99), and just as the self-interested passion corrects itself through the artifices of justice (PS 272), the "peculiar point of view" that we inhabit not only creates the central problem of morality, it also provides its own solution to that problem through its role in the sympathy mechanism. Because we have a distinctive location in the world, we can sympathetically acquire the sentiments of others and thereby overcome the limitations of our distinctive location.

Since Baier's contributions to contemporary moral philosophy use Hume's sympathy-based moral theory as a model, my interpretation can also be seen to second her approach, in that it highlights the attractions of a neo-Humean project. An adequate account of morality must make sense of two ostensibly conflicting demands. It must show how it is that morality is impartial—how every person can be thought of as equal—but it must also acknowledge the distinctive features that make us different from one another—our individual characters and perspectives, our social affiliations and identities. Too often, contemporary moral theorists (e.g. neo-Kantians, rational choice theorists, and consequentialists) emphasize the former demand at the expense of the latter, leaving us with only a desiccated notion of the self. Those who recoil from these theories (e.g., neo-Aristotelians and neo-Hegelians), in contrast, emphasize our social constitution only to lose sight of the importance of pluralism and impartiality. Hume, I think, offers a way out of this bind. Given that a robust notion of the self is at the center of his sympathy-based "system of ethics" (T 3.3.6.1, SBN 618), it cannot be said that he overlooks the individuality of persons; at the same time, his discussion of why we must adopt a moral point of view to correct our sympathetic responses in moral judgment demonstrates his sensitivity to the need for impartiality in morality.

NOTES

I had the benefit of discussing several early drafts of this paper with Annette Baier while I was her student at the University of Pittsburgh. But I am indebted to her for much more than this. Her deep understanding of Hume's philosophical contributions stirred my interest in his work; her grasp of how the history of philosophy should be investigated allowed me to see the philosophical importance of historical studies; and, most importantly, her distinctive philosophical voice has provided me with a model of what a philosopher should be—scholarly, dynamic, humorous, and fully engaged with the world.

I also owe thanks to Jennifer Whiting and Stephen Engstrom, each of whom offered many useful comments and criticisms of earlier versions of this paper. I presented one such version at the 22nd International Hume Conference, Park City, Utah, July 1995; Kathleen Schmidt was the commentator on that occasion, and I thank her for the lively discussions we had throughout the conference.

1. Annette C. Baier, *A Progress of Sentiments: Reflections on Hume's* Treatise (Cambridge, MA: Harvard University Press, 1991). Further references to this text will be made parenthetically as PS.

2. David Hume, *A Treatise of Human Nature*, 2nd ed., ed. L. A. Selby-Bigge and P. H. Nidditch (Oxford: Clarendon, 1978); and *A Treatise of Human Nature*, ed. David Fate Norton and Mary J. Norton (Oxford: Clarendon, 2000). This text will be cited parenthetically as T, followed by the relevant book, part, section, and paragraph numbers as given in the Norton and Norton edition, and then as SBN, followed by the page numbers as given in the Selby-Bigge and Nidditch edition.

3. See especially Baier's presidential address for the Eastern Division of the American Philosophical Association, "A Naturalist View of Persons," in Annette C. Baier, *Moral Prejudices: Essays on Ethics* (Cambridge, MA: Harvard University Press, 1995), 313–26, and more generally the other essays in that volume, as well as those in her *Postures of the Mind: Essays on Minds and Morals* (Minneapolis: University of Minnesota Press, 1985).

4. Norman Kemp Smith, *The Philosophy of David Hume* (London: Macmillan, 1941).

5. Annette C. Baier, "Hume, The Women's Moral Theorist?" in *Moral Prejudices*, 54–57.

6. See Donald C. Ainslie, "The Problem of the National Self in Hume's Theory of Justice," *Hume Studies* 21 (1995): 289–313, for a discussion of Hume's treatment of nationality and national characters.

7. See Baier's discussion of what Hume calls the principle of comparison (PS 149–50). I agree with her claim there that sympathy is internal to the operations of comparison; Mercer, in contrast, takes comparison to work without involving sympathy. See Philip Mercer, *Sympathy and Ethics: A Study of the Relationship between Sympathy and Morality with Special Reference to Hume's* Treatise (Oxford: Clarendon, 1972), 32 ff.

8. Hume later notes two other slight variations in his account of pure contagion and human sympathy, which arise from differences in the causal inference of the first step. First, he thinks we tend to sympathize more easily with stronger and negative passions, such as affliction and sorrow, than with subdued and pleasing ones (T 2.2.7.2, SBN 369), presumably because the former passions leave more obvious signs, thus facilitating a causal inference. Second, he thinks that sometimes we sympathize with sentiments that do not exist. When we think that someone is in circumstances which ought to elicit a particular sentiment, we infer an idea of it, regardless of whether or not the communicant knows about those circumstances. If we later find out that the communicant is not moved by the circumstances in question, we might come to see our sympathy as only "partial" and thus reject the idea of his affection that we had inferred and the sympathy consequent to it. On the

other hand, we might decide that the absence of indications of emotion on the part of the communicant means that he is especially stoical; this will, Hume thinks, only increase the intensity of our sympathetically received sentiment (T 2.2.7.5, SBN 370–71). At the start of Part 3 of Book 3, in the brief review of his earlier account of sympathy, Hume seems especially open to sympathy with nonexistent sentiments: "[W]hen I perceive the *causes* of any emotion, my mind is convey'd to the effects, and is actuated with a like emotion" (T 3.3.1.7, SBN 576).

9. See Ainslie, "The Problem of the National Self," for a discussion of what is presupposed in our ability to sympathize with the public.

10. I have taken the labels "human" and "social sympathy" from a passage in Hume's *History*, vol. 5, chap. 55. When discussing the 1641 uprising by the Irish against their English rulers, Hume describes how the hatred by the former of the latter "on account of their religion, and . . . their riches and prosperity" led to "an universal massacre . . . of the English." "In vain was recourse had [by the English] to relations, to companions, to friends: All connexions were dissolved, and death was dealt by that hand, from which protection was implored and expected." Hume goes on to say that during the insurrection, religious precepts served "not to stop the hands of these murderers, but to enforce their blows, and to still their hearts against every movement of *human* or *social sympathy*" (David Hume, *The History of England*, ed. William B. Todd [Indianapolis: Liberty/Classics, 1987], 341–43; emphasis mine). I take him to be saying in this passage that the victims of the slaughter could not rely on either the communication of their evident distress when they were contiguous to their murderers—that is, on human sympathy—or on the preexisting social connections they had once shared with them—that is, on social sympathy.

11. We have seen that resemblance plays a role in each of the steps of the sympathy mechanism, both as a precondition for the causal inference in the first step, and as a relation by which vivacity is transferred in the second step. Hume's point here is subtle. Because of the role of resemblance in the first step, he thinks that there is a *potential* for us to sympathize with any human (and perhaps even some animals) (T 2.2.12.6, SBN 398), in that when she or he is contiguous to us, human sympathy or pure contagion will be possible. Nonetheless, because of the role of resemblance in the second step, there is a *tendency* for us to sympathize only with those with whom we share a socially significant common feature.

12. The relevant passage states: "Benevolence [consequent to extensive sympathy] . . . arises from a great degree of misery, or any degree strongly sympathiz'd with: Hatred or contempt [consequent to limited sympathy] from a small degree, or one weakly sympathiz'd with . . ." (T 2.2.9.15, SBN 387). The phrase "any degree strongly sympathiz'd with" seems to me to get at the possibility of intentional sympathy because it is presented as an *alternative* to the kind of strong sympathy that arises from the strength of the original sentiment, such as "a great degree of misery."

Mercer, in his discussion of extensive sympathy, misses out on Hume's subtle introduction of intentional sympathetic communication (Mercer, *Sympathy and Ethics*,
36–43).

13. Kemp Smith, *The Philosophy of David Hume*, v, 74–75, 555 ff.

14. See, among others, Mercer, *Sympathy and Ethics*, 29–30; J. L. Mackie, *Hume's
Moral Theory* (London: Routledge and Kegan Paul, 1980), 159–60 n.; Don Garrett,
"Hume's Self-Doubts about Personal Identity," *Philosophical Review* 90 (1981): 337–58;
and John J. Jenkins, "Hume's Account of Sympathy—Some Difficulties," in *Philoso-
phers of the Scottish Enlightenment*, ed. V. Hope (Edinburgh: Edinburgh University
Press, 1984), 91–104.

15. Ronald Butler is the only commentator I have come across who has recognized that Hume's use of "intimate" in these contexts is significant; see Ronald J.
Butler, "'I' and Sympathy," *Proceedings of the Aristotelian Society Supplement* 49
(1975): 1–20.

16. Jenkins, "Hume's Account of Sympathy," 93.

17. Similarly, Hume shows no anxiety about the effect that his retraction of
the argument about personal identity might have on his use of the "indirect" passions of pride and humility in Book 3 (as concomitants of the moral sentiments [T
3.1.2.5, 3.3.1.3; SBN 473, 575]), despite their involving the idea of self as their objects (T 2.1.2.2, SBN 277). In *Treatise* 3.1.1, Hume indicates his general attitude
about going over in detail in Book 3 the material that he is borrowing from Book 2
by saying: "It would be tedious to repeat all the arguments, by which I have prov'd
that reason is perfectly inert, and can never either prevent or produce any action or
affection" (T 3.1.1.7, SBN 457–58); here he refers back to the arguments in "Of
the influencing motives of the will" (T 2.3.3).

18. I argue for this interpretation of Hume's treatment of the indirect passions in Donald C. Ainslie, "Scepticism about Persons in Book II of Hume's *Treatise*," *Journal of the History of Philosophy* 37 (1999): 469–92.

19. This point is made especially clear when Hume declares that an impression accompanies every idea (although often secretly) (T 2.3.8.4, SBN 373–74).

20. Garrett, "Hume's Self-Doubts," and also his *Cognition and Commitment in
Hume's Philosophy* (New York: Oxford University Press, 1997), 167–69.

21. In the course of his discussion of abstract ideas, Hume discusses what Descartes and others who followed the "way of ideas" called "inadequate" ideas—ideas
that fail to capture the relevant details of their objects. Hume gives the example of
a large number, such as 1,000, the idea of which does not usually contain enough
detail to distinguish it from, say, the idea of 1,001. Hume thinks that in some cases
the inadequacy of an idea is harmless, because we have the capacity to make an idea
adequate when the details are necessary. In mathematics, for example, our mastery
of the decimal system allows us to distinguish 1,000 and 1,001. The capacity we

have to correct the faulty use of abstract ideas by bringing to mind relevantly different instantiations is, Hume thinks, somewhat similar to our corrections for the inadequacy of our ideas (T 1.1.7.12, SBN 23).

It is true that the idea someone has of her mind will not usually be "adequate" to the complexities of the perceptual system constituting her mind throughout its life. She will form an idea of a complex set of interrelated perceptions, including most of those she is experiencing at that time and many memories. But, when necessary, she can alter the idea to include ones that have been left out of this "inadequate" idea. This does not, however, make the "true idea" into an abstract idea.

22. Waxman, however, argues that Hume does not need to rely on language in his account of abstraction. See Wayne Waxman, *Hume's Theory of Consciousness* (New York: Cambridge University Press, 1994), 105–15.

23. Garrett's own interpretation of the Appendix has to do with how certain perceptions—passions, tastes and smells, and certain other secondary qualities—are "no where" (T 1.4.5.10, SBN 235). He thinks that Hume is left with no way to explain how these perceptions are integrated into one person's mind-bundle rather than another person's, since two people could have qualitatively indistinguishable nonspatial perceptions simultaneously (Garrett, "Hume's Self-Doubts," and *Cognition and Commitment*, 180–85). But if this was Hume's problem in the Appendix (and I doubt it, for various reasons that I have detailed in Donald C. Ainslie, "Hume's Reflections on the Simplicity and Identity of Mind," *Philosophy and Phenomenological Research* 62 [2001]: 557–78), it is hard to understand why Hume did not take his invocation of the "idea, or rather impression" of self to be jeopardized, since, for Garrett, Hume takes it to be derived from the idea of self as a bundle of perceptions.

24. Nicholas Capaldi, "Hume's Theory of the Passions," in *Hume: A Reevaluation*, ed. D. Livingston and J. King (New York: Fordham University Press, 1976), 185; and *Hume's Place in Moral Philosophy* (New York: Peter Lang, 1989), 179.

25. Capaldi, "Hume's Theory," 189; *Hume's Place*, 243.

26. Ironically, earlier in the article in which Capaldi "exposes" this contradiction, he writes: "To a large extent, Hume's older and less sympathetic commentators seemed content to expose apparent contradictions in his work. On reflection, these contradictions always turn out to be conflicts between what Hume said and what he should have said if he would remain consistent with his commentator's preconceptions. One may view these lapses, as is usually done, as regrettable, or one may view these alleged contradictions as invalidation of the standing preconceptions about Hume" (Capaldi, "Hume's Theory," 172).

27. Some interpreters take Hume's definition of the self as the object of pride and humility—"that succession of related ideas and impressions, of which we have an intimate memory and consciousness" (T 2.1.2.2, SBN 277)—to be the same as the definition of mind in "Of personal identity" (Terence Penelhum, *Hume* [New

York: St. Martin's, 1975], 87; Mackie, *Hume's Moral Theory*, 160; Capaldi, *Hume's Place*, 168 ff.). I have argued that this cannot be the case in Ainslie, "Scepticism about Persons." Briefly, the problems with abstruseness that I noted above make it unlikely that the idea of mind is what we think of when feeling pride or humility. And when Hume does describe what happens when we feel these passions, he says that our attention turns, not to contemplate our minds, but to "our own qualities and circumstances" (T 2.1.5.6, SBN 287). Furthermore, Hume's use of the modifier "intimate" in his definition of the self as object of pride and humility (T 2.1.2.2, SBN 277) shows that he thinks we come to think of only *some* of our experiences when in the grip of this passion, not all of them.

28. See Jane McIntyre, "Personal Identity and the Passions," *Journal of the History of Philosophy* 27 (1989): 545–57, for some speculations about what Hume means by these two kinds of personal identity.

29. The identity of the Hume Society and the identity of its executive committee can corroborate one another without their being the same as one another.

30. Of course, all of us have complicated social locations springing from many different commitments and qualities. I write as though who someone is could be exhausted by being a philosopher, a generous person, a Briton, or a labourer, only in order to simplify exposition.

Note that who someone is can make a difference to her sympathetic tendencies even if she does not have a conception of herself as that kind of person. Hume points out that when people who share a common concern do not recognize the similarity between them, they will nonetheless sympathize with one another's sentiments more easily than with people who do not share the concern (T 2.2.4.6, SBN 354).

31. Baier makes a somewhat similar point in a different context. In discussing Hume's inability to find an impression-source for the idea of a substantial soul (T 1.4.3.3, SBN 232–33), she suggests that, once the notion of substance is demystified (T 1.1.6.2, SBN 16), such an impression might be "derived from the manner of appearing of *all* a person's impressions, along with her ideas." It would "arise only occasionally, when a somewhat painful effort of reflection is made, such as that in 'Of personal identity'" (PS 128). My interpretation of the "idea, or rather impression" of self in terms of the manner in which our perceptions appear, however, does not involve taking this impression to offer support for a substantial soul of any sort, nor would I take any effort to be involved in perceiving what is, for me, an *ever-present* impression.

32. Baier, *Postures*, 3.

33. Consider another way to put this point: Let the *formal* aspects of a perception be those having to do only with its external relations (i.e., succession or contiguity) to other perceptions; let the *material* aspects of a perception be those having to do with its content (what it is a perception of). Then, whereas our per-

ceptions of space and time would depend on only the formal manner of appearances of perceptions, our "idea, or rather impression of ourselves" would depend on the material manner of appearances of perceptions.

34. Garrett, "Hume's Self-Doubts," 341.

35. The term "intimate" appears in several difficult interpretive contexts in the *Treatise:* in connection with the awareness of self involved in the sympathy mechanism (T 2.1.11.6, SBN 317; cf. T 2.1.11.8, 2.2.4.7, 2.3.7.1, SBN 320, 354, 427); in connection with introspection and the investigation of mind (T 1.4.6.1, 1.4.6.3; SBN 251, 252); and in connection with the definition of self as the object of pride and humility (T 2.1.2.2, 2.1.5.3, 2.2.1.2; SBN 277, 286, 329). (Other uses of this term that are of note can be found at T 1.3.8.6, 1.3.8.15, 1.4.2.7, 1.4.2.38, 2.2.2.15; SBN 101, 106, 190, 206, 339.) I doubt that a consistent reading can be found to make sense of Hume's usage across these contexts.

36. Consider, for example, our perceptions of our body; these are almost always with us, but only rarely at the center of our thoughts. Recall that by including a section on pride and humility in our bodies (T 2.1.8), Hume indicates that bodily qualities play a central role in defining us as persons.

37. I offer my interpretive solution to this perennial problem in Hume scholarship in Ainslie, "Hume's Reflections."

38. Note that the bundle view of the mind first appears at a crucial point in "Of scepticism with regard to the senses" (T 1.4.2.39, SBN 207); if Hume meant to reject the whole bundle view, and not just the account of our belief in the mind's identity, he would have had to revisit the argument from the earlier section in the Appendix.

39. Throughout "Of personal identity," Hume uses the terms "self," "person," and "soul" as synonyms for "mind." In Book 2, Hume treats "person" and "self" as interchangeable terms.

40. Just as Hume treats ideas before discussing impressions, despite the causal priority of the latter to the former, he treats personal identity (T 1.4.6) before discussing embodied, socially-located persons (in Book 2), despite the priority of the latter to the former. (A similar reversal of the expected order of exposition occurs in Book 3, where the discussion of the artificial virtues precedes the discussion of the natural virtues.)

41. See Hume's comment in the first *Enquiry* to the effect that determining when, exactly, thinking begins in a human life is a "frivolous" question. David Hume, *An Enquiry Concerning Human Understanding*, in *David Hume: Enquiries Concerning Human Understanding and Concerning the Principles of Morals*, 3rd ed., ed. L. A. Selby-Bigge and P. H. Nidditch (Oxford: Clarendon, 1975), 22 n.; and *An Enquiry Concerning Human Understanding: A Critical Edition*, ed. Tom Beauchamp (New York: Oxford University Press, 2000), section 2, para. 9, n. 1.

CHAPTER 9

Hume's Voyage

JANET BROUGHTON

Annette Baier's *A Progress of Sentiments*[1] is marvelous: fresh, powerful, and stimulating. In what follows, I want to look at some of its large-scale claims as they bear on Book One of Hume's *Treatise*,[2] and to argue that we can preserve much of what is novel and persuasive about Baier's reading of Book One while adding shadows and shadings to the relatively bright picture of human nature that she thinks Hume has painted.

Permeating Baier's book is the conviction that the *Treatise* narrates a "progress," and that we cannot appreciate Hume's philosophical undertaking if we ignore the sort of book that the *Treatise* is. To say that the book narrates a "progress" is to say several things, as I understand it.

First, it is to say that the book has a shape, that it is not simply a compendium of arguments and claims. Baier reads Hume as having reasons for putting the first parts first and the later parts later. (It is amazing how many readers lack Baier's sensitivity to this point.)

Second, it is to say that the sections and parts and books of the *Treatise* have a narrative order. In this respect the *Treatise* would be more like Descartes' *Meditations*, for example, than his *Principles*. This suggests that we should think of the *Treatise*'s order as a sort of temporal sequencing, at least where there are no literary cues to some more complex narrative order.

So the lower-numbered pages will generally contain an account of thoughts that come earlier in a sequence of thoughts, and the higher-numbered parts tell us about later thoughts.

Third, because the *Treatise* narrates a sequence of thoughts, earlier claims and arguments may well be displaced by later ones, or be modified by them in some other way. I will come back to this point; for now, let me just note an important interpretative maxim that arises from it. Just because Hume says something does not mean it is his view of the subject he is writing about. In this respect, too, the *Treatise* is like Descartes' *Meditations:* Descartes writes that he is "compelled to admit that there is not one of [his] former beliefs about which a doubt may not properly be raised; and this is not a flippant or ill-considered conclusion, but is based on powerful and well thought-out reasons."[3] But that is not his view, of course.

I agree wholeheartedly with these three points, and in the rest of this paper I simply take them for granted. What I do want to explore is a fourth point implicit in the idea that the *Treatise* narrates a progress, and that is the idea that it narrates a successful journey, one that moves us from a less-good position to a better one by way of a sequence of intermediate steps aimed at doing just that. As Baier sees it, the narrator begins in ignorance of the human ideal to which we should aspire. That is our less-good beginning position. If he investigates an inherited ideal—call it a dispassionate, rationalist ideal—he will come to recognize its dangers and its inadequacy. Its dangers are those of radical skepticism, and it is by seeing the skepticism at the end of the rationalist path that the inquirer is enabled to see what is wrong with the path itself. And that helps him to keep moving in the right direction: in turning away from the rationalist ideal, he is encouraged to endorse a different one—call it a sentimental ideal—and to recognize its adequacy and fruitfulness. This step eventually gets him to the better position that is our hoped-for destination.

When I refer to Book One as a progress, I will have in mind all four of these points: shapeliness, narrative sequence, revisability, and achievement of an improved and positive understanding. When I refer to it as an inquiry, I will be thinking just of the first three points: shapeliness, narrative order, and revisability. So I can put the main claim of this paper this way: Book One narrates an inquiry, but not a progress.

To support this claim, I am now going to turn to three tasks. The first is to describe some parts of Baier's interpretation in more detail. The second is to raise some critical questions about it. And the third is to answer these questions by explaining how I think Hume could be narrating an inquiry that is not a progress. This will be to explain where I think we ought to add shadows and shadings to Hume's picture of the human understanding.

Baier sees the first three parts of Book One as all of a piece: a constructive account of the human understanding undertaken by an inquirer who quite properly takes himself to be located in a community of perceivers and language-users who see and talk about each other, and see and talk about a world of other objects, both animate and inanimate (e.g., PS 32–33). Hume's study of human nature can therefore appeal to many facts—"experiments," "observation" (T xix)—about people and things. And what his study uncovers is the very small role played in our ideas, reasonings, and beliefs by "reason," where that means our faculty of demonstration and intuition, and the extremely large role played by custom, association, and the feeling-like aspect of perceptions that Hume calls their force, liveliness, steadiness, firmness, vivacity, or vividness. Let us use the term "sentimental theory" for a theory of the human understanding that brings out the central roles of custom, association, and vividness. For Baier, Hume's main aim in the first three parts of Book One is to develop a sentimental theory of the human understanding.

This general perspective on Parts One, Two, and Three informs many of the more specific interpretative claims Baier makes about them. In places where many of Hume's recent readers have seen skepticism—for example, in Hume's famous account of causal inference—Baier sees instead a sentimentalist correction of philosophers' characteristic preoccupation with the powers of reason. Saying that reason does not give us our causal beliefs does not make Hume a skeptic: he need not be saying that our causal inferences are unreasonable or groundless; he need only be saying that they are not propelled by the faculty that enables us to see that two plus two makes four. Similarly for Hume's claim that causal beliefs arise from the workings of the imagination: that claim identifies the causal origins of such beliefs but does not imply that they are unreasonable.

Baier, however, does not deny that Hume is concerned in Part Three with large-scale questions about the source of the reasonableness of our reasonable causal beliefs. She does think that in the first three parts of Book One, Hume is willing to raise a large question about our causal inferences, and that is the question how it is possible that the workings of the imagination should have normative force.

For Hume, we can put that question in a more specific form: how is it that a person will have good reasons for his beliefs when his imagination operates according to the "[r]ules by which to judge of causes and effects" (T 173)? Let me quickly survey those rules. Some of them simply spell out consequences of Hume's first definition of cause: we should identify an object as the cause of another object only if the first is contiguous to and prior to the other, and only if objects like the first are regularly followed by objects like the second. But other rules go further: "The same cause always produces the same effect, and the same effect never arises but from the same cause"; "where several different objects produce the same effect, it must be by means of some quality, which we discover to be common amongst them"; the "difference in the effects of two resembling objects must proceed from that particular, in which they differ"; "[w]hen any object encreases or diminishes with the encrease or diminution of its cause, 'tis to be regarded as a compounded effect"; and "an object, which exists for any time in its full perfection without any effect, is not the sole cause of that effect" (T 173–74). Hume describes these rules as "all the LOGIC I think proper to employ in my reasoning" (T 175); by following them, "we may know when [objects] really are [causes or effects to each other]" (T 173). I will refer to these rules as causal inference rules.

Baier sees Hume as willing to entertain the question how these rules can have normative force, how it is that following them gives us reasonable beliefs. She argues that for Hume, mental causes amount to good reasons when they can "bear their own survey" (PS 96; T 620); "[t]he [causal inference] rules that Hume enunciates and endorses . . . get their normative force from the fact that reasoning conforming to them has just been demonstrated to be capable of being turned successfully on itself" (PS 92). This is "successful reflexivity"; it allows Hume to "promote" habits into rules with genuine normative authority (PS 91). These are very suggestive claims and might be elaborated in several ways, but the main idea, I take it, is that Hume's sentimental theory explains or predicts its own credibility. I will return to these ideas of norms and reflexivity later.

For Baier, Part Four has a very different character from that of the first three parts, but it, too, represents progress, even though it does not simply develop further the discoveries of the earlier parts. Rather, in Part Four, the inquirer tries out a different sort of inquiry, one that has a different set of background assumptions and perhaps even a different set of data to which the inquirer can appeal.

In Part Four, Baier claims, Hume takes up the position of the "Cartesian intellect" (PS 21) or "determined solipsist" (PS 114) and engages in a "highly intellectual reflection of intellect on intellect and on its sensory data" (PS 106). The results are disastrous. Our prereflective idea of objects arises from a "gross illusion" (T 217) and is "contrary to the plainest experience" (T 210); our philosophical response to these problems is a "confusion of groundless and extraordinary opinions" (T 218). Further reflection shows us that "there is a direct and total opposition betwixt our reason and our senses" (T 231): it is impossible "for us to reason justly and regularly from causes and effects, and at the same time believe the continu'd existence of matter" (T 206). The bad news just keeps coming: "our aim in all our studies and reflections" is to be "acquainted with that energy in the cause, by which it operates on its effect" (T 266); but "when we say we desire to know the ultimate and operating principle, as something, which resides in the external object, we either contradict ourselves, or talk without a meaning" (T 267). To recognize fully the predicament in which these conclusions leave us is to recognize that there is no rational policy of belief to be adopted: "[w]e have . . . no choice left but betwixt a false reason and none at all" (T 268).

Baier argues that these despairing and skeptical conclusions are not Hume's view of the human understanding. Hume as author is executing the narrative strategy of taking up a point of view different from that of the main persona. This allows him to distance himself from this alternative point of view and to reach the despairing skeptical conclusions simply as part of a *reductio* of the cramped conception of human nature from which they emerge.

Suppose that a rationalist theory of the human understanding were correct. Then the human understanding would mainly be an intellect plus a faculty of sense perception. But by steps Hume lays out, any belief held by such a human being would be as reasonable as a contradiction. Hume does not just lay these steps out; he also takes up the perspective of someone holding the rationalist theory. To see why he does this, try it yourself. Suppose yourself to be a human being who holds a rationalist theory and follows out the steps Hume has indicated. You would have to regard as unreasonable all your beliefs derived from reason or the imagination, and so *inter alia* you would have to regard as unreasonable your own basic belief that the human understanding is an intellect plus a faculty of sense perception. Your theory would dictate its own rejection.

I think it is in this sense that Baier sees Part Four as showing how the rationalist conception of the understanding self-destructs. She then sees the final few pages of Book One as the inquirer's transition back to the sentimental conception of human nature developed in Parts One through Three. The inquirer returns to this conception both in the sense that he again endorses it as a correct account of human nature, and in the sense that he understands himself, the inquirer, to have the various powers and tendencies the sentimental theory ascribes to people. Therefore he understands his inquiry as one that can freely draw upon these faculties. Such an inquiry will not end in self-destruction; on the contrary, it will issue in self-approval.

To summarize: In Parts One, Two, and Three, Hume inquires into the human understanding from a perspective innocent of special philosophical presuppositions. He reaches as his conclusion a broad and detailed theory of human understanding, the theory I have been calling the sentimental theory. This theory allows him to claim normative authority for some of the operations of the human understanding, because it permits successful reflexivity. In Part Four, Hume inquires further into the human understanding by taking up the perspective of the rationalist inquirer, who regards the human understanding as mainly intellectual and sees the philosopher as confined in his inquiries to the contents of his own mind. But the deeply negative outcome of that inquiry, its dramatic reflexive failure, shows the inadequacy of its starting point. Seeing this confirms us in our endorsement of the sentimental theory, and returns us to that theory as we prepare to inquire into the passions and into morals.

Let me begin my reflections on this interpretation by looking more closely at Baier's claim that the successful reflexivity of the sentimental theory allows Hume to "promote" habits into rules with genuine normative authority. Let us try to see how this works:

Question (1): How do we form causal beliefs?

Answer (1): We form them through habit, which works as follows: [insert sentimental theory].

Question (2): If a person formed his causal beliefs in the way described by Answer (1), how would he answer Question (1)?

Answer (2): He would answer by giving Answer (1); that is, he would answer that we form causal beliefs through habit, which works as follows: [insert sentimental theory].

I take it that at minimum, Baier is claiming that if it is good to form causal beliefs in the way the sentimental theory says we do, then the person described in Question (2) must give Answer (1) as his answer to Question (1). It is at least a necessary condition for normativity that the theory predict its own endorsement.[4]

But something is amiss in this series of questions and answers. The sentimental theory is a causal account of bad causal reasoning as well as good causal reasoning. Hume aims to explain what goes on in the mind of a Newton, to be sure, but he also wants to explain what goes on in the mind of someone who, while reading the *Meditations*, maintains that Frenchmen have no solidity, or who believes in the healing powers of the bones of long-dead martyrs. If the person we are asking about in Question (2) is prejudiced or superstitious, then he will probably not answer Question (1) by giving the sentimental theory. To bring about successful reflexivity, the person in Question (2) has to be one who reasons according to only one of the several patterns of reasoning that the sentimental theory explains.

Then let us focus just upon the reasoning-patterns of a Newton or a Boyle. If we do, the notion of successful reflexivity might look like this:

Question (1): What are the rules according to which (say) scientists regulate their causal beliefs?

Answer (1): Those rules are as follows: [insert causal inference rules].

Question (2): If a person formed his causal beliefs in the way described by Answer (1), how would he answer Question (1)?

Answer (2): He would answer by giving Answer (1), that is, he would answer that those rules are as follows: [insert causal inference rules].

The trouble here is that this all floats free of the particular account Hume has given of the workings of our minds: it does not turn on acceptance by the person in Question (2) of any of the distinctive features of Hume's theory of the human understanding. Hume's theory is compatible with the claim that some people's beliefs are regulated by the causal inference rules, but this is a much weaker claim than the one for which Baier argues.

My first question, then, concerns what exactly it is that is reflexively endorsing itself here. But I also have a second question about the claim that in the first three parts of Book One, normativity can be understood as connected with successful reflexivity. Does Hume try to make *any* connection in Book One between normativity and reflexivity? In Parts One, Two, and Three, I see no signs that Hume ever entertains any question about whether or how the causal inference rules manage to articulate genuine norms for causal inference. He announces in the Introduction to the *Treatise* that he is going to do for human nature what great scientists had recently done for nonhuman nature. He cheerfully adopts their method of inquiry, as he understands it; only the subject matter is to be different. He is well aware of two complications. One is that his subject matter will include all the ways the human mind can work, not just what happens when it is working well. The other is that because he himself, in conducting this inquiry, is a mind busily reasoning away, a good theory must explain *inter alia* the workings of the theorist's own mind in the production of the theory.

But none of this is to say that Hume sees the norms of scientific inquiry as somehow themselves in need of grounding or validating, or that in Book One he aims to produce such a grounding or validation. One the contrary, the first three parts of Book One seem to me to proceed upon the *assumption* that we ought to reason as scientists reason: that when we adhere to the causal inference rules, we reason carefully and well, and provide ourselves with good reasons for our beliefs. Hume's exploration of the human understanding helps him to articulate the rules, but he gives no specific signs of thinking they are in need of validation, or of thinking he can provide them with validation.

My third question focuses not on the first three parts and their relation to the norms of scientific inquiry, but on Part Four and its devastating skeptical conclusions. For Baier, these conclusions follow from features of a special perspective that Hume takes up in Part Four. This is a perspective distinguished by its solipsism and by its tendency to identify the human understanding with the human intellect. It is also a perspective that Hume repudiates, Baier argues, once he sees the skeptical failure in which it results, for its failure, she claims, is the failure to achieve successful reflexivity.

These are rich and interwoven interpretative claims. The strand I want to tease out and examine is the one that says the argumentation of Part Four arises out of a different perspective from the perspective of Parts One, Two, and Three. I want to give my reasons for thinking that in Part Four Hume does not take up the stance of a "determined solipsist" (PS 114), and that he does not engage in a peculiarly "intellectual reflection of intellect on intellect and on its sensory data" (PS 106).

I will focus here on the second section of Part Four. It is a very long and complex investigation of our idea of physical objects, and in many ways it is Part Four's centerpiece. The first point I want to make about it is that it is an investigation into the causal origins of our idea of physical objects and of our belief in their existence. Hume poses the same kind of question about our belief in the objective physical world that he had posed in Part Three about our causal beliefs. Compare these passages:

> Since it appears, that the transition from an impression present to the memory or senses to the idea of an object, which we call cause or effect, is founded on past *experience*, and on our remembrance of their *constant conjunction*, the next question is, Whether experience produces the idea by means of the understanding or of the imagination; whether we are determin'd by reason to make the transition, or by a certain association and relation of perceptions. (T 88–89)

> Reason can never shew us the connexion of one object with another, tho' aided by experience, and the observation of their constant conjunction in all past instances. When the mind, therefore, passes from the idea or impression of one object to the idea or belief of another, it is not determin'd by reason, but by certain principles, which associate together the ideas of these objects, and unite them in the imagination. (T 92)

> The subject . . . of our present enquiry is concerning the *causes* which induce us to believe in the existence of body. . . . [W]e . . . shall consider, whether it be the *senses, reason*, or the *imagination*, that produces the opinion of a *continu'd* or of a *distinct* existence. (T 187–88)

We may . . . conclude with certainty, that the opinion of a continu'd and of a distinct existence never arises from the senses. . . . [O]ur reason neither does, nor is it possible it ever shou'd, upon any supposition, give us an assurance of the continu'd and distinct existence of body. That opinion must be entirely owing to the IMAGINATION: which must now be the subject of our enquiry. (T 192–93)

Furthermore, in Part Four Hume continues to aim at explaining not just how we get a certain idea, but also why we believe it to be true; indeed, he exerts himself to explain our belief in bodies by fitting it into the theory of belief he had developed in Part Three: "[i]t has been prov'd already, that belief in general consists in nothing, but the vivacity of an idea; and that an idea may acquire this vivacity by its relation to some present impression" (T 208). In Part Four, Hume's naturalistic explanations also invoke tendencies of the imagination that he had not much explored earlier, but they are tendencies of the *imagination*, and take their place within the sentimental theory.

The tendency of the imagination that does the most work in Part Four is our tendency to take ourselves to have had one series of perceptions, (A), when really we have had a different series of perceptions, (B). This tendency arises when having series (A) feels much like having series (B): "[t]he thought slides along [a] succession [of related objects] with equal facility, as if it consider'd only one object; and therefore confounds the succession with the identity" (T 204). Hume says that he is here elaborating a claim he had actually tried out earlier, in Part Two of Book One, and it is worth taking a quick look at the earlier passage.

Hume begins that passage by remarking that when he explained the principles of the association of ideas in the imagination, he made no use of "imaginary dissection of the brain" (T 60) to explain why the mind works that way. But, he adds, there are "mistakes that arise from these [associative] relations," and he feels he cannot "rest contented with experience" that tells us these mistakes occur; he wants to give an "account" of them (T 60). The account he gives is this:

as the mind is endow'd with a power of exciting any idea it pleases; whenever it dispatches the spirits into that region of the brain, in which the idea is plac'd; these spirits always excite the idea, when they run precisely into the proper traces, and rummage that cell, which belongs to the idea. But as their motion is seldom direct, and naturally turns a little to the one side or the other; for this reason the animal spirits, falling into the contiguous traces, present other related ideas in lieu of that which the mind desir'd at first to survey. This change we are not always sensible of; but continuing still the same train of thought, make use of the related idea, which is presented to us, and employ it in our reasoning, as if it were the same with what we demanded. (T 60–61)

This is an unusual passage, the only one in the whole *Treatise*, I think, that makes "an imaginary dissection of the brain." For our purposes, what is significant about it is that it does not show us a solipsistic inquirer, austerely examining intellect by intellect. Hume is drawing as fully as he ever does upon the richly populated realm that Baier describes as the realm of the sentimental theorist, and he is as fully engaged as he ever is in giving a naturalistic—empirical, scientific—explanation of the human understanding, broadly construed. He is happily importing all this into the explanatory project at the heart of Part Four, and his doing so underlines the difficulty of seeing him as working from a radically different perspective than that of the first three parts.

My last question about Baier's reading is a more tentative one. If Hume is narrating a progress, then why does he tell us about his investigations of the deformed theory *after* showing how he developed the rich and successful theory? If he were taking up two different perspectives, wouldn't the narrative have been shapelier if it had begun by showing the failure of the traditional philosophical conception, and then continued by showing how, with a shift of perspective, we can reach a successful conclusion to our inquiry after all?

That, in a way, is how Baier sees the shape of the final and highly dramatic section of Part Four, where the solitary despair to which the rationalist conception drives Hume gives way in the final few pages to the equanimity of the sentimental theorist. But why would someone who had achieved a rich and successful theory of the human understanding have been tempted in the first place to take up the rationalist perspective, and to treat the human understanding as precisely what he has discovered it not to be? I think it is no accident that Baier begins *A Progress of Sentiments* by giving us a close reading of that last section of Book One. On her understanding of Book One, its last section would actually be a natural start for Hume's inquiry.

I have raised four questions about Baier's reading of Book One. The first is whether the notion of successful reflexivity can be made to work with the sentimental theory. The second is whether Hume really allowed room for the question about normativity to which successful reflexivity would have been the answer. The third is whether Hume takes up a new and distinctively rationalist stance in Part Four, and the last question concerns the narrative shape of Book One. I now want to turn to the possibility that Book One narrates an inquiry but not a progress, and that Hume sees the human understanding as a more troubling set of faculties than Baier thinks.

Suppose for a moment that I am right about Parts One, Two, and Three. This would mean that in those parts, Hume never questioned the propriety of the causal inference rules and therefore never thought we could or should promote habits into rules. By reading Hume in this way, we would leave completely untouched most of Baier's specific interpretative claims about the first three parts. We could—and I think should—still see Hume as helping himself to a rich set of "experiments" and "observation" (T xix), still see him as engaged in the construction of a sentimental theory, and still see him as deflating various philosophical pretensions—all without seeing him as any sort of arch-skeptic.

So we would be adding no shadows or shadings in those first three parts. If anything, we would be brightening the picture slightly, by attributing to Hume a cheerful, unquestioning, and ordinary assumption that by following the scientists' method—by following the rules of causal inference—we will acquire reasonable beliefs and form good theories.

But suppose for a moment that I am also right about Part Four, and that in it Hume is extending the sentimental theory to account, among other things, for our forming the idea of the continued and distinct existence of bodies, and for our applying that idea to the objects of our senses. What are we to make of the fact that this extension of the sentimental theory ends in extravagantly skeptical conclusions? Baier can explain these conclusions neatly: they show the failure of reflexivity for the rationalist conception, and they thereby enjoin us to reject that conception and return to the successfully reflexive sentimental theory. But I am saying the skeptical conclusions emerge from the sentimental theory, from a continuation of the scientifically guided inquiry into the human understanding. How can that be?

Here is where I think we must add the shadows and shadings. Let me show a bit more specifically how I would add them in two key spots. Then I will step back and look at the general picture to which I think Hume's inquiry leads us.

Let us first look at Hume's account of our belief in the continued and distinct existence of body. This belief is a fiction, Hume says, and it arises out of operations of the imagination that are intrinsically defective, since they involve mistaking one sequence of experiences for another. In Parts One, Two, and Three, Hume used his developing sentimental theory to deflate the views of certain philosophers. Here in Part Four, though, the sentimental theory explains our belief in the continued and distinct existence of body, but the explanation constitutes a criticism not just of philosophers but of us all.

In Part Three, for example, Hume punctures the claim that every change in a thing *must* be brought about by an antecedent cause, and Locke, for one, ought to be troubled by this result. But it is open to Locke to give up his pretentious modal claim and to settle for the claim that all changes in things *are* brought about by antecedent causes. He could have given up his philosophical claim and its attendant ambitions and have adopted a more sober, scientific, and modest view both of causality and of our knowledge of it. But in Part Four, there is no appealing position for Locke to fall back to, or for anyone to fall back to. Indeed, Hume in a way sympathizes here with Locke for making a philosophical distinction between "ideas" and bodies: Locke at least was sensitive to an absurdity in our ordinary conception and was trying to avoid it. But his attempt fails: the absurdity is simply there, in the idea any of us tries to form of a physical object.

So our basic conception of the physical reality around us is at once unavoidable and deeply flawed. This is one conclusion of Hume's scientific investigation of the human understanding, and it amounts to one sort of shading we must add to his portrait of us.

But worse is to come. As Hume goes on to argue, reflection upon our absurd belief in physical objects shows us that our causal inferences, so happily performed and explained in the earlier Parts of Book One, cannot, after all, be reasonable. Hume's argument here is a difficult one, and I want to sketch it in just enough detail to indicate its strategy.

In Part Four, section 4, Hume argues that the distinction between primary and secondary qualities is the outcome of good causal reasoning concerning our sense perceptions.

> 'Tis certain, that when different impressions of the same sense arise from any object, every one of these impressions has not a resembling quality existent in the object. . . . Now from like effects we presume like causes. Many of the impressions of colour, sound, &c. are confest to be nothing but internal existences, and to arise from causes, which no ways resembles them. These impressions are in appearance nothing different from the other impressions of colour, sound, &c. We conclude, therefore, that they are, all of them, deriv'd from a like origin. (T 227)

But he goes on to argue that the conception of objects that possess just primary qualities is an empty one. It does not seem to be empty: we take ourselves to have the conception of a moveable, solid, extended object. But motion cannot be conceived without extension or solidity, and extension cannot be conceived without color or solidity. Color is excluded from the conception because it is a secondary quality. So the primary-quality conception of an object depends upon the independent conceivability of solidity. But

> [t]he idea of solidity is that of two objects, which . . . cannot penetrate each other. . . . Solidity, therefore, is perfectly incomprehensible alone, and without the conception of some bodies. . . . Now what idea have we of these bodies? The ideas of colours, sounds, and other secondary qualities are excluded. The idea of motion depends on that of extension, and the idea of extension on that of solidity. 'Tis impossible, therefore, that the idea of solidity can depend on either of them. . . . Our modern philosophy, therefore, leaves us no just nor satisfactory idea of solidity; nor consequently of matter. (T 228–29)

As he stresses in the most despairing passages of the last section in Book One, Hume thinks this argument cuts as much against the reasonableness of all of our causal inferences as it does against the reasonableness of our belief in the physical world. It is not "possible for us to reason justly and regularly from causes and effects, and at the same time believe the continu'd existence of matter" (T 266). But it is one and the same "principle" that is responsible for both sorts of belief; the two "operations" of the imagination "are equally natural and necessary in the human mind" (T 266). And Hume says that leaves us no way to "adjust those principles together" (T 266). At best we "successively assent to both, as is usual among philosophers," but we must then ask ourselves "with what confidence [we can] afterwards usurp that glorious title [of philosopher], when we thus knowingly embrace a manifest contradiction" (T 266).

So, I would argue, the negative results Hume reaches in Part Four not only entail that we regard some of our inevitable beliefs as absurd; they also mean that we must revise our prior cheerful assumption that we would have reasonable causal beliefs so long as we kept to the rules of causal inference. Hume did not think he was showing up our causal inferences as unreasonable by showing that they are caused by our imaginations; I am in complete agreement with Baier on that important point.[5] But I do not think that Part Three ends his ongoing investigation of the imagination, and the extension of this investigation in Part Four leads him to take back earlier assumptions and conclusions. Central among them is the assumption that many of us often manage to be reasonable in the beliefs we hold.

So I think we must see a retrospective shadow cast back from Part Four onto the first three Parts. This is the second sort of shading I want to add to Hume's picture of the human understanding. For Hume, the outcome of naturalistic inquiry into the human understanding is that the human understanding operates according to principles—those developed in the sentimental theory—that make reasonable belief in almost anything impossible. And this is a dark outcome indeed.

Or is it? I want now to reflect a little on the different interpretations of Hume I have been discussing: Baier's, and the alternative I have just sketched. At the beginning of this paper I said that I thought Book One was the narration of an inquiry but not of a progress. There is an obvious sense in which, on my view, Hume fails to reach a positive account of the human understanding. There is nothing positive *about* the human understanding: all the news about it is bad. But there is another sense in which Hume might have felt he did give a positive account of us, and that is the sense in which his account, though leading to a negative assessment of us, is definite and complete. That is, he has applied the methods of science to the human understanding, and from that has built up the sentimental theory, a very detailed account of how the understanding works. So even though the theory as a whole implies that we rarely, if ever, hold reasonable beliefs, it is still a good theory. It tells us some truths about ourselves, and even if some of those truths are bleak, arriving at the theory constitutes progress of a sort.

I think it is very hard to judge whether this is a good way to read Hume. For my taste, the last section of Book One, upon which judgments like this must mainly rest, is much too short. I want Hume to have given us a far finer anatomy of his melancholy.

That said, I will venture the opinion that this is not the best way to read Hume. For one thing, it implies that he was insensitive to what happens when we apply the negative outcome of the sentimental theory to the theory itself. If we cannot form reasonable beliefs by following the rules of causal inference, then we cannot think it reasonable to believe the sentimental theory, which is built up by following those very rules. For textual reasons that I will not belabor here, I think Hume is very sensitive to the instability, in this sense, of the theory (see, e.g., T 186–87).

For another thing, Hume seems explicitly to reject a scenario that this "progress of a sort" interpretation invites. The scenario is that we put together all the pieces of the sentimental theory and think through their consequences; we take in the awful truth about ourselves; and then we decide upon the policy of suspending judgment about nearly all that we believe. We may foresee that this is a policy we will soon forsake, but given our self-understanding, it is the only rational policy available. But Hume will have none of this. There is no rational policy for judgment, suspended or otherwise: "[w]e have . . . no choice left but betwixt a false reason and none at all. For my part, I know not what ought to be done. . . . I can only observe what is commonly done; which is, that this difficulty is seldom or never thought of; and even where it has once been present to the mind, is quickly forgot, and leaves but a small impression behind" (T 268).

Let me close by reflecting further on this forgetting, inanition, or blank with which we acknowledge the incapacities of our minds. In a remarkable couple of pages, Hume goes on to describe a sequence of moods and dispositions that his skeptical conclusions precipitate. Perhaps "humors" is the best term for what he describes: he speaks of his "philosophical melancholy and delirium" (T 269), of his subsequent "spleen and indolence" (T 270), and finally of the eventual "returns of application and good humour" (T 273). Hume is aroused from his "spleen and indolence" by the revival of his natural curiosity, and as it revives, he finds that his temperament is more suited to letting science, rather than superstition, be his guide. At the very end of Book One, Hume once again declares himself a scientist of man.

I think it is helpful to recognize that Hume uses irony to indicate the almost indescribable mixture of detachment and commitment with which he once more takes up the scientific inquiry into human nature. But instead of developing that point here, I want instead to say a little about the simple fact that at the end of Book One, Hume *does* pick his inquiry back up. He has two more books to go, one about passions and the other about morals. And in those books he emphatically does not reach the frightening conclusions I believe he reached in Book One.

Shall we say, then, that Books Two and Three narrate a progress of sentiments? "Sentiments" certainly continues to be the perfect word. What about "progress"? Well, yes, but with two caveats: keep moving and don't look down! For example, we can regard ourselves as making progress if we inquire how we can take satisfaction in other people's "tables, chairs, scritoires, chimneys, coaches, saddles, ploughs" (T 364), and if we explain that phenomenon by invoking the workings of sympathy. But we had better not stop to inquire how we form the idea of an objective world of tables and chairs, saddles and ploughs. And we had better not look down, either, lest we begin to follow out the underlying question of how our commonplace observations of life can lend reasonableness to our belief in the theory of sympathy.

But isn't it difficult to keep moving and to keep our eyes trained ahead on our quarry? Hume did not think so: he thought it was the most natural thing in the world, and that the pleasures of philosophy, like those of hunting, lie mainly in the forward motion of the chase (T 448 ff.).

NOTES

1. Annette Baier, *A Progress of Sentiments: Reflections on Hume's "Treatise"* (Cambridge, MA: Harvard University Press, 1991). Further references to this book will be made by giving page numbers in the body of the paper.

2. David Hume, *A Treatise of Human Nature*, ed. P. H. Nidditch (Oxford: Oxford University Press, 1990). Further references to this book will be made by giving page numbers in the body of the paper.

3. René Descartes, *Meditations on First Philosophy*, in *The Philosophical Writings of Descartes*, vol. II, ed. and trans. J. Cottingham, R. Stoothoff, and D. Murdoch (Cambridge: Cambridge University Press, 1984), 14–15.

4. There are places where Baier gives an even richer account of successful reflexivity, and in some of those passages she suggests that successful reflexivity is also sufficient for normativity. The claim I am focusing on, however, is just the claim that it is necessary.

5. See my "Hume's Skepticism about Causal Inferences," *Pacific Philosophical Quarterly* 64 (1983): 3–18.

CHAPTER IO

Artifice, Desire, and Their Relationship

Hume against Aristotle

ALASDAIR MACINTYRE

Why return to topics in Hume's moral philosophy that have been subject to as much and as minute examination as any in the history of philosophy? I do so in hope of throwing some light on how debate between rival Humean and Aristotelian positions may be conducted with most profit to philosophical enquiry. My concern is with Hume's uses of his distinction between the natural and the artificial and his account of the relationship between these, in order to ask what their place is in Hume's overall philosophical enterprise and to contrast his positions with those of Aristotle. I shall not argue for the superiority of one to the other—although it will be evident that I write from one particular Aristotelian point of view—but I shall argue for the importance of confronting the differences between the two rival positions systematically and not only in a piecemeal, problem-by-problem way.

I

Hume was a moralist as well as a moral philosopher. Of Charles I, Hume wrote in chapter 59 of *The History of England* that "his virtues predominated

192

extremely above his vices" and that "his dignity was free from pride, his humanity from weakness, his bravery from rashness, his temperance from austerity, his frugality from avarice," although Hume qualifies this praise by
noting the king's ungracious manner, his superstition, his "deference to persons of a capacity inferior to his own," and his liability to "hasty and precipitate resolutions."[1] Although no other sketch of an individual's character is as extended as the account of Charles I, pithier judgments abound.
The councils of James I "were more wise and equitable in their end, than
prudent and political in the means." Oliver Cromwell was "this fanatical
hypocrite," while Francis Bacon was "admired for the greatness of his genius,
and beloved for the courteousness of his behavior," yet lacked the strength of
mind to keep his "intemperate desire of preferment" in check and by his
prodigality laid himself open to the temptation to take bribes. *The History
of England* is a history of moral character. What, then, are the standards
governing Hume's moral judgments? He had already explained them in the
Treatise.

Moral approbation is given to those judgments and actions which express natural impulses and sympathies that are common and natural to
human beings: "we always consider the *natural* and *usual* force of the passions, when we determine concerning vice and virtue; and if the passions depart very much from the common measures on either side, they are always
disapprov'd as vicious" (T 483).[2] Deviations from this standard of moral approbation are of at least two kinds. First, "some defect or unsoundness of the
passions" (T 488) may be such that, for example, we allow self-interested desires too influential a part in determining our actions. In the natural course
of things our tendencies to this kind of immorality are often corrected either
by our interactions with others or by the influence upon our judgments and
actions of the impersonal standpoint of that shared evaluative language in
which we have learned to give voice to our moral approvals and disapprovals
(E 228).[3] But such lapses into excessive self-interest are not the only source
of deviation from the standards of moral approbation.

We may instead be influenced by the adoption of motivating beliefs
which interpose themselves between our natural impulses and sympathies
and our actions, so that we are no longer pleased or pained as are "the rest
of mankind." The lives of those thus influenced Hume calls "artificial," to
mark their deviation from the standard of nature.[4] Not all artificiality is,
on Hume's view, deviant. The rules and institutions of justice are notably

artificial constructions, but it is natural sentiment and sympathy that motivate us to conform to them. The artificiality of deviant lives, such as those
of Diogenes the Cynic and Pascal, is by contrast a result of the beliefs that
motivate the actions of those who lead such lives. Such was the influence
upon Diogenes of philosophical beliefs and upon Pascal of religious beliefs
that what pleased or pained them was not the same as what pleases and
pains those whose actions are governed entirely by natural sentiment and
sympathy.[5]

Annette Baier has drawn our attention to the importance of Hume's
discussion of motivating beliefs in Book One of the *Treatise:* "Firm beliefs
about what is good can activate the will and influence the passions almost
as strongly as do present pleasures."[6] A belief, that is to say, may present the
passions with objects not hitherto entertained as objects of possible attraction or aversion, so that some new attraction or aversion is elicited and some
new motivation established. Not every idea is capable of so moving us, for,
were this to be so, the mind "would never enjoy a moment's peace and tranquility" (T 119). But it is clear that a range of very different beliefs may so
motivate and that, since different individuals will encounter and accept different and sometimes incompatible beliefs, there will be a corresponding
range of differences in what pleases and pains individuals.

Hence there will be an important contrast between those whose moral
judgments and actions give expression to sentiments and sympathies natural to human beings and those whose moral judgments and actions to some
significant degree give expression to passions informed by and directed toward intentional objects supplied—artificially supplied—by different motivating beliefs. The former, when responding to the same actions in the same
circumstances (on the relevance of circumstances, see *A Dialogue*), can be
confidently expected to concur in their approvals and disapprovals, because
of the "uniformity in the *general* sentiment of mankind" (T 547 fn.), a uniformity ascribed in the *Enquiry* to "some internal sense or feeling, which virtue has made universal in the whole species" (E 173). The latter will be apt
to disagree both with the generality of humankind and with each other, and
it is this disagreement that is exemplified in the contending enthusiasms of
Diogenes and Pascal.

Suppose now that someone who had already become aware that her or
his moral judgments do in fact conform to the standard of the natural and
usual is confronted by the rival claims of these and other conflicting moral

ideals. Such a one may then enquire just what it is, on Hume's view, that makes the standpoint of the generality of humankind superior to such alternatives as those presented by Diogenes and Pascal. James King has supplied three closely related answers to this question. The first is that the attitudes and practices of those guided by natural sympathies and sentiments, those who, in the words of Palamedes in *A Dialogue*, "adhere to the maxims of common life and ordinary conduct," are corrigible in a way that artificial lives are not: "Experience and the practice of the world readily correct any great extravagance on either side."[7] King thus contrasts the openness to change of the one with the inflexibility of the other.[8] But on Hume's account, not all change would be accounted a correction. And the only available standard by which a change may be judged a correction rather than an aberration is the standard provided by "the *natural* and *usual* force of the passions." So the appeal to corrigibility presupposes the very standard that is in question, and the force of that appeal will depend upon whether or not we already accept that standard.

King's second answer is that morality in its history has generally been just what Hume declares it to be and that artificial moral systems therefore lack continuity with "our historical morality."[9] Perhaps this is so, perhaps not. But, even if it is so, it is clear that the force of this consideration, too, will depend upon whether or not we already accept the very standard that is in question. For it is only if we identify with and judge in accordance with the standpoint of the generality of humankind that we will be disposed to give these particular continuities in the history of morality this kind of weight. From any rival standpoint it will be deviation from and discontinuity with the morality that has prevailed in these episodes of continuity that will be valued.

Note that I am not disagreeing with King that, in general, openness to correction by experience and continuity with inherited moral tradition may on occasion be important characteristics for judging between the claims of rival and contending moral systems. What I am arguing is that, if these characteristics are understood in specifically Humean terms, as they must be to preserve the consistency and integrity of a Humean position, the appeal to them will not strengthen, because it already presupposes, Hume's account of the standard of moral judgment. King's third suggested reply is not question-begging in this way, but it brings to light a further difficulty. In the course of an acute, courteous, and apt criticism of my own earlier and too brief discussion of these issues,[10] King pointed out that I had neglected to notice that "Hume holds that an artificial system is not an alternative moral response, but an alternative to a moral response."[11] So someone who enquires why it is better to judge in accordance with the standard of "the *natural* and *usual*" might be told that judgments which depart from this standard, as all artificial judgments do, are not moral judgments, but expressions of merely idiosyncratic alternatives to morality. Yet those convinced by this reply have a problem.

For if they were now to offer as a reason in support of their particular moral judgments, that those judgments conform to the standard of the *natural* and *usual* rather than to some idiosyncratic nonmoral standard, those judgments would no longer be the direct expression of their natural sentiments and passions, but instead would be the direct expression of their belief that we ought to judge in such a way as to give expression to those sentiments and passions. And the interposition of such a belief between their natural responses and their judgments would, by Hume's criterion, make their motivation artificial. It follows that even if moral judgments do generally conform to the standard of the natural and the usual, neither conformity to that standard nor any further reason adduced in support of that standard can function as a reason for particular moral judgments or for particular actions in accordance with those judgments. Except in our instrumental reasoning, when we judge that some particular course of action will effect some particular outcome which it would be virtuous for us to bring about, we can have, if Hume is right, and as he himself insisted in the *Treatise*,[12] no reasons for our judgments as to how we should act. And Hume's own moral portraits in the *History* and in *A Dialogue* must therefore invite responses of sympathetic agreement in feeling rather than any concurrent reasoning. The condemnations of Diogenes and Pascal are themselves no more than expressions of feeling.

To this it may be said not only that it is unsurprising, but that it is scarcely a criticism. It is, after all, Hume himself who insists upon the limitations of reason and defines those limitations so as to make this kind of conclusion inescapable. The moral portraits of the *History* and the critique of artificial lives in *A Dialogue* stand or fall with Hume's fundamental theses about the relationship of reason to the passions. It would be difficult to disagree. But perhaps the groundlessness of Hume's rejection of artificial lives reveals a weakness in those fundamental theses. This is the possibility that I want to entertain in this paper.

The type of artificial life with which I will be concerned is neither that of the Jansenist not that of the Cynic. It is rather the type of life commended in the *Nicomachean Ethics*, a type of life about which Hume is remarkably silent. In his third year at Edinburgh University, Hume would have been introduced to Aristotle's ethics and politics, but his writings exhibit only occasional traces of this introduction. In his earliest extant essay his use of the expression "a just mean" may be intended as an allusion to Aristotle, and in the *Enquiry* he quotes "the Peripatetics" as holding that "a due medium" is "the characteristic of virtue" (E 231). His essay "The Populousness of Ancient Nations" has incidental references to the *Ethics*, the *Politics*, and the *Generation of Animals*, but only as a historical source.[13] And there are a small number of other passages in which Aristotle either is or may be referred to, but never as a major contributor to moral philosophy. So in the face of this noteworthy silence it may be worthwhile to confront Hume with Aristotle and to consider both how Hume would have had to characterize Aristotle's point of view and how Aristotle would have had to characterize Hume's.

II

"[I]t appears evident," wrote Hume, "that the ultimate ends of human actions can never, in any case, be accounted for by *reason*, but recommend themselves entirely to the sentiments and affections of mankind, without any dependence on the intellectual faculties" (E, Appendix I, 293). He illustrates his point by citing explanations of action in which an agent, having first accounted for his doing x by avowing that he desires y and that he judges x to be a means to y, accounts for his desire for y by declaring that he is pleased by y—or perhaps pained by the absence of y—thus terminating his explanation. "If you demand *Why? It is the instrument of pleasure*, says he. And beyond this it is an absurdity to ask for a reason."

Set alongside this is what Aristotle asserts in the *De Anima:* "Now intelligence [*nous*] does not move without desire [*orexis*]. For wish [*boulēsis*] is [a species of] desire [*orexis*], and whenever someone is moved in accordance with reasoning, she or he is indeed moved in accordance with wish [*boulēsis*].

But desire [*orexis*] also moves contrary to reasoning, for appetite [*epithumia*] is [a species of] desire [*orexis*]" (433a22–26). The translation of *boulēsis* by "wish" is conventional, but not altogether happy. Irwin contrasts *boulēsis*, *epithumia*, and *thumos* by saying that "Rational desire, wish, *boulēsis*, is for an object believed to be good," while "Appetite, *epithumia*, is nonrational desire for an object believed to be pleasant," and "Emotion, *thumos*, is non-rational desire for objects that appear good, not merely pleasant, because of the agent's emotions."[14]

Aristotle's conception of *prohairesis*, that act from which the actions of the virtues (and the vices) issue, is also relevant. He speaks of *prohairesis* as "deliberative desire [*orexis bouleutikē*]" in which "the reason must be true and the desire right" (*Nicomachean Ethics* 1139a23–24). The conventional translation of *prohairesis* by "choice" is, as Irwin notes,[15] misleading, since Aristotle allows for the occurrence of choice without deliberation. What is distinctive about "*prohairesis*" is, according to Irwin, that it is not only the outcome of deliberation, but also of "a wish, a rational desire for some GOOD as an END in itself."[16]

What these passages from Aristotle and Irwin's apposite glosses on them bring out, first of all, is the contrast that Aristotle draws between the good and the pleasant as objects of desire. This is a contrast that Hume cannot allow: "good and evil, or in other words, pain and pleasure" he says in the *Treatise* (T 439), and consistently with this, he never speaks of a good except as that which pleases or is a cause of that which pleases or of an evil except as that which pains or is a cause of that which pains. So there can be no desire for goods independent of desire for pleasures. It follows that Hume is unable to make another distinction, one between two different kinds of relationship in which pleasure may stand to good.

I may on occasion treat pleasure itself as a good, that is, I engage in some activity, just because it or its consequences are pleasant. But I may also on occasion take pleasure in having achieved some good, where the good is an end valued just because and insofar as it is good, and the pleasure is incidental to or, as Aristotle puts it, supervenes upon the end (*Nicomachean Ethics* 1174b33). Aristotle is as aware as Hume is of the ubiquitous and pervasive parts that pleasure and pain play in the practical life (1104b2–1105a16), but his standpoint allows us to recognize complexities which Hume's idiom obscures from view, among them that, just because what pleases and pains the virtuous differs from what pleases and pains the vicious, we cannot make pleasure into a neutral standard by reference to which we can demonstrate that the life of virtue is superior to the life of vice. Diderot, in *Le Neveu de Rameau*—written, but not published in Hume's lifetime, nor indeed in Diderot's—demonstrated this once and for all by the splendid defense of the pleasures of the intelligently vicious life that he put into the mouth of the younger Rameau. Hume, by contrast, follows a long line of engaging but naïve moralists in inviting his honest readers to consider how much greater their pleasures are than are those of sensible knaves (E 282–83).

This identification of goods with causes of pleasure and evils with causes of pain was perhaps forced upon Hume by his moral epistemology. That epistemology and the psychology that Hume developed from it require us to find a source for our motivations and our expressive judgments and behavior in some type of internal impression from which passions arise, and pain and pleasure do seem to be just such impressions. Hence, goods and evils can find a place in Hume's scheme only by being identified either as pleasures and pains or as causes of pleasures and pains, thus conceived. Does this Procrustean treatment of goods and evils give us reason to reject at least some features of Hume's epistemology? Part of the attraction of Hume's moral epistemology has been its naturalism, that is, its foundation in a psychological and sociological account of human nature. And the fear of those who have been thus attracted has at least sometimes been that, if "good" is not construed as naming a property definable in terms of pleasure and pain, it would have to be defined as the name of some property that could not be accommodated within a naturalistic scheme. Naturally enough, therefore, those would-be naturalists who have rejected the detail of Hume's moral epistemology and its accompanying psychology, for example, his identification of virtue with "the power of producing love or pride" and vice with "the power of producing humility or hatred" (T 575), have taken the only other course that seemed guaranteed to avoid the nonnaturalism that they feared: they have preserved the expressivism of Hume's account of particular judgments of virtue and vice, so that according to them "good" no longer names a property, whether "natural" or "nonnatural," but they have generally detached that expressivism from Hume's psychology. It may be, however, that we can avoid the unfortunate conflation of the good with the pleasing without resorting to either nonnaturalism or expressivism. Indeed it is the claim of this paper that Aristotle has shown us how to do so. But the force of that claim depends on the evaluation of a second thesis that emerges from the texts of Aristotle that I have quoted.

This second thesis is that desire for one's good or for what contributes to one's good is rational desire. Desires may fail to be rational in two ways. First, those who allow themselves to be moved by *epithumia*, so that their aim is pleasure *qua* pleasure, on occasions when they need for the sake of their ultimate good to achieve some good other than pleasure, are moved by desire contrary to reasoning (see *De Anima* 433a25–26, quoted above). When desire moves in accordance with reasoning, that reasoning need not be something that such individuals have actually rehearsed to themselves on this or that particular occasion. It is indeed the reasoning that justifies their practical conclusion that this particular action ought to be done here and now, if this or that particular good is to be achieved, some good whose achievement in this particular situation is that which will best contribute to the agent's overall good. And it must be the agent's own reasoning in this sense, namely, that it is the reasoning that the agent her or himself would articulate as her or his own, if that agent were to have occasion so to articulate it, and if that agent possessed the necessary powers of articulation. But the inarticulate may be virtuous as well. And it is possible for an inarticulate agent to have directed her or himself, at the level of practice, toward the end for the sake of which she or he acts, and in so doing to have implicitly grasped the *archē*, the first principle of the reasoning justifying the action, without having been able to make that reasoning explicit. Indeed, no one, however articulate, can first achieve a practical grasp of that type of principle by reflective reasoning. "Reason is not the teacher of first principles," wrote Aristotle, with reference to both mathematics and actions; it is virtue that is the "teacher of correct belief about the first principle" (*Nicomachean Ethics* 1151a17–19). And in the case of actions, virtues are acquired only through habituation (1103a14–26), a type of habituation that issues in true beliefs about the relevant goods.

For Aristotle, then, our initial natural responses are generally morally and politically inadequate. We can only understand that inadequacy after those initial responses have been transformed so that they are informed and directed by true beliefs about goods. From Hume's standpoint, what Aristotle commends as rational practice is of course just one more artificial form of life, one more idiosyncrasy to be catalogued. And this judgment could only be reinforced by considering a second way in which Aristotle supposes that our desires can fail to be rational.

Boulēsis is desire for what we take to be our good, but what appears to us to be our good may not in fact be such. Even if I am directed by *boulēsis* rather than by *epithumia*, my desires may, as a result of false judgment, fail to direct me to that good which, if I were rational, I would try to achieve. What makes it contrary to reason, on Aristotle's view, to desire what I falsely take to be my good? The answer can be framed in straightforwardly Humean terms. That such and such is or is not my good here now is a matter of fact, and matters of fact belong to the province of reason. Practical reasoning that has among its premises a false judgment as to goods is unsound reasoning.

To this, the Humean may retort that no claim about matter of fact can move us to action. Only some passion or desire can do that. And to this, the Aristotelian reply is to agree: no action without *orexis*. But among the species of *orexis* is *boulēsis*, and the objects of *boulēsis* are specified by the agent's beliefs about her or his good. To assign this function to the agent's beliefs about her or his good is, of course, once again to incur the Humean charge of artificiality in motivation, a charge to which the Aristotelian cannot but plead guilty. And what is thereby made clear is that what makes it impossible for Hume to find application for any concept of rational desire is not only his conflation of goods with pleasures or causes of pleasure and of evils with pains or causes of pain. It is also his distinction between artificial and natural motivation.

III

There is, however, one significant respect in which Aristotle's standpoint differs from those of Diogenes and Pascal, Hume's exemplars of artificial lives and manners. Pascal's "illusions" were, on Hume's account, the outcome of "religious superstition," while Diogenes' "illusions" were produced by "philosophical enthusiasm." It is not just that in their lives beliefs operated so as artificially to inhibit or distort their natural motivations, but also that their particular beliefs derived from false religion and misguided philosophy. But the beliefs about our good which, on Aristotle's account, are presupposed by and find expression in our practical judgments and our actions are, initially for everyone, and throughout their lives for many, pretheoretical beliefs, convictions arrived at—at least in the first instance—through practical training.

There is, says Aristotle, general agreement on giving the name *"eudaimonia"* to the human good, even although there is disagreement as to what it consists in. What then is it about which there is this disagreement? It is the nature of human flourishing. In thinking about that nature, we do well to begin by considering the indispensability of the concept of flourishing for our understanding of the lives and activities of members of other species. Students of nonhuman animal behavior generally presuppose rather than spell out in explicit terms what it is for a member of the particular species whom they are studying to flourish *qua* member of that species. But a contrast between the course of normal and natural development for a dolphin or a gorilla or a cheetah in some particular environment and the variety of factors that may frustrate or interrupt that development is inevitably part of the presupposed background when explanations of the histories of particular individuals or groups are advanced. And we can generally identify both those types of relationship and experience that contribute to the achievement of their flourishing by individuals and groups of such nonhuman species and the characteristics that such individuals and groups have to acquire in order to flourish. In ancient Greek it would not have been linguistically odd to speak of the *aretai*, the virtues, of such nonhuman animals. Yet it may be thought that the application of the concept of flourishing to dolphins or gorillas or cheetahs is uncontroversial in a way that the application of the concept of human flourishing cannot be. For unresolved disagreement about the standards by which individuals or societies are to be evaluated in respect of their flourishing or their failing to flourish is a salient feature of any extended discussion of this topic. Yet here we need to distinguish between two kinds of disagreement, namely, those that are always incidental to and sometimes ineliminable from serious and sustained enquiry, whether practical or theoretical, and those that are generated by a variety of other types of cause.

Human beings are by their nature enquiring animals, and their enquiries cannot but direct them toward the question: how should we live, if we are to flourish, and how are we to identify and then confront those harms and dangers that threaten the possibility of our flourishing? By the different ways in which they live, human beings from different cultural and social backgrounds already presuppose different and rival answers to this question.

And, if and when they come to the point of making those answers explicit, they also often disagree on how the question is to be framed. Thus, in periods in which systematic enquiry on how to answer this question is generated, both the initial disagreements that groups and individuals bring to the debate and the disagreements that develop in the course of the enquiry have to be taken into account. But this does not mean that some answers are not better than others or cannot be shown to be better as a result of rational debate. And it does not mean that individuals and groups may not arrive at conclusions which they have good reason to accept as the best conclusions so far to emerge from such enquiry, conclusions that they may have even better reason to accept, if subsequently those conclusion are able to withstand— doubtless with some revision and emendation—not only internal criticism, but also each further challenge that is presented to them from some rival point of view. Disagreement about what human flourishing consists in does not then of itself show that there is not application for that concept.

Consider now disagreements with other sources. It is a central Aristotelian thesis that failure or frustration in achieving the kind of life which exemplifies *eudaimonia* is in some types of case inseparable from misconception of and false beliefs about both the human good and subordinate goods. It would, for example, be impossible to conceive of the life that takes money-making for its ultimate end as the best life for human beings without some failure both in those particular virtues that prescribe certain attitudes toward money, such as liberality, and in those several virtues that require us to place other goods above money and to recognize acquisitiveness as such, *pleonexia*, as a vice. And it would be equally impossible to conceive of the life directed towards the achievement of honors as its ultimate end as the best kind of life for human beings without a failure, symptomatic of more than one vice, to distinguish between those whose judgments concerning desert and merit ought to be respected by rational agents and those whose judgments on these matters are corrupted or confused.

Aristotle's scheme of the virtues and vices is thus explanatory as well as prescriptive, and it purports to explain some types of disagreement about the nature of human flourishing. But these are not Aristotle's only explanatory resources. To flourish, individuals require citizenship in a *polis*—or in whatever form of political community corresponds to the *polis* in their particular social order—and the possibilities of individuals flourishing are enhanced or diminished by how their particular political community fares.

But the well-being of a *polis* depends on certain preconditions, and in the *Politics* Aristotle considers both the material and the educational preconditions of such well-being, including the need for an adequate supply of pure water (1330b3–7 and 11–17) and the kind of regimen necessary for the health of citizens (1335a5–11). Aristotle observes that the recognition of health as a good is apt to vary with the health of the individual making the judgment (*Nicomachean Ethics* 1095a24), but he never brings into adequate or indeed any explanatory relationship those failures in achieving a true conception of the human good that are due to individual vices and those that are due to the absence of one or more of the preconditions for the well-being of a *polis*. Aristotle's account is therefore incomplete, although it is not difficult to envisage ways in which it could be completed. What makes this kind of incompleteness important?

The answer is not just that Aristotle's ethics and politics are explanatory as well as prescriptive. It is that the soundness of its prescriptive claims depends in key part on the success of its explanatory claims. This is something ignored or even seemingly denied in some recent interpretations of Aristotle's ethics whose authors have focused on the perspective and situation of the agent, at the expense of attention to the presuppositions of an Aristotelian account of that perspective and situation. It is true that a well-habituated agent, in directing herself or himself to the performance of that action which the virtues require in this particular situation, will often have in mind only that this proposed action is to be done just because it is what justice or courage or temperateness requires, and will generally not take into account in her or his immediate deliberations that it is also to be done for the sake of achieving *eudaimonia*, the kind of life that constitutes human flourishing. Yet, on Aristotle's view, an action cannot be that which is immediately required by the virtues, unless it is also that action which in this particular situation best contributes to the achievement of *eudaimonia*, either as a constitutive part of a flourishing life or as a means to some future activity or state that is part of such a life. And for this to be true, a particular account of the causes and effects involved in the genesis of this particular action must be true. Agents, their passions and actions, their social relationships, and the ends which they pursue individually and in concert with others are *causally* interrelated. We need to remember that Aristotle's ethics and politics claim that the theoretical articulation of a mode of practice would be impossible, if the psychology of agents and the structure of their social relationships were not of a certain kind. Aristotle's ethics and politics are therefore vulnerable to refutation by empirical findings of the psychological and social sciences, and, where they are relevant, of biological science. And, if Aristotelianism is to be capable of solving some of its own internal problems—those arising from the incompleteness and the need for revision of its explanatory accounts—it will have to draw on resources afforded by those sciences. In this sense, then, Aristotelian ethics is naturalistic: its conception of human goods and human flourishing finds application within an explanatory scheme of cause and effect. This causality is to be understood in terms of Aristotle's fourfold classification of causes, and explanation is to be understood correspondingly.

One large and continuing obstacle to thinking of Aristotelianism in these terms has been the modern division of academic labor between philosophy and the natural and social sciences. Philosophy, including moral philosophy, is taught in the large majority of colleges and universities as a wholly conceptual, nonempirical form of enquiry, distanced from and independent of the psychological, social, and historical sciences. Political philosophy, under the rubric "political theory," is indeed taught in political science departments, but usually in a manner that insulates it from the findings of empirical political science. Study of and commentary on Aristotle's *Ethics* and *Politics* therefore generally proceed without reference to and without impact upon psychological and social enquiry.

A second and related obstacle derives from the fact that, on an Aristotelian view of the practice of the virtues, it is only possible to understand their nature by first having been initiated into and habituated in that practice. This follows from the Aristotelian claim that how one judges about the virtues, practically or theoretically, depends upon whether and how far one is virtuous, a claim that, as I noticed earlier, has an important part to play in the explanation of disagreement. It follows that we cannot teach Aristotle's ethics and politics from an evaluatively neutral standpoint. *Either* it is taught from some standpoint external to the relevant type of practice, in which case it is no longer in fact Aristotle's ethics and politics that are being taught, but a rendering of them into some form of theory detached from practice, allegedly capable of being understood and evaluated prior to and independently of any engagement with practice; *or* it is indeed taught as the theoretical expression of the relevant type of practice, practice in which teacher and students are equally participants, in which case there is no place for it in the contemporary academic curriculum. For that curriculum is one in which moral theory is systematically severed from, and studied in independence of, practice.

In both these respects, Humean moral philosophy is at analogous disadvantages. Hume's moral theory is, as I suggested earlier, the philosophical counterpart of his history. The moral judgments that find application in *The History of England* are just those which Hume had distinguished in the *Treatise* from a variety of types of deviant judgment. Hume's moral commitments and his philosophical understanding of the virtues are to some significant degree inseparable. It does not follow, of course, that someone who accepts the substance of Hume's philosophical position cannot also quarrel with some of Hume's moral and political positions. A contemporary Humean can and should disown, for example, Hume's embarrassing male eighteenth-century attitudes toward women with no more difficulty than a contemporary Aristotelian can and should disown Aristotle's even more embarrassing male fourth-century attitudes. Nonetheless, Hume presents himself, just as Aristotle does, as a teacher of morals as well as of moral philosophy, a role for which there is no place in the conventional curriculum of modern academic philosophy.

Moreover, Hume's claims require support from and are open to refutation by the findings of the psychological, social, and historical sciences, just as much as are Aristotle's. Hume proposes to us a politics as well as an ethics and a social psychology of both. The presentation of Hume's thought under the constraints imposed by the dominant contemporary conception of philosophy—that is, philosophy understood as a purely conceptual enterprise, independent of the enquiries of psychology and the social sciences—is bound, therefore, to offer us a greatly diminished and distorted Hume, one who in moral philosophy is sometimes nothing more than an ancestor for modern expressivism.

Happily, the notable flowering of twentieth-century Hume scholarship has provided the resources for rescuing Hume from this fate, just as the best of Aristotelian scholarship—including some Thomistic Aristotelian scholarship—has provided the means for rescuing Aristotle from attempts to recommend his thought in fashionable late-twentieth-century terms. Annette Baier's *A Progress of Sentiments* is the most remarkable achievement so far of this work of scholarly interpretation. "Hume," she writes, "was initiating not the science (in our sense) of psychology, either introspective or experimental, but a broader discipline of reflection on human nature, into which Charles Darwin and Michel Foucault, as much as William James and Sigmund Freud, can be seen to belong."[17] And her own work has itself been a notable contribution to that broader discipline. But it is not a discipline for which the structures of the conventional curriculum afford anything like adequate space, any more than it provides the space for the development of Aristotelian modes of enquiry in contemporary terms.

What is thereby excluded is not only the comprehensive presentation of two very different ways of reconceiving the relationships between philosophy and the human sciences, but also the possibility of any systematic and ongoing debate between the protagonists of an Aristotelian ordering of enquiry, the protagonists of a Humean study of human nature, and the defenders of the established academic order.

IV

One focal set of issues in that debate would concern the distinction which provided the starting point for the arguments of this paper, namely, that between the natural and the artificial. So it may be appropriate to conclude by raising some further questions about this distinction. It is a commonplace that both Aristotle and Hume speak of nature and the natural in different ways and senses and that both show themselves well aware that they are doing so. Aristotle, for example, contrasts natural dispositions to virtue with genuine virtues (*Nicomachean Ethics* 1144b1–14). The difference between the two is that the latter require a capacity for practical reasoning, a capacity developed only by habituation. But this development accords with and is required by our specific nature as rational animals. In one sense of "natural," therefore, it is natural for us to go beyond the natural virtues (in another sense of "natural") to the genuine virtues.

For Hume, too, the natural is generally not to be identified with the merely untutored. But while, for Aristotle, the natural development of human beings requires the acquisition of sets of beliefs whose part in generating action has the effect of making their way of life, in Hume's terms, artificial, Hume understands the natural development of human beings as one in the course of which they have to avoid both such distortions as those due to excessive self-love or violent passions, and such distortions as are due to the replacement of their natural impulses and motivations by artificial impulses and motivations deriving from such beliefs. Natural development, that is to say, requires conformity to certain constraining conditions. This led J. L. Mackie to argue that what Hume calls the natural virtues are themselves "another set of artificial virtues" since "interpersonal, impartial, objectifying approval," which is characteristic of the natural as well as of the artificial virtues, is contrived to serve the same social ends as that served by the artificial virtues.[18] And Annette Baier endorses Mackie's view that some measure of artifice is essential in arriving at the standpoint of the natural virtues.[19]

Nonetheless, the type of artifice required by the natural virtues has a distinctive function, namely, that of preventing interference with or inhibition of the expression of sentiments that, were their social circumstances and their inherited custom the same, would issue in one and the same set of judgments by all human beings who are not victims of religiously or philosophically grounded illusions. The natural condition of humankind is one of moral agreement and hence derives from what Hume takes to be an observable uniformity of moral sentiment. This is why the natural is, on Hume's view, also taken to be the usual and the artificial the unusual. Indeed, "there is such an uniformity in the *general* sentiments of mankind" as to render "of but small importance" questions concerning in what sense it is that "we can talk of a *right* or a *wrong* taste in morals, eloquence, or beauty" (T 547 fn.).

In Hume's explanatory scheme, then, the distinction between nature and artifice is used to explain those differences and disagreements in moral and aesthetic judgments that are not due to the different situations of those making such judgments, to differences in inherited habits and customs, or to individual psychological differences. So, part of Hume's explanation of the differences between certain ancient polities and those of modern Europe is that "ancient policy was violent, and contrary to the natural and usual course of things." He contrasts Spartan and Roman attitudes by saying that the Roman republic was "supported on principles somewhat more natural."[20] Hume's ambitions are very similar to Aristotle's. Both aspire to recognize the full extent of moral, social, and cultural diversity and conflict. Both aspire simultaneously to draw from the resources of philosophical enquiry grounds for asserting one particular set of moral and evaluative positions as that which alone gives expression to human nature rightly understood. Both recognize that their enterprise must therefore be on a large scale; it must embrace in a more or less integrated way a range of topics that comprehend the entire study of human nature. And the scale of their enterprises is part of what makes it so difficult to provide a compelling account of how we should adjudicate between their rival claims.

Contemporary philosophy for the most part avoids this problem by treating large-scale and systematic philosophies from the past as assemblages of particular theses and arguments directed toward the solution of particular present-day philosophical problems. And, up to a certain point, this has been a rewarding strategy. Hume's view of reason and the passions or Aristotle's account of the practical syllogism, for example, are matched against contemporary desire-and-belief accounts of action. Or, Aristotle's or Hume's conception of causality is treated as a rival to contemporary conceptions. But this piecemeal treatment of problems characteristically issues in apparently ineliminable philosophical disagreements and in a number of rival solutions to each set of problems, each with its own protagonists.[21] There are too few constraints upon what is to be accounted a solution to a problem.

This suggests that, while we can never afford to neglect what is to be learned from such piecemeal approaches, we also need to take seriously the systematic character of the Aristotelian and Humean enterprises and to confront system with system, placing our emphasis on the interrelated character of the different theses and arguments defended by each. It is this task with which I have tried to make a beginning in this paper.

NOTES

1. David Hume, *The History of England*, vol. 5 (Indianapolis: Liberty Classics, 1983), chap. 59, 542.
2. T followed by the page number refers to David Hume, *A Treatise of Human Nature*, ed. L. A. Selby-Bigge and P. H. Nidditch (Oxford: Clarendon Press, 1978).
3. E followed by the page number refers to David Hume, *An Enquiry Concerning the Principles of Morals*, in *Enquiries*, ed. L. A. Selby-Bigge and P. H. Nidditch (Oxford: Clarendon, 1975).
4. David Hume, *A Dialogue*, in *Enquiries*, 343.
5. Hume, *A Dialogue*, 342–43.

6. Annette Baier, *A Progress of Sentiments* (Cambridge, MA: Harvard University Press, 1991), 159.

7. Hume, *A Dialogue*, E 341.

8. James King, "Hume on Artificial Lives with a Rejoinder to A. C. MacIntyre," *Hume Studies* 14 (April 1988): 80–81.

9. King, "Hume on Artificial Lives," 80.

10. Alasdair MacIntyre, *After Virtue*, 2d ed. (Notre Dame, IN: University of Notre Dame Press, 1984), 230–33.

11. King, "Hume on Artificial Lives," 84.

12. See T II, iii, 3.

13. David Hume, "Of the Populousness of Ancient Nations," in *Essays Moral, Political and Literary*, ed. Eugene F. Miller (Indianapolis: Liberty Classics, 1985).

14. See Terence Irwin's "Annotated Glossary" in *Nicomachean Ethics*, trans. Terence Irwin (Indianapolis: Hackett, 1985), 394.

15. Irwin, "Glossary," 393.

16. Irwin, "Glossary," 392; the capitals are Irwin's, and his reference is to *Nicomachean Ethics* 1111b26, 1113a2, and 1113a15.

17. Baier, *Progress*, 25.

18. J. L. Mackie, *Hume's Moral Theory* (London: Routledge and Kegan Paul, 1980), 129.

19. Baier, *Progress*, 178–79.

20. Hume, "Of Commerce," in *Essays Moral, Political and Literary*, 259.

21. See on this my *Three Rival Versions of Moral Enquiry* (Notre Dame, IN: University of Notre Dame Press, 1990), 10–14.

CHAPTER 11

Hume and Morality's "Useful Purpose"

DAVID GAUTHIER

I

"Or what theory of morals can ever serve any useful purpose, unless it can show, by a particular detail, that all the duties which it recommends, are also the true interest of each individual" (E.IX.II, 280)?[1] Is Hume right to insist that duty is contained within interest? And does his own theory show that it is?

To discuss these questions, I want to draw a distinction that Hume ignores. Consider the duty, or presumed duty, of promise-keeping. Is it contained within interest if (1) it is in one's interest to be a promise-keeper— someone who acknowledges the duty of promise-keeping and is thereby motivated to keep his promises, or (2) it is in one's interest to keep one's promises—if acts of promise-keeping are at least normally in one's interest? One may believe that the benefits of being reputed a promise-keeper outweigh the costs of actually keeping promises, and that one is most likely to be reputed a promise-keeper if one actually is a promise-keeper. In this case, one will think it in one's interest to be a promise-keeper even though particular acts of promise-keeping are frequently costly. The dutiful disposition will be contained within interest, even if the dutiful actions are not.

212 ß PERSONS AND PASSIONS

So, I shall divide Hume's question into two. What theory of morals can serve any useful purpose unless it can show (1) that the dutiful dispositions it recommends are the true interest of each individual, or else (2) that the dutiful actions it recommends are the true interest of each individual? When I ask if Hume is right to insist that duty is contained within interest, I am primarily concerned with whether dutiful dispositions must be in one's interest.[2] In considering his views, however, it will be necessary to keep both in mind.

But why does it matter? Why need duty be contained within interest, in either of the senses I have distinguished? First, why does it matter for Hume? If we may suppose that the account of moral motivation in the *Treatise* is in the background of Hume's argument in the *Enquiry*, then what may seem a partial answer is easily found. For in the *Treatise*, Hume insists that *"no action can be virtuous, or morally good, unless there be in human nature some motive to produce it, distinct from the sense of its morality"* (T.III.II.I, 479). No action can be a duty, then, unless there is some motive to produce it distinct from the sense of duty. Duty does not afford an original motive to action. Hence, a theory of morals must show that the duties it recommends are the object of some prior, nonmoral motive.

But why should the motive be interest? Again, a partial answer is suggested by the *Treatise*. Hume claims that it is only our interest in justice, arising "when men observe, that 'tis impossible to live in society without restraining themselves by certain rules" (T.III.II.VI, 533), that originally motivates just behavior. But although the artificial duties of justice, promise-keeping, and allegiance require this foundation in interest, why must all our duties be contained within it? For Hume recognizes that we are naturally disposed to benevolence, gratitude, and other estimable traits of character.

II

To continue, we need to understand Hume's view of moral motivation. He does not deny that a person can be motivated to act by an appeal to duty, but he supposes that duty can be motivationally effective only as a stand-in for some nonmoral disposition. We are naturally disposed to gratitude, and, because it contributes to making us agreeable to our fellows, we morally approve this disposition and consider it a virtue. A person who finds herself without the usual disposition to gratitude will disapprove of this lack and hate herself, as Hume argues, on that account; she may be led to act as if she were grateful, either to develop her sense of gratitude or to conceal her want of it (see T.III.II.I, 479). This is moral motivation; in effect, it enlists moral approval and disapproval to supply the lack of a virtue.

But what of disapproved dispositions—vices? A person who finds herself with a vice will disapprove of it. Will she then hate herself for her vicious disposition, and be led to act as if she did not possess it, either to weaken it or to conceal its existence? Hume does not consider the role of moral motivation in relation to vices. If he were to offer the account I have just suggested, however, he would need to amend his claim that when a person performs "an action merely out of regard to its moral obligation, . . . this supposes in human nature some distinct principles, which are capable of producing the action, and whose moral beauty renders the action meritorious" (T.III.II.I, 479). In the case of vice, a person would not be morally motivated to produce an action which some distinct principle is capable of producing, but rather motivated not to produce such an action. Perhaps, however, Hume would be willing to say that when a person refrains, out of moral obligation, from performing some action, there must be some distinct principle capable of producing that action, whose moral ugliness would render the action opprobrious.

A theory of morals must be able to show that the duties it recommends are the objects of nonmoral motivation. But whatever Hume may think, we should not equate all nonmoral motivation with interest, much less "true interest." And even if we do, we do not yet have a clear account of the link between the utility of a moral theory and the relation between duty and interest. I suggest we seek this account in the view of Christine Korsgaard, who interprets Hume as employing the test of *reflective endorsement* for the assessment of moral claims.[3] To serve a useful purpose, a moral theory must become the object of reflection, and its claims must then be reflectively endorsed. But reflection proceeds from some standpoint. For Hume, she claims, there are two relevant standpoints, one determined by the interest of the agent, the other by his moral capacity itself.[4] In the question with which we began, Hume is drawing attention to the former standpoint. The duties recommended by a moral authority must be endorsed when the agent reflects on them from the perspective determined by his true interest.

Korsgaard introduces the further idea of *reflexive* endorsement, which arises when we consider whether morality endorses, or approves of, itself.[5] I shall return to this kind of endorsement, which must be quite different from the reflective endorsement of interest, but the latter is my immediate concern. Why is reflective endorsement relevant as a test for a moral theory? Introducing it as a test seems merely to assume that duty must be contained within interest. No justification for this has yet been offered.

The question with which I began immediately precedes Hume's purported demonstration that his own moral theory passes the test it imposes. In the discussion leading up to this question, Hume speaks of "our interested *obligation*" to "merit or virtue," and proposes "to inquire whether every man, who has any regard to his own happiness and welfare, will not best find his account in the practice of every moral duty" (E.IX.II, 278). Clearly, then, we should understand a person's "true interest" as consisting in "his own happiness and welfare," so that the endorsement of interest concerns well-being, and not whatever a person might take an interest in, unless the satisfaction of his interest affects his well-being. This seems to me to limit the test of interest in a way that makes it unsuitable for Hume's purpose. For I argue that, although a first-person test of the form that Hume proposes is appropriate, a test with the limited content of personal well-being is too narrow. Hume, after all, insists that morality cannot be derived simply from self-love, but rather requires the presence of other sentiments, all of which we may take as affecting the scope of a person's interests. And so if the practice of every moral duty promotes the realization of a person's interests, broadly defined as those things in which he takes an interest, then he has reason to endorse the practice from his own standpoint.

The appropriateness, and indeed necessity, of a first-person test may best be understood in terms of Bernard Williams' insistence that "Practical deliberation is in every case first-personal, and the first person is not derivative or naturally replaced by *anyone*."[6] He goes on to say that "I can stand back from my desires and reflect on them, and this . . . can be seen as part of the rational freedom at which any rational agent aims. . . . [But t]he *I* of the reflective practical deliberation is not required to . . . be committed from the outset to a harmony of everyone's deliberations. . . . The *I* that stands back in rational reflection from my desires is still the *I* that has those desires."[7]

Williams' view is hardly uncontroversial. But, although I cannot argue the matter here, I believe that it is nonetheless sound. Practical deliberation addresses the question of what to do from the standpoint of the doer; neither Kantians nor utilitarians, it seems to me, have grasped this fundamental point. What others who view the situation from quite different standpoints would endorse is not of any direct relevance, although nothing precludes the deliberator from introducing these considerations, or any others, in an effort to answer his question. If there is a weakness in Williams' account, it is in its emphasis on desire. Although the I that reflects is, no doubt, also an I with desires, it need not privilege its desires in its deliberations. I want to insist that the rational freedom realized in deliberation frees a person from any direct dependence on desire and leaves open the possibility that reflection will lead the agent to quite new concerns—which may give rise to desires but are not grounded in them. But however desires enter practical deliberation, they need not do so as egoistic or agent-directed. This is the basis for my unwillingness to allow Hume the standpoint of interest, conceived in terms of personal well-being, as central to reflective endorsement. If a moral theory is to serve any useful purpose, it must show that the duties it recommends are binding from the standpoint of rational deliberation—a standpoint from which the person's true well-being will usually be of deep, but not necessarily exclusive, concern.

We should suppose, therefore, that Hume's question has been reformulated to remove any pressure on "true interests," while retaining the perspective or standpoint of the agent. I shall speak of the deliberative endorsement of moral duties, and I shall suppose that it is normally motivationally efficacious, either indirectly in ratifying the appropriate natural motivation, or directly, since endorsement would be pointless if one did not normally act in accordance with it. On the face of it, morality itself will then play, as Hume insists, a secondary motivational role. I shall consider in due course whether its role is actually secondary, and whether we should agree with Hume's particular account of that role.

III

In agreeing with Williams, I am supposing that Hume is right to seek to contain duty, if not within interest (as Hume construes it), then within the framework of deliberative endorsement. This is to subject morality to a nonmoral test. At a later point, I will consider whether such a test is appropriate, and whether it compromises the status of morality. But for the present I turn to my second question: does Hume succeed in showing that morality receives deliberative endorsement? And since my concern is primarily with Hume's account, I shall grant him what I have just denied, namely, that deliberative endorsement must proceed within the framework of the agent's interest, truly conceived. So, does Hume's theory succeed in showing that duty must receive the endorsement of interest?

For Hume, moral approbation is of course directed to those mental qualities that are "*useful* or *agreeable* to the *person himself* or to *others*" (E.IX.I, 269). And he suggests that "it would surely be superfluous to prove" that characteristics useful or agreeable to the person, or those "*companionable* virtues" which are agreeable to others, "are desirable in a view to self-interest" (E.IX.II, 280). As for qualities useful to others, such as "the enlarged virtues of humanity, generosity, beneficence," Hume insists that should we be "apprehensive lest these social affections interfere, . . . with private utility. . . . [W]e are but ill-instructed in the nature of the human passions" (E.IX.II, 281). He claims that "the immediate feeling of benevolence and friendship, humanity and kindness, is sweet, smooth, tender, and agreeable"; they "are . . . attended with a pleasing consciousness or remembrance," and almost assure us of the "good-will and good wishes" of others, who would "show a jealousy of our success in the pursuits of avarice and ambition" (E.IX.II, 282). Thus, he makes light of any hesitation we might have about acknowledging our interest in those traits of character which receive our moral approbation—with the notorious exception of justice.

But should Hume be so sanguine? I think not. No doubt, qualities useful to oneself will receive the support of self-interest. But qualities which may make a person agreeable in the company of some may make him or her loathsome in that of others. Partiality to one's friends makes one useful to certain others and may, in suitable circumstances, be recommended by self-interest, but is not always compatible with fair dealing. One may take pleasure in one's forthrightness and willingness to speak one's mind on every occasion, but such traits may give offence to others, and be a detriment to advancing one's aims.

Hume asks us to "let a man suppose that he has full power of modelling his own disposition, and let him deliberate what appetite or desire he would choose for the foundation of his happiness and enjoyment" (E.IX.II, 281). Of course, the outcome of such deliberation will reveal those characteristics that he would favor from the standpoint of self-interest. But these need not be the characteristics that, given the kind of person he is, he actually finds agreeable. No doubt he would choose characteristics that would make him agreeable and useful to some other persons, but there is no reason to think that he would aim indiscriminately at the agreeable and useful. It seems unlikely that Andrea Dworkin and Rush Limbaugh, were they modeling their dispositions, would choose those characteristics that would make them agreeable to each other. Indeed, since what is agreeable or useful to some is disagreeable or harmful to others, persons must be selective in aiming at the agreeable and useful.

Hume presupposes a harmony that human life does not exhibit, whether within each individual or among different individuals. His account of moral approbation and his view of the relation between moral approbation and deliberative endorsement ignore the centrality of conflict—and conflict, among persons, is one of the foundations of morality. Hume is no doubt right to reject the idea of a penitential morality, "full of austerity and rigour" (E.IX.II, 280). But he clearly recognizes that "'tis impossible [for men] to live in society without restraining themselves by certain rules" (T.III.II.VI, 533). Neither every form of agreeableness nor every form of usefulness ultimately proves conducive to the social harmony of which morality is one of the main pillars. These qualities themselves must be restrained, not to achieve a gloomy asceticism, but to make social life mutually beneficial and acceptable.

IV

Hume must show that moral approbation, although logically independent of interest, is directed at characteristics which a person would in fact choose with a view to his interest. He does not succeed, even when he restricts himself to traits of character that are directly agreeable or useful. His argument does not improve when he comes to the one virtue which, as even he acknowledges, is troublesome for his position—justice. Here, the "sensible knave" enters the account with his claim that "in particular incidents, an act of iniquity or infidelity will make a considerable addition to his fortune, without causing any considerable breach in the social union and confederacy" (E.IX.II, 282). The sensible knave is of course right in what he says. We must consider whether what he has said is enough.

The sensible knave agrees "That *honesty is the best policy*, may be a good general rule." He does not claim that one always or even usually does better to act in a dishonest or unjust way. But he insists that the rule "is liable to many exceptions; and he . . . conducts himself with most wisdom, who observes the general rule, and takes advantage of all the exceptions" (E.IX.II, 282–83). The sensible knave thus holds that the dutiful *actions* which justice recommends are not all of them in the true interest of the individual, and therefore the *policy* of being just, although "a good general rule" (E.IX.II, 282), should be rejected in favor of one that recommends actions insofar as they are in the individual's interest.

At the outset of this paper I distinguished between dispositions that were in the agent's interest and actions that were in his interest. But the sensible knave rejects the relevance of this distinction. In claiming that one should observe the general rule but take advantage of all the exceptions, he is, in effect, assuming that the disposition which is in the agent's true interest is the one which leads him to act on each occasion in his interest. In response, Hume declines to argue on the knave's terms, but attends instead to the "inward peace of mind, consciousness of integrity, a satisfactory review of our own conduct" (E.IX.II, 283), which, he claims, attend justice. He emphasizes "above all the peaceful reflection on one's own conduct" (E.IX.II, 284). And while this reflection attends, as Hume says, to conduct, it depends on awareness of the underlying disposition or traits of one's character. Insofar as we think ourselves to be persons disposed to justice, and so see in our conduct not an accidental but an intentional conformity to the virtue, our reflection affords us satisfaction and peace of mind. Or so Hume claims.

Gerald Postema has discussed Hume's reply to the sensible knave at length. He notes that the knave must keep "a central governing principle of . . . [his] life . . . from public knowledge." But this prevents him from receiving from others "the confirmation essential to one's own sense of self." Even if he successfully deceives others and thereby receives their approbation, he knows that their approval is "in sharp contrast with . . . [his] own judgment of himself," so that he cannot interpret their approval as an affirmation of what he is. And without this affirmation, he cannot reflect on his own conduct "without inward conflict. . . . He cannot bear his own survey."[8] But Postema argues that Hume has implausibly overstated his case, for he himself recognizes that one's social contacts are limited, and that one needs only the affirmation of family and friends, not that of all of the members of society to whom justice is owed. Perhaps a Stalin could not experience inner peace, but a man who deals honorably with those in his own social circle may find little to unsettle him in reviewing his rapacious behavior toward those outside that circle.

Postema's criticism may, however, be of greater concern to us than it would have been to Hume. For Hume limits the boundaries of justice to those who maintain "intercourse for mutual convenience and advantage" (E.III.I, 192). Beyond these boundaries, social rules and constraints would serve no useful purpose and would not be the object of moral approbation. He might then argue that the community within which one seeks the confirmation essential to one's sense of self is the community within which justice is binding. But is this a plausible claim? The community of affirmation, as we might call it, is surely much more circumscribed than the community of advantage. Those on whom we depend for our sense of self are a more limited, more intimate group than those on whom we depend, and who reciprocally depend on us, for mutual well-being. Perhaps the members of the small tribes of hunter-gatherers who were our remote ancestors enjoyed coincident communities of affirmation and advantage, but we depend, if not, like Blanche Dubois, on the kindness of strangers, then on their willingness to treat with us in order to ensure mutual benefit.

This willingness affords Hume a better answer to the sensible knave than any he actually offers. Briefly, if a person wants to be accepted by others in cooperative arrangements for mutual advantage or benefit—and such acceptance is surely in one's interest—then she needs to be regarded by her fellows as one who may be trusted to refrain from acts of iniquity or infidelity, and so as one who is genuinely disposed to justice. And the best way to be regarded as just is indeed to be just. Even though the just person's actions may sometimes prove contrary to her own interest, or would not, considered in themselves, receive her deliberative endorsement, yet she may expect, given the way in which others regard her, to enjoy opportunities that others would deny her if she were always disposed to pursue her own concerns. And she may reasonably expect the value of these opportunities to outweigh the costs incurred in her receiving them.

Hume does not offer this argument in response to the sensible knave. But there seems no reason why we should not offer it on his behalf. Within the community of advantage, each of us wants to be regarded as trustworthy and fair, not solely by our intimates and familiars, but by all with whom we might come to interact, friends and strangers alike. Each wants a certain reputation, and, the argument goes, the best way to gain this reputation is to deserve it. To be sure, some persons will no doubt gain an undeserved reputation for probity and thereby be able to take advantage of their trusting fellows, but their success, if success it be, runs contrary to the reasonable expectations a person should entertain in forming her character (or that others should entertain in training her character). And of course, some persons will be raised in circumstances which give them little control over their characters, and others in circumstances which either blind them to the benefits of trustworthiness or deny them its benefits. The argument is not addressed to these persons, but to the *sensible* knave, who has the normal opportunity to shape or model his own character and who lives in a community in which mutual trust has taken root and affords mutual benefits.

This argument may be usefully connected with Hume's insistence, in the *Treatise*, that "There is no passion . . . capable of controlling the interested affection, but the very affection itself, by an alteration of its direction" (T.III.II.II, 492). He continues by noting "that the passion is much better satisfy'd by its restraint, than by its liberty." The claim here cannot reasonably be understood as the claim that on some occasions, one furthers one's interest better by restraint, for this is clearly false. Rather, I suggest, what Hume recognizes is that one furthers one's interest better by being the sort of person who characteristically exercises restraint, because in being that sort of person, one fits oneself for mutually advantageous interactions with others. And so he supposes that one redirects one's interest, by disposing oneself to restraints imposed by obligations of justice, allegiance, and promise-keeping. These I take to encompass what the sensible knave challenges in the *Enquiry*, although he names only the first.

In her response to my paper "Artificial Virtues and the Sensible Knave," Annette Baier emphasizes the importance of redirection of interest in Hume's argument. In her reading of the *Treatise*, she claims that "there are four successive versions of the interested passion" (which she identifies with "the passion for increase"), where the succession is determined by "the changes in what the salient scarce goods are," brought about by the successive artifices or social conventions of property, transfer, promise (or contract), and government.[9] At each stage, the new convention brings with it a new obligation, and this obligation is grounded in the need for each to internalize the convention in her own conduct if she is to realize her share of the benefit. Baier supposes that what I am terming "internalizations" are treated by Hume as redirections. I have no quarrel with this, provided we are clear about what redirection involves. As I have noted, in the passage in which Hume introduces an alteration of direction, he also speaks of restraint. It is not enough to suppose that the interested passion redirects itself to a different set of goods, or to actions that would secure them, related to new artifices or conventions. Rather, this redirection requires restraint in the pursuit of the former set of goods, one which affects the agent's opportunities in such a way that the objective pursued, "the acquiring possessions," as Hume puts it (T.III.II.II, 492), is better satisfied. Thus Baier is right to insist that, with the introduction of promises, persons must redirect their interest to encompass reputation—the reputation of trustworthiness—as a good. However, it is necessary to note that although this concern with reputation requires one to forego opportunities to benefit oneself directly in acquiring material possessions, it may also be expected indirectly to yield one greater opportunities to benefit.

Consider again the two interpretations of Hume's question with which I began. If we agree that our interest is redirected by social conventions, should we then suppose that Hume may claim that the dutiful actions his theory recommends are in the true interest of each individual, because these actions are the outcome of redirected interest? Or should we suppose rather that dutiful actions require the restraint of interest, but that the dutiful dispositions his theory recommends are in the true interest of each individual, because they are the result of interest redirected in the light of social conventions? On my interpretation, Hume should claim the latter. He should, as I have said, grant the sensible knave that particular acts of iniquity or infidelity may, on occasion, directly serve the interest of the agent, but then deny that the disposition to perform such acts may reasonably be expected to serve her interest. He should recognize, as he does, that interest must be restrained, and insist that the fact of being disposed to exercise such restraint itself better satisfies interest.

It may seem misleading to speak of interest both as redirected and as restrained, since if interest were genuinely redirected, it would not then need to be restrained. But I have distinguished two roles of redirection and restraint, and I have suggested that we think of interest as redirected from acts to dispositions, which then restrain interest in acts. However, a clearer formulation of what I believe to be Hume's view could be expressed in terms of deliberative endorsement. The person disposed to justice is guided in her deliberations by considerations of what is just, not only by considerations of what advances her interests or, more generally, her particular concerns. In being disposed to justice, she comes to endorse actions she would not otherwise endorse. And so, we may say that she redirects her deliberative endorsements. She does not redirect her concerns, which she expects to advance more effectively, albeit indirectly, but she does restrain the direct pursuit of her concerns. Thus instead of supposing that one thing—interest—is both redirected and restrained, I treat deliberation as redirected, and concerns, which include interests, as restrained.

Let me now return to my earlier claim that Hume should tie duty to deliberative endorsement but should not rest that endorsement solely on interest. The argument in support of restraining dispositions may easily be detached from its Humean basis in personal interest and extended to embrace whatever concerns individuals acknowledge. As long as each sees her concerns as capable of being advanced through cooperation with her fellows, then there will be structures of constraint in place, embracing the virtues of justice, promise-keeping, and allegiance; these she can endorse. Of course, this is not to say that any set of social conventions will gain acceptance; each person must be able to see that her own concerns are benefited by the conventions, and benefited commensurately with those of her fellows. History should convince us that the artifices Hume considers—property and exchange, promise and contract, government—need not be devised to entitle each person to expect to benefit in the pursuit of her concerns. But we may agree with Hume that they may be so devised, and if they are, they invite the deliberative endorsement of each person.

v

Let me focus the discussion by asking how far Hume succeeds in exhibiting morality within the framework of deliberative endorsement, given that for him this involves an appeal to true interest. I suggest that he actually does better with justice than with some of those virtues whose deliberative status he finds unproblematic. For even if his own defense of justice is unconvincing, we have seen that a better one is available to him. But as long as he supposes that moral approbation is directed at whatever traits of character are pleasing or useful, either to their possessor or to others, he allows it too much scope. Given that, as I have noted, what is pleasing to one person or in one context may be displeasing to another person or in other circumstances, and similarly, what is useful to one person or in one context may be detrimental to another person or in a different context, approbation needs to be selective if it is to provide a coherent and harmonious assessment of a person's character. And we should not expect such an assessment to be easily or readily attained.

Suppose we agree with Hume that our initial tendency is to approve dispositions that are pleasing or useful, whether to their possessor or to others. But suppose we are displeased by the contradictions that arise in our approbation when the same act or disposition has both pleasing and displeasing, or both useful and harmful, effects. Hume will have no difficulty in supposing both that we are motivated to make our moral approbation harmonious, and that morality approves itself reflexively insofar as this harmony is realized. The reflexive test, therefore, allows us to distinguish sound from misdirected moral approbation; we approve rightly of what we approve of approving.

Moral approval, on this account, is quite distinct from deliberative endorsement. But by restricting genuine moral approval to what satisfies the reflexive test, we have weakened a strong objection against supposing that the character traits or dispositions which morality recommends will also be deliberatively endorsed. We could weaken this objection still further if, as I argued earlier, we let deliberative endorsement invoke all of an agent's concerns and not (as Hume does) merely those identified with interest. Even so, we have no reason to assume that, on Hume's account, moral approval and deliberative endorsement will always coincide. I shall return later to the importance of this.

Nevertheless, I argue that incorporating the reflexive test adds plausibility to Hume's account of moral motivation. Recall that he considers that the motivational role of duty is to substitute for the want of the usual motive to virtuous action. Generosity, which naturally motivates us to share our goods with others, is a virtue. We are aware of the benefits the generous person confers on his fellows, and so approve of generosity, and, we may reasonably assume, approve of our approving it, for it fits harmoniously with other agreeable and useful characteristics. A person who lacks natural generosity will wish to avoid the moral self-disapproval associated with that lack, and so will be moved to act as if he were generous; in this way, the thought of duty is effective.

I noted earlier that for Hume, moral motivation is of relatively secondary importance; it comes to the fore only in circumstances where the agent may easily lose sight of her interest in a social convention—as the sensible knave does. But, as I have now argued, Hume overlooks its role in resolving the incoherence and disharmony present in much of our indiscriminate approval and disapproval of acts and dispositions. This disharmony reflects an underlying conflict among the traits of character that naturally influence our behavior. In the face of this conflict, moral approbation plays both an adjudicative and a motivating role. A person who is disposed, say, to extravagant spending, and finds himself welcomed in some circles on this account, may nevertheless reflexively curb the favorable view of himself that this welcome encourages and come to disapprove of his excess. Hating himself for what he judges to be a vice, he curbs his desire to spend beyond his means; he is moved by "a certain sense of duty" (T.III.II.I, 479), as Hume would have it. But note that here, a sense of duty does not strengthen or serve as a substitute for the usual and appropriate nonmoral motivation; rather, it weakens and serves as a counter to what may be a usual but nevertheless inappropriate nonmoral motivation. In the absence of his reflexive moral disapproval, the extravagant person would have no effective curb on his tendency to overspend. Thus, moral approbation can have a more extensive, and somewhat different, motivational role than Hume himself recognizes.

Much would need to be done to work out the details of this Humean account of moral approbation, and only by doing so could we say more precisely how far it meets the test of deliberative endorsement. But I shall not attempt to do this. I want rather to reflect on the overall plausibility and adequacy of such an account. In introducing the idea of a reflexive test, in which morality considers whether it approves itself, I have been influenced, as I noted previously, by Christine Korsgaard's recent account of Hume's moral theory. But I have not followed Korsgaard in some of the details of her account. Korsgaard supposes that moral approval of justice depends on the general effects of just and unjust actions, and finds a problem in sustaining this approval in those particular instances in which, for example, an unjust act would have beneficial consequences.[10] In contrast, I suppose that moral approval, like deliberative endorsement, is addressed to the consequences of possessing the relevant disposition, and so, in the case of justice, of being a just person. It is not addressed solely to the effects of the actions motivated by the disposition, although these, of course, are among the consequences. Other considerations, such as the effects of possessing such a disposition on a person's reputation, will also be relevant. Someone may recognize that a particular just action may not have good consequences, and yet favor it because it expresses a just disposition, the possession of which she morally approves.

V I

My interpretation—and emendation—of Hume's account seems to offer an attractive way of relating moral approval and deliberative endorsement. It does not reduce moral approval to a particular kind of deliberative endorsement; the standpoint of moral approbation retains its independence. It provides a distinct and significant role for moral motivation. But attractive as it may be, does it relate moral approval and deliberative endorsement in the right way? Why should approbation have to satisfy a nonmoral test? Some, of course, would argue that deliberative endorsement, understood as an exercise of practical reason, and carried through fully, is not a nonmoral test. This is Kant's position, which many persons continue to find plausible. But Kant builds universality into deliberative endorsement, whereas Hume and I restrict it to the standpoint of the agent. And on the face of it, the agent's standpoint does not provide a moral test—although we shall shortly see reason to think otherwise.

I want to distinguish a stronger and a weaker form of the nonmoral test. The stronger form, which has been the focus of my discussion, is that a theory of morals must show that each virtue, and hence each morally approved character trait, receives deliberative endorsement. The weaker form is that a theory of morals must show only that each virtue does not face deliberative rejection; this may be further weakened by requiring merely that each virtue not face deliberative rejection by most persons. A theory of morals which failed this doubly weak test would represent moral virtues in frequent opposition to those character traits that would serve an agent best in realizing his concerns. I shall not speculate on what reasons, if any, might

226 PERSONS AND PASSIONS

lead us to accept a theory which failed the doubly weak test. I merely note that were we to accept such a theory, we would do well to abandon morality.

Hume, I suggest, would have done well to employ the doubly weak test. Since he does not seek to moralize rationality or to rationalize morality, he could admit that for some persons, true interest would exhibit indifference or, in rare cases, opposition to some virtues. He would, of course, insist that for most persons, true interest would pronounce favorably on most virtues. This would be quite enough to ensure that his theory of morals had a useful purpose. But what could he say about the negative cases? What need he say about them?

His message should be addressed to us—to those whose moral sentiments form "the *party* of humankind against vice or disorder" (E.IX.I, 275). Our task is threefold: to seek to cultivate and strengthen the moral sentiments as widely as possible, to support social practices and attitudes that bring the interests and concerns of most persons into fuller harmony with their moral sentiments, and to sanction, both formally and informally, those who choose the role of the sensible knave. It is, we might say, our practice, and not Hume's preaching, that will convert the knaves, if anything will. Those whose interests lead them to neglect their moral duties need not be mistaken. However, we have an interest in making them mistaken, both negatively, by punishing their neglect (and so making it contrary to their interests), and also positively, by changing the circumstances that reward and hence encourage that neglect. Hume could then say that a theory of morals must show that every morally approved character trait would be deliberatively accepted by most persons as one to develop in themselves and to promote in others.

I began with Hume's question, "What theory of morals can ever serve any useful purpose, unless it can show, by a particular detail, that all the duties which it recommends, are also the true interest of each individual?" I first proposed that we understand this as requiring the theory to show that every dutiful disposition which it recommends is in every individual's true interest. The theory may then allow that particular dutiful acts, considered in themselves, are contrary to one's interest. I then urged that we remove the egoistic pressure exerted by "interest" and seek to relate dutiful dispositions to deliberative endorsement, taken as reflecting all of a person's concerns, and not necessarily only his interests. I supposed that the dutiful dispositions or virtues recommended by Hume's theory are those dispositions to approve (and disapprove) which themselves are approved—which satisfy the reflexive test of moral approval. And finally, I proposed that the test of endorsement be weakened, so that we require only that the theory show that every dutiful disposition or virtue is one that most persons on reflection will accept for themselves and encourage in their fellows.

The attractiveness of this account is, I believe, clear. Nevertheless, it seems to me to establish the tie between morality and deliberation in a way that is inadequate. Hume treats the two as quite separate: "Having explained the moral *approbation* attending merit or virtue, there remains nothing but briefly to consider our interested *obligation* to it, and to inquire whether every man, who has any regard to his own happiness and welfare, will not best find his account in the practice of every moral duty" (E.IX.II, 278). Although morality's claim upon us requires that it has a useful purpose, for Hume this purpose is extraneous to moral approval, considered in itself. If this purpose provides the ultimate claim that morality makes on us, then that claim is a nonmoral one. I raised earlier the question whether subjecting morality to a nonmoral test is appropriate. For Hume, it would seem that it is appropriate, but only because morality in itself lacks authority.

I urge instead that a deliberative test is appropriate for morality because rational deliberation itself has a moral dimension. We may begin from the idea that, in deliberating, a person ultimately decides what it makes sense for her to do by developing a conception of a fulfilling life and relating her decisions to it. Morality does not enter this account until we consider interaction among persons and recognize the fundamental problem posed by such interaction, namely, that if each does what makes sense in her own terms, the outcome is frequently less than optimal. It is worse for each person, considered in that person's own terms, than at least one of the possible outcomes that would result were each to act differently. It then makes sense for each person to agree with her fellows to develop and sustain in herself, and to encourage in others, constraining dispositions that reorient each person's deliberations toward what makes mutual sense, and so is useful to all. These constraining dispositions, which prepare each person to be a welcome participant in mutually beneficial interactions, give rise to the duties that invite reflexive moral approval. Each refines her sense of what is truly useful so that she comes to approve those dispositions that pass the test of agreement. And since these dispositions give rise to actions that have come to receive her deliberative endorsement, she approves of her approving. What a person rightly approves, then, is determined by what she rationally endorses. Hume distinguishes explaining the moral approbation we extend to virtue from exhibiting our interested obligation to it. Although he is right to insist that moral approbation and interested obligation are not in themselves the same, he fails to consider the deeper deliberative endorsement in which they are shown to be united.

NOTES

1. E and T refer to *An Enquiry Concerning the Principles of Morals* and *A Treatise of Human Nature*, respectively. Roman numerals indicate section and part (*Essay*) or book, part, and section (*Treatise*). Arabic numerals indicate pagination in the editions edited by L. A. Selby-Bigge: *A Treatise of Human Nature* (Oxford: Clarendon Press, 1888); *Enquiries* (Oxford: Clarendon Press, 1902).

2. In *Morals by Agreement* I claimed that a theory that showed that duty was contained within interest would be "too useful," in doing away with the need for duty. There, I was concerned with the second of the two questions I have just distinguished. That dutiful dispositions are in one's interest does not enable us to replace particular appeals to duty with appeals to interest.

3. Christine N. Korsgaard, *The Sources of Normativity* (Cambridge: Cambridge University Press, 1996), 49–66.

4. Korsgaard, *Sources*, 55.

5. Ibid., 61–65.

6. Bernard Williams, *Ethics and the Limits of Philosophy* (Cambridge, MA: Harvard University Press, 1985), 68.

7. Ibid., 69.

8. Gerald J. Postema, "Hume's Reply to the Sensible Knave," *History of Philosophy Quarterly* 5, no. 1 (1988): 35.

9. Annette Baier, "Artificial Virtues and the Equally Sensible Non-Knaves: A Response to Gauthier," *Hume Studies* 18, no. 2 (1992): 432–33.

10. Korsgaard, *Sources*, 89.

CHAPTER 12

Reflection and Well-Being

ROBERT SHAVER

What is it that Hume believes does give authority to some habits of thought and some social customs; what is it that converts them into normative rules? My answer to this question . . . is "surviving the test of reflection". . . . The most authoritative survey is that of the "whole mind," of which the operation being examined will usually be merely one among others. . . . The questions become "Would we perish and go to ruin if we broke this habit? Do we prefer people to have this habit of mind, and how important do we on reflection judge it that they have it?" What ultimately get delegitimized are such modes of thought or extensions of some mode of thought beyond some limited domain as are found "neither unavoidable to mankind, nor necessary, or so much as useful in the conduct of life." The approved habits are seen to be useful or agreeable. . . . They are the ones that "bear their own survey," that is, the surveyor of the representative of the "party of humankind," concerned for its well-being.[1]

Annette Baier voices this view in many places.[2] Of it there are various pressing questions. One might ask whether this is Hume's view, or whether surviving reflection is the right view of how normative status is acquired, or whether reflection should be tied to well-being.

My concern is the last question. Baier is no friend of deontology, and so it is no surprise that she sees well-being as what satisfies reflection. But others—notably Christine Korsgaard—employ the reflection test to support deontology. In section I, I consider two ways of linking reflection and well-being. In section II, I consider Korsgaard's argument for linking reflection and deontology, and indeed for thinking that making out a connection to well-being is not even *one* way of satisfying reflection.[3] I argue that Korsgaard is wrong.

Three preliminaries are worth mentioning.

First, I want to consider well-being in a sense such that it is not part of one's well-being that one is equal to others, or that one keeps promises, or that one is punished for one's crimes. Following a distinction made by Larry Temkin, I take considerations of equality or promise-keeping or retribution to be suggestions for the proper evaluation of outcomes rather than suggestions for the proper theory of well-being.[4] I take pleasure, or preference satisfaction, or (some) "objective list" accounts to provide the latter.

Second, I take an appeal to well-being to be an appeal to the well-being of all concerned. I leave aside rational egoism.

Third, I sometimes describe one who holds that *only* an appeal to well-being satisfies reflection as a "welfarist." I follow Amartya Sen, aside from substituting "well-being" for "utilities": welfarism is the view that "[t]he judgment of the relative goodness of alternative states of affairs must be based exclusively on, and taken as an increasing function of, the respective collections of individual utilities in these states." Welfarism as so defined is compatible with preferring a distribution that fails to maximize the sum total of well-being, but not compatible with preferring a distribution that brings a drop, offset by no gains, in individual well-being. Welfarism is, for example, compatible with a version of the difference principle that concerned well-being rather than primary goods, but incompatible with strict egalitarianism.[5]

I

Hume is a welfarist. His official argument for welfarism in the *Enquiry* presents the useful and the agreeable as systematizing our judgments of praiseworthy and blameworthy traits. This argument is a staple of welfarism.[6] It may be the best argument. But given the opposition to welfarism, it has obviously sometimes failed to convince.[7] There remains, however, a core thought which may motivate trying the systematization argument in the first place, and which may survive its rejection. (This thought may also underlie attributions of benevolence, but not, say, justice, to an ideal observer.) The thought is that there is something suspicious about bringing about a drop, offset by no gains, in individual welfare. Two ways of fleshing out this thought follow.

Hume sometimes employs what might be called the strategy of distance. This asks one to consider some practice, not as a familiar participant, but as an outside observer. It supports linking reflection and well-being because the outside observer comes to see the value of the practice when he sees a connection between the practice and well-being. Thus Hume describes the habits involved in justice as follows: "I may lawfully nourish myself from this tree; but the fruit of another of the same species, ten paces off, it is criminal for me to touch. Had I worn this apparel an hour ago, I had merited the severest punishment; but a man, by pronouncing a few magical syllables, has now rendered it fit for my use and service."[8] These habits seem as puzzling as religious habits: "A fowl on Thursday is lawful food; on Friday abominable: Eggs in this house and in this diocese, are permitted during Lent; a hundred paces farther, to eat them is a damnable sin. This earth or building, yesterday was profane; to-day, by the muttering of certain words, it has become holy and sacred."[9] But Hume resolves the puzzle about justice by noting that its habits are "absolutely requisite to the well-being of mankind and existence of society." Religion remains puzzling. It is "frivolous, useless, and burdensome."[10] Reflection on justice reveals its connection to well-being and so resolves puzzlement about it, leading us to endorse the habits of justice. Reflection on religion fails to reveal conduciveness to well-being, and so religious habits remain puzzling and unendorsed.[11]

One might object that the strategy of distance is inappropriate. Surely we should not adopt the viewpoint of outsiders, who do not understand the nuances of our practices as we do. The reply is that looking from a distance is intended as a check on misguided practices. It is appropriate when we have reason to fear that our practices suffer from, as Baier puts it, "the taint of special interest, the less powerful poison of special tastes, the contaminant of . . . religious or prior theoretical prejudice."[12] The satisfaction of the outsider is some reassurance that the practice does not suffer from these defects.[13]

The strategy of distance does not, however, provide an easy route to link reflection uniquely with well-being. Nor does it provide the check on deontological practices that Hume and Baier might anticipate. For many will claim that puzzlement about a practice can be removed by other means. Consider two suggestions.

(1) Ross claims that "[i]f we compare two imaginary states of the universe, alike in the total amounts of virtue and vice and of pleasure and pain present in the two, but in one of which the virtuous were all happy and the vicious miserable, while in the other the virtuous were miserable and the vicious happy, very few people would hesitate to say that the first was a much better state of the universe than the second."[14] Ross thinks many would choose the first even were the total pleasure greater in the second: "[S]uppose that A is a very good and B a very bad man, should I then . . . think it self-evidently right to produce 1,001 units of good for B rather than 1,000 for A? Surely not."[15]

(2) Ross asks the reader to "[s]uppose . . . that the fulfillment of a promise to A would produce 1,000 units of good for him, but that by doing some other act I could produce 1,001 units of good for B, to whom I have made no promise, the other consequences of the two acts being of equal value; should we really think it self-evident that it was our duty to do the second act and not the first? I think not."[16] In each case, Ross suggests that an observer would not be puzzled.

One might object that the observers in these cases are not distanced. A distanced observer is one who wonders about the point of retribution or promise-keeping, not one who already understands the practice. But this points to a problem. For the strategy of distance to support connecting reflection and well-being, the outside observer must view promoting well-being as resolving puzzlement about the practice. The outsider must be like us—or most of us—in this respect. He cannot be so distanced that he does not see how a tie to well-being could remove puzzlement. But the outsider cannot be too similar to us, for then he will fail to provide any check on our practices. What the welfarist needs is an observer who is like us in seeing the value of well-being, and unlike (some of) us in not seeing the value of anything else. But if so, the process is rigged. It does not help against, say, the retributivist to note that an outsider who values only well-being—who

reacts, as Sidgwick does, with "an instinctive and strong moral aversion"—
would be puzzled by punishment in which "no benefit result[s] either to
[the criminal] or to others from the pain."[17]

Hume has a reply. He is anxious to reject the hypothesis that "the sentiment of justice . . . like hunger, thirst, and other appetites . . . arises from a
simple original instinct in the human breast."[18] This is exactly the objection
his critics make. Kames, for example, claims that "[t]here is a peculiar connection betwixt a man and the fruits of his industry felt by every one. . . . We
are led by nature to consider goods acquired by our industry and labour as
belonging to us . . . and we have a sense or feeling equally clear of the property of others."[19] Hume objects that distinctions of property are too complex, too varied, and too obviously designed by us for a specific purpose to
be instinctive.[20] Benevolence is hard-wired; the sentiment of justice is not.[21]
Given this, Hume can draw a distinction between outsiders. The appropriate
outsider has only hard-wired sentiments. He is appropriate since his task is
to judge additional sentiments—the "artificial" sentiments, "artificial" in the
sense that they are "purposely contriv'd and directed to a certain end."[22] This
is one way to spell out the intuition that rights, promises and the like, unlike
well-being, are inventions in need of justification.

It may not, however, be the best way. For Hume does not think that
benevolence is the only relevant instinct. There are others: resentment, the
"love of life," parental affection, "the desire of punishment to our enemies,"
gratitude, pity, self-love, "affection between the sexes."[23] Resentment and
the desire to punish, in particular, are likely to make the outsider unpuzzled
by practices, such as retributive punishment, that bring about a drop in well-
being uncompensated by any gain. The same point can be made in terms
of the "natural" virtues, since these include "equity."[24] Others go further:
Nietzsche takes as instinctive "[h]ostility, cruelty, joy in persecuting, in attacking, . . . in destruction."[25] Darwin gives evidence supporting both Hume
and Nietzsche.[26]

The problem can be illustrated by reference to Hume's comments on
punishment. Often, he seems to adopt a welfarist position: punishment is
justified by its utility.[27] Elsewhere, he notes, without disapproval, our retributive sentiments.[28] Paul Russell suggests that there is no inconsistency: the
institution of punishment is justified by its utility; the question of whom to
punish is decided by our retributive sentiments.[29] Russell notes that Hume
differs here from Smith, in that Smith gives complete authority to these

234 of PERSONS AND PASSIONS

sentiments; utility plays no role.[30] Russell sees the issue between Hume and Smith as turning on the involuntariness of our retributive practices.[31] But the more pressing issue is whether Hume has an argument for limiting the role of the retributive sentiments, given that he, like Smith, takes them to be instinctive. Russell suggests that for Hume, "punishment requires some adequate 'general justifying aim,'" and that "it is the sign of a civilised and humane mind (or society) that such retributive impulses are controlled and curbed in such a way that we can ensure that they serve only socially desirable ends."[32] But it is unclear why Smith should agree to the claim that, if our retributive practices are (fairly) voluntary, they must be justified by appeal to welfare. That is, given that our retributive sentiments share with benevolence an instinctive base, it is unclear why benevolence occupies a privileged position as the needed justifier. (Hume does give arguments to show why benevolence, rather than self-love, generates our moral distinctions. Benevolence is suitably general, univocal, and comprehensive.[33] But these characteristics do not separate benevolence from Smith's retributive sentiments.)[34]

There is another worry. Those who wish to attribute benevolence to the distanced observer probably do not do so because they find benevolence instinctive. Were they persuaded that malice was instinctive, they would not be led to attribute malice as well. Nor do they suppose that their argument hangs on an inquiry into what is really instinctive. Their key distinction is not, I think, between the instinctive and the added, but rather between the uncontested and the contested. Benevolence is special, not because it is instinctive, but because it is unchallenged.

This suggests a different way of understanding the observer, and a different argument for privileging well-being. In the debate between Hume and Ross, both agree that well-being is good. No one, as Sidgwick notes, wants "the paradoxical position of rejecting happiness as absolutely valueless."[35] Indeed, as Sidgwick argues, those like Ross, who care about distribution for its own sake, must value something other than the distribution itself. Otherwise, they have nothing to distribute that, by their own lights, matters.[36] Ross can be described as adding something valuable—distribution, or promise-keeping—to what all agree has value, namely, well-being. The characteristic welfarist thought is that this addition requires defense, in a way that the initial claim (that well-being has value) does not. It requires special defense for two reasons. First, it is a contested addition. All agree that well-being is valuable; not all agree that Ross's promise should be kept, or with retributive punishment. Second, it is a suspect addition. It requires the reduction of (part of) what even Ross finds valuable.[37] This is the force behind the familiar worry that retributivists are simply malicious. The worry need not be a serious suspicion that malice is what really motivates Ross. It is rather the suspicion that the justification he can offer is really no better than the justification a malicious person might offer. Thus Sidgwick fears that the retributivist wants a "purely useless evil," inconsistent with benevolence.[38] Of course nothing here shows that Ross *cannot* offer a better justification. The point is rather that he needs to give some justification, in a way that someone who thinks that well-being matters need not.

At this point, the welfarist becomes skeptical. He is skeptical that much can be said in favor of promise-keeping or retribution. (The paucity of argument is particularly obvious in Ross, with his repeated appeals to what we see, or do not see, to be self-evident.) True, the welfarist may be unable to provide a defense of valuing well-being that goes past a bare intuition. If both the welfarist and Ross are faced with the need to justify what they value, they might well be driven to the same unhappy claim: "We just do value this." The welfarist argument turns on preventing this interrogation of both parties. One party, the argument claims, is a suspect; the other is not.

The welfarist argument can be put in terms of what Temkin calls "the Slogan": "One situation cannot be worse (or better) than another in any respect if there is no one for whom it is worse (or better) in any respect."[39] Temkin notes that the Slogan has great intuitive appeal. It underlies, for example, the conviction that it is irrational to prefer an outcome, D, that is Pareto-inferior to some other outcome C.[40] The welfarist treats any violation of the Slogan as suspect. Consider a problem that Temkin poses for the strict egalitarian. "C is a world where half are blind, D a world where all are. One *could* always transform C into D by putting out the eyes of the sighted. . . . [For many,] [t]hat D is more equal than C gives one *no reason at all* . . . to transform C into D; and only a hardened misanthrope, or someone motivated by the basest form of envy, could think otherwise."[41] (Temkin later writes: "Do I *really* think there is some respect in which a world where only some are blind is worse than one where all are? Yes."[42]) The welfarist argues that preferring D to C, even in some respect, is, as a violation of the Slogan, suspect. The strict egalitarian must show how his rationale is better than malice or envy. The welfarist again supposes that Temkin will not have much to say, and concludes that strict egalitarianism has not been defended adequately.[43]

It is worth noting that this reasoning helps to make sense of Bentham's argument for utilitarianism. Bentham sees many opponents of utilitarianism as "partizan(s) of the principle of asceticism," "approving of actions in so far as they tend to diminish . . . happiness; disapproving of them in as far as they tend to augment it."[44] This strikes the reader as misguided: opponents of utilitarianism need not be ascetics, and asceticism is not a popular position. But Bentham's point may be that opponents of utilitarianism (or at least welfarism) have no more justification for their position than ascetics do. Of course an opponent of welfarism can suggest principles, other than asceticism, that differ from utility. But here Bentham sees "caprice"—the "mere averment of . . . unfounded sentiments," foisted on us in a "despotical" fashion.[45] Bentham's worry may be, again, that attempted justifications of principles other than utility will fail. Here the reader quickly asks whether Bentham has anything more impressive to say in favor of utility, and is disappointed to find that he does not. Caprice, it seems, is everywhere. But Bentham might reply that utility needs no defense; he claims that a proof of the principle of utility is "needless," perhaps because there has never been anyone "who has not on many, perhaps on most occasions of his life, deferred to it."[46] Bentham could mean, as he says, that a proof of the principle of utility is "impossible," without thus putting utility and its rivals on a par. The rivals need a proof; utility, because not challenged, does not.[47]

I want to point out, without reply, two problems for this argument.

(1) Some do not agree that well-being is always good. They do not value well-being derived from sadism or envy, for instance.[48] There may also be agreement that well-being is good only when the particular theory of well-being is left unspecified.

(2) Some might object that scepticism about additions to well-being is a welfarist prejudice. The worry is that any scepticism is driven by a prior conviction that well-being alone matters, rather than by doubts specific to (say) the retributivist proposal. Ross may just appeal to intuition, and so is open to the charge of caprice. But those, like Kant, who share Ross's enthusiasm for retribution and promise-keeping, without sharing his intuitionism, have a great deal more to say. Whether this objection is persuasive depends on *what* more there is to say. In the next section, I consider one Kantian attempt to say more.

The results of this section may look meager, even if the objections can be met. Burden of proof arguments are unsatisfying. It seems cheap to defend welfarism by sheltering well-being from critical scrutiny, while exposing all alternatives to such scrutiny. I think, however, that the argument has some worth. In today's climate, it would be an achievement to put the burden of proof on the anti-welfarist. And once the burden is there, it may prove crushing, given that philosophers are much better at criticism than construction.

II

Korsgaard shares Baier's method, which she calls "reflective endorsement." "If the problem is that morality might not survive reflection, then the solution is that it might. If we find upon reflecting on the true moral theory that we still are inclined to endorse the claims that morality makes on us, then morality will be normative" (49–50).[49] The method proceeds by fending off challenges to morality. It does so by showing the connection between morality and well-being. "[T]he normative question . . . is whether we have reason to be glad that we have [moral] sentiments. . . . The question is whether morality is a good thing for us" (50). "The concern is that morality might be bad or unhealthy for us. . . . We reply to the challenge by showing that morality's claims are not going to hurt us or tear us apart" (61; also 76). Reflective success comes when "there is *no intelligible challenge* that can be made to [morality's] claims" (66). Yet Korsgaard holds that "the logical consequence of the theory of normativity [held] by Hume . . . is the moral philosophy of Kant" (51; also 20).

To motivate this unlikely conclusion, Korsgaard imagines a Humean lawyer handling the estate of a late wealthy client. The lawyer had helped her client draw up a will that gives the money to medical research. But she finds a later, valid will, drawn up by the client himself, that redirects the money to his worthless nephew. She could simply destroy this will: the practice of respecting wills is approved of only because of its utility, and honoring the later one lacks utility. She would disapprove of herself for destroying it—but she also knows that she would disapprove only because of the usual consequences of injustice, absent here.

She has asked herself whether her feeling of disapproval is really a *reason* . . . not to do the action, and in this case she has found that it is not.

238 PERSONS AND PASSIONS

She only disapproves of injustice because it is usually counterproductive. But this act, isolated and secret, will be useful in every way. So now she thinks she has a reason to do it.

Or does she? Why should reflection stop there? We said that she was a convinced Humean, so she rejects realism. She therefore does not think that the fact that an action is useful is in and of itself a reason for doing it. . . . So why should she be moved by utility, any more than by disapproval? Perhaps she now finds that she is *inclined* to be moved by the thought of utility, but that is no more a reason than the fact that she was *inclined* to be moved by disapproval before. She can also ask whether this new inclination is really a reason for action. What is to stop her from continuing to ask that question, from pushing reflection as far as it will go? (88–89)

Now, it is unclear how this example shows the need to move from Hume to Kant. I canvass four possibilities.

(1) At times, Korsgaard suggests that the reflective endorsement method leads to Kant because it leads one to test particular impulses, and not, as in Hume, dispositions, by the test of reflection. "If the reflective endorsement of our dispositions is what establishes the normativity of those dispositions, then what we need in order to establish the normativity of our more particular motives and inclinations is the reflective endorsement of those. . . . But [this] is exactly the process of thought that, according to Kant, characterizes the deliberations of the autonomous moral agent" (89; also 91). This, however, does not lead to Kant any more than it leads to act utilitarianism, and so Korsgaard must intend more.

(2) Korsgaard notes that "the difficulty . . . is not, strictly speaking, a difficulty with the reflective endorsement strategy. It arises most immediately from something particular to Hume's view: the fact that the moral sentiments are supposed to be influenced by 'general rules,' rules which do not hold in every case" (88). On this reading of the lawyer example, the problem parallels familiar difficulties with rule utilitarianism. But then the example fails to show any problem for a reflective endorsement theorist whose sentiments are influenced simply by the well-being produced by the possible acts at hand. Korsgaard herself rules out the interpretation under consideration: "the difficulty does show us something important about the

reflective endorsement method" (88)—something explicated in the long passage from pages 88–89 quoted above.

(3) Korsgaard might stress the role played by the falsity of realism.[50] The lawyer is confronted by competing inclinations. If utility were "in and of itself a reason," as the realist thinks, the choice between inclinations would be easy. But since the reflective endorsement strategy is an alternative to taking any considerations as in and of themselves reasons, this route to a decision between the inclinations is blocked. Kant, Korsgaard claims, provides an answer to the question "[w]hat brings . . . reflection to a successful end?" that does not rely on any concession to realism (97). Reflection reaches a successful end when one finds a maxim one can will as a law (104, 113).

Yet on this reading, adopting the categorical imperative test is undermotivated. For there appears to be a much simpler way (at least in principle) to bring reflection to a successful end, while still avoiding realism. Suppose that the lawyer is, after reflection on the point of justice, "inclined to be moved by the thought of utility." Korsgaard objects that this "is no more a reason than the fact that she was inclined to be moved by disapproval before." But the lawyer can reply that it *is* more a reason, because it is an inclination held in light of more information. Her inclination of disapproval is less a reason, because it is an inclination that depends upon her first, less informed, thoughts. These thoughts depend on her "forget[ing]" that her disapproval is to be explained by the usual consequences of injustice—again, absent here (88). Once she sees that destroying the will is "useful in every way" and remembers that her disapproval of destroying it is explained by facts about usefulness, she rejects her first inclination. Reflection reaches a successful end when further information would not change the verdict. This is quite compatible with the rejection of realism: one can hold that reflection is satisfied by seeing a connection to utility, without explaining this by adding that utility is in and of itself a reason.

(4) Korsgaard writes that "the activity of reflection has rules of its own. . . . [P]erhaps the most essential is the rule that we should never stop reflecting until we have reached a satisfactory answer, one that admits of no further questioning. It is the rule, in Kant's language, that we should seek the unconditioned" (257–58). She identifies "the worry that nothing will count as reflective success" with "the fear that we cannot find what Kant

called 'the unconditioned'" (94). "The unconditioned" is what stops a regress argument:

> We can keep asking why: "Why must I do what is right?"—"Because it is commanded by God"—"But why must I do what is commanded by God?"—and so on, in a way that apparently can go on forever. This is what Kant called a search for the unconditioned—in this case, for something which will bring the reiteration of "but why must I do that?" to an end. The unconditional answer must be one that makes it impossible, unnecessary, or incoherent to ask why again. (33)

"Pushing reflection as far as it will go," then, requires asking "Why?" until some regress-stopping answer is reached.[51]

This suggestion faces a dilemma. Korsgaard might take her "rule of reflection" to exclude stopping a regress by appeal to something contingent— something that might have been otherwise—or she might not. (a) If she does take appeal to something contingent to be inadequate, then she must justify doing so; her rule becomes a serious departure from ordinary practice, very different from the characterization of the reflective endorsement method given initially. (b) If she does not exclude stopping a regress by appeal to something contingent, then an appeal to what we would continue to desire given increasing information seems capable of stopping the regress, and reflection can be satisfied without any passage to Kant. I take these options in turn.

(a) Say that, for Korsgaard, an appeal to something contingent is inadequate to stop a regress. It is unclear why failing this challenge is worrisome. Consider Hume's presentation of a similar regress:

> Ask a man *why he uses exercise;* he will answer, *because he desires to keep his health.* If you then enquire, *why he desires health,* he will readily reply, *because sickness is painful.* If you push your enquiries farther, and desire a reason *why he hates pain,* it is impossible he can ever give any. This is an ultimate end, and is never referred to any other object. . . . It is impossible there can be a progress *in infinitum;* and that one thing can always be a reason why another is desired. Something must be desirable on its own account, and because of its immediate accord or agreement with human sentiment and affection.[52]

On the present horn of the dilemma, Korsgaard takes Hume's inability to answer the question "why do you hate pain?"—other than by appeal to our natures—as a problem, just as an inability to show that morality is "good for us" would be a problem. But she needs to explain why these two problems are on a par.

One might say that they are on a par because one must always be able to answer a "why" question. But this is insufficient; it is what some children believe, until they are taught otherwise. The norm we accept and teach is, I think, that a failure to answer a "why" question is telling when some definite and serious challenge is in the air.[53] Korsgaard seems sympathetic to this norm when she sums up Hume's view as being "we have *no reason not to be* the best version of what we are"—Hume proceeds, on this view, by defeating definite challenges (66). Similarly, in the initial descriptions of the reflective endorsement method, the "intelligible challenge" concerns discovering that morality is "bad or unhealthy for us." And, as Korsgaard notes, where morality is challenged by Nietzsche and Freud, the challenge has a particular and serious content—morality is a means of controlling our natural impulses that makes us hate our impulses, and in time hate ourselves (159).[54] One might recommend a new norm, which directs us to keep asking "why," even with no definite or serious worry in mind. But then one needs an argument in favor of accepting such a norm.

Korsgaard is guilty of bait-and-switch. The reflective endorsement method is attractive when, as advertised, the reflection consists of fending off definite and serious challenges, and in particular challenges to the connection to well-being. But the version of reflective endorsement that Korsgaard relies on to motivate the passage to Kant is much less attractive, relying, as it does, on a bare regress argument.

It is worth noting that, when pressed on the issue of contingency, Korsgaard reverts to seeing the challenge as connected to well-being rather than taking the form of a regress. Bernard Williams objects that for Korsgaard, "nothing will serve as an adequate normative resource in . . . reflectio[n] unless 'I just happen to . . .' *cannot even intelligibly* be applied to it."[55] Part of Korsgaard's reply is that

[s]uppose the knavish lawyer proposes that she just happens to have a moral sense constructed in such-and-such a way . . . and so her moral distaste for the unjust but useful action needs no further justification.

242 PERSONS AND PASSIONS

The answer is that accepting the role of nature in the construction of our values, and so accepting the element of arbitrariness and contingency that lies at their basis, does not commit us to accepting everything that nature provides, or as being unable to distinguish the sick from the healthy. . . . [W]e sometimes find that there is in the end nothing more to say than that this is how it is, this is what nature and history have made of us. [For example,] [t]he human delight in certain effects of light, colour, and sound . . . may not admit of further justification. . . . But . . . [s]ometimes [our passions and values] are revealed to be neurotic or phobic or fetishistic or self-contradictory. . . . This is the result that Freud and Nietzsche and in a way Hume feared . . . and this is what I claim happens to the knavish lawyer. (253–54)

Suppose, then, that the lawyer drops her disapproval of destroying the will. Or suppose she says, right off, that she just happens to have a moral sense that approves only of the useful. Here Korsgaard does not, and cannot plausibly, raise the challenge that the lawyer is sick, neurotic, phobic, fetishistic, or self-contradictory. Instead, if she is going to complain, she must complain that this answer is inadequate because it is contingent.

(b) Say that the appeal to something contingent is adequate to stop a regress. Then Korsgaard needs to explain why Hume's answer regarding pain does not suffice. She must, in other words, explain why Hume's appeal to our nature does not count as discovering "the unconditioned." The "unconditional answer must be one that makes it impossible, unnecessary, or incoherent to ask why again." This is just what Hume claims for his answer. Korsgaard admits that "we sometimes find that there is in the end nothing more to say than that this is how it is." She also rejects the claim that "even contingent beings must in some sense be necessary," which again suggests that ending up with a contingency is unproblematic (34). If so, our contingent satisfaction upon seeing a connection to well-being can be unproblematic.

Of course one can ask why we should care that our natures make us dislike pain. This sort of question was sometimes asked by rationalists with a theological bent. Thus Balguy, for example, agrees with Hutcheson that we possess an instinct to help others. But he does not agree that this instinct is the "true ground and foundation" of morality.[56]

[I]t seems an insuperable difficulty in our author's scheme, that virtue appears in it to be of an arbitrary and positive nature, as entirely depending upon *instincts*, that might originally have been otherwise, or even contrary to what they now are, and may at any time be altered or inverted, if the Creator pleases. If our affections constitute the *honestum* of a morality, and do not presuppose it, it is natural to ask, what was it that determined the Deity to plant in us these affections rather than any other?[57]

Hume did not find this a natural question. Disbelief in God makes Balguy's worry hard to formulate. One might want an explanation of why we have the natures we do, of the sort Darwin aims to provide. Or one might criticize one part of our nature from the viewpoint of another part, as Nietzsche, Freud, and Hume do. But neither of these approaches leads us to ask "why should we care about our natures?" Both approaches lead us to endorse those parts of our natures that survive criticism from the rest of our natures.[58]

There is a further worry about Korsgaard's rule, independent of the dilemma. In a work on the sources of normativity, one can hardly assume a rule such as "seek the unconditioned." This rule requires justification. If Korsgaard simply stipulates this rule, then the strategy she describes Clarke as deploying against Hobbes can be turned against her: if one rule, such as "keep your covenants," can be stipulated, other rules can be stipulated too (28–29, 46). Worse, offering a stipulation here is inconsistent with the reflective endorsement strategy, which works by asking what we find acceptable rather than, with Korsgaard's realist, by finding normative facts beyond our sentiments. Seeking the unconditioned might, then, be seen as a part of our nature—as a desire. But if so, it need not be a desire shared by everyone, particularly when it is understood as excluding appeal to contingencies. It begins to look like a quirk of Kantian psychology—Kant's attempts to link it with "Reason" notwithstanding.

(Doubts about the need to search for the unconditioned also block one of Korsgaard's arguments against realism. She notes correctly that realists such as Clarke, Price, and Nagel argue by refuting challenges to normative claims (31, 41, 41 n. 67, 41 n. 69). Nagel, for example, argues that Mackie and Harman fail, and so there is no general reason to doubt the existence of moral reasons.[59] Korsgaard, however, objects that realism is "an expression of confidence and nothing more" (41; also 38–40, 48). Realism "refuses to answer the normative question," since "the normative question arises when our confidence has been shaken" (39, 40; also 34). For example, "if someone falls into doubt about whether obligations really exist, it doesn't help to say 'ah, but indeed they do. They are *real* things'" (38). We "can *always* ask: . . . must I really do this?" (47, emphasis in original; also 43). On Korsgaard's first, correct, construal of realism, realists do not simply express confidence in some normative claims. They reply to challenges to these claims; if they defeat these challenges, they take the claims to be justified. This procedure can be described as a mere expression of confidence and as an avoidance of the normative question only because Korsgaard construes the normative question—"why must I do this?"—as not raising any definite challenge. The person who doubts the existence of obligations gives no reason for doubt; if he did, the realist would try to remove it. It is because realists do not try to answer "why must I do this?" where no challenge is suggested that they seem, to Korsgaard, to be blithely confident.)

I conclude that Korsgaard fails. The problem does not lie—or at least need not lie—in familiar worries about the workings of the categorical imperative test itself. The problem is rather that Korsgaard fails to make good her claim that the reflective endorsement method leads past Hume and Baier to Kant. It does not follow, of course, that *no* rationale for departing from welfarism will succeed. But recording her failure is a start in what I take to be the right, welfarist direction.

NOTES

I wish to thank Jack Bailey, Bob Bright, Ken Gemes, Iain Law, and especially Joyce Jenkins, along with audiences at the University of Manitoba and at the 1998 Hume Conference in Stirling, for comments or discussion.

1. Annette C. Baier, *Moral Prejudices* (Cambridge, MA: Harvard University Press, 1994), 81–82.

2. Baier offers the test of reflection in, for example, *Moral Prejudices*, 86; *Postures of the Mind* (Minneapolis: University of Minnesota Press, 1985), 98, 103, 164, 224–26, 266; *A Progress of Sentiments* (Cambridge, MA: Harvard University Press, 1991), 284–85. Sometimes she sees the test more narrowly, as reflexivity. See, for example, *Postures,* 172, 259–60, *Moral Prejudices*, 268, *Progress*, 55, 91–100, 215–16,

277, 284–85, 287–88. But it is clear that reflexivity is merely a minimal form of reflection, necessary but not sufficient for justification. See, for example, *Postures*, 226, *Moral Prejudices*, 173–74, 326 n. 38. For a helpful statement of the distinction between the reflection and reflexivity tests, see Christine M. Korsgaard, *The Sources of Normativity* (Cambridge: Cambridge University Press, 1996), 49–50, 60–65.

3. Korsgaard does not say this explicitly, and much of what she says grants that there is a connection between reflection and well-being. She is arguing, however, for Kantianism, and Kant does seem to hold that making out a connection to well-being fails to satisfy reflection at all. In any case, Korsgaard's position would remain interesting even if she disagrees with Kant here, in that she provides an argument in favor of (non-uniquely) linking reflection and deontology.

4. Larry Temkin, *Inequality* (Oxford: Oxford University Press, 1993), 258, 263–64, 267–68, 272, 274 n. 47, 275–77.

5. See Amartya Sen, "Utilitarianism and Welfarism," *Journal of Philosophy* 76 (1979): 468.

6. It is made most famously by Sidgwick, who credits Hume: see Henry Sidgwick, *The Methods of Ethics* (Indianapolis: Hackett, 1981), 423–25.

7. For a quick statement of worries, directed at Hume's version of the systematization argument, see C. D. Broad, *Five Types of Ethical Theory* (London: Routledge and Kegan Paul, 1930), 97–99.

8. David Hume, *An Enquiry Concerning the Principles of Morals*, ed. L. A. Selby-Bigge and P. H. Nidditch (Oxford: Clarendon, 1975), 199; also *A Treatise of Human Nature*, ed. Selby-Bigge and Nidditch (Oxford: Clarendon, 1978), 515–16, 524–25.

9. Hume, *Enquiry*, 198. For a similarly distanced treatment of Laud's consecration of a church, see Hume, *History of England*, ed. William Todd (Indianapolis: Liberty, 1983), 5:224–26, and Donald Siebert, *The Moral Animus of David Hume* (Newark: University of Delaware Press, 1990), 107–8.

10. Hume, *Enquiry*, 199.

11. Michael Gill has criticized Baier's account of Hume. Gill notes that Baier frequently sees Hume as offering a reflexivity test: a trait must be able to bear its own survey. Gill objects that Hume usually settles normative worries by appeal to well-being, not reflexivity. But Hume may think the reflexivity test is passed only when the practice scrutinized is shown to produce well-being. For example, the moral sentiment approves of itself only when it finds that possessing moral sentiment is beneficial. See Gill, "A Philosopher in his Closet: Reflexivity and Justification in Hume's Moral Theory," *Canadian Journal of Philosophy* 26 (1996): 239–45.

12. Baier, *Postures*, 145.

13. At the close of an attack on utilitarianism that relies on a nonutilitarian understanding of the virtues, Philippa Foot notes that utilitarianism may seem attractive because "[i]t cannot be enough to say that we *do* have such things as rules of

justice in our present system of virtues: the question is whether we should have them, and if so why we should." She goes on to write that "[i]n its most persuasive form," this thought "involves a picture of morality as a rational device developed to serve certain purposes." Her objection is that this picture of morality is "a consequentialist assumption" that one should reject. But her initial worry—that we should ask whether we should have a certain system of virtues—survives this rejection. For one need not think of morality as a device to have the worry that some particular moral code is bad for us. Even if morality, properly understood, has no extra-moral purpose, one can worry that obeying it frustrates too many of our extra-moral purposes. Thus Korsgaard, for example, who shares Foot's dislike of picturing morality as a device, is very exercised by the worry that morality is bad for us (see below). For Foot, see "Utilitarianism and the Virtues," *Mind* 94 (1985): 208–9. For Korsgaard's dislike of picturing morality as a device, see "The Reasons We Can Share: An Attack on the Distinction between Agent-Relative and Agent-Neutral Values," *Social Philosophy and Policy* 10 (1993): 25, 49–51.

14. W. D. Ross, *The Right and the Good* (Indianapolis: Hackett, 1988), 138; see also 26–27, 58, 136–37.

15. Ibid., 35.

16. Ibid., 34–35.

17. Sidgwick, *Methods*, 281.

18. Hume, *Enquiry*, 201.

19. Lord Kames, *Essays on the Principles of Morality and Natural Religion* (Edinburgh: A. Kincaid and A. Donaldson, 1751), 105, 108; also 107, 112, 119. See also Thomas Reid, *Essays on the Active Powers of the Human Mind*, in *Philosophical Works* (Hildesheim: Georg Olms Verlag, 1967), 2:653, 661, 662.

20. Hume, *Enquiry*, 201–3; also *Treatise*, 528–29.

21. J. J. C. Smart is tempted by a similar thought: "the obligation to keep promises seems to be too artificial, to smack too much of human social conventions, to do duty as an ultimate principle." See Smart and Bernard Williams, *Utilitarianism: For and Against* (Cambridge: Cambridge University Press, 1973), 6; also 68.

22. Hume, *Treatise*, 529, also 474, 484, 489, 526, 577; *Enquiry*, 306, 307 n. 2.

23. Hume, *Treatise*, 398, 417, 439, 570; *Enquiry*, 201, 303; *Essays*, ed. Eugene F. Miller (Indianapolis: Liberty, 1985), 479; *Natural History of Religion*, in *Dialogues and Natural History of Religion*, ed. J. C. A. Gaskin (Oxford: Oxford University Press, 1993), para. 1.

24. Hume, *Treatise*, 578. This is noted by Baier, *Progress*, 260.

25. Friedrich Nietzsche, *On the Genealogy of Morals*, trans. Walter Kaufmann and R. J. Hollingdale, in *On the Genealogy of Morals and Ecce Homo*, ed. Kaufmann (New York: Vintage, 1994), II.16 para. 2.

26. Charles Darwin, *The Descent of Man and Selection in Relation to Sex* (Akron, OH: Werner, 1874), 98–129. Darwin emphasizes the social affections, since he is trying to explain the moral sense, but see 114 n. 27 for envy and hatred, and 119 and 124 for torture and cruelty.

27. Hume, *Treatise*, 526; *Essays*, 594–95.

28. Hume, *Treatise*, 348, 376–77, 418, 439, 591. I take these references, and those in the previous note, from Paul Russell, *Freedom and Moral Sentiment* (Oxford: Oxford University Press, 1995), 137, 139, 150 n. 5.

29. Russell, *Freedom*, 140–42.

30. Ibid., 142–43.

31. Ibid., 147–49.

32. Ibid., 146, 148.

33. Hume, *Enquiry*, 228–29, 271–74.

34. Hume may agree. He sometimes notes that resentment, along with benevolence, has some of the suitable characteristics for generating moral distinctions. See *Enquiry*, 218, 222, 225, 286.

35. Sidgwick, *Methods*, 406.

36. Ibid., 393. Ross agrees; see *Right*, 135–36.

37. For a similar point, see Shelly Kagan, *The Limits of Morality* (Oxford: Clarendon, 1989), 16–18. The addition may be suspect for a further reason. F. C. Sharp argues that retributivism, in particular, does not cohere with the rest of our impartial, benevolence-directed moral practices, since it ignores the interest of the victim of the retribution. It is also parasitic on these other practices, since "it demands retaliation only when the person to be punished has acted in violation of eudemonic standards." See Sharp, "Hume's Ethical Theory and its Critics II," *Mind* 30 (1921): 154–55, and *Ethics* (New York: Century, 1928), 137.

38. Sidgwick, *Methods*, 72.

39. Temkin, *Inequality*, 256, emphases omitted.

40. Ibid., 249.

41. Ibid., 247–48. Temkin stipulates that welfare is distributed equally in D, unequally in C.

42. Ibid., 282. On balance, he does not approve here—"[e]quality is not all that matters"—but in other cases of leveling, he does. See 274.

43. Dennis McKerlie writes that "[t]here is no obvious reason for saying that the claim that inequality is bad must be supported by an argument while the claim that suffering is bad does not require that support." But he goes on to note that strict egalitarians have not done much to show that their egalitarianism fits "the considered moral judgments of ordinary people." Surely this is an obvious reason for taking strict egalitarianism, but not the badness of suffering, to require argument. See "Equality," *Ethics* 106 (1996): 277–78.

44. Jeremy Bentham, *Introduction to the Principles of Morals and Legislation*, ed. J. H. Burns and H. L. A. Hart (London: Athlone, 1970), II.IV, III, emphases omitted.

45. See Bentham, *Principles*, I.XIV, II.XI–XIV, XIV n. R. M. Hare's treatment of "ideals" as mere preferences reflects the same worry. See, for example, the exchange between Richard Brandt, Peter Singer, and Hare in *Hare and Critics*, ed. N. Fotion and D. Seanor (Oxford: Clarendon, 1988), 149–52, 220–21, 269–70. For an earlier version of the same thought, see Sharp, "Hume's Ethical Theory," 155, and *Ethics*, 502.

46. Bentham, *Principles*, I.XI, XII; also I.XIII, II.VIII, X.

47. In one respect my argument follows Smart, who writes that "[t]here is *prima facie* a necessity for the deontologist to defend himself against the charge of heartlessness, in his apparently preferring abstract conformity to a rule to the prevention of avoidable human suffering" (*Utilitarianism*, 6; also 5, 67, 72). Smart, however, thinks noncognitivism is needed to show how his repeated appeals to benevolence support utilitarianism and defeat the deontologist. Noncognitivism is needed to prevent the deontologist from claiming that his principles "can be *seen* to be true" (6). This is wrong: one might combine noncognitivism with deontology by noting, for example, that just as we like benevolence, we also like justice; and the deontologist might be defeated by giving a (cognitivist) argument against his claims. My argument, unlike that of Smart, tries to say what is special about benevolence. And its claim that the goodness of well-being is uniquely uncontested, which is intended to show the special place of benevolence, is neutral between cognitivism and noncognitivism.

48. See, for example, Sen, "Welfarism," 473–74, 477–78; Temkin, *Inequality*, 268; G. E. Moore, *Principia Ethica* (Cambridge: Cambridge University Press, 1903), 209–10; John Rawls, *A Theory of Justice* (Cambridge, MA: Harvard University Press, 1971), 30–31.

49. Parenthetical references in the text are to Korsgaard, *Sources*.

50. For Korsgaard, a (substantive) realist holds that "[o]bligation is simply there, part of the nature of things. . . . Some actions are simply intrinsically right. . . . There are correct procedures for answering moral questions *because* there are moral truths or facts which exist independently of those procedures. . . . It conceives ethics as a branch of knowledge, knowledge of the normative part of the world" (30, 31, 36, 37; also 41 n. 68, 44, 46).

51. See also Korsgaard, "Morality as Freedom," in *Kant's Practical Philosophy Reconsidered*, ed. Yirmiyahu Yovel (Dordrecht: Kluwer, 1989), 27–31.

52. Hume, *Enquiry*, 293.

53. For one development of this Austinian approach to moral theory, see Mark Timmons, "Outline of a Contextualist Moral Epistemology," in *Moral Knowledge?* ed. Mark Timmons and Walter Sinnott-Armstrong (Oxford: Oxford University

Press, 1996), 293–325. Baier may find this approach congenial, given some of her comments on trust. See *Moral Prejudices*, 159, 194, 197.

54. She quotes Nietzsche: "Have [value judgments of good and evil] hitherto hindered or furthered human prosperity? Are they a sign of distress, of impoverishment, of the degeneration of life?" (49) Nietzsche has an idiosyncratic view of what counts as well-being. But it seems he would be satisfied by seeing a connection between morality and well-being so understood. (He thinks, of course, that the dominant moralities not only fail to be connected to well-being, but inhibit well-being.)

55. Bernard Williams, "History, Morality, and the Test of Reflection," in Korsgaard, *Sources*, 214–15.

56. John Balguy, *The Foundation of Moral Goodness*, in *British Moralists: 1650–1800*, ed. D. D. Raphael (Indianapolis: Hackett, 1991), 1:389.

57. Ibid., 1:390.

58. J. B. Schneewind notes that some of the voluntarists, although not themselves atheists, had the same attitude. See "Voluntarism and the Foundations of Ethics," *Proceedings and Addresses of the American Philosophical Association* 70 (1996): 34–36.

59. Thomas Nagel, *The View from Nowhere* (New York: Oxford University Press, 1986), 143–49.

CHAPTER 13

Friendship and the Law of Reason

Baier and Kant on Love and Principles

SERGIO TENENBAUM

Annette Baier has been unsparing in her criticism of Kant's ethical theories, especially on the grounds that Kant has failed to provide a proper place for human nature and sentiment in his account of morality. This place is illicitly occupied in Kant's philosophy by an unfeeling reason, and more particularly by the various formulations of the categorical imperative. This distorted view of reason's place in our moral lives leads Kant to a flawed conception of moral theory. In *Postures of the Mind*, Baier claims that Kantian ethics takes the job of a moral theory to be giving "guidance in concrete human situations, perhaps with the help of a body of professionals, heirs to the casuists, whose job is to show how a given moral theory applies to a case."[1] The formulations of the categorical imperative, especially the "Formula of the Universal Law" (FUL),[2] are supposed to be the tools that Kant hands to those heirs to the casuists. FUL then does the same job that Christian teachings did when applied by the original casuists: "The casuist who applied Christian moral teaching to concrete, sometimes novel, human situations, were a bit like judges who, given an accepted body of statute law and precedents, applied these to the case before them."[3]

Much attention has recently been paid to the role of judgment in Kant's ethics.[4] The observation that judgment has a role to play in applying the categorical imperative allows us to avoid the error of thinking that Kant took FUL to be a formula that can be mechanically applied, one that does not require more judgment than applying an algorithm to a particular instance. But this mistake is, of course, not one that Baier makes.[5] The allusion to our need for the help of the heirs to the casuists leaves no doubt that this is not Baier's concern. Her concern is rather that the principles might be of no help: finding a unifying principle of morality will not necessarily enlighten our decisions, with or without the help of judgment "sharpened by experience."[6] That is, Baier suggests that the search for ultimate principles might be futile, and the belief that universal principles are necessary tools of moral reasoning might be just a dogma.

The danger of futility might seem all the more serious when we note that FUL is a formulation of a principle that, according to Kant, already guides ordinary reason (*gemeine Vernunft*).[7] If we are guided by it anyway, how could its explicit formulation help us in our moral reasoning? No doubt we can only gain by an increase in our knowledge, and our awareness of FUL might throw light on some issues in the same way as any other improvement in our understanding of issues related to morality. But why should we expect that the explicit formulation of a principle that guides us in any case could provide us with a systematic method of settling difficult issues?

I will begin by drawing attention to the evidence that for Kant, the main function of the explicit formulation of the categorical imperative is not to provide us with definite guidance in applying the categorical imperative to particular cases. In fact, we should not expect the formulation of the categorical imperative to provide any guidance of this kind. It might happen to give such guidance on some occasions, but we should not think of this as the function that FUL is supposed to perform. The formulation of the categorical imperative is part of Kant's main project of tracing the origin of human cognitions to their proper faculties. In particular, this formulation traces the origin of our moral judgments to the faculty of reason; it locates what we might call "the mark of rationality" in our ethical life.[8]

Once these proper disclaimers on the role of the formulations of the categorical imperative are in place, we can look at another criticism Baier levels against Kant. According to Baier, Kant is a "misamorist," that is, someone who distrusts "the claims of love"⁹—someone who takes love to be a barrier to, rather than an essential part of, our moral life. Much recent literature has tried to rescue Kant's account of friendship from various criticisms. My discussion here, however, will have a different focus. I want to examine a certain complaint that is not explicit in Baier's essay "Unsafe Loves," but which I believe to be the ground on which the complaint of her article rests: the allegation that Kant's moral theory leaves no cognitive role for our sentiments. In defense of Kant, one might say that the moral law might tolerate or encourage certain feelings (or at least corrected versions of these feelings), but it must treat them as blind forces that merely happen to lead us in the right direction. No matter how much tolerance or encouragement we allow for, we do not regain the sense that our feelings can be moral educators or instruments of moral insight. Nor do we have the sense that by, for instance interacting with others, loving and being loved, we gain an insight into morality, which could not be provided simply by internalizing a principle. The inadequacy of Kant's account of friendship would thus be a consequence of the general inadequacy of his views on the role of sentiments in moral cognition. However, once we are no longer hostage to the notion that the formulation of the categorical imperative is a tool for modern casuists, we can identify a wider cognitive role for sentiments. Experience and our natural feelings will have an important role to play in our cognition of what the categorical imperative demands in particular cases, a role that goes beyond their obvious functions (such as, for example, allowing us to recognize particular cases to which the categorical imperative applies). In fact, I will argue that Kant's discussion of friendship is the best instance of Kant's recognition of this function of our affective capacities.

I

At first, nothing seems more obvious than the importance of finding a principle of morality. Although one can be skeptical about the *possibility* of finding such a principle, it is hard to object to the *desirability* of doing so. Kant himself seemed somewhat irked by the fact that the importance of such a principle was not obvious to one of his reviewers (cf. KpV 14n). There is no doubt that the formulation of the categorical imperative performs an important function. At the very least, FUL shows what unifies different moral judgments. However, few people think that this is the *only* function of FUL. It seems that the categorical imperative should also have a guiding function, in helping us achieve better judgments in particular cases. Again, at this level of generality, it is hard to oppose such a claim. A better understanding of the nature of morality would probably not be a hindrance, and would likely be an aid, in developing our capacity for moral judgment. But the categorical imperative is also thought to give the kind of systematic guidance that John Rawls seems to take his theory to be providing; it is a theory whose major aim is to settle our differences on moral issues:

> If the scheme as a whole seems on reflection to clarify and to order our thoughts, and *if it tends to reduce disagreements and to bring divergent convictions more in line*, then it has done all that one may reasonably ask.[10]

The importance of this kind of principle can hardly be underestimated. A tool that would determine clearly what our ordinary understanding had left obscure would, no doubt, be a desirable tool. And it is tempting to think that an ethical theory that cannot deliver a tool of this kind is rather worthless. However, it is hard to believe that a principle as simple as the categorical imperative could even begin to be such a tool, no matter how much room one leaves for judgment in Kant's ethics. Here it seems difficult not to share Baier's skepticism about finding such a principle, or her suspicion that the idea that any moral guide must consist of universal and explicitly formulated rules is a prejudice "whose self-evidence does not survive self-consciousness."[11] In fact, once we accept that the categorical imperative already guides the judgment of ordinary understanding, it is hard to see how the formulation of the categorical imperative could provide any further guidance. It is far from clear that making explicit a rule that implicitly guides us would help us judge the particular cases falling under the rule.

Our skepticism should increase when we look at how Kant describes the function of the moral philosopher. By providing a formulation of the categorical imperative, the philosopher has isolated the *a priori* source of morality. So Kant says:

> Not only are moral laws together with their principles essentially different from every kind of practical cognition in which there is anything empirical, but *all moral philosophy rests entirely on its pure part*. When

applied to man it does not in the least borrow from acquaintance with him (anthropology) but gives *a priori* laws to him as a rational being. (G 389; emphasis mine)

Kant often admonishes fellow philosophers for trying to locate the source of morality in empirical principles. But such confusion is widespread, and it is what separates (true) philosophy from ordinary reason: "For philosophy is distinguished from the cognition of ordinary reason in that it presents in a separate science [*in abgesonderter Wissenschaft*] that which the latter conceives only confusedly" (G 390; translation amended). Given the contrast in this quote, I take it that Kant is using "confusedly" (*vermengen*) to mean "mixed with other cognitions."[12] If this is the main confusion that bewitches popular systems of morality, and if the avoidance of this confusion is what sets philosophy apart from ordinary reason, then it is hard to see how it could be the task of the philosopher to help in *applying* these principles. If the philosopher has to isolate the pure source of morality, she will search for its most abstract version, one that is not mixed with anything empirical. Thus, since FUL abstracts from anything empirical, it is farther removed from application to the particular conditions of human nature than are the precepts of ordinary reason, in which the presentation of the categorical imperative is already mixed with empirical cognitions.

Take, for instance, the precept "You should show respect and gratitude toward your parents." Let us assume, for the sake of the argument, that this is an incontrovertible principle; ordinary reason can easily determine that this is a valid moral precept. The philosopher knows that this is not one of the basic principles of morality, since its truth depends on the empirical conditions of human nature. This precept itself is quite vague, and so even if it is incontrovertible, some of its applications might be controversial. It might not be clear, for instance, whether refusing a request to let your parents live in your house in their old age counts as a violation of this principle. In trying to settle this issue, would a direct appeal to FUL help? It seems far from clear that it would. More likely, it would at best show us how the principle itself is justified rather than help with its application; that is, FUL would probably have *its* application to the particular matter in hand mediated by the principle "We ought to show gratitude to our parents."

Of course, one might think that I have missed an obvious use of the categorical imperative. A particular precept might be wrongly identified as having the seal of approval of morality, when in fact it does not. Respecting one's parents might *not* be something that morality demands at all. Here it is important to note two ways in which mistakes can occur in the choice of more basic precepts. First, despite being guided by the correct fundamental principles of morality, we might have used bad principles of application, wrong factual beliefs, or faulty inferences. In such cases, the formulation of the categorical imperative could not help us. Factual beliefs and principles of application depend on empirical principles that fall outside the scope of the categorical imperative. Faulty inferences are certainly not a matter of failing to be in possession of the correct moral principle.[13] On the other hand, if our specific precepts are wrong because they stem from incorrect moral principles, then the formulation of the categorical imperative can certainly eradicate them. I might have a mistaken conception of what the fundamental principle (or principles) of morality is (or are); that is, I might wish to do the morally right thing, but still be mistaken about what morality requires at the most fundamental level. However, this latter type of mistake is not one that Kant seems to think is even *possible*. When we look at the list of moral shortcomings presented by Kant in *Religion Within the Limits of Reason Alone*, nothing like that shows up. In fact, this work speaks against it. The fundamental choice of one's character described in *Religion* is between an ordering of the principles of morality and self-love, that is, between the categorical imperative and the unrestrained pursuit of one's own happiness,[14] and there is no doubt that ordinary reason does not mistake this principle of happiness for a fundamental moral principle.[15] There is no suggestion that a mistaken moral principle could be the fundamental principle of our choices. It is important not to ascribe to Kant a concern with competing moral outlooks that he did not have. Kant rather optimistically claims that even the bully will see the justice of his beating (KpV 61), and the murderer will not complain that the death penalty is too harsh a sentence (MS 334). In fact, Kant often alludes to the ease with which ordinary reason discovers what morality demands, and sometimes even proclaims its advantage over the thought of philosophers:

And the most extraordinary thing is that ordinary understanding in this practical case may have just as good a hope of hitting the mark as that which any philosopher may promise himself. Indeed it is almost more certain in this than even a philosopher is, because he can have no principle other than what ordinary understanding has, but he may easily confuse his judgment by a multitude of foreign and irrelevant considerations and thereby cause it to swerve from the right way. (G 404)

This should be no more surprising than the fact that we do not expect complex arguments in nonformal areas to be made simpler by trying to reconstruct their most basic premises (not just the premises we happen to agree about), using only fundamental rules of derivation. Typically, a complex piece of reasoning would make this task an endless and impossible one. A complex argument usually involves a large share of accumulated wisdom; representing this using only these meager resources would involve a great number of steps, and would call upon a highly developed capacity to apply the relevant concepts and principles. No doubt, appeal to basic premises or fundamental rules of derivation can sometimes throw light on a difficult issue, but a systematic use of the above method would be ludicrous.

It is interesting to compare Mill's view on the principle of utility in this context. A possible objection to the principle of utility is that its application is not humanly possible; given the amazing complexity involved in calculating the effect of a typical action on the general happiness and the relatively short span in which we have to make a decision, any attempt to be guided by the principle of utility seems impractical. Mill's answer to this objection is illuminating. Mill suggests that one should almost never appeal to the principle of utility; the rules of morality we already have embody the experience of humankind in applying the principle of utility.[16] One might claim that the principle of utility is useful in that it can be appealed to when the rules conflict. But here, too, it would not typically work. Controversial issues, such as legislation on hate speech, abortion, and so forth, might be controversial precisely because the utility calculation in those cases is particularly baffling. Again, it might be true that, from time to time, appeal to the principle of utility, as to any other account of morality, would help us see through bias and prejudice or clarify an issue. But this is far from accepting the idea that direct appeal to the principle of utility could be used as a systematic method for settling controversial issues.[17] It is important to note that the emphasis on "calculating" here is misleading. The problem is not that we are faced with a sum of too many addends, but rather that the principle of utility does not tell us what counts as more or less happiness in an individual, let alone how to compare the happiness of various individuals.

One may argue that the sources of confusion are multiple, and that an explicit formulation of the principle might at least close one door. For instance, a faulty inference may be best exposed with the help of the explicit formulation of the categorical imperative. I have nothing against this claim. There is no reason not to expect that a clearer understanding of the nature of morality could improve our judgment in moral matters. This applies to Kant's work, but also to Hume's or any other philosopher's, insofar as he or she puts forth a genuine contribution to the field. It is, however, a far cry from claiming that the role of moral principle is to serve as a systematic test to which we can appeal whenever disagreement threatens or a new case shows up—a far cry from thinking that the main role of FUL is to serve as the basic tool for those modern heirs of the Christian casuists. In fact, the truth of this claim does not even make us hope that this sort of direct appeal to FUL will even be of *widespread* utility in improving our judgment. Our long experience of morality and of being implicitly guided by this principle teaches us the application of the categorical imperative to various occasions that depend on our knowledge of the world and of human nature. In controversial issues, it should rarely be the case that direct appeal to the principle (as opposed to the more particular lessons it has taught us throughout centuries of moral reasoning together with experience) would settle the issue. It is unlikely that we have missed something that could flow so smoothly from the most abstract formulation of this principle.

Why should we be concerned about formulating the categorical imperative if its use as a tool for the casuists is quite limited? Of course, this is no place to undertake a detailed examination of Kant's work on the categorical imperative. I will simply give an answer in broad outline. First, we must note that FUL is arrived at by asking a specific question: "What sort of law can that be whose presentation (*Vorstellung*) must determine the will without reference to any expected effect, so that the will can be called absolutely and without qualification good" (G 402)? In the *Critique of Practical Reason*, Kant says that the first question concerning such a critique is, "Is pure reason sufficient of itself to determine the will, or is it only as empirically conditioned that it can do so?" For Kant, these two questions are equivalent. To say that the will is good absolutely and without qualification is to say that the determination of its object is not empirically conditioned. But if the determination of the will is not empirically conditioned, then the will must be determined absolutely *a priori*, that is, by reason alone.[18]

The formulation of the categorical imperative, therefore, allows us to trace our moral cognitions back to their legitimate origin in the faculty of reason (as opposed to a "chimerical idea" or a "phantom of the brain" [G 445]). A similar project can be found in Kant's theoretical works. There Kant tries to show that the categories have their legitimate origin in the understanding (they are not just "bastards of the imagination"). Formulating a principle is, of course, only part of the project. We might need to prove its objective reality, or its compatibility with other cognitive principles (such as the law of universal causation). However, showing that all moral cognitions are expressions of a formal principle such that, in virtue of its form, reason must prescribe it if it prescribes anything unconditionally, is an important step. Tracing back the origin of morality to reason also traces it back to other related concepts, such as those of freedom and self-legislation. Not only do we locate the origin of moral cognition in reason, but by doing so, we determine the basic properties of a will whose cognition stems from the faculty of reason.[19]

These are the gains that an explicit formulation of the categorical imperative provides with respect to what Kant calls "the motives of speculation regarding the source of practical principles" (G 390). These are not gains to be sneered at. The explicit formulation provides the basis of our practical self-understanding, and as such, can easily find its home among the intellectual projects worth undertaking. Moreover, as noted above, improving our self-understanding certainly cannot hurt the practical aims of morality. However, such gains cannot, by themselves, explain Kant's claim that his project is also a corrective to the fact that "morals are liable to all kinds of corruption" (G 404).

At the end of the first section of the *Groundwork of the Metaphysics of Morals*, Kant explicitly discusses the practical advantages of a metaphysics of morals. Philosophy is supposed to help deliver us from a "natural dialectic, i.e. a propensity to quibble with these strict laws of duty, to cast doubt upon their validity, or at least upon their purity and strictness" (G 405). It turns out that philosophy has a practical use after all:

> Ordinary reason is forced to go outside its sphere and take a step into the field of practical philosophy . . . *on practical grounds themselves*. There it tries to obtain information and clear instruction regarding the *source* of its principles and the correct determination of this principle *in its op-*

position to maxims based on need and inclination, so that reason may escape from the perplexity of opposite claims. (G 405; emphases mine)

The need for a critique of our practical cognitive faculties, just as of our theoretical ones, is the result of a dialectic in which these faculties find themselves entangled. In the case of practical reason, it is a *practical* dialectic, one involving the claims that are made on our *will*. The apparent plausibility of the claims of self-interest is what has to be combated, not any confusion about the demands of the claims of morality. The threat concerns the failure of the principle of morality to determine our will, not uncertainty about its contents.

Such a project, however, commits us to the claim that our moral pronouncements are instantiations of FUL; they are more particular forms of this abstract formulation. In many cases, this is (at least according to Kant) a rather trivial matter. Kant's examples in the *Groundwork* are cases in point. Kant chooses them not because he regards them as particularly controversial, but, I think, quite the opposite: because they make it all too easy to see (so he thinks) that a certain course of action would not conform to FUL. At any rate, the claim that the categorical imperative is the supreme principle of morality commits us to the claim that all our moral decisions can be seen as instances of FUL. This commitment need not show itself in direct derivations of our duties from certain principles, but it should be apparent in the way we give and ask for moral reasons, for instance, in the way that the demand for universality shows up in our reasoning. Particularists are often keen to point out that we cannot find a nontrivial universal principle of clear application that will be valid on all occasions. However, if FUL is supposed to represent a commitment, rather than a decision procedure, it will be immune to this sort of criticism. Even if it is true that a certain feature of an action that seems to render it immoral according to FUL might show up in an action that is not immoral, this would not be a fatal blow to FUL. It would only indicate that we are committed to rethinking these situations in such a way that only one of them is indeed compatible with acceptance of FUL. This commitment might be demonstrated, for instance, in the fact that we never rest content in merely saying that a moral factor that was relevant in one case is simply not relevant in another. If I think that breaking a promise makes an action immoral in one case, but I allow that breaking a promise in a different circumstance is not immoral, I do not think that my duties of justification can be fulfilled *merely* by saying "that an action is an instance of breaking a promise is sometimes morally relevant, but not always." Rather, I am committed to finding a relevant difference. In Kant's terminology, I try to conceive of the two actions as governed by different maxims.

This point can be made more clear if we think about a long-standing objection against Kant. It has been a challenge to the ingenuity of philosophers to try to find counterexamples to FUL. A standard source of counterexamples is the possibility of generating coordination problems by universalizing perfectly innocent maxims. For instance, if I like to do my shopping when no one else is doing theirs, in order to avoid the hassle of long lines, I might find to my shock and surprise that I have been violating a perfect duty. Suppose my maxim is this: "In order to avoid lines when I shop, I shall shop only at a time when no one else is shopping." Assuming a certain scarcity of available store hours, we could not conceive, it seems, that everyone would be able to act from this maxim.

However, it is easy to tinker with maxims to avoid those embarrassing conclusions. For instance, there is no problem with this maxim: "Before entering every shop I shall take a peek inside, and if I find that there is someone inside, I shall turn around and go; otherwise, I'll shop." The problem with this solution is that it seems as if we are tinkering with the maxims to make the action permissible. With enough tinkering, any action might turn out to be permissible.[20] However, this "objection against tinkering" makes sense only if we think of FUL as primarily a deliberative tool. Under the interpretation I have been advancing here, this "tinkering" can be seen as the working out of our commitment to have our moral practice bear the mark of rationality. Insofar as ordinary reason can figure out on its own the demands of morality, reconceiving these demands in terms of maxims that conform to the formulations of the categorical imperative is not mere tinkering with maxims, but a presentation of its insight in a form that makes it clear that this insight has a rational source. Of course, this is not to say that ordinary reason is infallible in this regard. And difficulties in reconceiving one's moral commitments in this way might signal a problem with these commitments. But this is only one source of evidence that something has gone awry with our moral judgments; discovering that they are often self-serving, that they are connected to prejudice or anger, or that they are in conflict with the judgment of other reasonable people may be symptoms of the same problem. Once again, there is no guarantee that those difficulties of regimenting our moral insight in accordance with FUL will be a particularly important means of correcting our mistakes in judgment.

II

Kant has often been chastised for not providing a proper place for human nature and sentiment in his account of morality. Certain features of his moral theory appear to lend support to this charge: Kant argues that our understanding of morality is exhausted by our knowledge of a principle of pure reason, that is, the categorical imperative. Kant, no doubt, would claim that no account of morality based on empirical incentives could provide us with a genuine principle of practical reason, and he often emphasizes the purely rational source of the moral law. Moreover, he repeatedly asserts that it is the wish of all rational beings to see themselves rid of their inclinations, and thus of all forms of nonrational motivation.[21]

Other aspects of Kant's work suggest a more sympathetic role for the sentiments in our moral life. In his famous response to a criticism raised by Schiller, Kant makes it clear that sentiment and morality cannot completely diverge:

> If one asks what is the aesthetic[22] character, the temperament, so to speak, of virtue, whether courageous, hence joyous, or fear-ridden and dejected, an answer is hardly necessary. This latter slavish frame of mind can never occur without a hidden hatred of the law. And a heart which is happy in the performance of its duty (not merely complacent in the recognition thereof) is a mark of genuineness in the virtuous disposition.[23]

I will argue in the following sections that Kant's views do accord a proper role to the interaction between reason and sentiments in our understanding of morality, and in the attainment of moral insight. This possibility, I believe, has been made plausible by the arguments from the previous section. If we think that direct application of the categorical imperative is not the main tool of actual moral deliberation, then we might conclude that there is a role for sentiments here. Indeed, in light of the arguments of the previous section, we might think that we *ought* to find a role for our sentiments here, for pure reason offers nothing other than the most abstract formulation of the categorical imperative.

Kant certainly takes the categorical imperative to be the sole principle of morality, and this principle of morality is, so to speak, a product of un-aided reason. Yet, contrary to appearances, Kant's commitment to these claims does not prevent him from providing for a cognitive role for senti-ments in our moral life. This cognitive role is worked out most clearly in Kant's account of friendship, and in particular, his views on the relationship between friendship and the categorical imperative. By examining this rela-tionship, I aim to show how sentiments and the abstract moral law combine to shape crucial aspects of our conception of the good in Kant's moral phi-losophy. In particular, I will try to demonstrate that our affective feelings toward our friends provide us with subordinate maxims, maxims that guide us in applying the categorical imperative, and so have a positive role to play in specifying what counts as a moral life. At the end of this section, I hope to have shown that Baier's insights are compatible not only with Kant's ac-count of friendship, but also with the thought that Kant has correctly un-derstood the cognitive role of sentiments and their relation to the rational principle of morality.

One might think that Kant's moral theory is incompatible with the ideals of friendship and, in general, incapable of dealing with human rela-tions, because of its demands for impartiality.[24] According to some of these criticisms, Kant's claim that friendship constitutes what he calls a "moral ideal" must, at least, be contrary to the spirit of the rest of the enterprise.[25] Such criticisms have been addressed elsewhere, so I will not try to offer an explicit answer to them here. Many of these responses have also been rather successful in explaining how, for Kant, sentiments are not merely obstacles and hindrances to the moral law. [26] As I indicated above, my concern is more specific: I want to investigate whether Kant can allow for a proper *cogni-tive* role for our sentiments. These investigations will also address some of Baier's objections to Kant's account of friendship—objections that are not answered in the literature.

Kant speaks of true friendship as an ideal set for us by reason. And, according to Kant, we have a duty of friendship, a duty to adopt this ideal (MS 469). Thus, perfect friendship must conform to rational norms, and is, in a sense, the highest expression of these rational norms, as we will see in a moment. But how do we come to know that we have such a duty, and what kind of duty is that of friendship? What is the relation between the duty of friendship and the natural friendly feelings whose onset seems to predate our awareness of a duty of friendship?

One answer that we might be tempted to give to this last question is "none." Kant carefully distinguishes between different kinds of friendship, and disdains the kinds of friendship that he attributes to the "rabble" (cf. MS 471). The friendship that it is a duty to strive for must, one might say, be derived from the moral law and thus from pure practical reason. But if this is so, it might seem that how we feel toward certain people is irrelevant both to our understanding of friendship as a duty and to the cultivation of a friendship according to duty.[27] If this were a consequence of Kant's account of friendship, it would certainly fail to provide us with an example of how our sentiments can contribute to our understanding of morality (or to our moral agency). Some of Kant's texts might seem to support this reading. Kant says that friendship as an ideal "is not derived from experience"(VE 217 [202]), and that "friendship cannot be an affect, for affect is blind in its choice, and after a while it goes up in smoke" (MS 471).

It is true that Kant says that friendship, at least the perfect friendship that it is our duty to strive for, is not derived from experience. Friendship is an "idea," and this means for Kant that it is a standard against which we can judge empirical objects.[28] But experience could not provide the standard itself, nor the grounds for accepting this standard as a proper way of evaluating actual friendships. Experience could only tell us how certain friends actually behave, or how people actually behave, but not that they ought to have friends, nor how they ought to behave toward their friends.

However, accepting this claim does not imply that experience cannot contribute to the formation of this idea, and in particular it does not imply that we cannot see the contribution of human sensibility in the formation of this idea. It might be the case that unaided reason is the ground of the idea of friendship; however, reason cannot, by itself, specify its full content. We can get a better sense of how Kant could accept the idea that the duty of friendship cannot be fully known by merely contemplating the moral law, and at the same time hold that the idea of friendship is not derived from experience, if we look at the following passage from the introduction to the *Metaphysics of Morals*:

a metaphysics of morals cannot dispense with principles of application, and we shall often have to take as our object the particular nature of man, which is known only by experience, in order to show in it what can be inferred from universal moral principles. But this will in no way detract from the purity of these principles or cast doubt on their *a priori* source. This is to say, in effect, that a metaphysics of morals cannot be based upon anthropology but can still be applied to it. (MS 216–17)

Of course, to say that we might need to rely on empirical knowledge to apply the moral law is very far from accepting the idea that our sentiments make any serious contribution to our understanding of the moral law. In order to apply *modus ponens* to the empirical world, we need to know what kinds of conditionals and conditions are true, and this knowledge is certainly empirical knowledge. But it is a formidable leap to infer from this trivial point that our empirical knowledge contributes in any way to our understanding of logic. The last sentence of this quotation might suggest that Kant does not wish to concede anything beyond a similar, trivial point with respect to the relation between empirical knowledge and our understanding of the moral law.

However, even though it is true that the contribution of principles other than those of pure reason in the realm of morality can only be as principles of application, we are not thereby committed to belittling their role in our understanding of morality in general, and our duty of friendship in particular. The very mention of "principles of application" suggests that applying the moral law is not as straightforward a matter as applying a rule like *modus ponens*. If the conditions of application of the moral law were obvious, and if they amounted to merely replacing some variables with the appropriate information, we would have no more need of principles of application in the case of the moral law than we have in the case of *modus ponens*.

By looking at one of Kant's own examples of lack of judgment, we can clearly see that the role of sentiments goes beyond merely providing us with material for application of the FUL, and that they play a truly cognitive role in the realm of morality:

A physician . . . may have at command many excellent pathological . . . rules, even to the degree that he may become a profound teacher of them, and yet, none the less, may easily stumble in their application. For . . . he may be wanting in natural power of judgment. (KrV, B173)

Imagine a school of medicine in which, during the first years, students learned only from books, with no practical training, the latter being left to the last two years of teaching. A student who left before the two years of practical training would certainly not be a very good doctor. His short-comings would be "due to his not having received . . . adequate training for this particular act of judgment" (KrV, B173).

Because medicine is a practical science, we would consider someone's knowledge of medicine deficient if his knowledge of biological theory were unimpeachable, but if he did not know that being unwilling to run a marathon did not count as being in a lethargic state. However, we should not be misled by this example to downplay the contribution of "judgment sharpened by experience." Medical textbooks do not try to separate the contribution of each faculty, let alone isolate the work of pure reason. Thus, many of the rules contained in those books are already rules of application based on judgment; that is, they are rules generated when the faculty of judgments tries to apply more general rules to cases in which the application of the rule is not obvious. Kant explicitly states that judgment performs such a role in morality by providing us with subordinate maxims: "Ethics inevitably . . . leads to questions that call upon judgment to decide how a maxim is to be applied in particular cases, and indeed in such a way that judgment provides another (subordinate) maxim" (MS 411).

It is also helpful to remember that we can form no determinate idea of how perfectly rational beings would follow the moral law. It is not clear, for instance, how the rule against suicide (or self-termination) would apply to them. There is no "system of nature" that would collapse on the assumption that self-termination is permissible. The same holds for beneficence; it is a form of inconsistent willing for us not to be beneficent, but this does not seem to apply for beings without needs, even if they have the power to help finitely rational beings like us. A similar point can be made for finitely rational beings whose inclinations are radically different from ours, but who are also subject to the moral law. Since we can assume that they have needs, we can also assume that some kind of maxim of beneficence binds them; but since we know nothing about the nature of their needs, we have no determinate idea of what such a maxim would prescribe.

Thus, if pure reason provides only a very abstract principle, the contribution of our sensible nature can be at least partly constitutive of our understanding of the duty of friendship. If applying the moral law requires making difficult judgments, then the fact that our sentiments could make a genuine contribution only to the application of the moral law does not in any way threaten the cognitive role these sentiments play in the formation of our understanding of what counts as a life guided by the categorical imperative. An agent might require more than abstract knowledge of these rules to know what would count as a life lived according to these rules in particular circumstances, or even to know what counts, for a particular kind of rational being (such as a rational being with human sensibilities), as following these rules. For those rules whose application is not a matter of course, principles of application provide guidance that is not straightforwardly contained in the more abstract rule.[29]

At least with respect to the duties of virtue, there is no doubt that, for Kant, the application of the highly abstract categorical imperative is no obvious matter and requires the exercise of judgment. As noted above, judgment provides subordinate maxims that serve as principles of application of the moral law. The moral law enjoins us, for instance, to make the ends of other human beings our own. However, an understanding of the moral law is not enough to explain how we should go about adopting other people's ends. It is a fairly straightforward consequence of, for instance, the ideal of the kingdom of ends that we make the happiness of others our end.[30] The idea of a kingdom of ends enjoins each rational being to think of every other rational being as a legislator in the kingdom of ends, and thus to make their ends his own.[31] But there is no obvious way to apply this injunction to particular actions. Every selfish action could be seen as pursuing my ends *only on this occasion*, as opposed to disregarding the ends of others.[32] Thus, in and of itself, no action I undertake—at least as long as it does not conflict with any other duty—is obviously incompatible with my having adopted the general maxim of beneficence. Disregarding the ends of others *on this particular occasion* could always be the result of an overriding need of my own, rather than a failure to make someone else's end my own.

Given the complexity of adjudicating the demands of my needs and those of others, I need subordinate maxims that will help me identify the proper demands of the duty of beneficence. I cannot evaluate the proper place of these claims without good exercise of judgment about human nature, and about the importance of different needs for different persons. The moral law cannot provide us with an understanding of the place of the different elements in the conception of the good of different human beings, nor can it help us adjudicate their different claims. Yet, without this understanding, we cannot have subordinate maxims with any content. In particular, I need to know when the satisfaction of my needs should be foregone, in order to satisfy the needs of others, given the conditions of human nature. As we can see from this case, principles of applications are those principles that will help us determine what counts as a life guided by the categorical imperative for rational beings who are also *human* beings.[33]

Among the conditions of human nature is the fact that we are not perfectly virtuous, and thus, to use Kant's form of expression, that which I give might not be returned to me. Our friendly feelings and our capacity to cultivate friendships provide us with an understanding of a certain possibility of human nature—that is, that I take a natural interest in the ends of my friend. In loving someone, I already find myself making someone else's end my own. The idea of the kingdom of ends permits us to see how this form of human sensibility can be developed to form a moral ideal, one according to which our subjective needs are taken to be objective ends. Consequently, on the ideal of friendship, the needs of my friend ought to make the same demands on my will as do my own. This ideal prescribes that we form perfect friendships, friendships in which the love of a friend for another is limited only by the requirement of mutual respect. This is an ideal of *human* nature. Friendship might not be an available option for other rational beings; they might recognize moral ideals that are unintelligible to us in view of our human nature. They might have other ways of sharing ends or managing to live in accordance to the principle of beneficence that depend on quite different natures. So, the moral ideal of friendship is not accessible by pure reason alone, but requires that our affective capacities reveal to us a particular form of making the ends of others our own.

Friendship, for Kant, requires the interaction of love and respect. This interplay of love and respect is an important example of how sentiments and reflection guided by the moral law cooperate in the specification of what counts as a life lived according to the maxim of beneficence, and thus according to the categorical imperative. We naturally feel affection toward certain people; these feelings are possible only because we have some natural inclinations or some natural dispositions to form such inclinations. Our inclinations, however, can be shaped by habit and thus by the exercise of reason. For instance, Kant argues that a person who is beneficent from duty will end up loving the recipients of her beneficence. Kant interprets the biblical command "Love your neighbor as yourself" as follows:

> [It] does not mean that you ought immediately (first) to love him and (afterwards) by means of this love do good to him. It means, rather, *do good* to your fellow, and your benevolence will produce love of man in you (as an aptitude of the inclination to beneficence in general).[34]

In the same way, we have "an indirect duty to cultivate the compassionate natural (aesthetic) feelings in us." However rational activity can help shape our aptitude for love, this aptitude is nonetheless part of human sensibility. Of course, it is not necessarily the case that love is the result of our virtuous willing. Love can be "pathologically" determined—that is, determined by the contingent, nonrational aspects of our faculty of desire. We may love someone who was never the object of our virtuous willing. Moreover, even the extent of our love for our fellows is largely determined by various aspects of human nature—Kant claims, for instance, that "it is not man's way to embrace the whole world in his good will" (VE 222 [206]).

Respect, on the other hand, has no pathological manifestation. Respect can be effected only by the moral law (cf. KpV 76–78). Kant equates respect with consciousness of the "immediate determination of the will by the law" (G 401n), or with "morality itself, regarded subjectively as a drive" (KpV 76). So, we can think of respect as our awareness of the moral law insofar as it can determine us to act. It might seem strange that we talk about respect for a friend, since, as we would expect from the above definitions of respect, and as Kant himself emphasizes, the only proper object of respect is the moral law (G 401n and KpV 76).

However, a person can be at least indirectly the object of respect insofar as the moral law resides in that person—or, in other words, insofar as she is a rational agent. Respect for others can be thus understood as "the *maxim* of limiting our self-esteem by the dignity of humanity in another person" (MS 449). To show respect for a particular person is to have one's self-esteem limited in this way, and thus we can say that reason must shape our friendly feelings and our inclinations arising out of friendship so that friendship does not demand a suspension of morality. In other words, the work of reason over sentiments has to make sure (at least in the ideal case) that our friendly feelings will not be the source of commitments that *compete* with the moral law. Rather, they must turn out to be the source of projects and commitments that *express* the moral law.

Respect and love make different contributions to the moral ideal of friendship. The feeling of respect in a friendship is the direct product of the activity of reason, of the understanding of the moral law. Respect is the expression of the moral law in our sensible nature, and Kant equates it with our consciousness of our duty (MS 464). On the other hand, our affectionate feelings toward our friends owe much more to our natural inclinations. Although they are capable of being corrected and encouraged by our consciousness of the moral law, they cannot be wholly grounded in this consciousness.

The duty of friendship can thus be seen as a specification of the maxim of beneficence, made possible through the cooperation of some sensible aspects of human nature. The categorical imperative could not prescribe such a duty, if it were not for our natural capacity to engage in the kind of sensible relations with other people that make us take the kind of interest that we take in the welfare of our friends. Although the duty of friendship cannot be arrived at by a straightforward application of FUL, the categorical imperative guides us in singling out our friendly feelings as setting morally worthy ends, and provides us with a framework for the proper cultivation of such feelings. That is to say, insofar as we think that a particular ideal of friendship is an expression of a moral ideal, we are committed to the possibility of accounting for it as an instantiation of the principle of beneficence. And accounting for this ideal is not to account for some raw, indiscriminate feeling, but rather for our sensibilities developed under the guidance of our rational nature. If Kant is right, then, our friendly feelings, when properly corrected by reflection, provide us with determinate ends that constitute our conception of what could count as living a life guided by the categorical imperative.

III

It might be worth looking into some objections to this account of the role of sentiments in Kant's account of friendship. One might object that even if

Kant allows for such a role, his commitment to the overriding character of morality will prevent him from seeing that our sentiments, especially in the case of friendship, can be *better* guides than the moral law. Some might argue that friendship is a form of human relationship that does not need to be patrolled by the strict rules of morality. [35] It is immoral to use other people's rightful property as if it were my own, but friends would not (or should not always) feel harmed if their friends violate this requirement— my friend will not be offended if I use his car, without his express consent, to pick up my sister stranded in a bad neighborhood. Finally, if it is true that friendship involves relaxing the claims of morality, there would be no way that Kant could count friendship as any kind of practical ideal. For Kant, nothing can legitimately relax the strict claims of morality.

However, we should not be misled by the demand that the rules of morality be "strict." Suppose I want to send an open letter to a paper that will denounce someone, but since I am afraid of his revenge, I do not want to sign my name. I know that the paper will not publish an anonymous letter, so I decide to sign someone else's name. This is indeed a shameful thing to do. It would certainly not make it any better if the name I sign was my friend's; if anything, this would make it worse. I cannot say "Moral rules are not so strict among friends, so it is not so bad to exploit my friend," or even, "at least it is better than exploiting a stranger." To say that the rules of morality are strict is to say that nothing can cancel their overriding character, including friendship, and this seems to be confirmed by the example above.[36] But, what I can expect of an intimate friend might be relevant in determining what I can or ought to do or refrain from doing. Indeed, there might be nothing wrong about using my friend's car without her manifest consent in circumstances in which I would not use a stranger's car without asking permission. In certain contexts, the fact that someone is my friend would require, to use this imprecise manner of speaking, that I follow the rules of morality *more* strictly. Suppose I am informed of a poorly advertised but desirable job opening for which I am reasonably qualified. I might know of another person who is more qualified for the job, a person whom I have never met and to whom I am in no way related, and who, I suspect, might not be aware of this opening. At least in certain circumstances, it would not be a violation of my duty not to inform this person of this job. However, in the same circumstances, it would be a serious moral failing not to inform this person of this job opening if this person happened to be one's best friend.

An observation that Kant makes in another context seems to apply here as well. Kant claims that Aristotle mistakes the difference between the miser and the spendthrift person. The difference is not that the latter does the same thing as the former does, but to a lesser degree. The difference must be in their *maxims* (MS 404). Here too, the difference between how one treats one's friends and how one treats strangers is best accounted for by the fact that these different actions fall under different maxims, not by the need to be more or less bound by the restraints of morality. In fact, Kant seems to be in a particularly good position to explain why we might be tempted by this improper way of speaking to claim that in the first case, the moral rules seem to be "looser" for our friends, and in the second case, "stricter." The ideal of friendship is an ideal of taking my friend's end as my own, of always sharing each other's ends. Although real friendships fall short of this ideal, I know that I can expect that my friend will share my end when I need to rescue my stranded sister, in a way that I cannot expect from a stranger. And it may be consistent with thinking of a stranger as a fellow human that I do not inform her of job opportunities I covet. I may be allowed to give my interests significantly more weight than those of a stranger's without violating the principle of beneficence. But I could not be guided by the ideal of friendship if I let my interests weigh so much more heavily against my friend's in such a case.

A more serious threat implicit in this objection is that Kant's account of friendship might turn out to be too "intellectualist": since it gives such an important role to reflection and the limiting conditions of the moral law, it cannot account for the more affectionate, humane forms of friendship which are truly valuable. If this turns out to be the case, despite our attempts to identify the contribution of sentiments, it would certainly lend credence to the suspicion that Kant's ethics cannot accommodate in any plausible way the role that sentiments play in our moral lives. Indeed, Kant often describes the role of respect in a way that cannot but foment such suspicions and might seem quite repugnant. The following is a prime example: "Love can be regarded as an attraction and respect as a repulsion, and if the principle of love bids friends to draw closer, the principle of respect requires them to stay at proper distance of each other" (MS 470). It seems plausible to object that friendship does not require a principle that keeps friends at a proper distance; this is a principle that leads people away from friendship into cold indifference.

The requirement for respect and lack of excessive familiarity might bring to mind the picture of a friend who refuses to forgo a whole array of formalities—someone, for example, who will not come to visit her friend if her shirt is not properly ironed. The above discussion of Kant's notion of respect should have made it clear, however, that this cannot be what Kant means. The distance that respect establishes cannot be different from the distance that the moral law requires. To say that respect imposes a certain "distance" between friends amounts to no more than to say that friends remain two different persons with autonomous wills. This is, in itself, a quite plausible claim, even if one wants to take issue with the way in which Kant marks this distance—or with the particular restrictions that Kant thinks the moral law imposes on friendships.

If, on the one hand, some inclinations can be shaped by reflection to conform to the moral law and be part of a moral ideal, then these same inclinations, abstracted away from reflection, might carry with them some temptations to deviate from the moral law. Reflection teaches us that friendship as an ideal would involve a greater amount of mutual love than we encounter in the world, but also that not everything that is done out of love can meet with our approval.

In particular, love might tempt us to erase the boundaries between persons and to disregard the autonomy of each will. Indeed, this temptation is a natural outgrowth of these same aspects of love that make love part of a moral ideal. The more I care about my friend, the more I see her happiness as playing a role in my life similar to the role of my own happiness. Those who love each other come to a (partial) union, and this union is partly constitutive of the ideal of friendship. The idea of friendship, Kant says, is one "in which self-love is superseded by a generous reciprocal love" (VE 217 [201]). However, I would violate the demand of respect for my friend if I not only *adopted* her ends, but also took myself to be capable of *setting* her ends. No matter how much I care for her well-being, it is the exercise of *her* judgment that determines her ends; we remain two different agents with two different bodies and differently constituted conceptions of the good. Thus, the boundary between persons must remain in place if I am still to regard my friend as an agent—if my actions are to be compatible with recognizing her exercise of judgment as constituting her good. The duty of respect is, for Kant, the recognition of another as a person, or as an agent:

"The duty of respect . . . is contained in the maxim not to degrade any other man to a mere means to my ends" (MS 450; cf. MS 462). I cannot commit my friend to political causes, no matter how noble they are; I cannot use her body as if it were just a continuation of mine; and I cannot determine for her what her happiness consists in, no matter how well-intentioned I am. Given that the principle of respect is what makes us treat our friends as *agents*, its claims will be limiting conditions of the claims of love. The principle of love draws friends closer by making a friend's end one's own, but the principle of respect keeps us at a proper distance by reminding us that we can make our own only those ends that our friends have already recognized as *their* ends. The limits imposed by respect allow us to see the ideal of friendship as a moral ideal, and the maxims of my actions that have their source in a conception of friendship as ones prescribed by the moral law.

One may have suspicions that some of Kant's text does not fit the account given here very well. Kant's discussion of friendship often seems to suggest that, at least in this case, our sentiments have no such role; indeed, it seems to suggest that the ideal of friendship is an ideal formed independently of these sentiments. One passage quoted earlier may seem to be especially difficult to reconcile with attributing any positive role to our friendly feelings in the formation of any moral ideal: "friendship cannot be an affect, for affect is blind in its choice, and after a while it goes up in smoke" (MS 471).

However, when we look at what Kant means by "affect," we see that this passage is compatible with my interpretation, and perhaps lends further support to it. According to Kant:

> Affects belong to *feeling* insofar as, *preceding reflection, it makes this impossible or more difficult.* Hence an affect is called *precipitate* or *rash* and reason says . . . that one should *get hold of* oneself. (MS 407) [37]

Friendship based on affect is thus exactly the kind of friendship that does not or cannot heed the principles that we set ourselves upon reflection. It is a kind of infatuation that is blind in its choice, *because it makes reflection impossible.* In fact, exactly because of this incompatibility with reflection, no kind of affect will last for long; it will be a mere impulse, whose claim will go away as soon as we take hold of ourselves again.

IV

We can now turn to some of Baier's objections to Kant's account of friendship. Baier claims that Kant does not regard friendship as having intrinsic
value, but only as being an instrument, "and a risky one," whose purpose is
to correct judgment. [38] Certainly, some of what Kant says seems to commit
him to this view:

> To have a friend whom we know to be frank and loving, neither false nor
> spiteful, is to have one who will help us to correct our judgment when it
> is mistaken. This is the *whole* end of man, through which he can enjoy
> his existence. (VE 222 [206]; emphasis mine)

However, we should not be confused here by what Kant means by the
"whole end of man." Correct judgment cannot but be the whole end of man,
since it amounts to attaining the right view, both in the theoretical and the
practical realm. It is doing right and thinking right. But this does not rule
out the fact that part of what we judge is that we should care about our friends
for their own sake. To say that we always aim at judging right does not rule
out the possibility that to care for our friends for their own sake *is* to judge
rightly. The following remark of Kant, however, is considerably harder to
integrate in an attractive picture of friendship: "It is very unwise to place
ourselves in a friend's hand completely, to tell him all the secrets which might
detract from our welfare if he became our enemy and spread them abroad"
(VE 224 [208]).

Baier points out that we cannot praise friendship and at the same time
enjoin people to avoid the risks of trusting others: "if all the world (except
the misamorist philosophers) is to keep loving lovers, it will have to come
to accept risks too."[39] We can begin to rescue Kant by noting that the idea
that we should not entrust our friends with our secrets in light of certain
prudential considerations is incompatible with what he says in the *Metaphysics of Morals*. There, he argues that human beings have a "need to *reveal*
themselves to others" (MS 471), and that this need can only be realized
through moral friendship, which Kant defines as the "*complete* confidence
of two persons in revealing their secret feelings and judgments to each
other" (MS 472; emphasis mine). The text leaves little room to doubt that
Kant thinks that we ought to pursue such friendships. More interestingly,

this kind of friendship is not considered by Kant to be a mere ideal, "but (like black swans) actually exists here and there in its perfection" (MS 472). It is important to avoid leaving the impression that Kant simply changed his mind between the *Lectures on Ethics* and the *Metaphysics of Morals*. In the *Lecture on Ethics*, he says: "Each of us needs a friend, one in whom we can confide unreservedly, to whom we can disclose *completely* all our dispositions and judgments, to whom we can communicate our *whole* self [dem er sich *völlig* kommunizieren kann]."[40]

This apparent inconsistency might justify certain textual gymnastics. We might say that Kant is not warning us against trusting a friend in general, but rather warning us that we should not trust a friend whom we would have reason to believe would betray our trust. The passage immediately following the one that warns us against telling all our secrets lends some credence to this reading: "In particular, we ought to place no weapon in the hands of a hot-headed friend who might be capable of sending us to the gallows in a moment of passion" (VE 224 [208]). It seems reasonable enough that Kant will warn his students against making themselves the victims of the outbursts of such a friend. No doubt one wonders, in such cases, whether it is not the best advice to avoid friendship with this kind of person altogether. However, there is nothing wrong with Kant's warning, and it should not be confused with an injunction against seeking friends in whom we can confide fully.[41]

The natural inclinations of love that express themselves in friendship allow us, under the scrutiny of reason, to think of an ideal realization of the maxim of beneficence, in which we make the ends of our friends our own. In friendship, we are fellow legislators in the kingdom of ends. Kant says that in friendship, all that I give I receive back (VE 207 [201]). In fact, what I get back is more than what I could possibly have by myself. For, in friendship, self-love, freedom, and sympathy all find their highest expression.

It might now seem that we have gone too far in attempting to make room for a positive role for sentiments in Kant's moral philosophy. If our inclinations have such an important role to play, why should we say that a rational being wishes to get rid of his or her inclinations? However, recognizing that our sentiments have a positive role in our moral life is compatible with recognizing that they can also turn out to be hindrances. Empirical motives do not necessarily coincide with the ends of morality. A wish to be rid of our inclinations should be understood as no more than a wish not to be tempted to act immorally. This wish can only be what we could call an "aspectual wish"; that is, we can only wish to get rid of our inclinations *insofar as they are threats* to the commands of the moral law. However, we cannot unqualifiedly desire or make this wish the end of our actions. In fact, Kant himself warns against this temptation: "*Considered in themselves* natural inclinations are *good*, i.e., not reprehensible, and to want to extirpate them would not only be futile but harmful and blameworthy as well" (R 58).

Our sentiments can and often do lead us away from the path of virtue. For Kant, it is this recognition—not the fact that the philosopher is in a particularly good position to settle moral disputes—that underscores the practical significance of the philosopher's task of tracing the source of our moral cognitions to the faculty of reason. As Kant engages in this task, it is natural that the positive role of sentiments will be left aside. However, this should not make us lose sight of Kant's keen awareness of the extent to which human finitude requires reliance upon our sensible nature.

NOTES

I thank Annette Baier for many insightful comments on an ancestor to this paper, and for her invaluable mentoring. I would also like to thank Jennifer Nagel, Hans Lottenbach, Stephen Engstrom, and the editors of this volume for very helpful comments on various drafts of this paper.

1. Annette Baier, "Theory and Reflective Practices," in *Essays on Mind and Morals* (Minneapolis: University of Minnesota Press, 1985), 207.

2. "Act as if the maxim of your action were to become by your will a *universal law of nature*" (G 421). For the rest of this section, I will discuss only FUL, but my claims should also apply to the other formulations.

3. Baier, "Theory and Reflective Practices," 207.

4. See, especially, Barbara Herman, "The Practice of Moral Judgment" in her *The Practice of Moral Judgment* (Cambridge, MA: Harvard University Press, 1993), 73–93.

5. I agree with Marcia Baron that this is a mistake that can be easily dismissed. See her *Kantian Ethics Almost Without Apology* (Ithaca, NY: Cornell University Press, 1995), 9.

6. See G 389. References to Kant's works are to the appropriate volume of *Kant's gesammelte Schriften, herausgegeben von der Deutschen* (formerly *Königlichen Preussischen*) *Akademie der Wissenschaften* (Berlin: Walter de Gruyter [and predeces-

sors], 1902), with the exception of the *Critique of Pure Reason* and *Lectures on Ethics*. References to the *Critique of Pure Reason* are to the standard B pagination of the second edition. References to the *Lectures on Ethics* are to *Eine Vorlesung über Ethik*, edited by Gerd Gerhardt (Frankfurt am Main: Fischer Verlag, 1990). Specific works are cited by means of the abbreviations below. I have used the English translations mentioned below with occasional minor changes. I have provided the page number of the German edition and the English translation (the latter in parentheses) whenever the latter did not include the German pagination in the margins.

APH *Anthropology from a Pragmatic Point of View*, trans. Victor Lyle Dowdell, revised and edited by Frederick P. Van de Pitte (Carbondale: Southern Illinois University Press, 1978).

G *Grounding of the Metaphysics of Morals*, trans. James Ellington (Indianapolis: Hackett Publishing Co., 1981).

KrV *Critique of Pure Reason*, trans. N. Kemp Smith (New York: St. Martin's Press, 1965).

KpV *Critique of Practical Reason*, trans. L. W. Beck (Indianapolis: Bobbs-Merrill, 1956).

VE *Lectures on Ethics*, trans. Louis Infield (Indianapolis: Hackett Publishing Co., 1981).

MS *Metaphysics of Morals*, trans. Mary Gregor (New York: Cambridge University Press, 1991).

R *Religion Within the Limits of Reason Alone*, trans. Theodore M. Greene and Hoyt H. Hudson (New York: Harper & Row, 1960).

L *Logic*, trans. R. Hartman and W. Schwarz (New York: Dover, 1974).

TP *On the Proverb: That May Be True in Theory, but Is of No Practical Use*, trans. Ted Humphrey (Indianapolis: Hackett Publishing Co., 1983).

7. See, for instance, G 404.

8. As we will see below, this is not to say that the explicit formulation of the categorical imperative has *no* practical function to perform.

9. Annette Baier, "Unsafe Loves," in *Moral Prejudices* (Cambridge, MA: Harvard University Press, 1994), 48.

10. John Rawls, *A Theory of Justice* (Cambridge, MA: Harvard University Press, 1971), 53, emphasis mine. It is important to note that doubts about the possibility of finding *ethical* principles that can perform this job are not necessarily doubts about the possibility of finding *political* principles that can settle disputes in the context that Rawls is interested in.

11. Annette Baier, "Doing Without Moral Theory," in her *Postures of the Mind: Essays on Mind and Morals* (Minneapolis: University of Minnesota Press, 1985), 235. Baier calls this a "Kantian" prejudice.

12. This is how he often uses *"verwirren."* See, for instance, KrV, B9 and KrV, B11. See also L 34–36.

13. No doubt faulty inferences might be thought to be more likely without an explicit formulation of the categorical principle. I will come back to this point shortly.

14. See R 35.

15. Indeed this is a speculative mistake made by some philosophers (that is, they *misdescribe* the fundamental principle of morality), but not by ordinary reason. Kant says that this mistake "can maintain itself only in the perplexing speculations of the schools which have temerity enough to close their ear to that heavenly voice in order to uphold a theory that costs no brainwork" (KpV 35). See also KpV 35–36. For more on this issue, see my "Speculative Mistakes and Ordinary Temptations: Kant on Instrumentalist Conceptions of Practical Reason," *History of Philosophy Quarterly* 20 (April 2003): 203–23.

16. Cf. John Stuart Mill, *Utilitarianism* (Indianapolis: Hackett Publishing, 1979), 23–24.

17. I am ignoring for the moment the potential that either the principle of utility or FUL have to serve as tools of radical reform; that is, tools for reforming tenets of ordinary morality that are more or less generally accepted. Since I am not optimistic about the prospects of either in this regard, I will ignore this issue.

18. According to Kant, "knowledge through reason and *a priori* knowledge are the same thing" (KpV 12).

19. Thus, the concept of freedom is introduced in the main text of the *Critique of Practical Reason* with the following task: "Granted that the mere legislative form of maxims is the sole sufficient determining ground of a will, find the property (*Beschaffenheit*) of the will which is determinable by it alone" (KpV 28).

20. Herman argues that this is a problem for the practical interpretation of FUL. See *The Practice of Moral Judgment*, 137–40. But given what I say below, I do not think it is a fatal problem for this interpretation.

21. See KpV 118 and G 428. This is indeed a striking claim, and I will try to reconcile it with my interpretation of Kant only at the end of this paper.

22. "Aesthetic" should here be understood not as relating to categories of the beautiful, but rather as relating to that which pertains to *sensibility* (in the same way as the term is used in the *Critique of Pure Reason*).

23. R 23–24n (19–20n). See also MS 484–85.

24. See, for instance, Bernard Williams, "Persons, Character and Morality," in his *Moral Luck* (New York: Cambridge University Press, 1981), and Julia Annas, "Personal Love and Kantian Ethics in 'Effi Briest,'" in *Friendship: A Philosophical Reader*, ed. Neera Kapur Badhwar (Ithaca, NY: Cornell University Press, 1993), 155–74.

25. This is Julia Annas's position. See her "Personal Love and Kantian Ethics in 'Effi Briest.'"

26. See, for instance, Marcia Baron, "Impartiality and Friendship," *Ethics* 101 (1991): 836–57, and "Was Effi Briest a Victim of Kantian Morality?" in Badhwar, *Friendship*, 174–91; Barbara Herman, "Integrity and Impartiality," in *The Practice of Moral Judgment*, 23–44; Christine Korsgaard, "Creating the Kingdom of Ends," in her *Creating the Kingdom of Ends* (Cambridge: Cambridge University Press, 1996), 188–221.

27. It is interesting to note that Kant divides friendship into many kinds, but never distinguishes between a friendship based on sentiment, on the one hand, and a friendship according to reason, on the other. The closest he gets to such a distinction is that between moral and aesthetic friendship. A friendship is a moral friendship insofar as two friends trust each other to the point that they can confide in each other all their judgments and feelings (consistent with mutual respect; see MS 471). Kant's use of the phrase *"merely* moral" (*bloße moralische*, MS 472; emphasis mine) to talk about a certain friendship insofar as it consists *only* in this kind of confidence suggests that moral friendship is a *part* of friendship in its "purity and completeness" (MS, 470), which it is a duty to strive for. In the *Lectures on Ethics*, Kant seems to suggest that this kind of confidence is possible only within an aesthetic friendship. He makes it clear there that the highest form of friendship is the friendship of sentiment (see VE 221–22 [205–206]), and I think there is no evidence that he later changed his mind on this issue.

28. See VE 218 (202). Compare with KrV, B372–74. Kant distinguishes between an idea and an ideal, but since this distinction is not important for our purposes, I will assume that there is no difference between an idea and an ideal of friendship.

29. Kant was certainly aware of the fact that applying a rule is ultimately not a matter of finding more rules to apply a certain rule, or, as he says, "further rules cannot always be added to guide judgment in its subsumptions (for that could go on infinitely)" (TP 275). Even if we have principles of application, these will, in turn, require judgment for their own application, and judgment cannot be guided by rules. See also KrV, B171–72, and APH 199.

30. I will use the phrase "maxim of beneficence" to mean the maxim that I shall make the happiness of others my end.

31. Although I will be relying here on the idea of the kingdom of ends, Kant thinks that the principle that we should make other people's ends our own is a consequence of the categorical imperative under any formulation (after all, all the formulations should be equivalent).

32. This does not need to be the result of "cheating" in the use of this procedure, but merely the result of considering each occasion at a time without reflecting on one's general patterns of conduct and general disposition for beneficence.

33. This also explains why, in the *Doctrine of Virtue*, Kant does not attempt to derive our duties directly from the categorical imperative. The *Doctrine of Virtue* is

concerned with exactly those duties that require principles of application. If we could determine these duties by straightforward applications of the categorical imperative, we would not need principles of application.

34. MS 402. This also explains Kant's response to Schiller. A person who acts from a good will would tend to have the inclination to act as duty prescribes.

35. John Deigh makes this point in "Morality and Personal Relations," in his *Sources of Moral Agency* (Cambridge: Cambridge University Press, 1996), 1–17. I have also borrowed the following example from this paper.

36. Samuel Scheffler argues that it is probably too much to expect that moral norms are always overriding. See his *Human Morality* (New York: Oxford University Press, 1992), 56. And when demands of friendship come to the fore, this expectation might seem particularly problematic. But since, for Kant, the realm of morality simply is the realm of unconditional principles of action, we would be changing the subject if we were to abandon this expectation.

37. Kant also defines "affect" as the "feeling of pleasure or displeasure that does not give rise to reflection (the representation of reason of whether one should submit to it or reject it)" (APH 251), and as "surprise through sensation, whereby the composure of mind is suspended. . . . Therefore . . . it quickly grows to a degree of feeling which makes reflection impossible" (APH 252).

38. Baier, "Unsafe Loves," 36.

39. Ibid., 48. Baier includes Kant among the misamorists.

40. VE 221–22 (205–206), all emphases mine. It must be pointed out that a few sentences later, Kant says that "we have certain natural frailties which ought to be concealed for the sake of decency, lest humanity be outraged. Even to our best friend we must not reveal ourselves, in our natural state as we know it ourselves. To do so would be loathsome." Whether or not one thinks that Kant is being excessively prudish here, the reserve that Kant calls for here has nothing to do with distrusting a friend.

41. What counts as reasonable distrust toward a friend will, of course, depend on the circumstances. In particular, it will have a lower threshold in a historical context in which one has much more to fear from disclosure of one's secret judgments and feelings.

CHAPTER 14

Cruelty, Respect, and Unsentimental Love

MICHELE MOODY-ADAMS

The categorical imperative, Nietzsche complained in *The Genealogy of Morals*, retains a certain "odor of blood and torture."[1] Kant's understanding of moral guilt, Nietzsche continued, developed out of a "material" conception of debt according to which unpaid debts could be compensated by inflicting pain on the body of the debtor—sometimes even by cutting from that body what seemed "commensurate" with the size of the debt. On the resulting conception of morality, every instance of moral wrongdoing can be paid back through the suffering of the offending party.[2] Nietzsche thus thought that Kant's view licensed the moral judge—usually the self-scrutinizing faulty agent, but sometimes an external assessor, or even the penal institutions of political society—to extract some equivalent of a pound of flesh.[3] Because Nietzsche believed that the disposition to inflict such suffering (and the pleasure that he thought was bound up with it) amounted to cruelty, he considered Kant's moral conception to be unreservedly—and objectionably—cruel.

Yet Nietzsche also believed that some intertwining of guilt and suffering was fundamental to most moral views, and he sought to unmask the cruelty of these views as part of a challenge to their fundamental values. Liberated from conventional morality's allegedly cruel demands, the sovereign

Nietzschean agent would place little importance on familiar values such as love, friendship, and trust. Nietzsche's attack on pity, as Martha Nussbaum argues, is rooted in a Stoic ideal of the person who cares for nothing that he cannot control and who so insulates himself against pain and loss that he becomes incapable of genuine love.[4] There is thus an important irony informing Annette Baier's skillful effort, in "Moralism and Cruelty: Reflections on Hume and Kant," to reiterate essentially Nietzschean allegations about the cruelty of Kant's moral views.[5] Like Nietzsche, Baier charges that Kantian pressures for moral conformity are cruel. She contends, for instance, that Kant's retributive theory of punishment uncritically equates the Germanic concept of *Blutschuld* with the deliverances of reason.[6] She nonetheless rejects Nietzsche's broader challenge to conventional morality. She defends the moral importance of care—and of forms of trust that are possible only in caring relationships. Moreover, she persuasively argues that vulnerability to potentially "unsafe loves" is an essential ingredient of any life worth living.[7] Baier holds, further, that any cruelty associated with conventional moral demands can sometimes be preferable, as the lesser of two evils, to the total absence of any such demands. Morality must sometimes risk "angry cruelty," she urges, if society is to protect itself against murderers, rapists, and the like.[8]

Yet Baier believes that Kantian pressures for moral conformity cause unnecessary cruelty, especially in comparison with the sympathy-based morality described by Hume. She maintains, for instance, that Kant's conception of moral criticism embodies an inhumane demand for moral perfection and may well damage the faulty agent's virtues as well as his vices.[9] Humane moral criticism, in Baier's view, would not be aimed at the entire person—as Kantian moral criticism is—but, as Hume suggests, at the "faulty aspect of the person."[10] Baier also rejects the conception of responsibility that underlies Kant's moral theory. A Humean always looks for "the social fault behind the individual fault," she urges, because responsibility for moral evil is always shared and is not "localizable" in individual agents.[11] She allows that it may sometimes be essential to take "forceful protective measures" against individual agents. As a Humean, however, she justifies the infliction of suffering only when there is evidence that some good is likely to come of it.[12] Morality can be both effective and humane, Baier adds, if we follow Hume's preference for moral pressure with "a light touch"—relying on laughter, for instance, more often than "hectoring commands."[13] Baier ultimately doubts whether Kant could have appreciated the force of these objections, since she believes that he wrongly considered masturbation and suicide, rather than cruelty, as the worst that a human being might do.[14] These doubts reinforce her preference for Hume's understanding of cruelty—an approach summed up in her contention that Hume regarded cruelty as "the worst vice."[15] Kant's presumed failure to understand the moral weight of cruelty, along with the cruelty allegedly caused if one accepts a Kantian view of morality, leads Baier to insist that Kant's moral theory is deeply flawed.[16]

Anyone who regards cruelty as a basic moral failing, however, should actually prefer Kant's view to Hume's. To begin with, as I argue in section 1 of this essay, Hume never provides an adequate account of cruelty or of the moral relevance of the suffering it causes. He is mainly concerned with the moral status of certain kinds of cruelty, rather than with the moral wrong of cruelty in general. Moreover, those passages which purport to analyze the morality of cruelty as such prove to be concerned with only a narrow subset of cruelty's effects. Most of Hume's discussion concerns the consequences cruelty has for the cruel person's character—almost to the exclusion of serious attention to the suffering of the victims of cruelty. As a result, his account is virtually indifferent to those aspects of cruelty which are central to understanding why it is morally reprehensible.

The second formulation of Kant's categorical imperative, as I argue in section 2, provides a better analysis of cruelty and a richer understanding of the moral wrong of cruelty than anything available on a Humean view. I maintain that cruelty has two essential elements: the intentionally inflicted injuries suffered by cruelty's victims, and the intentions of the perpetrators in inflicting suffering. Further, intentionally inflicted suffering constitutes cruelty only when it embodies an intention to treat another merely as a means. But Kant's view is indispensable to explaining the moral wrong of such intentions, and of any conduct embodying such intentions. Kantian notions prove particularly useful in analyzing what Philip Hallie describes as "institutionalized cruelty"—the kind of cruelty embodied (perhaps in different ways) in the horrors of the Nazi Holocaust, in several ancient and modern slave systems, and in the systematic torture sometimes used by political regimes. To be sure, some features of Kant's view are deeply problematic: his applications of the categorical imperative to political and legal contexts, for instance, are sometimes objectionable on the terms of Kantian moral notions themselves. But Kant's occasional moral myopia cannot vitiate the importance of those Kantian notions that help illuminate cruelty's moral status.

Finally, I argue in section 3 that though morality with a light touch may be the best defense against some kinds of moral failures, a Kantian morality of "hectoring commands" is still the best defense against cruelty. Kant's view also yields the most appropriate moral response to those who suffer the worst effects of cruelty. In particular, Kantian respect for persons seems to be the philosophical expression of the "unsentimental love"—as Hallie describes it—that motivated a village of Huguenots in Vichy France to save thousands of people (mostly children) from Nazi death camps. I hope to show, then, that Kant's view, not Hume's, is the most effective and humane bulwark against cruelty.

I

Baier's conviction that Hume's approach to cruelty is superior to Kant's relies, in part, on her interpretation of one of the few passages in which Hume explicitly considers the problem: a passage in Book III of the *Treatise* analyzing the "angry passions." There, Hume first notes that there are occasions on which anger and hatred are not subject to moral disapproval, and that their absence may sometimes even be taken as a sign of "weakness and imbecility." Yet,

> [w]here these angry passions rise up to cruelty, they form the most detested of all vices. All the pity and concern which we have for the miserable sufferers by this vice, turns against the person guilty of it, and produces a stronger hatred than we are sensible of on any other occasion.[17]

According to Baier, this passage shows that Hume considers cruelty to be "the worst vice."[18] But the scope of Hume's concern here is far narrower than her interpretation suggests. The subject of the passage is the moral disapproval not of cruelty as such, but of cruelty that arises from anger and hatred. Yet, according to the *Oxford English Dictionary*, on the two most common senses of "cruelty" considered as a character trait, cruelty is either simply a "disposition to inflict suffering," or else a "delight in or indifference to the pain and misery of others." On neither of these common understandings does a disposition have to arise from angry passions in order to constitute cruelty.[19] Common conceptions of cruelty fail to capture the complexity of the cruel agent's disposition and intentions. Cruelty is not simply a disposition to inflict suffering, nor is a cruel person necessarily one who delights in or is indifferent to the suffering of others. Yet the common understandings of cruelty rightly allow that not all cruelty is angry cruelty.

Anger and hatred are obviously at the root of much of the cruelty that conventional morality seeks to prevent. The frustrated babysitter who angrily shakes a crying child, or a gang of teenage boys who vent their hatred in gay-bashing, are rightly subjects of moral condemnation. Yet cruelty sometimes arises from anger that is morally more complex. In a recent California criminal case, a man was charged with malicious cruelty to animals for brutally beating a dog with a baseball bat, upon learning that the dog had severely mauled his infant son.[20] The prosecutor argued that the father's grief could not justify his efforts to carry out a kind of vigilante justice. In the end, however, the jurors voted to acquit, apparently believing that the father's actions amounted to excusable cruelty. But surely it makes sense to ask whether the father's vengeful anger was a morally appropriate response to his son's injuries, and to question the readiness to express vengeful anger in the manner that the father ultimately chose. Even if morality demands forgiveness in this case, the father's angry passions seem to have exploded in just the kind of cruelty that morality should seek to contain or prevent.

But cruelty does not always arise from anger or hatred—and this is a matter of genuine moral importance. Kant recognized, in the *Lectures on Ethics*, that a child who tortures animals for pleasure is as serious a source of moral concern as an angry babysitter or a group of hate-filled adolescents. Appealing to imagery in Hogarth's engravings of "The Four Stages of Cruelty," Kant argued that a child who starts by cruelly torturing a dog or cat for sport might be headed—in Kant's words—for the "culmination of cruelty" as an adult, in murder.[21] This concern would seem hyperbolic, but for revelations about more than one serial killer whose childhood cruelty to animals was not taken seriously enough. Even cruelty that is explicitly a vehicle of hatred may offer its perpetrators a kind of pleasure. Moreover, the most hate-filled institutions of cruelty sometimes require for their continued existence and operation the participation of people who are primarily motivated, not by hatred, but by pleasure derived from inflicting suffering. The *Treatise* passage does not mention the regularity with which terrible cruelty may be motivated by terrible pleasure, and this omission suggests that the passage was not concerned with the viciousness of cruelty as such. In the final paragraph of "Moralism and Cruelty," Baier revises her interpretation of this critical passage, referring to Hume's "reflective judgment that angry cruelty is the worst vice."[22] But she does not comment on the difference between condemning angry cruelty and condemning cruelty as such, nor on what it might mean that Kant saw, as Hume did not, that some of the worst expressions of cruelty are motivated by sadistic pleasure and not by any kind of anger or hatred.[23] There is an even deeper problem with Hume's discussion, however—even considered more narrowly as an account of angry cruelty, rather than cruelty as such. Consider the paragraph that immediately follows the passage cited above:

> Even when the vice of inhumanity rises not to this extreme degree, our sentiments concerning it are very much influenc'd by reflexions on the harm that results from it. And we may observe in general, that if we can find any quality in a person, which renders him incommodious to those, who live and converse with him, we always allow it to be a fault or blemish, without any farther examination.[24]

The passage purports to be concerned with beliefs about "the harm that results" from "the vice of inhumanity," and with the role that such beliefs play in the moral assessment of the vice. One might thus expect some mention of the harm done to cruelty's immediate victims—to the shaken baby or the battered gay person, the concentration camp inmate or the domestic slave. Yet Hume turns instead to discuss the tendency of angry cruelty to render the agent of cruelty "incommodious" to those with whom he must "live and converse." When we enumerate the good qualities of a person, Hume continues, "we always mention those parts of his character, which render him a safe companion, an easy friend, a gentle master, an agreeable husband, or an indulgent father."[25] This crucial passage never even considers the harm actually done to those who suffer cruelty's most direct effects. But how is it possible to appreciate the moral gravity of cruelty, or even to understand what cruelty is, without really considering the suffering of cruelty's most immediate victims?[26]

Of course, cruelty does moral harm to the cruel person. Self-deceiving refusals to admit the possibility of such harm often allow the cruel person to rationalize such practices. Moreover, such rationalizations have played a central role in sustaining some of the worst institutionalized cruelty of the modern era. Philip Hallie finds a terrifying example of this phenomenon in a speech given by Himmler to a session of his SS subordinates, in which Himmler insisted that, despite their murderous actions, "we suffered no harm . . . in our character."[27] Still further, Hume's account contains much-needed reminders of how difficult it can be to contain habits of cruelty. A striking episode in the Argentinian film *The Official Story* (1985) bears out the importance of Hume's caution that the calm of everyday domestic life may be destroyed by habits of cruelty first practiced elsewhere. The film tells the story of a wealthy Argentinian couple (during the reign of the military junta) who may be raising a child of one of Argentina's "disappeared." The wife has long affected ignorance—in Aquinas's phrase—of the child's likely origins and of her husband's ties to the torture and killing. But after an encounter with a woman who believes that her missing adult daughter may have been the child's biological mother, the wife's moral discomfort prompts her to confront her husband with a demand that they return the child to her biological family. Angered by the suggestion that he might lose the daughter he has grown to love, the husband smashes the wife's head against a wall and repeatedly crushes her fingers in a door. The angry cruelty in this scene is a moving depiction of the domestic consequences of cruelty practiced elsewhere. Nonetheless, the worst expressions of cruelty are more often reserved for those who have somehow been segregated—physically, socially, conceptually, or legally—from the cruel person's sphere of everyday life. In such circumstances, any violence that breaks through the moral calm of everyday life is likely to be less extreme than the background cruelty with which it is linked. Hume's focus on the domestic impact of cruelty is thus incapable of accounting for much of what makes the most extreme cruelty morally reprehensible.

In her postscript to "Moralism and Cruelty," Baier suggests that we might look elsewhere in Hume's writings for a more satisfactory account of cruelty—specifically, to Hume's discussion of ancient slavery in his essay "Of the Populousness of Ancient Nations."[28] But the discussion of cruelty in that essay confirms the inadequacy of Hume's approach. Pondering "the influence of slavery on the populousness of a state," Hume argues that if physical conditions are roughly equal, wherever one finds the "most happiness and virtue, and the wisest institutions, there will also be the most people."[29] Thus he seeks to determine whether slavery is a "wise" institution, conducive to the happiness and virtue of those who accept it.[30] In the course of this inquiry, Hume does remark on the cruelty of several practices associated with ancient slavery, including the (Greek) practice of extorting testimony from slaves by means of torture, and the (Roman) practice of leaving old and sick slaves to die of starvation and exposure. He also observes, though all too briefly, that the lives of anyone likely to be subject to such "exquisite torments" and "inhuman sports" could hardly have been "comfortable."[31] Yet the essay goes on to condemn slavery not for its cruelty to those subjected to it, but for the fact that "every man of rank was rendered a petty tyrant" as a consequence of the social acceptance of slavery. Hume even claims that "[t]he little humanity, commonly observed in persons, accustomed, from their infancy, to exercise so great authority over their fellow-creatures, and to trample upon human nature, were sufficient alone to disgust us with that unbounded dominion."[32]

To be sure, Hume is not alone in emphasizing the moral importance of cruelty's effects on those who perpetrate it. Nineteenth-century British and American abolitionists, for instance, often echoed this insistence on the harm that slavery did to the character of slaveowners. But the moral force of abolitionist arguments was inseparable from the abolitionists' attention to the sufferings of slaves themselves. That concern embodied the recognition that one cannot understand the real cruelty of slave systems if one simply overlooks—or treats as incidental—the suffering of those over whom "unbounded dominion" is cruelly exercised. The shortcomings of Hume's discussion thus suggest two important maxims to guide any adequate analysis of cruelty. First, it is not possible to understand the real cruelty of any practice without attending to the harm done to its victims. Second, it is impossible to illuminate the moral wrong of cruelty without attending to the full range of its effects.

II

How should we understand the effects of cruelty and their moral importance? It is sometimes claimed that the central case of cruelty involves the infliction of physical pain, and that only by a metaphorical extension of the concept can we make sense of the idea of cruelty that involves no physical pain. It is thus essential, on this view, to distinguish cruelty that involves physical pain from cruelty that does not. Judith Shklar, for instance, distinguishes cruelty involving the infliction of physical pain from what she describes (somewhat misleadingly) as "moral cruelty"—by which she means a "deliberate and persistent humiliation" that eventually renders its victims unable to trust themselves or others.[33]

Yet the truth about cruelty is more complex. Consider a child who suffers both physical and verbal abuse from his parents. Suppose, further, that the nonphysical abuse involves persistent verbal browbeating—including, perhaps, name-calling and screaming, as well as unrelenting and unmitigated criticism of even the child's smallest failings. This kind of abuse obviously can severely undermine a child's self-confidence and have lasting psychological effects that might be, in some important sense, more agonizing than the effects of any physical abuse suffered by the same child. One need not be a child to experience extreme mental anguish, of course. Repeated sexual infidelity may cruelly demolish the self-esteem of a trusting spouse or long-time companion. Stephen Sondheim's aptly titled song, "Every day a little death," describes the subtle processes by which infidelity can become mental cruelty. But children typically have fewer opportunities for relief from any mental cruelty they might suffer, and while there are obvious difficulties with interpersonal comparisons of suffering, a child's experience of mental cruelty will often be more severe—and more damaging—than an adult's. Of course, as Baier notes in "Moralism and Cruelty," it is not entirely clear how to compare the suffering caused by physical brutality with the mental anguish caused by psychological abuse.[34] But surely the mental cruelty experienced by a severely abused child makes it reasonable to question the idea that physical cruelty should be taken as the central case of cruelty.

The complexity of cruelty goes even deeper, however. Some of the worst agony caused by childhood physical abuse, for instance, is probably not physical at all, but psychological. Indeed, the very fact that a child might suffer severe physical abuse by a parent is likely to be a source of extraordinary psychological distress for an abused child, even very early in the child's conscious life. This is due, in large measure, to the kind of trust that children typically invest in their caretakers. As Baier observes in "Trust and Antitrust," parents do not normally need to work very hard in order to win an infant's trust; infants simply seem ready, in her words, "to impute good-will to the powerful persons on whom they depend."[35] Parents who physically abuse their children violate this trust, and children whose parents subject them to severe physical abuse will experience great anguish at such violations. It seems likely, in fact, that mental anguish will eventually become a constant accompaniment of the physical pain caused by repeated physical violence. Shklar cautions at one point that we must not confuse the pain of mental anguish—for instance, the humiliation of what she calls "moral cruelty"—with physical brutality.[36] Yet physical brutality is often experienced as cruelty precisely in virtue of its capacity to cause such "confusion." Even Shklar recognizes that physical cruelty typically combines physical brutality with mental anguish: she defines physical cruelty as the "willful inflicting of physical pain on a weaker being in order to cause anguish and fear."[37] An adequate definition of physical cruelty would help make sense—as Shklar's definition does not—of the reasons for which physical cruelty typically causes this intertwining of physical pain and mental anguish. But recognizing the importance of this phenomenon provides the key to understanding what cruelty, in general, really is and why it is morally reprehensible.

To understand this point, it will help to first consider the circumstances under which we forgive, or even welcome, the infliction of extreme physical suffering. Major surgery to cure or treat serious injury or disease, for most people, would constitute just such circumstances—even though a major surgical procedure may require actions that, in a different setting, would constitute physical brutality. Of course, it is not morally irrelevant that a modern surgeon almost always uses some kind of anaesthesia. Even with anaesthesia, however, the aftermath of major surgery may include lasting physical pain and even more lasting mental anguish; this is often the case, for instance, in back surgery or in the surgical treatment of breast cancer. There is nonetheless an important moral difference between the intentional infliction of suffering in pursuit of a legitimate medical purpose and the intentional infliction of suffering that constitutes cruelty. Moreover, there is special moral opprobrium reserved for the doctor whose practices cruelly ignore this distinction: Robert Jay Lifton's account of the special horrors of Nazi medicine vividly suggests why.[38] Taken together, these considerations reveal that the essence of cruelty is not any particular kind of suffering, or even the fact that some suffering (physical, mental, or both) is intentionally inflicted; its essence is the intentional infliction of suffering as a way of degrading or devaluing the being who is made to suffer. Etymologically, as Philip Hallie observes, the word "cruelty" has its origins in the Latin *crudus* (which has links to the notions of raw flesh and bloodshed), and this has always suggested a connection between cruelty and the spilling of blood.[39] But, as Hallie also notes, appeals to etymology can only yield a superficial understanding of cruelty. It is the effort to degrade and devalue another by means of intentionally inflicted suffering that turns any kind of intentionally inflicted suffering into cruelty.

What do notions like "devalue" and "degrade" mean in these contexts? I take the view, which is in essence the view defended by Kant, that to devalue or degrade someone is to try to use her merely as a means. Moreover, following Onora O'Neill, I assume that there is a fairly simple way to recognize what it is to use another merely as a means: it is a matter of trying to involve another in some action to which she would not—and often, could not in principle—consent.[40] In episodic cruelty (such as a rape, or an incident of gay-bashing or baby-shaking), as well as cruelty that is typically extended in time (such as torture or child-abuse), victims are clearly subjected to forms of suffering to which they would not consent. Such actions deny the moral worth of beings by overriding their capacity to consent or dissent. To be sure, an account that appeals to the idea of consent may seem incapable of making sense of the idea of cruelty to oneself, and thus unable to answer Nietzschean concerns about the allegedly self-lacerating demands of Kantian moral reflection. But any account of cruelty will have difficulty analyzing the idea of cruelty to oneself, since the person who inflicts suffering on himself so often seems to do so in a willing indulgence of masochistic pleasure.[41] Where self-inflicted suffering can be distinguished from willing masochistic indulgence, the most helpful analysis will show that such suffering constitutes cruelty only when the subject attempts to somehow deny his value as a person—that is, to devalue himself—by means of it.

My definition of cruelty has several important implications. First, it allows a straightforward explanation of why extreme cruelty may sometimes involve no physical violence at all. We need only acknowledge that the suffering inflicted by a nonphysical assault might express as powerful an intention to degrade or devalue as anything expressed by the infliction of physical pain. The lasting psychological effects of a childhood of verbal abuse, for instance, may severely undermine a person's capacity for self-confidence and self-trust. My account also makes sense of those cases where a nonphysical assault other than verbal abuse embodies a particularly vicious effort to degrade or devalue another. Consider someone with a severe phobia who is repeatedly and unwillingly subjected to viewing the object of that phobia, with the intention of causing extreme psychic distress. This kind of visual assault on the phobic's psyche would surely constitute a case of extreme cruelty.

But, second, because my account focuses attention on the special nature of the cruel person's intention—as well as on the suffering which embodies that intention—it helps explain the complex fashion in which physical cruelty may link physical pain with mental anguish. Physical cruelty often produces mental distress simply by making the victim feel helpless and afraid. But cruelty has such effects because of the way it seeks to override or ignore another being's capacity to consent, and thereby embodies an intention to devalue and degrade. In other cases, the mental anguish associated with physical cruelty is principally a function of the perpetrator's success in getting the victim to internalize the perpetrator's conception of degradation. The worst mental anguish suffered by some rape victims, for example, is caused by the psychologically destructive belief that their worth as persons has somehow been diminished by the attack. Such notions are even more destructive when a rape victim seeks to blame herself, by wondering what she might have done to "deserve" the attack. Child abuse may also encourage its victims to assume that they must be bad or worthless, and so somehow deserve the abuse they suffer. In such cases the child internalizes the cruel parent's faulty conception of his value—usually as a means of trying to make sense of his suffering.

A third important implication follows from the idea that the intention to devalue or degrade by means of suffering is a central element of cruelty. On my view, whenever the intention to cause suffering embodies an effort to devalue or degrade, we have a case of cruelty—even if the victim does not succumb to the perpetrator's effort at degradation, and indeed even if the victim is in no way aware of that effort. These considerations explain why shaking a crying baby, for instance, is so clearly a case of cruelty, even though a baby has no sophisticated capacity to articulate dissent, and little (if any) awareness of the cruel person's intentions. Violently shaking a baby in order to get him to cease crying involves treating the baby as a mere means. It carries out a scheme of action to which one could not in principle consent, because it fundamentally endangers the very capacity to consent.

But my account makes it equally clear that intentionally inflicting suffering on an aware and articulate person who does not succumb to the effort to degrade him or her still constitutes cruelty: it counts as cruelty simply because of the intention embodied in the perpetrator's actions.

Some commentators suggest, perhaps unwittingly, that it is the essence of cruelty (especially extreme, nonepisodic cruelty of the familial or institutional sort) to crush a person's self-respect, maim a person's sense of dignity, or otherwise effectively humiliate the sufferer.[42] Yet parental abuse, for example, is no less cruel if the victim of that abuse manages to survive to adulthood with her self-respect and self-trust intact. To be sure, even an experience of episodic cruelty, such as a rape or a gay-bashing, may severely damage the self-respect of its victim. But some who survive such attacks prove remarkably able to resist the perpetrators' efforts to degrade and humiliate them, and such attacks are no less cruel for that fact. In one of the most intriguing debates about American history, it has been claimed that the cruelty of American slavery produced in its victims and their descendants a set of character traits that embodied a lack of self-respect and a lasting sense of personal and group humiliation.[43] Critics such as Orlando Patterson deny that there is historical evidence to show that any slaves ever internalized the conception of degradation held by their masters.[44] On my view, the truth of such criticisms would in no way diminish the moral wrong of any slave system embodying such a conception.

There are degrees of cruelty, to be sure. The extreme cruelty of Nazi medicine, for instance, would obviously be at one end of the moral spectrum, while at the other would be something like the cruelties of one child teasing another in the playground. Moreover, even though some instances of psychological abuse may be more cruel than some forms of physical abuse, it is certainly possible that the most extreme degradation is most often associated with the infliction of extreme physical suffering. Yet it is also worth stressing Hallie's contention that cruelty typically requires some kind of disparity in power between perpetrator and victim, and that extreme cruelty requires an extreme imbalance in power.[45] The link between cruelty and power helps to explain why the cruelty of a parent who abuses a child, for instance, is likely to be more extreme, and morally more reprehensible, than the cruelty of marital infidelity. Hallie rightly suggests that legal and political institutions which cement imbalances in power will often be associated with the worst excesses of cruelty.

The practices I have subsumed under the term "institutionalized cruelty" are in some respects quite different from each other. Some cases of institutionalized cruelty represent the culmination of historically rooted efforts to elevate vicious prejudices to the status of requirements on collective action, as in the Holocaust. In other circumstances, institutionalized cruelty is part of an effort to protect practices that promote the interests of some dominant group, as in the cruelty that often developed in socially sanctioned institutions of slavery. Political torture is still a third kind of institutionalized cruelty, which typically expresses a community's willingness (explicit or implicit) to accept the violent suppression of dissent in the belief that "stability"—at any cost—is in the best interest of the community. But whatever its purposes, the excesses of institutionalized cruelty are always attempts to devalue and degrade, and these excesses depend for their effectiveness on an imbalance of power. The most extreme expressions of such efforts will obviously have the most extreme consequences for their victims. This is why Kant is right to follow Hogarth in considering murder as the culmination, or "perfection," of cruelty. Moreover, Kant's view—not Hume's—offers the clearest condemnation of the effort to devalue another by using him merely as a means to further ends which he cannot be expected to share. Kant's view thus yields a clearer understanding of the moral wrong of cruelty, as well as a deeper of appreciation of what cruelty is.

Critics of Kant's views may be concerned that any account relying on Kantian notions is ultimately inadequate to explain the moral wrong of cruelty to animals. This is an especially difficult problem since, as noted above, Kant vehemently stressed the moral dangers of cruelty to animals. Kant's conviction that animals are mere things requires him to hold that the moral duty to avoid cruelty to animals is only an indirect duty to humanity. This stance may seem insufficient to take seriously the suffering of animal victims of cruelty. Yet it should be recalled that the concerns which generated the most vehement criticisms of Kant's approach to cruelty do not put concern for cruelty to animals at the center of the debate. For Baier, as well as for Nietzsche, it is the cruelty associated with Kantian moral criticism that elicits the strongest objections. But only a being with the capacity for morality could experience any cruelty that might be associated with pressure for moral conformity—and even Hume does not claim that animals have the capacity for moral concern and action. Merely wondering about the cruelty of pressures for moral conformity—as Baier most clearly does—commits one to an account of cruelty that already excludes nonhuman animals. Thus, one need not provide a satisfactory analysis of the moral wrong of cruelty to nonhuman animals in order to adequately answer Baier's, and Nietzsche's, objections.[46]

A Humean may still seek to rebut the charge that Kant's view provides a better analysis of cruelty to humans than any Humean notions could. I have argued that Hume typically ignored the suffering that cruelty causes its human victims, as well as the intention to devalue or degrade which that suffering embodies. But even if Hume had understood the nature of cruelty, his view would still be poorly suited to make sense of the moral wrong of cruelty. The shortcomings of a Humean approach to institutionalized cruelty are particularly instructive. Hume would argue that the content of morality in any given society is fixed by a combination of natural ends and socially established patterns of normative expectations. In more Humean language, there are both natural and artificial virtues. The moral rules that emerge from socially established normative expectations may be—as Baier observes—the product of custom and tradition, of self-interest and instrumental reason, and even of historical accident and the chance workings of human imagination.[47] But such a conception lacks the resources for defining an appropriately critical stance on the means by which a community's practices might be claimed to justify institutionalized cruelty.

Baier seeks to show otherwise, on the grounds that, for a Humean, morality is ideally the outcome of efforts to eliminate "contradictions in the 'passions' of sympathetic persons" who are aware of "their own and their fellows' desires and needs."[48] Yet this appeal to Hume's notion of sympathy must confront an important difficulty. One of the defining features of insitutionalized cruelty, as I have argued, is its dependence upon the physical, social, or legal segregation of its victims. But Hume argues in the *Treatise* that when the subject under consideration is, in his words, too "remote," our capacity for extensive sympathy with others will prove limited.[49] Hume certainly allows for the possibility of a "progress in sentiments"—he allows, that is, that deficiencies in the capacity for extensive sympathy might be corrected. Such corrections, however, seem to depend on what Hume describes in the *Enquiry* as the "general preferences and distinctions" enshrined in the moral language of one's own society.[50] If critical distance on a community's conventional moral practices must await awareness of "contradictions in the passions of sympathetic persons," then victims of institutionalized cruelty will have to wait a very long time indeed.

Even more tellingly, Hume seems to speak in his own voice when one of the characters in his short work, "A Dialogue," observes that "[t]here are no manners so innocent or reasonable, but may be rendered odious or ridiculous, if measured by a standard unknown to the person."[51] This character goes on to caution that we should not "try a Greek or a Roman by the common law of England," but should allow him to "defend himself by his own maxims, and then pronounce."[52] Such passages simply confirm what emerges virtually everywhere in Hume's writings: Hume's conception of morality provides no firm ground for understanding, and then condemning, the moral wrong of extreme institutionalized cruelty. Yet it is with respect to such matters that the strengths of Kant's conception are most obvious. It is, of course, an open question whether the rational structure described in the *Groundwork* (and redescribed in the second *Critique*) can be shown to be objectively valid. But, if I am right, anyone concerned to understand and combat unnecessary cruelty has reason to hope that something very like that structure might be objectively valid.

What of Baier's concern that Kantian pressures for moral conformity are themselves the embodiment of unnecessary cruelty? To begin with, Kantian moral criticism demands no whips and scourges. Any suffering it may cause must surely pale by comparison to the suffering caused by many moral failures to which that criticism responds. More fundamentally, the readiness to hold a person morally to blame for some genuine moral wrong recognizes the faulted person's status as an agent capable of choice, and therefore as a being worthy of respect. If I am right that cruelty to human beings occurs when suffering is inflicted as a way of degrading, devaluing, or otherwise denying the genuine worth of the sufferer, then it is fundamentally impossible for moral criticism to constitute cruelty. Moral criticism of others may give way to self-righteousness, and moral self-criticism may be transformed into self-indulgent wallowing in guilt, but such attitudes are no longer consistent with the requirements of morality. Suffering produced by such attitudes may well embody an intention to degrade, but the resulting cruelty is then not a product of genuine pressures for moral conformity.

Equally important, it is an open question whether Baier rightly understands the nature of our moral failings. She would look for the social fault behind the individual fault, rejecting the idea that the individual agent is really the locus of responsibility. But while there are important links between human agency and what is often called culture, cultures survive only through the survival of individual agents who make choices about how their cultures ought to survive. In fact, any culture that worked to impair its members' capacities for judgment and choice would be creating the conditions for its own demise.[53] Cultures must be distinguished from "total" institutions—in Goffman's phrase—that are typically designed to limit or (in extreme cases) even to destroy their victims' capacity for choice. Baier makes a compelling case in her essay "How Can Individualists Share Responsibility?" for the reasonableness of a concept of collective responsibility. But judgments of collective responsibility—for instance, in cases of culturally sanctioned wrongdoing—make sense only because being a member of an ongoing culture always requires the exercise of choice.[54] Moreover, there can surely be different degrees of responsibility for some culturally sanctioned wrong, but only because responsibility can be localized in assignable individual agents.

Kant's defense of the retributive theory of criminal punishment is morally more problematic than his conception of acceptable moral criticism. The theory licenses what Bentham once called "non-remissible" punishments—which make it difficult, if not impossible, to restore to a person some semblance of a normal life should we learn that she has been wrongly convicted. The readiness to rely on such punishments, in spite of human fallibility, may suggest a willingness to use a convicted person, regardless of actual guilt, merely as a means to the venting of vengeful anger. Kant is thus far from convincing in his claim that the non-remissible punishments likely to be justified by the retributive theory are required by the categorical imperative.[55] Contrary to Nietzsche's claim, then, it is not the categorical imperative which retains an odor of blood and torture, but only some of Kant's unconvincing claims about its implications.

III

It is nonetheless true, as Baier argues, that Kant is insufficiently attentive to the value of moral pressure with a "light touch." Even Konrad Lorenz, writing about the so-called "fighting instinct" in humans, reminds us that humor can be a powerful ally of morality. The satirist who mocks the insincerity of others and the reflective person who gently mocks herself, Lorenz claims, provide strong inducements to honesty with ourselves and others. He also insists on the persuasive power of humor, especially for those whose "skepticism and sophistication" leave them unmoved by the claims of express moral argument: satire, he once claimed, "is the right sort of sermon for today."[56]

Yet while humor can be a powerful ally of morality, it can sometimes be a powerful enemy as well. Lorenz believes that laughter may be derived from instinctive patterns of aggressive behavior—evolving as ritualizations of "a redirected threatening movement"—and that it can quite easily turn into "a very cruel weapon."[57] When laughter is "undeservedly" turned against a defenseless person, he continues, it is capable of causing grave injury. He is especially insistent that it is "criminal" to laugh at a child. Baier is aware, in "Moralism and Cruelty," of the possible hurtfulness of laughter and of the possible cruelty of any suffering that laughter may cause.[58] But her account is insufficiently attentive to the grounds on which the hurt caused by laughter might actually constitute cruelty. Here one seems to need something like Freud's notion of the comic, which recognizes, for instance, that we sometimes make a person comic in order to make him contemptible and bereft of dignity.[59] Yet if we want to understand why it is morally wrong to try to deprive another of her dignity, we need, once again, to look to Kant's second formulation of the categorical imperative. Lorenz cautions, further, that the capacity to share in laughter with others—sometimes simply as a benign aid to the cementing of social bonds—may also reinforce a group's shared aggressiveness toward outsiders. This suggests that there is often a link between laughter and those dangerous social conditions that may give rise to extreme expressions of cruelty. Humor is, therefore, no more intrinsically humane than the "hectoring commands" which Baier associates with Kant's view.

Some of Kant's demands on moral reflection are, admittedly, quite harsh. Kant cautions against moral smugness and self-righteousness with the insistence, in the *Groundwork*, that we can never know whether we have acted from genuinely moral motives or whether we have simply been pursuing the purposes of the "dear self." In *Religion Within the Limits of Reason Alone*, Kant contends that a bad man's duty is not only to become better in the future, but to have been better in the past. He thus rejects the widespread belief that immoral actions are sometimes the result of an agent's bad "consitutive luck." Whatever the past experiences of the person who behaves immorally, every immoral action (in Kant's view) "must be regarded as though the individual had fallen into it directly from a state of innocence."[60] Such claims set very high standards for moral reflection and moral action, and failure to live up to them may induce mental anguish even in the morally upright person. Yet if Kant is right, as I think he is, such suffering could hardly constitute cruelty. Cruelty is the infliction of suffering with the intention of degrading or devaluing the sufferer. The agent who sincerely acknowledges her genuine failures to meet the demands of morality simply affirms the value of the human capacity for moral action. Excessive guilt may, of course, produce moral paralysis; in other cases, it may minister to a masochistic self-indulgence. But moral paralysis and masochistic self-laceration could hardly be required by Kantian moral notions because they cannot genuinely affirm respect for persons. More important still, as Nietzsche understood all too well, "pain is the most powerful aid to mnemonics."[61] The very harshness of Kantian moral criticism, then, suggests that Kant's conception provides morality's best defense against cruelty.

Kant's account may also provide the best response to those who have suffered from cruelty's worst effects. Hallie's account of the people of Le Chambon-sur-Lignon—like Pierre Sauvage's moving film, *Weapons of the Spirit*—tells the story of a village of 3,500 French Protestants who, during the Nazi occupation of France, helped save the lives of about 6,000 people—mostly children whose families had been killed in concentration camps. Hallie maintains that these villagers acted out of an "unsentimental, efficacious love."[62] They saw "no alternative" to their actions, he continues; "they saw what they did as necessary, not something to be picked out for praise."[63] Of course, there are important and complex religious dimensions to the unsentimental love out of which these villagers acted.[64] But the richness of fundamental Kantian ideas—from the notion that respect for persons requires kindness "done from duty," to the idea of the necessity of duty—suggests that Kant's conception might be properly interpreted as a secular, philosophical expression of that unsentimental love.[65]

There is much to be learned from Baier's richly textured reconstruction of Hume's moral views: far more about the importance of caring and trust, for instance, than could possibly emerge from these reflections on the problem of cruelty. It may even be true that Kant is rightly faulted for failing to recognize the moral importance of certain kinds of caring and trust.

In particular, Kant may have been insufficiently attentive to the ways which in caring (and the kinds of trust that emerge only in caring relationships, such as that between a parent and child) help develop one's capacity to fulfill important positive duties to others, and possibly even to ourselves. But if we want—in Judith Shklar's phrase—to "put cruelty first," it is Kant's view, and not Hume's, to which we should turn.

NOTES

1. Friedrich Nietzsche, *The Genealogy of Morals and Ecce Homo.* ed. and trans. Walter Kaufmann (New York: Vintage Books, 1969), II-6.

2. Ibid., II-4.

3. Nietzsche's criticisms suggest that the "equivalents" may be psychological as well as physical and (more generally) material.

4. Martha Nussbaum, "Pity and Mercy: Nietzsche's Stoicism," in *Nietzsche, Genealogy, Morality: Essays on Nietzsche's On the Genealogy of Morals,* ed. Richard Schacht (Berkeley: University of California Press, 1994), 139–67; see 161.

5. Annette Baier, "Moralism and Cruelty," which originally appeared in *Ethics* 103 (April 1993): 436–57. All references are to the version reprinted, with an additional "Postcript," in Baier, *Moral Prejudices* (Cambridge, MA: Harvard University Press, 1994), 268–93. See 277.

6. Ibid., 273.

7. See Baier, "Moralism and Cruelty," and "Trust and Antitrust," also in *Moral Prejudices.*

8. Baier, "Moralism and Cruelty," 289; 272–73; 288–89.

9. Ibid., 274.

10. Ibid., 274.

11. Ibid., 288.

12. Ibid.

13. Ibid., 289.

14. Baier cites Kant's discussion of "Duties to Oneself" in the *Lectures on Ethics* (esp. p. 125 of the Infield translation—see note 21 below); and sec. 7 of the *Doctrine of Virtue* (Pt. II of the *Metaphysics of Morals*). See "Moralism and Cruelty," 269; 334 n. 2.

15. Baier, "Moralism and Cruelty," 269.

16. This stance is most fully suggested by Baier's arguments in the postscript to "Moralism and Cruelty," esp. 290–91.

17. David Hume, *A Treatise of Human Nature*, ed. L. A. Selby-Bigge, rev. P. H. Nidditch (Oxford: Oxford University Press, 1978), 605–6.

18. Baier, "Moralism and Cruelty," 269.

19. This is the sense, for instance, in which Nietzsche seems to lament the cruelty of conventional morality, and even of conventional religious asceticism.

20. The case was decided in Los Angeles, California, October 1995.

21. Immanuel Kant, *Lectures on Ethics*, trans. Louis Infield (Indianapolis: Hackett Publishing Co., 1981), 239–40. Hogarth's title for the third engraving in his series is "Cruelty in Perfection." See *Hogarth's Graphic Works* (New Haven: Yale University Press, 1970), vol. 2, Plate 203 (cat. no. 189).

22. Baier, "Moralism and Cruelty," 290.

23. At one point in the second *Enquiry*, Hume makes the intriguing suggestion that "[a]bsolute, unprovoked, disinterested malice has never perhaps place in any human breast; or if it did, must there pervert all the sentiments of morals, as well as the feelings of humanity." *Enquiries Concerning Human Understanding and Concerning the Principles of Morals*, ed. L. A. Selby-Bigge, rev. P. H. Nidditch (Oxford: Clarendon Press, 1975), sec. v, pt. ii. But Hume never pursues the links between such "unprovoked, disinterested" malice—as a phenomenon separate from sadistic pleasure, as well as anger and hatred—and its occasional manifestations in cruelty.

24. Hume, *Treatise*, 606.

25. Ibid.

26. The shortcomings of Hume's views on this matter—despite the idiosyncratic nature of his concept of the virtues—may reveal a weakness inherent in virtue theories generally. The virtue theorist's emphasis on perfecting the character of the moral agent often leads to the neglect of genuine concern about the external manifestations of one's character traits. Virtue theories may, thus, be incapable of adequately explaining the moral wrong of cruelty.

27. Philip Hallie, "From Cruelty to Goodness," in *Vice and Virtue in Everyday Life*, ed. C. Sommers and F. Sommers (New York: Harcourt Brace and Jovanovich, 1993), 13.

28. Baier, "Moralism and Cruelty," 292.

29. Hume, "Of the Populousness of Ancient Nations," in *The Philosophical Works of David Hume*, 4 vols., ed. T. H. Green and T. H. Grose (Darmstadt: Scientia Verlag Aalen, 1964), vol. 3, 384–85.

30. Ibid., 385.

31. Ibid., 386.

32. Ibid., 385.

33. Judith N. Shklar, *Ordinary Vices* (Cambridge, MA: Harvard University Press, 1984), 37.

34. Baier, "Moralism and Cruelty," 269.

35. Baier, "Trust and Antitrust," 107.

36. Shklar, *Ordinary Vices*, 37.

37. Ibid., 8.

38. Robert Jay Lifton, *The Nazi Doctors: Medical Killing and the Psychology of Genocide* (New York: Basic Books, 1986).

39. Hallie, "From Cruelty to Goodness," 11.

40. Onora O'Neill, "A Simplified Account of Kant's Ethics," in *Matters of Life and Death*, ed. Tom Regan (New York: Random House 1986). Reprinted in *Contemporary Moral Problems*, 3rd ed., ed. James White (New York: West Publishing 1991), 26–30.

41. I do not deny that one may be cruel to oneself. I do contend, however, that it is difficult to offer a general analysis of such cruelty—and possibly even more difficult to distinguish genuine cruelty to the self from a willing indulgence of masochistic tendencies.

42. Hallie's analysis is particularly prone to this tendency, though Hallie also seems to recognize that not everyone who is the victim of extreme cruelty need actually suffer the loss of dignity that he rightly laments.

43. Stanley Elkins, *Slavery: A Problem in American Institutional and Intellectual Life*, 3rd ed. (Chicago: University of Chicago Press, 1976).

44. Orlando Patterson, *Slavery and Social Death* (Cambridge, MA: Harvard University Press, 1982), 97.

45. Hallie, "From Cruelty to Goodness," 15.

46. Certain actions and practices constitute morally reprehensible forms of cruelty to animals (possibly involving institutionalized, as well as noninstitutionalized cruelty). But, as I have argued, I need not provide an analysis of the moral wrong of cruelty to animals in order to answer Baier's and Nietzsche's objections to Kant's moral views.

47. Baier, "Hume, the Women's Moral Theorist?" in *Moral Prejudices*, 55.

48. Ibid., 55–56.

49. Hume, *Treatise*, 499.

50. Hume, *Enquiry Concerning the Principles of Morals*, 228, 274.

51. Ibid., 330.

52. Ibid.

53. This point is defended at greater length in Michele Moody-Adams, "Culture, Responsibility, and Affected Ignorance," *Ethics* 104 (1994): 291–309.

54. A familiar criticism of the concept of collective responsibility charges that the notion is incompatible with serious attention to individual responsibility. I cannot pursue the point here, but I think that this criticism misunderstands the fundamental requirements for any attribution of collective responsibility.

55. The failure of Kant's defense of nonremissible punishments—including the death penalty—does not, however, show that there is no plausible (non-Kantian) argument for some or all of such punishments.

56. Konrad Lorenz, *On Aggression*, trans. Marjorie Kerr Wilson (New York: Bantam Books, 1971), 286–87.

57. Ibid., 284

58. Baier, "Moralism and Cruelty," 285–86

59. Sigmund Freud, *Jokes and Their Relation to the Unconscious*, trans. James Strachey (New York: W. W. Norton, 1963), 189.

60. Immanuel Kant, *Religion Within the Limits of Reason Alone*, trans. J. Silber, (New York: Harper Collins, 1960), 36.

61. Nietzsche, *On the Genealogy of Morals*, II-3, p. 61.

62. Hallie, "From Cruelty to Goodness," 18.

63. Ibid., 21.

64. I do not deny the specifically religious nature of the villagers' actual motivation. But one may plausibly wonder whether one who does not share the Huguenot belief in a divine requirement to "love thy neighbor as thyself" (the Christian conception of agape) might nonetheless display unconditional and unsentimental love for human beings. This legitimate moral concern underwrites the search for a secular analogue—and a specifically philosophical expression thereof—of the Huguenot's religious conviction.

65. At one point, Kant claims that central ideas implicit in the categorical imperative provide the most plausible interpretation of "passages from Scripture in which we are commanded to love our neighbor and even our enemy. For love out of inclination cannot be commanded; but kindness done from duty—although no inclination impels us, and even although natural and unconquerable disinclination stands in our way, is practical . . . residing in the will and not the propensions of feeling, in principles of action and not of melting compassion." Kant, *The Groundwork of the Metaphysics of Morals*, trans. H. J. Paton (New York: Harper and Row, [1785] 1964), 13.

CHAPTER 15

Trust as an Affective Attitude

KAREN JONES

In this paper I defend an account of trust according to which trust is an attitude of optimism that the goodwill and competence of another will extend to cover the domain of our interaction with her, together with the
expectation that the one trusted will be directly and favorably moved by
the thought that we are counting on her. The attitude of optimism is to be
cashed out not primarily in terms of beliefs about the other's trustworthiness, but rather—in accordance with certain contemporary accounts of
the emotions[1]—in terms of a distinctive, and affectively loaded, way of seeing the one trusted. This way of seeing the other, with its constitutive patterns of attention and tendencies of interpretation, explains the willingness
of trusters to let those trusted get dangerously near the things they care
about. This account is presented and defended in the first two sections of
the paper.

Any account of what trust is sets constraints on what can be said about
the justification conditions of trust. Thus, if a theorist analyzes trust as
(perhaps among other things) a belief that the one trusted will have and
display goodwill toward the one who trusts, then that theorist has com-

mitted herself to saying that trust is justified only if the one who trusts is justified in forming the belief constitutive of trust. In the third section of the paper, I take up the question of the justification conditions of trust. While a full account of the justification conditions of trust is beyond the scope of this paper, I identify the key variables affecting the justifiedness of trust. An account of trust that makes affect central has an unexpected payoff: it is able to view a wide range of our trustings—including many of those undertaken for instrumental reasons—as justified. Moreover, it is able to do this without taking a stance on evidentialism, or the doctrine that we should not believe anything without sufficient evidence. Since trust is not primarily a belief, it falls outside the scope of the evidentialist thesis.

It is necessary, first, to get clearer about the target of my investigation. The word "trust" is used in a variety of expressions, ranging from "Trust you to do something like that!" to "We trust you have enjoyed your flight with Air New Zealand," to "Othello's trust in Iago was misplaced." In the first sentence "trust" is used ironically, although it brings with it from its nonironic uses the idea of expectations having been met, while in the second it politely conveys something intermediate between an expectation and a hope. Sometimes the word "trust" is used to convey any sort of delegated responsibility, especially one where checking up is difficult or precluded. Thus a politician of such egregious ethical turpitude that she has long since ceased to be trusted by any of her constituents can nonetheless, on the exposure of some new failing, be said to have once again violated the public's trust. My task is thus not to explicate the meaning of the word "trust" wherever it occurs, since there is no one common phenomenon that all uses of the word "trust" pick out. Instead, my target is the sense conveyed in our third example: "Othello's trust in Iago was misplaced." That is to say, my target is interpersonal trust. But this is not a narrow target: it is the trust always found in friendship, often found between professionals and their clients, sometimes found between strangers, and sometimes, even, between people and their governments. My task is therefore an explanatory task, the success of which is to be tested by how well it lets us understand this everyday phenomenon—how well, that is, it can account for the similarities and differences between interpersonal trust relations of the sorts just listed.

I. AN ACCOUNT OF TRUST

1.1 The Basic Model

Trusting is composed of two elements, one cognitive and one affective or emotional. (I say "affective" rather than "noncognitive" because affective states can themselves contain a significant cognitive component.) Roughly, to trust someone is to have an attitude of optimism about her goodwill and to have the confident expectation that, when the need arises, the one trusted will be directly and favorably moved by the thought that you are counting on her. If A's attitude toward B (in a given domain of interaction) is predominantly characterized by optimism about B's goodwill and by the expectation that B will be directly and favorably moved by the thought that A is counting on her, then A has a trusting relationship with B (within that domain). There can be moments of trust within relationships that are not, in general, characterized by trust, although if the attitude and expectation are too fleeting, it would not be correct to say that A trusts B. The attitude and expectation characteristic of trust combine to explain why trusters are willing, when the need arises, to rely on those they trust.[2]

In the standard case, the confident expectation that the one trusted will respond directly and favorably to the thought that the truster is counting on them is itself grounded in the attitude of optimism; thus the attitude of optimism is central. This account of the two aspects of trust requires further elaboration and refinement. It also needs to be shown why we should think that both are necessary for trust and why we should think that together they amount to a satisfying account.

First, though, I should explain what I mean by "optimism," for the word has connotations that are apt to be misleading. The attitude of optimism is directed at the goodwill of another. I can trust someone with whom I'm engaged in a very difficult endeavor even though I have no optimism about the success of our joint task; thus, trust does not involve a general tendency to look on the bright side. However, trust does lead one to anticipate that the other will have and display goodwill, and this is the aspect of optimism that I want to highlight—the way optimism leads us to anticipate a favorable outcome. Throughout, though, I do not want "optimism" to suggest a general tendency to look on the bright side. With that in mind, we can turn to the task of refining our characterization of trust.

At the center of trust is an attitude of optimism about the other person's goodwill. But optimism about goodwill is not sufficient, for some people have very good wills but very little competence, and the incompetent deserve our trust almost as little as the malicious. (Almost, but not quite, for the incompetent might sometimes get things right, whereas the malicious will get things right only to the extent that they are incompetent.) Thus, we should say that trust is optimism about the goodwill and competence of another. The position requires additional refinement: except perhaps with our most trusted intimates, the optimism we bear is seldom global. This is not to say that the optimism itself is qualified and instead of being unreserved optimism is a qualified or restricted optimism. What is qualified is not the optimism itself, but the domain over which it extends. So, for example, the optimism we have about the goodwill and competence of strangers does not extend very far. We expect their goodwill to extend to not harming us as we go about our business and their competence to consist in an understanding of the norms for interaction between strangers. For a man to run up at full speed behind a woman on an ill-lit street is to display a lack of such competence, and, even if he was simply out for a late night run and meant no harm, he has given the woman reason to distrust him. When we trust professionals, from plumbers to physicians, we expect of them a technical competence (and minimal decency). However, the competence we expect in trusting need not be technical: when we trust a friend, the competence we expect them to display is a kind of moral competence. We expect a friend to understand loyalty, kindness, and generosity, and what they call for in various situations.

There are a number of reasons why we might think that a person will have and display goodwill in the domain of our interaction with her. Perhaps she harbors friendly feelings toward us; in that case, the goodwill is grounded on personal liking. Or perhaps she is generally benevolent, or honest, or conscientious, and so on. The formulation is meant to be neutral between these reasons for thinking that a person's goodwill extends to cover the domain of our interaction.

It might be thought odd to claim that trust centrally involves an affective attitude, but this analysis is borne out by considering distrust. Distrust is trust's contrary and is synonymous with wary suspicion. Distrust is pessimism about the goodwill and competence of another (again, relativized to a certain domain), but to be pessimistic about someone's goodwill is to expect that it is likely that she will harm your interests, and thus to treat her warily and with suspicion.

The analysis is further borne out by considering a parallel between trust and self-confidence. It seems intuitively correct to say that self-confidence involves an affective attitude. To have self-confidence is to be optimistic about one's competence (in the domain in question) and to have the expectation that one will be able to bring about a favorable outcome. Sometimes we use the phrase "trust yourself" as roughly interchangeable with "be self confident." There seems, though, to be an important difference between the two: with self-confidence, and its lack, self-doubt, we are worried about our capacity, rather than our will. "Trust yourself" has application precisely because parts of ourselves can sometimes stand in the kind of external relation to other parts that makes their interaction more like the interaction between two persons. We need to trust ourselves when we are worried about the possibility of self-sabotage, about the possibility that some not fully conscious part of ourselves might he operating from motives other than our professed ones.

While trust essentially involves an attitude of optimism that the good-will and competence of another will extend to the domain of our interaction with her, it is not exhausted by such an attitude. The affective element of trust needs to be supplemented with an expectation, namely, the expectation that the one trusted will be directly and favorably moved by the thought that someone is counting on her. Being directly and favorably moved by this thought may not give the one trusted an overriding motive; acting on such a thought, could, for example, be tempered by other concerns or by thinking that what the one who trusts is counting on is not, under the circumstances, in her own best interests. Nevertheless, one is not trustworthy unless one is willing to give significant weight to the fact that the other is counting on one, and so will not let that consideration be overruled by just any other concern one has. For this reason, one would not trust if one thought that the fact that one was counting on someone, while always being taken into account, would nonetheless be reliably overridden by other considerations. Were that the case, then, from the point of view of the truster, the other would appear unwilling to give enough weight to the thought that she was counting on her. If someone thought another would give this much weight and not more to the thought that she was being counted on, then she would not willingly rely on her if the need to do so were to arise. However, the truster's expectation need not amount to an expectation of actual performance in every case. Someone doesn't show herself untrustworthy simply because there are occasions on which the thought that someone is counting on her is not a consideration that she can let prevail. Further, when the attitude and expectation lead the truster to willingly rely on the one trusted, there may be (though there does not have to be) some vagueness about what it is the truster is counting on her for. There may be a number of ways of adequately responding to the thought that you are being counted on, which is why trusting is associated with discretionary powers.[3]

The qualification "directly" in "directly and favorably moved by the thought that someone is counting on her" is required to distinguish trusting from certain cases of mere reliance. I might, for example, know that you will be moved by the thought that I am counting on you because you fear my retaliation if you let me down. If I believe that you will be directly moved by fear and only indirectly moved by the thought that I am counting on you, our relationship is not, on my analysis, one of trust.

There are two ways to see that an expectation has to be added to the affective component of trust in order to have an adequate account: by considering unwelcome trust and by considering the ways in which a reliably benevolent person's actions and motives might yet fall short of the actions and motives that we would demand of someone we trust.

We do not always welcome trust. Sometimes someone's trust in us can feel coercive. When it does, we don't usually complain about the person's having an attitude of optimism about our goodwill and competence, or even about her displaying such optimism in her interaction toward us, for it is rare that we would find such an attitude unwelcome. (Although there can be such cases: as when, for example, we find it impertinent that someone has attributed goodwill to us with respect to a particular domain of interaction.) In the standard case, however, what we object to when we do not welcome someone's trust is that, in giving it, she expects that we will be directly moved by the thought that she is counting on us and, for one reason or another, we do not want to have to take such expectations into account, across the range of interactions the truster wants. (If we are morally decent, we do not find the trust common between strangers coercive, because what is demanded of us is minimal.) We would rather that the one trusting did not expect us to respond to her counting on us because we would rather not have her count on us. We may, for example, feel that we cannot live up to her expectations, or we may have reservations about what such expectations will amount to in a given case, or we may feel that too many people are already counting on us and that one more is a burden we would rather not have.

Perhaps not everyone will be convinced by this argument. It might be thought that we never object to someone's trust, as such, but only to their entrusting certain things to us. When someone entrusts something to our care they expect us to respond to the fact that they are counting on us. Cases of objectionable or unwelcome trust are always cases of unwelcome entrusting, as when, for example, you burden me with your secrets. Thus, having the expectation that another will be directly moved by your counting on them is part of entrusting but, for all that's been said so far, not part of trusting. (When I discuss Baier's account of trust, I'll return to the connection between trust and entrusting in more detail.) However, we can see that this objection cannot be right, for I can find your trust a burden even when you have not entrusted anything in particular to me. Moreover, since we can entrust where we don't trust (I might know, for example, that you will take good care of whatever I entrust to you because you wouldn't dare do otherwise), it seems that if entrusting *sometimes* involves the expectation that the other will be directly moved by the thought that we are counting on them, then that expectation must be part of our trusting rather than our entrusting.

The second consideration in favor of supposing that trust must involve an expectation as well as an attitude is that someone who isn't at all directly moved by the thought that you're counting on them but is, let us suppose, reliably benevolent toward you, is reliable rather than trustworthy. Suppose that the only operative motive in your interaction with me is concern about my well-being. Regardless of what I count on you to do, you do it only if it maximizes my well-being, and if it does that, you would do it anyway, whether or not I counted on you to do so. I would be justified in having an attitude of optimism about your goodwill while refraining from seeing you as trustworthy.

It might be objected that it is only in cases where optimism about goodwill is grounded in perceived benevolence that we need also attribute to the truster the expectation that the other will be directly and favorably moved by the thought that she is being counted on. To demand it in all cases, or even in the majority of cases, is to make one's analysis overly narrow and vulnerable to counterexample. But this seems to me mistaken. Consider trust in physicians.[4] The objection asks, "Isn't it enough for me to count as trusting my physician if I view her as a person of integrity and competence who cares about the interests of her patients? Why must I also expect that she will be responsive to my counting on her?" The answer is that we hope that what the physician takes to constitute acting with integrity and takes to constitute the interests of her patients will be, at least in part, shaped by the expectations of those patients. And if a physician refuses to allow the expectations of her patients to shape her understanding of what, here and now, good medical practice consists in, her patients would not be justified in trusting her. (This explains why a physician might have reservations about having someone as her patient: if she feels that she will have objections to living up to her patient's expectations, she will think it difficult to maintain the proper relationship of trust.) For this reason, it would be a mistake to think that the ideally moral are always properly trusted. While it might be true that the ideally moral are properly trusted by those who are themselves ideally moral, it doesn't follow that they are properly trusted by those who are not.

I have claimed that trust is composed of two elements: an affective attitude of optimism about the goodwill and competence of another as it extends to the domain of our interaction and, further, an expectation that the one trusted will be directly and favorably moved by the thought that you are counting on them. Our expectation is, in the typical case, grounded in the attitude of optimism. That is to say, we expect that the other will react favorably to our counting on them because we are optimistic about their goodwill. Our expectation is usually grounded in the very same evidence that grounds our attitude of optimism. Thus the attitude of optimism is central.

1.2 The Attitude of Optimism

We now have a sketch of an account of trust. But it remains a sketch insofar as we do not yet have a firm grip on what is meant by saying that trust is, among other things, an affective attitude of optimism about the goodwill of another.

According to one influential account of the emotions, held in various forms by Rorty, Calhoun, and de Sousa,[5] emotions are partly constituted by patterns of salience and tendencies of interpretation. An emotion suggests a particular line of inquiry and makes some beliefs seem compelling and others not, on account of the way the emotion gets us to focus on a partial field of evidence. Emotions are thus not primarily beliefs, although they do tend to give rise to beliefs; instead they are distinctive ways of seeing a situation. In resentment, for example, the object of resentment might be seen as a "manipulative exploiter."[6] Similarly, the claim being advanced here is that the attitude of optimism constitutive of trust is a distinctive way of seeing another. This way of seeing the other is constituted by a distinctive trusting cognitive set, which makes one's willingness to rely on the other seem reasonable.

The cognitive set constitutive of trust restricts the interpretations of another's behavior and motives that we consider. It also restricts the interpretations we will consider as possibly applying to situations and the kinds of inferences we will make about the likely actions of another. Consider the following exchange:

> IAGO: My lord, you know I love you
> OTHELLO: I think thou dost;
> And, for I know thou'rt full of love and honesty
> And weigh'st thy words before thou givest them breath,
> Therefore these stops of thine fright me the more;
> For such things in a false disloyal knave
> Are tricks of custom; but in a man that's just
> They're close dilations, working from the heart
> That passion cannot rule. (*Othello*, 3.3.117–23)

Othello trusts Iago and interprets his words and behavior in the light of his trust. Had Othello not trusted Iago, he would have been able to see Iago's speech and the very fact of his interference for what they were, malicious attempts to harm him. Trust restricts the interpretations we will consider as possibly applying to the words and actions of another. When we can—and sometimes even if doing so requires ingenuity—we will give such words and actions a favorable interpretation as consistent with the goodwill of the other. Trusting thus functions analogously to blinkered vision: it shields from view a whole range of interpretations about the motives of another and restricts the inferences we will make about the likely actions of another. Trusting thus opens one up to harm, for it gives rise to selective interpretation, which means that one can be fooled, that the truth might lie, as it were, outside one's gaze. Because we impute honorable motives to those we trust, and typically do not even stop to consider the harms they might cause if they have dishonorable motives, we are willing to rely on those we trust. The harms they might cause through failure of goodwill are not in view because the possibility that their will is other than good is not in view. What in the absence of trust would be taken to be a reason for jealousy, for wary suspicion, or for action to protect my interests will not be so taken when there is trust.[7]

It is because the one trusted is viewed through the affective lens of trust that those who trust are—usually cheerfully, and often on the basis of the smallest evidence—willing to risk depending on the one trusted. Someone might object that it is possible to have this distinctive way of seeing another without trusting her. You might see her in this way, but resist the appearance, and struggle to keep nontrusting interpretations in mind. We can see the force of this objection by considering a possible parallel with phobic emotions. If I have a phobic fear of spiders, I still fear them, even though, let us suppose, once I'm aware of my fear I make every effort to resist the patterns of salience and tendencies of interpretation that constitute fear.[8] If trust, on account of having an affective component, has features in common with emotions, it should be the case that there can be "phobic" trusting, but this, the objection continues, is implausible. To reply to this objection we need to consider the difference between trusting someone, however briefly, and having a relationship with that person that is predominately characterized by trust. In many circumstances, these will amount to the same thing, as, for example, when I trust a stranger in a momentary meeting: there is no relationship beyond the momentary that could be distrusting. Let us look at an example to see how this reply evades the objection.

Suppose that I have a friend who is particularly charming and particularly irresponsible. Time and time again she lets me down, and time and time again I forgive her and resume a relationship, promising myself that this time I will be more cautious, this time I will not count on her, this time I will remember to think of the ways in which I make myself vulnerable to her, and this time I will take measures to protect myself. I won't trust her again. For all my resolution, I might nonetheless find myself trusting her. It's true that whenever I become aware of doing so, I will resist the impulse and will once again be on my guard. At one extreme, I might only become aware of my having again trusted when I am again let down. I would say of myself that I find myself trusting her, even though, when I think about it, I'm aware that I shouldn't. Our relationship, for that time period, would have been characterized predominantly by trust. At the opposite extreme, my caution might undermine my tendency to view her with trust so that no sooner do I find myself viewing her that way than I call myself to attention and remind myself of all the reasons not to trust her: in this circumstance, I would not be willing to depend on her when the need arises. Here, I'm inclined to say that I don't trust her, although I fight the tendency to do so: I do not go far enough along with the patterns of salience and tendencies of interpretation that partly constitute trust for it to be the case that I trust her. Even when caution dominates, there is, though, the possibility of momentary trust—trust that is unnoticed and would be withdrawn as soon as it were noticed—and there will be momentary trust whenever I'm not quick enough to catch myself and reject the view of her that I have adopted. When I'm not quick enough at catching myself, my view of the other can give rise to the risk-taking behavior characteristic of trust. In this kind of case, our relationship is not one characterized by trust, but for all that, it can have moments of trust. Usually, when we say that A trusts B (within a certain domain), we mean that A's relationship with B (within the domain in question) is predominantly characterized by trust's distinctive way of seeing someone, and not merely that on occasion A sees B through the lens of trust. Thus, there is some truth in the claim that when I reject the appearances trust gives rise to, I don't trust, but this does not force us to say that trust requires more than a distinctive way of seeing someone; although a trusting relationship (which is usually what we have in mind when we say that A trusts B) requires a consistent pattern of such interpretations. This solution to the objection is preferable to saying that trust requires us to have an endorsed attitude toward another, because we are generally not aware of our trusting and seldom bring it sufficiently clearly before our minds to endorse or reject it.

1.3 Clarifying the Distinction between Trust and Reliance

While trust is always a possible attitude to take toward a person, we sometimes rely on people instead of trusting them. So, for example, I can rely on someone to behave in a certain kind of way because I have evidence that it is likely that she will behave in that way out of, say, habit, fear, vanity, or stupidity. As Baier notes, trust is not a precondition for relying on someone.[9]

Trusting is not an attitude that we can adopt toward machinery. I can rely on my computer not to destroy important documents or on my old car to get me from A to B, but my old car is reliable rather than trustworthy. One can only trust things that have wills, since only things with wills can have goodwills—although having a will is to be given a generous interpretation so as to include, for example, firms and government bodies. Machinery can be relied on, but only agents, natural or artificial, can be trusted.[10]

Some cases of reliance are not grounded in perceived features of a person's psychology at all. Sometimes we adopt a policy of not checking up on people because to do so would be too time-consuming or too expensive. It's better to allow a few people to cheat on the coffee sign-up sheet than to devise a cheat-free method for collecting the coffee money. Devising a cheat-free method would simply take more time and cost more money than it would be worth.

There are some additional things that need to be said about the difference between trust and reliance. Sometimes we rely on things because we have no choice but to do so; thus we can be forced to rely on something when we are unable to predict that the event on which we rely will occur. However, if we have a choice about the matter, we will rely on someone only to the extent that we would be willing to make a prediction that the favored outcome will occur. In Section 3, we shall see that things are otherwise with trust: we can be justified in trusting even when we would not be justified in predicting a favorable action on the part of the one trusted. Our evidence for trusting need not be as great as the evidence required for a corresponding justified prediction. In this respect trusting is more like hoping than like predicting.

2. ADVANTAGES OF THE ACCOUNT

As we have seen, trust is to be distinguished from reliance in that trusting requires an attitude of optimism about the goodwill and competence of another as it extends to the domain of our interaction with them, and, in addition, trusting requires an expectation that the other will be directly moved by the thought that we are counting on them. It still needs to be shown that this account is adequate as an account of trust. An adequate account of trust should be able to explain at least the following three fairly obvious facts about trust: that trust and distrust are contraries but not contradictories,[11] that trust cannot be willed,[12] and that trust can give rise to beliefs that are abnormally resistant to evidence.[13] Because my account places an affective attitude at the center of our understanding of trust, it is able to explain all these things.

Given that trust and distrust both involve attitudes, it should be the case that together they do not exhaust the possible stances we can take toward another's goodwill and competence. Optimism and pessimism are contraries but not contradictories; between them lies a neutral space. As a consequence, the absence of trust is not to be equated with distrust, for one may fail to trust without actively distrusting—one may simply not adopt any attitude at all toward the goodwill and competence of another. In between trust and distrust are found various forms of relying on and taking for granted which are not grounded in either optimism or pessimism about the other's goodwill.

Affective attitudes look toward features of the world that would make them justified and can no more be sincerely adopted in the face of a known and acknowledged absence of such grounds than a belief can be adopted in the face of a known and acknowledged lack of evidence. Because trust involves an affective attitude, it is not something that one can adopt at will: while one can trust wisely or foolishly, trust cannot be demanded in the absence of grounds for supposing that the person in question has goodwill and competence and will be likely to take into account the fact that one is counting on them. This is not to say that there can never be an element of decision in adopting beliefs or attitudes. We can, for example, decide that the evidence we now have is enough to support the belief, but we can't just decide to believe regardless of the evidence.[14] While trust cannot be willed, it can be cultivated. We cultivate trust by a selective focus of attention toward the grounds for trust and away from the grounds for distrust.

Trust gives rise to beliefs that are highly resistant to evidence. While affective attitudes can't be willfully adopted in the teeth of evidence, once adopted they serve as a filter for how future evidence will be interpreted. If I trust you, I will, for example, believe that you are innocent of the hideous crime with which you are charged, and I will suppose that the apparently mounting evidence of your guilt can be explained in some way compatible with your innocence. Of course this resistance to evidence is not limitless:

given enough evidence, my trust can be shaken and I can come to believe that you are guilty. When my trust is shaken, I will come to see you in quite a different light: that certain shortness of temper that never seemed so important before, seemed always to be able to be explained away, now seems highlighted. I can come to see that, yes, you could have done what you are charged with, and, perhaps, even more strongly, that, yes, it is the sort of thing you would do. But in coming to see you in this way, without trust, I undergo a significant shift in the patterns of my attention with respect to your character and in my habits of interpretation of you, your character, and your motives.

If, as I have claimed, trust has an affective component and emotions are partly constituted by patterns of salience and tendencies of interpretation, it should come as no surprise that trust gives rise to beliefs that are highly resistant to evidence. For the same reason, trust and distrust have a tendency to seek out evidence for themselves and so to be, to a degree, self-confirming.

Bearing in mind these three facts that an account of trust ought to be able to explain, I turn now to Baier's account of trust in "Trust and Anti-trust." According to Baier, trusting is a matter of entrusting. Trusting is analyzed as a three-place predicate: A trusts B with valued thing C.[15] Baier acknowledges that there are three difficulties with her account: It involves a degree of regimentation in that it may sometimes be difficult to specify exactly what is entrusted (236). It might suggest a greater degree of consciousness and explicitness than our trusting relations typically display, so we need to guard against interpreting the model in this way (240). And finally, it seems to overlook plain, non-goods-relativized, trust. But we might think that we should first trust before we entrust. (Baier herself notes this [259] but thinks that we flatly rule out entrusting anything whatsoever to someone or some group of persons only when our interests are in complete opposition.)

I want to test an entrusting model against the three commonplace facts about trust mentioned earlier. It turns out that, because the model leads us to focus on the disposition of cared about objects at the expense of focusing on attitudes, it has problems explaining at least two of the three commonplaces; furthermore, with our attention drawn outward toward these objects, it is easy to lose sight of the crucial element of optimism about the goodwill of another. Trust becomes insufficiently distinguished from (mere) reliance.

It seems that one either entrusts valued thing C to B or one does not. If not entrusting is distrusting, then trusting and distrusting are contradictories. But it seems that while one has to either entrust or not, trust and distrust do not exhaust the options, and so trust and distrust are not to be equated with entrusting and refraining from entrusting. Explaining why trust and distrust should be contraries but not contradictories is thus at least a prima facie problem for an account that analyzes trust in terms of entrusting. There may, though, be a way to preserve this distinction within an entrusting model. Perhaps trust involves a positive handing over of the thing entrusted, and distrust involves a positive refusal to hand over, a deliberate withholding of, the good in question, or, perhaps, purposive action to *protect* the valued thing. Trust and distrust could then be seen as contraries, for there is room for a neutral position in which one neither hands over the valued good nor holds it close to oneself. How good a reply this is depends on what it is that is being entrusted to another. There are three stances to take toward, say, you and the family silver: I may lend it to you, lock it up when I know you are visiting, or take no special precautions over it. It is less clear that there are three stances to take toward one's own self when walking down the street, and so it's not clear that this reply is fully satisfying.

The second commonplace that an account of trust must he able to explain is that trust cannot be willed. Baier notes this fact: "'Trust me' is for most of us an invitation which we cannot accept at will—either we do already trust the one who says it, in which case it serves at best as reassurance, or it is properly responded to with, 'Why should I and how can I, until I have cause to?'" (244). But why cannot one trust at will? If trust is entrusting it seems that I should be able to entrust at will, simply by handing over the relevant good. I may not feel very comfortable about it, but unless a feeling is built into the analysis of trust, that seems beside the point. Entrusting is an action and actions are, paradigmatically, things that can be willed. If, however, trusting involves an attitude, and attitudes cannot be adopted at will, we have an explanation for why one cannot trust at will.

Put just like this, the objection is surely unfair. We must cash out the "trust" as it occurs in the entrusting model's "A trusts B with valued object C." Perhaps without a belief in the reliability of the goodwill of another we cannot trust but instead can only rely on them. Baier says that the difference between trusting and relying on is that when we trust we rely on the goodwill of others toward us, whereas we may rely on others' "dependable habits, or only on their dependably exhibited fear, anger, or other motives compatible with ill will toward one, or on motives not directed on one at all" (234). So we are to view trust as entrusting on the basis of a belief about the goodwill of the other. Trust is the action in conjunction with the belief that specifies its reason. Such a belief would have to be based on evidence and so could not be summoned at will. However, when an entrusting model is adopted, the significance of confidence in the goodwill of the other easily falls from view. This is because we can entrust where we don't, on my account, trust. That goodwill drops out of the picture when we focus on entrusting is shown in Baier's discussion of the moral rightness or wrongness of trust relations. The cases she considers as trust relationships appear to lack this element of reliance on the goodwill of another: "Where the truster relies on his threat advantage to keep the trust relation going, or where the trusted relies on concealment, something is morally rotten in the trust relationship" (255). I would suggest that in a situation such as this you haven't a morally rotten trust relationship, you haven't a trust relationship at all; instead you have a case of mere reliance. Optimism about goodwill is central to trust, but in situations like the one Baier describes, there is no goodwill. Trust does not seem to be sufficiently distinguished from relying on. Nor should this surprise us given that one can entrust where there is mere reliance. If I can rely on another's fear, my ability to control the purse strings, or the foolishness of another, I might be fully justified in entrusting them with something I care about, for I can know that they will not dare harm it or that it won't occur to them to do so. In such cases, confidence in some other aspect of a person's psychology has replaced confidence in her goodwill, but where this other thing is sufficient to ensure adequate performance, I need not also depend on her goodwill. This is not to say that relationships of reliance aren't sometimes mixed or can't depend on both kinds of elements.

Goodwill readily drops out of an entrusting model even when we attempt to include it, as Baier does. This is because we are led to focus on the disposition of cared-about objects rather than on attitudes toward a person, whom we might, as a consequence of holding such an attitude, willingly let get dangerously near things we care about. One of the chief motives for adopting an entrusting model—namely, that we be able to say what is in common and what is different between the various forms of trust, ranging as they do from trust in strangers to trust in intimates—can be accommodated within a nonentrusting model provided that we allow for variation in the domain over which the attitude extends. This lets us keep "plain trust" (259), as an attitude directed toward a person and as explanatory of the kinds of risks we might willingly expose ourselves to with respect to that person, while yet being able to make the same kinds of distinctions that an entrusting model can.

An entrusting model is silent about the third commonplace a theory of trust should explain. And this is so even when such a model is fully spelled out so that trust is entrusting on the basis of a belief that the other has goodwill. The belief that another has goodwill may lead us, in the first instance, to be doubtful about her guilt. This is perfectly reasonable insofar as the evidence that supports the belief that the other has goodwill is also evidence for the belief that the person couldn't have done such a thing— think of character witnesses in criminal trials. However, as a belief of a perfectly ordinary sort, it should not be abnormally resistant to evidence, and it should not lead us to hold additional beliefs that are themselves abnormally resistant to evidence.[16] But the beliefs we form on the basis of trust are abnormally resistant to evidence and so, in general, is the optimism about the goodwill of another that grounds such beliefs.

I conclude that an entrusting model does not sufficiently bring out the affective component in trust. In particular, it obscures the importance of optimism about the goodwill of another.

3. JUSTIFIED TRUSTING

Given the usefulness of trust, should we say that a trusting attitude is the rational default position and that we should tend to approach the world with a trusting cognitive set? Or should we say that in the light of the harms to which we are vulnerable when we trust unwisely, the rational default position is one of distrust? Or, finally, should we say that the rational default position is one of neutrality?[17] Appropriate default stance is too sensitive to climate, and to domain and consequences as they interact to affect the expected disutility of misplaced trust, for there to be useful generalizations here. Further, for the individual truster, the appropriate default stance is linked to her assessment of tendencies in her own trusting and distrusting.

In climates in which there is strong motive to be untrustworthy, it would require more evidence for our trust to be justified than in climates where there is little incentive to untrustworthiness. A final verdict on whether a particular act of trusting is justified will have to step beyond that particular case to examine general features of the social climate we inhabit. Thus I take it that at the height of the Chinese Cultural Revolution, the justified default position was one of distrust, and that it took more evidence to be warranted in moving from this position than it would take to warrant justified trusting in a more favorable climate. During those campaigns, people accused of being counterrevolutionary were subject to public shaming, beating, and incarceration. At the time, there was strong motive for people to be untrustworthy. Informers were held up as model citizens, and anyone who displayed goodwill toward someone who became a target of the campaigns was in danger of herself becoming a target. In such a climate, showing goodwill toward others was dangerous. In contrast, in an ideally moral climate, the interests of each would be harmonized so that trust could flourish. The motivation to be untrustworthy would diminish, and there would thus be grounds for the expectation that those we encounter are trustworthy.

Domain and consequences interact to determine which default stance is justified and how much evidence we need to move from that default stance. If I am to have the depth of trust that would make it reasonable to entrust you with a secret of mine, then I'll want to have quite a bit of evidence about your character. If, though, I am to trust you not to attack me in the street, I may need no particular evidence about your character at all. This might seem to be a counterintuitive result, since surely it is worse to be attacked in the street than it is to be embarrassed by a confidence indiscreetly betrayed. However, domain is here signaling likelihood of performance. We are all aware of the lively pleasures of gossip and of the strength of character required to resist them. In contrast, it is not hard to refrain from harming a stranger on the street; that just takes basic decency, a trait that we can assume is widely shared, unless the climate is sufficiently bad. Once we hold domain fixed, consequences become of the first importance: of course I'm going to need more evidence of your trustworthiness before I willingly tell you a secret that, if spread abroad, would be damaging to me, than before I tell you a secret whose disclosure would be merely embarrassing. It is not, therefore, that one or the other of domain or consequence is always the most important; rather what is important is how they interact to determine the expected disutility of misplaced trust (or distrust).

While climate, domain, and consequences are variables determining which default stance is justified that extend across agents, the fourth variable determining the appropriate default stance is agent-specific. Some agents have reason to be distrustful of their tendencies toward trust in certain domains. When we believe that we are poor affective instruments, either in general or across a specific range of cases, we should distrust our trust, or distrust our distrust, and demand a correspondingly higher amount of evidence before we let ourselves trust or distrust in the kinds of cases in question. Consider responses to physicians. We can imagine someone with a tendency to find authoritative and avuncular physicians trustworthy and physicians who acknowledge the tentativeness of their diagnoses and the limits of their art untrustworthy. Given how sexism shapes what we take to be signs of competence, we should be wary of our tendency to trust when an etiology of that trust tells us it is as likely to be caused by mannerisms of privilege as by marks of trustworthiness.

Because climate, domain, consequences of misplaced trust, and appropriate assessment of the tendencies of our own trusting and distrusting affect how much evidence is needed before our trust can count as justified, the question of the rational default position has no general answer. However, there is still an important question to be addressed: Are there any instances of apparently justified trust or distrust where we would not want to say that the person would be justified in having the belief that the other was trustworthy or untrustworthy? If there can be such cases, then if we advocated an analysis of trust which made trust fully or partly constituted by a belief about the other's trustworthiness, we would be forced either to reject evidentialism or admit that the cases weren't justified after all.

There are two places to look for examples of trust leaping ahead of the evidence: when trust is governed by forward-looking or instrumental considerations, and when trust is governed by backward-looking considerations of evidence but our responses seem to outstrip the evidence. Let's examine the forward-looking cases first.

Earlier I remarked that trust cannot be willed but that it can be cultivated. We might want to cultivate trust toward people in general, toward members of a certain group, or toward a particular person. Moreover, it seems that we can sometimes be justified both in attempting to cultivate trust and in the trusting that is the result of such cultivation. If trust and distrust are partly constituted by patterns of attention, lines of inquiry, and tendencies of interpretation, it should be possible to cultivate them by controlling our patterns of attention, our lines of inquiry, and our interpretations. Thus, while trust cannot be directly willed, we can will to pay attention to the kinds of things that are likely to support, create, or extend our trust, and we can will to refrain from focusing on the kinds of things that are likely to undermine and limit our trust.

Sometimes we set about cultivating trust because we think that by trusting, and displaying our trust, we will be able to elicit trustworthy behavior from the other. When we do this our hope is that by trusting we will be able to bring about the very conditions that would justify our trust. It might be thought that we do not need to inquire whether attempts at this sort of bootstrapping can be justified, for we need never actually trust on the basis of forward-looking considerations—all we need do is act *as if* we trusted. To actually set about trying to trust is to do more than is needed. It is a mistake, though, to think that acting as if you trusted will have the same results as acting on the basis of genuine trust, cultivated in the hope of bringing about trustworthiness. Acting as if you trusted and genuinely trusting could have the same result only on the assumption that there is no perceptible difference between the behavior that would be produced from trust and the behavior that would be produced from acting as if you trusted. But this assumption is implausible in the kinds of cases where one is most likely to adopt this sort of strategy in the first place. Trusting in the hope of eliciting trustworthiness is a pointless strategy to adopt with those with whom we have infrequent contact. In such circumstances our strategic trusting could not bear fruit. Instead, it is the kind of strategy a parent might use with a child, or a lover with her beloved. But it is precisely the frequency of contact between the one who would trust and the one she would elicit trustworthiness from that makes it implausible to suppose that merely acting as if you trusted could, on each of many separate occasions, result in behavior indistinguishable from the behavior of one who genuinely trusts. If this is so, then we do need to ask when, if ever, bootstrapping is justified.

Bootstrapping is not always possible and not always reasonable. It won't be possible if we cannot find sufficient foundation in evidence for our trusting. Despite our attempts to control our patterns of attention and our interpretations, we might be unable to find enough to focus on to support our trust. Our attempts at giving positive reinterpretations of those aspects of a person that might otherwise have tended to support the hypothesis that she is untrustworthy have the feel of fantasy and wish fulfillment. They do not ring true. Whenever trust can be achieved only through a fantasy construction, our trusting is unlikely to elicit trustworthiness from the other, for if fantasy is required to see the other as trustworthy, it is highly unlikely that the other has the potential for trustworthiness.

In addition to cultivating trust in order to elicit trustworthiness from another, we sometimes cultivate trust in order to realize a conception of ourselves. So, for example, the rape victim whose trust in others has been shattered might set about cultivating trust because she sees herself as someone who is free-spirited and bold, and she does not wish to be the kind of person who is timid, protective of the self, and on the lookout for betrayal. She does not want her horrible experience to lead to a change in herself. The trust that results from willful cultivation can be rational. Provided that its cultivation did not require fantasy and distortion, it can be reasonable to view it as keyed to real and perceptible features of the agent's situation.

The second sort of cases involve flash intuitive assessments that do not seem to be based on evidence sufficient to support a belief. Let us consider an example taken from Greenspan's *Emotions and Reasons*.[18] I find myself feeling suspicious of a salesman, worried that he will harm my interests, worried that he is not trustworthy. Let us suppose, further, that the salesman has been recommended to me by a friend whose judgment in such matters I believe to be reliable. On the basis of this recommendation, I believe that the salesman is trustworthy, yet I find myself unable to help viewing him with suspicion. I continue to see him as untrustworthy, although I am not yet prepared to abandon my belief that he is trustworthy. I cannot articulate why I view him with suspicion, except to say that there is something creepy about him, something in his manner that I don't like. Finally, let us suppose, although I don't know this myself, that I am not, in general, a reliable detector of untrustworthiness. My suspicion would not track untrustworthiness across a suitable range of counterfactual circumstances relevantly similar to the present one. Thus, as the example is set up, if having a justified belief requires being able to give an account of what justifies that belief, I haven't got a justified belief. Similarly, if having a justified belief requires having a belief that tracks the truth across some range of counterfactual circumstances, I haven't got a justified belief. And if having a justified belief requires having a belief formed by a reliable process and the absence of undermining beliefs, I haven't got a justified belief, for my belief that the salesman is trustworthy appears to undermine my perception of him as untrustworthy.[19] Thus, it seems that I wouldn't be justified in forming a belief that he is untrustworthy on the basis of my seeing him as untrustworthy.

If we think that trust and distrust are primarily beliefs, it seems that—regardless of any of the variables mentioned earlier—we would have to say that my distrust could not be justified. But it seems to me that, especially if the stakes are high, I might still be justified in following through with the lines of inquiry and patterns of salience that are constitutive of distrust.[20] This is because emotions and other affective states often do represent the world in the way it is: those we are suspicious of often are untrustworthy.[21] I do not mean to claim that distrust would have to be justified in cases of this sort, only that even though we've *decisively* shown the belief that the other is untrustworthy is unjustified, we haven't decisively shown that distrust is unjustified. To do that we would have to step back and examine the other variables affecting the justification of trust, and they could well return the verdict "justified." This example better lets us understand the importance of the truster's assessment of the tendencies in her own trust and distrust: the metajustification in terms of the worth of following up on affective appearances would not be available to those with reason to distrust their distrust.

If there can be cases of the sort I have described, then an account of trust that makes affect central has an unexpected payoff: it lets us say that such cases can be justified without confronting the evidentialist thesis. It is beyond the scope of this paper to argue the merits of evidentialism. It might well be that evidentialism is false—perhaps, for example, we can be justified in believing on instrumentalist grounds. But if, as I have argued, trust and distrust are not primarily beliefs, then trust and distrust cannot be used to unseat evidentialism.[22] Equally, though, evidentialism cannot be used to challenge our intuitions about when trust and distrust are justified.

NOTES

This paper originally appeared in *Ethics* 107 (1996): 4–25 and is reprinted by permission.

1. Amelie Rorty, "Explaining Emotions," in *Explaining Emotions*, ed. Amelie Oksenberg Rorty (Berkeley: University of California Press, 1980); Cheshire Calhoun, "Cognitive Emotions?" in *What Is an Emotion?*, ed. Cheshire Calhoun and

Robert C. Solomon (New York: Oxford University Press, 1984), 327–42; Ronald de Sousa, "The Rationality of Emotions," in Rorty, ed., *Explaining Emotions*, 127–52, and *The Rationality of Emotions* (Cambridge, Mass.: MIT Press, 1987).

2. The account I develop here is indebted to Annette Baier's account—in "Trust and Antitrust," *Ethics* 96 (1986): 231–60, and "The Pathologies of Trust," and "Appropriate Trust," delivered at Princeton University as the Tanner Lectures on Human Values (*Tanner Lectures on Human Values*, vol. 13 [Salt Lake City: University of Utah Press, 1992])—most significantly in the following ways: (i) in maintaining a distinction between trust and reliance, (ii) in acknowledging the importance of the competence of the other (Baier, "Trust and Antitrust," 239, and *Tanner Lectures on Human Values*, 111–12), and (iii) in recognizing that trust can be faked (*Tanner Lectures on Human Values*, 112). The difference in our positions will become clear in Sec. 2.

3. That trust involves discretionary powers is first noted by Baier ("Trust and Antitrust," 236–40). However, I think she rather overstates the case in claiming that trust always involves discretionary powers.

4. Thanks to the editors of *Ethics* for this example.

5. Rorty, "Explaining Emotions"; Calhoun, "Cognitive Emotions?"; and de Sousa, "The Rationality of Emotions," and *The Rationality of Emotion*.

6. For a discussion of the notion of cognitive sets and of the cognitive set involved in resentment in particular, see Calhoun, "Cognitive Emotions?"

7. Ronald de Sousa discusses Othello in the context of how control of perceptual focus can give rise to emotions and how jealousy affects our interpretation of situations (*The Rationality of Emotion*, 195–96).

8. For a discussion of spider and other phobias, see Calhoun, "Cognitive Emotions?"

9. Baier, "Trust and Antitrust," 234.

10. It is a consequence of my account, though, that when we say nonnatural agents trust, our usage is analogous to our usage in attributing trust to a natural agent; but insofar as it is metaphorical to attribute affective states to unnatural agents, the meaning is not precisely the same. (This is also true, though, when we attribute beliefs to nonnatural agents.) Sometimes government policies can enact something similar to the selective vision characteristic of trust, and the rationale for those policies can duplicate the expectation constitutive of trust. For example, a social welfare agency might decide not to use surveillance methods to eliminate cheating, on the grounds that the number of cheaters is likely to be small and can be further reduced by a policy of not checking since that would make the recipients feel they were being treated respectfully, and they would respond positively to such treatment. Here, the government agency would have been expecting its clients to respond favorably to the fact that they were being counted on. The agency's policy would have mimicked

the way optimism gives rise to selective interpretation in that the agency would have proceeded on the basis of the assumption that cheating was not something to be expected. Note that the rationale for the policy matters: it would not be correct to say that the agency trusts its clients if they simply thought checking up on them was cost-inefficient.

11. This is noted by Trudy Govier in "Trust, Distrust, and Feminist Theory," *Hypatia* 7 (1992): 16–33, 18.

12. This is noted by Baier in "Trust and Antitrust," 244.

13. This point is made by Judith Baker in "Trust and Rationality," *Pacific Philosophical Quarterly* 68 (1987): 1–13. Baker is concerned about the problem of reconciling trust with evidentialism, or the view that we should never believe anything without sufficient evidence. She claims that trust is "a kind of commitment, a state of the will" (10). (If this were right, though, it seems trust should be able to be willed.) Trust still essentially involves beliefs, although it is to be assessed primarily for strategic rationality. She attempts to resolve the tension in saying that trust involves beliefs but is primarily assessed in terms of goal-directed, rather than truth-directed, rationality by pointing out the importance of trust for friendship: "But if a result of becoming someone's friend, of one's trust, is that barriers to honesty are removed and the other person is open with us, then trust in their veracity will be merited and end-directed rationality will not be opposed to truth-directed rationality" (12). If believing makes it so, then the belief is justified. But, of course, believing does not always make it so, and so strategic and representational rationality won't always be in alignment. My account, which places an affective element at the center of trust, is able to finesse the evidentialist objection. I return to the issue of evidentialism in Sec. 3.

14. Of course, that we cannot adopt an attitude in the face of a known and acknowledged lack of grounds is not to say that our affective stances follow our beliefs in a timely fashion, nor that we don't sometimes find ourselves experiencing "spill-over" feelings, as happens, for example, with phobias.

15. Baier, "Trust and Antitrust," 236. For the remainder of this section, page references in the text are to this article.

16. In Baier's newer work on trust, the entrusting model is less emphasized, and she acknowledges that trust also involves an affective aspect, though she does not attempt a detailed account of it (*Tanner Lectures on Human Values,* 111–12). For Baier, the affective aspect is not central in an account of when trust is justified. In Sec. 3, I will claim that the affective aspect of trust is central for understanding when trust is justified.

17. Talk of default positions is compatible with the Sec. 2 claim that emotions look to the world for evidence. Consider anger: we can admit that anger can't be willed but still inquire whether it is better to be irascible, placid-tempered, or something in between.

18. Partricia Greenspan, *Emotions and Reasons* (New York: Routledge, 1988). Greenspan argues that suspicion can be justified when one would not be justified in forming a belief that the other is untrustworthy Her account of justification also stresses forward-looking conditions. However, she does not think that skepticism about our own capacity as an emotional instrument is especially undermining of the justifiedness of an emotion.

19. These three options are meant to exhaust the possible accounts of what makes a belief justified. The first is an internalist account and the others externalist accounts.

20. That is why this sort of example is best developed with cases of suspicion, since usually the costs of being wrong in our distrust are less than the costs of being wrong in our trust. But this is a generalization that admits of exceptions: there can sometimes be severe consequences of misplaced distrust.

21. In *Passions within Reason* (New York: Norton, 1988), Robert Frank presents an evolutionary argument for why emotions can have this role.

22. In "The Virtue of Faith," *Faith and Philosophy* 1 (1984): 3–15, Robert Adams claims that trust requires beliefs that go beyond the evidence.

CHAPTER 16

Trusting "First" and "Second" Selves

Aristotelian Reflections on Virginia Woolf
and Annette Baier

JENNIFER WHITING

I know how much we are liable to err in matters that concern us, and also how much
the judgements of our friends should be distrusted when they are in our favour.
—Descartes, *Discourses on the Method*

A true sceptic will be diffident of his philosophical doubts,
as well as of his philosophical convictions.
—Hume, *A Treatise of Human Nature*

My point of departure is a parenthetical and rhetorical question posed by
Annette Baier in "Trust and Antitrust." In a brief survey intended to sub-
stantiate her claim that moral theorists have paid sparse attention to the
topic of trust, Baier concedes that the importance of trust is implicitly recognized in Aristotle's discussion of friendship. Referring to Aristotle's conception of the friend as an "other self," she asks whether someone could
have as a "second self" someone he distrusts. And she seems to assume that
the answer is "obviously not." For she moves on immediately to "Aquinas
and other Christian moralists," noting simply that Aristotle's recognition of
trust is not only implicit but also limited in scope, applying only to trust
among friends.[1]

I myself tend to think that Aristotle's recognition of trust is both more explicit and wider in scope than Baier suggests. But I do not wish to dwell on these points.[2] I shall focus instead on her ready assumption that you cannot have as a "second self" someone you distrust. Baier has confirmed in conversation that she was indeed assuming this, and I want to challenge her assumption. In doing so, I will simply assume for the sake of argument her account of trust as a form of reliance primarily on the goodwill but also on the competence of another, and so take distrust as some sort of reluctance or refusal to rely on the goodwill and competence of another.[3]

There are two (not necessarily exclusive) ways to take Baier's assumption. To the extent that it is an assumption about what Aristotle himself would say, we may have to agree with Baier. For Aristotle speaks of the friend as an "other self" only in the case of character-friendship—the friendship of virtuous agents who love one another on account of their highly idealized virtues.[4] And his conception of virtue as inseparable from practical wisdom may be so exacting as to leave no ground for distrust among such friends, who are by hypothesis good-willed and ultra-competent.[5] So there seems little point to asking whether such agents would trust one another. And I suspect that this question about *ideal* agents would leave Baier cold.

But there is another, more interesting way to take Baier's assumption. We can take it to be at least partly *in propria persona:* she may be acknowledging in her own voice the existence and merits of a modest and more realistic variety of character-friendship, and doubting of such friends that they would or should distrust one another. This is how I propose to take Baier's assumption: I propose to modify Aristotle's conception of character-friendship so as to render it more acceptable to Baier, and then to ask whether there is room within this modified conception for distrust among character-friends. For this strikes me as a question that should be of interest to Baier.

I. THE MODIFIED ARISTOTELIAN VIEW

Laying claim to Baier's sympathies requires at least two modifications of Aristotle's view. First, Baier has moral objections to Aristotle's view that love of one's friends is ideally to be explained and justified by appeal to their virtues: she thinks that we love people for all sorts of reasons, and that this is a good thing. But it seems to me that we can bracket the genetic-cum-justificatory claim: however it comes about that virtuous people love one another, and whether or not they regard such love as justified primarily by appeal to virtue, the important point is that agents who value virtue as such will in fact—and should normatively speaking—love and value the virtue of their friends. Such agents will also recognize and value the ways in which the virtue of their friends may assist them in their own attempts to live virtuously: they may seek one another's advice in attempting to resolve "hard cases" and may even, in some cases, defer to one another's "authority" in certain domains.[6] These rudiments of character-friendship are all phenomena that Baier can and presumably does recognize, even if she rejects the general project of justifying and explaining love of one's friends by appeal to their virtue. And these rudiments of character-friendship obtain not only in intimate relationships, but also in less intimate relationships such as those among "civic friends" (which I propose to treat as generalized forms of character-friendship).[7]

The second modification required by Baier's sensibility is some sort of concession to the fallibility of character-friends, who are by hypothesis supposed to be virtuous. The point of introducing fallibility is to make room for distrust among character-friends. But too great a concession to fallibility will undermine their hypothesized virtue, with the result that we purchase distrust among character-friends at the expense of their virtue and so at the expense of their claim to be genuine character-friends. We should thus allow only modest concessions to fallibility. There is moreover a strategic reason for limiting concessions to fallibility: the more fallibility I allow, the easier my argument becomes. So in order to argue the most difficult case, I will abstain for present purposes from two reasonable concessions to fallibility.

First, although I think it reasonable to allow for some sort of character-friendship both among continent and even incontinent agents, I will not allow that here. For admitting character-friendship among such subjects makes the case for distrust of character-friends too easy: such friends may hesitate to rely on one another's acknowledged goodwill because they recognize one another's wills as weak. Second, although I think it reasonable to allow for some sort of character-friendship among individuals who recognize themselves as virtuous in some respects but not in others, I will not allow that here either. For admitting character-friendship among such individuals once again makes the case for distrust too easy: such individuals may rely on one another's goodwill in some domains but not in others.

332 §§ PERSONS AND PASSIONS

What I seek, then, are cases in which character-friends are generally correct in viewing themselves as virtuous (rather than merely continent) and in failing to see what they take to be flaws in one another's characters, but not unreasonable in thinking that a certain sort of distrust of one another is nevertheless warranted. I say "generally correct" so as to allow that some of their beliefs and attitudes may be to some extent mistaken. The important point is that they correct such mistakes more or less immediately upon recognition; they do not live with what they take to be mistaken beliefs and attitudes. So they are typically without what they take to be grounds for failing to trust one another. In what sense, then, would it be reasonable for them to distrust one another?

I have argued elsewhere that Aristotle's "other self" doctrine involves taking the virtuous person's attitude toward herself as a normative paradigm for her attitude toward her friends. [8] This seems to me to be an aspect of Aristotle's view to which Baier can and should be sympathetic. On this view, the virtuous person's attitude toward herself functions, in a way the nonvirtuous person's attitude toward herself does not, as a criterion for the acceptability of her attitudes toward her friends. I want to apply this criterion to the question whether we should allow for distrust of genuine character-friends. And I want to argue that we can allow genuinely virtuous agents to distrust their "second selves" as long as we allow them to distrust their "first selves." What we need, then, is an argument that it is sometimes appropriate for a virtuous agent to distrust her "*first* self"—an argument capable of supporting the conclusion that it is sometimes appropriate for her to distrust her "*second* self." [9]

I believe that a modest concession to fallibility affords such an argument. A virtuous agent, in spite of her inability to detect flaws in her current beliefs and attitudes, will want to allow for the possibility that *some* of her beliefs and attitudes are mistaken, perhaps even radically so. This is not to say that massive error is compatible with her hypothesized virtue, but only that willingness to entertain the *possibility* of such error is an important mechanism for establishing and maintaining correct beliefs and attitudes, and so an important component of virtue itself. Moreover, even if the virtuous agent's general conceptions are for the most part correct, there is no doubt room for error in applying them, especially in hard cases. But the reasonably virtuous agent who sees no flaws in her current beliefs and attitudes while recognizing the possibility of error faces a dilemma. To whom can she turn for assistance in discovering where she is mistaken? Surely not to those whose judgment she does not respect. But if, as of course she must, she relies on her own sense of virtue in deciding whose judgment she is to trust, she runs the risk of turning only to those who share with her the very beliefs and attitudes she seeks to examine—namely, her "other selves," who are most likely to *second* her judgment and least likely to help her detect her own errors.[10] One way of attempting to cope with this dilemma is to cultivate a certain sort of distrust of one's "second selves." Such distrust is ultimately a kind of distrust of one's "first self," so the importance of distrusting one's "second selves" *follows from* the importance of distrusting one's "first self."

Distrusting one's "second selves" is especially important where there is reason to think that membership in a certain group may systematically distort one's attitudes in ways that make it reasonable to distrust the views of one's own and other similarly situated selves. Such distortion can occur not only in attitudes ordinarily recognized as moral, but also in attitudes not ordinarily recognized as moral (for example, where scientific attitudes are influenced by the dominant paradigms of the scientific community to which one belongs). Moreover, such distortion can occur not only where attitudes are systematically distorted by membership in a dominant group but also where they are systematically distorted by membership in a subordinate group.

Consider first how membership in a *dominant* group may systematically distort one's attitudes. Consider, for example, a male athletic director or judge who notes how many more of his male than his female acquaintances display an active interest in sports, and concludes that it is acceptable for universities to provide fewer sports for women because women are naturally less interested in sports, but fails to notice that girls' interests in sports are as systematically discouraged from an early age as boys' interests in sports are encouraged.[11] This may be little fault of the judge or athletic director's own: perhaps he has no sisters or grew up in an atypical family where his sisters' athletic interests were in fact encouraged.

Consider next how membership in a *subordinate* group may systematically distort one's views. Consider, for example, a girl who grows up thinking that she does not enjoy sports because she has never had the opportunity to develop the skills that contribute to such enjoyment. Perhaps—if she is lucky—she will be provided with such opportunities in college and will discover that she really enjoys sports and is in fact quite good at them.

We might think that such girls, if they are "character-friends," would suffer from trusting one another's lack of interest in sports. A similar point can be made about the way in which young boys might, as members of a dominant group, suffer from trusting one another's lack of interest in allegedly feminine arts, such as ballet. (Think, for example, of Billy Elliott, the eponymous hero of Stephen Daldry's recent film.) The important point is that the distortions resulting from membership in a dominant group do not always serve its members' interests.

A striking and nonhypothetical example of the way in which membership in a subordinate group may distort one's attitudes is discussed by Amartya Sen, who compares male and female assessments of health in societies like that of India, where different standards of health are applied to men and women with the result that women in those societies come to view as "normal" or "healthy" for themselves conditions that women elsewhere regard as "abnormal" or "diseased" (conditions associated, for example, with malnutrition). Sen discusses one study in which Indian widows systematically expressed more positive evaluations of their own health than did Indian widowers, in spite of the fact that standard medical criteria revealed that the widows were generally *less* healthy than their male counterparts.[12]

These examples illustrate some of the ways in which membership in a certain group can systematically distort one's beliefs and attitudes. To see how the virtuous agent might seek to accommodate the possibility of distortion in her own beliefs and attitudes, let us turn to the familiar "paradox of the preface." The virtuous agent is like the intellectually honest author sitting down to write the preface of his latest book. Just as the intellectually honest author now believes of *each* of the claims that he makes in his book that *it* is true, so too, the virtuous agent believes of *each* of her current states of character and the actions to which it gives rise that *they* are correct. But like the intellectually honest author who also believes it overwhelmingly likely that he has made a mistake *somewhere*, the virtuous agent also believes it overwhelmingly likely that her present character is *not perfect*. Like the author who wants to acknowledge this fact in his preface, the agent wants to acknowledge this in her actions. Perhaps she ends up like (Plato's) Socrates, constantly submitting her beliefs and actions to elenctic examination. She will, of course, continue to act on those beliefs which survive examination. But she does not trust herself enough to suspend examination.[13]

The virtuous agent will adopt the same attitude toward the views of her "second self": she will constantly examine his views, both for his sake and as a means of examining her own. And she sees nothing objectionable in this. For she expects him to do the same for her. He feels the same way: he wants her to have the same sort of distrust of him that he has of himself.[14]

Think, once again, of (Plato's) Socrates, who regards having his false beliefs corrected as a great benefit.[15] Socrates expects his friends to feel the same way about having their beliefs corrected: when Crito offers to help him escape from prison, Socrates does not leap at the opportunity but insists instead on examining the beliefs which lead Crito to regard escape as the only honorable option. And there is no sign that Crito resents Socrates' cross-examination, in spite of the fact that Crito clearly takes his own reputation to be at stake. Here we seem to have a case in which character-friends regard it as reasonable to cultivate a certain sort of distrust of one another.[16]

The suitably skeptical auditor will no doubt object that simply allowing for the possibility of error does not amount to the relevant sort of distrust and that distrust of an "other self" must involve something like *positive suspicion* of error. It is of course true that failure to rely on the goodwill and competence of another can rest on a variety of attitudes, ranging from mere suspension of belief to positive suspicion of error. But to the extent that what is proposed is a policy of "checking up" on the beliefs and attitudes of our other selves, it seems appropriate to speak here of a kind of distrust. For the policy of "checking up" is practically opposed to the policy, characteristic of trust, of foregoing such "checking up."

One might nevertheless object that my argument trades on equivocation—that in moving from the "moral" example of trusting (or distrusting) someone's *will* to the "epistemological" example of trusting (or distrusting) someone's *beliefs*, I have changed the subject, and have thus failed to show that character-friends might reasonably distrust one another's *wills*, as distinct from one another's *beliefs*. I doubt, however, that Baier would sympathize with this objection, for she aims throughout her work to challenge the assumption that there is a sharp distinction between cognitive and motivational states. She refers, in an article devoted to challenging this distinction, to "the fact that truth is a moral and evaluative matter, and that epistemology is a branch of value theory."[17] And she says explicitly in "Trust and Its Vulnerabilities" that trust "shows us the inadequacy of attempting to classify mental phenomena into the 'cognitive', the 'affective' and the 'conative'."[18] This suggests that Baier would take trusting one's "first" or "second" self in the moral sense to *include* trusting one's "first" or "second" self in the epistemological sense; and that she would allow that distrusting one's "first" or "second" self in the epistemological sense can sometimes *amount to* distrusting one's "first" or "second" self in the moral sense.[19] This may in fact help to explain why Baier's account of trust includes reliance not only on the *goodwill*, but also on the *competence*, of another. Though one might interpret her account as insisting on two separable conditions, I think it more plausible to read it as insisting on the difficulty, at least in some cases, of separating the competence of another from the bent of his will.

One might still object that Baier is wrong to reject the distinction between cognitive and motivational states, and that she ought to be more sympathetic to the foregoing objection. But think, for example, of Crito. To the extent that his beliefs (such as his belief that he should help Socrates escape) may stem from inappropriate concerns (such as concern for his own reputation), it seems plausible to say that we cannot easily separate the examination of his beliefs from an examination of his motives and character: an indictment of such beliefs *is* a kind of indictment of his motives and character. Crito's problem is not simply that he has false *beliefs*; it is at least partly that he is the sort of person who *cares* too much about what people will think of him and not enough about what justice requires. It is partly because he has this sort of *character* that he *believes* as he does.

Another example that illustrates the difficulty of separating the cognitive from the motivational aspects of our wills is provided by Susan Glaspell's story "A Jury of Her Peers," a polemical piece written in 1927 to demonstrate the value of allowing women to serve on juries. The story—originally a stage-play entitled "Trifles"—runs roughly as follows. A woman is accused of strangling her husband, but the sheriff and prosecutor, both male, are unable to discover the motive they need to convict her. Their detached investigative attitude is what stands in the way. It differs markedly from the attitude of two local women, whose empathetic response to the accused allows them to recognize as clues things that the men dismiss as women's "trifles" and thus to identify the missing motive.[20] I do not mean to suggest that this story provides a complete response to the foregoing objection. Nor can I undertake a complete response here. We must return to the central issue of trusting "other selves." I hope, however, in examining that issue to continue to address the objection, if only indirectly, by introducing examples where it seems plausible to say that we cannot easily separate the cognitive aspects of trusting ourselves from the moral or motivational aspects.

2. VIRGINIA WOOLF'S CASE FOR DISTRUSTING ONE'S "FIRST" SELF

Let us turn then to one of the most eloquent cases ever made for self-distrust, both among dominant and among subordinate members of society. This is the case made by Virginia Woolf in *Three Guineas*, the radical sequel to *A Room of One's Own*. No summary can do justice to so rich a literary work, for which Woolf was hailed in the *Times Literary Supplement* as "the most brilliant pamphleteer in all of England."[21] But this work is relatively little known—perhaps on account of its provocative assimilation of ordinary British patriarchs to European fascists, and perhaps on account of the alleged anachronism of Woolf's "feminism" (to use a term that she herself eschewed). Quentin Bell, Woolf's nephew and official biographer, reported that "Maynard Keynes was both angry and contemptuous [of *Three Guineas*]; it was he declared, a silly argument and not very well written."[22] And E. M. Forster said in his memoriam for Woolf that "the cantankerous *Three Guineas*" was the "worst of her books."[23]

   Three Guineas is ostensibly a letter written on the eve of World War II by the daughter of an educated British man to another educated British man, who has written to her asking how in her opinion they are to prevent war. He proposes—as if she cannot formulate her own suggestions but can handle only multiple-choice questions—three measures: first, that she and her cohort (presumably the daughters of educated British men) sign a manifesto pledging themselves to "protect culture and intellectual liberty"; second, that she and her cohort join his society dedicated to the prevention of war; and third, that she and her cohort contribute funds to his society.[24] In the course of answering his letter, she explains that she must first—because their causes are inseparable from his—answer two other requests for funds: one from the treasurer of a women's college, and the other from the treasurer of a society devoted to helping the daughters of educated men find employment in the professions. Embedded in her letter to him, then, are drafts of her letters to each of these women. And in each case—including his own—she agrees to give one guinea to the relevant cause: hence the title, *Three Guineas.*

The letters focus on what conditions, if any, she will attach to her gifts. In her letter to the women's college, she emphasizes the failure of traditional male colleges to prevent war, and she considers attaching to her guinea the condition that the women's college be organized so as "to produce the kind of society, [and] the kind of people that will help to prevent war" (TG 33).

Now since history and biography—the only evidence available to an outsider—seem to prove that the old education of the old colleges breeds neither a particular respect for liberty nor a particular hatred of war it is clear that you must rebuild your college differently. It is young and poor; let it therefore take advantage of those qualities and be founded on poverty and youth. Obviously, then, it must be an experimental college, an adventurous college. Let it be built on lines of its own. It must be built not of carved stone and stained glass, but of some cheap, easily combustible material which does not hoard dust and perpetrate traditions. Do not have chapels. . . . What should be taught in the new college, the poor college? Not the arts of dominating other people; not the arts of ruling, of killing, of acquiring land and capital; they require too many overhead expenses: salaries and uniforms and ceremonies. The poor college must teach only the arts that can be taught cheaply and can be practised by poor people, such as medicine, mathematics, music, painting and literature. It should teach the arts of human intercourse, the art of understanding other people's lives and minds. . . . The teachers should be drawn from the good livers as well as the good thinkers. There should be no difficulty attracting them. For there would be none of the barriers of wealth and ceremony, of advertisement and competition which now make the old and rich universities such uneasy dwelling places—cities of strife, cities where this is locked up and that is chained down; where nobody can walk freely or talk freely for fear of transgressing some chalk mark, of displeasing some dignitary. But if the college were poor it would have nothing to offer; competition would be abolished. Life would be open and easy. People who love learning for itself would gladly come there. . . . Let us then found this new college; this poor college; in which learning is sought for itself;

where advertisement is abolished; and there are no degrees; and lectures are not given, and sermons are not preached, and the old poisoned vanities and parades which breed competition and jealousy . . . (33–35; the final ellipsis is Woolf's; the rest are my own)

The letter breaks off there, with three dots, because the author realizes that her proposal is unrealistic: women will need degrees and recognized credentials if they are to achieve the financial independence necessary to effectively oppose patriarchal support for war. So she agrees to give her guinea to the women's college with no conditions attached. But she has reservations about whether she can *trust* the college, in the absence of these conditions, not to reproduce in women the "old poisoned vanities . . . which breed competition and jealousy."

She turns, however, to the more important question of what conditions to attach to the guinea she intends to give to the society devoted to helping the daughters of educated men find employment in the professions. The final draft of her letter to the treasurer of this society dwells on the effects of the professions on their professors, effects in which, I submit, we cannot easily separate the cognitive from the affective:

> [The professions] make the people who practise them possessive, jealous of any infringement on their rights, and highly combative if anyone dares dispute them. Are we not right then in thinking that if we enter the same professions we shall acquire the same qualities? And do not such qualities lead to war? In another century or so if we practise the professions in the same way, shall we not be just as possessive, just as jealous, just as pugnacious, just as positive as to the verdict of God, Nature, Law and Property as these gentlemen are now? (TG 66)

So the author attaches two conditions to her gift: first, that the society swear to "insist that any woman who enters any profession shall in no way hinder any other human being, whether man or woman, white or black . . . from entering it; [but] shall do all in her power to help them" (TG 66); and second, that the society seek to ensure that women, when they adopt the professions, refuse to be separated from the four traditional teachers by which women have always been educated—namely, "poverty, chastity, derision and freedom from unreal loyalties" (TG 79–80).

I shall eventually discuss each of these "teachers." But to give some idea of what the author has in mind, consider her injunctions concerning the somewhat obscure "derision" and "freedom from unreal loyalties":

> By derision . . . is meant that you must refuse all methods of advertising merit, and hold that ridicule, obscurity and censure are preferable for psychological reasons, to fame and praise. Directly badges, orders, or degrees are offered you, fling them back in the giver's face. By freedom from unreal loyalties is meant that you must rid yourself of pride of nationality in the first place; also of religious pride, college pride, school pride, family pride, *sex pride* and those unreal loyalties that spring from them. (TG 80; emphasis mine)

The author's point is that women should not trust themselves with the wealth, pride, and fame traditionally sought by men. Her explicit rejection of sex-pride reveals that she is not arguing—as many have taken her to argue—for the moral superiority of women. She thinks that men have shown by their example that people *in general* should not trust themselves with such things.

The author returns finally to complete the original letter. She agrees to give a guinea, with no strings attached, to her correspondent's society for the prevention of war. But she refuses to join his society on the ground that, in doing so, she and her cohort would cease to occupy the different point of view which might enable them to make a distinctive contribution to the prevention of war. She recommends instead that the daughters of educated men form a society of their own in which the first duty would be "not to fight with arms" (TG 106); the next duties would be "to refuse in the event of war to make munitions or nurse the wounded" (TG 106), and "not to incite their brothers to fight, or to dissuade them, but to maintain an attitude of complete indifference" (TG 107). The author's use of the term "society" is self-consciously paradoxical. She never refers to the daughters of educated men as its "members," and she describes this so-called society in the following way:

> [it] would have no honorary treasurer, for it would need no funds. It would have no office, no committee, no secretary; it would call no

meetings; it would hold no conferences. If a name it *must* have, it *could* be called the Outsiders Society. (TG 106; emphasis mine)

The author's injunction that the daughters of educated men form an Outsider's Society is an extension of her injunction that they refuse to allow themselves to be separated from their four traditional teachers. I wish, therefore, to return to these teachers, paying special attention both to the issue of trust—especially *self*-trust—and to the career of Annette Baier. For she seems to stand in flagrant violation of these injunctions, which I take to be Woolf's own.

Baier, who earned a B. Phil. at Oxford and recently accepted an honorary doctorate from the University of Otago, was the first tenured woman in the philosophy department at the University of Pittsburgh, where she eventually served as a Distinguished Service Professor. She is one of a handful of women to have served as president of the Eastern Division of the American Philosophical Association in its first hundred years. In 1995 she was the first woman ever to give the prestigious Carus Lectures, lectures first given in 1925 by John Dewey.[25] I mention only a few of what seem to be her most flagrant violations of Woolf's injunctions. In these and other ways, Baier's career stands in sharp contrast to that of Virginia Woolf.

Woolf never had an academic education or formal academic appointment. She refused an honorary degree from the University of Manchester. She generally lectured only to women or to (mixed-sex) working-class audiences. She has in fact been criticized—on the ground that she hurt the cause of all women—for declining an invitation to become the first woman ever to deliver the prestigious Clark lectures at Cambridge University.[26]

So we should ask ourselves what Woolf would have thought of Baier's career. We should also ask ourselves what *we* should think of it. For even if Woolf would disapprove of Baier, it does not follow that we should agree: Woolf may be right about the importance of self-distrust, but wrong about the appropriate mechanisms. Moreover, it is not at all clear that Woolf would disapprove. For she was painfully aware both of the complexities and of the tensions within her own position. This is clear from the attitude expressed in *Three Guineas* toward poverty, the first of women's four traditional "teachers."

3. WOULD VIRGINIA WOOLF HAVE APPROVED
OF ANNETTE BAIER?

Economic considerations lead the author of *Three Guineas* to withdraw the conditions she is first inclined to impose on her gift to the women's college. Though tempted to require that they found an "experimental" college where there are no degrees and no distinctions of rank, she is stopped short by the thought that women will need recognized credentials in order to achieve the financial independence necessary if they are to develop minds and wills of their own with which to oppose war. So she withdraws this condition, thinking it best to forego such experiments until women are financially more secure. This realism belies Woolf's alleged naiveté and informs her revisionary concept of "poverty":

> By poverty is meant enough money to live upon. That is, you must earn enough to be independent of any other human being and to buy that modicum of health, leisure, knowledge and so on that is needed for the full development of body and mind. But no more. Not a penny more. (TG 80)[27]

There is considerable flexibility here. And in spite of the emphatic "not a penny more," it is unlikely that the author intends to rule out earning enough to help others achieve the same goals. For having and exercising the ability to provide such assistance may belong to the "*full* development of body and mind." So it is by no means clear that Woolf would have any intrinsic objection to a woman's accepting the financial perks associated with a distinguished professorship. It may all depend on the extent to which the woman can trust herself, once she is reasonably fully developed, to assist others in reaching the same goals.[28]

One might argue that Baier has proven herself trustworthy by putting her own research funds to the unorthodox use of paying for her *students* to attend conferences so that *they* could deliver papers. One might of course object that Baier has been insufficiently loyal to her sex, for she has provided such support indiscriminately to male as well as to female students. But there is no reason to think that Woolf would object to this. *Three Guineas* explicitly rejects "sex-pride," and Woolf herself supported the literary endeavors of many individual men—a practice implicitly explained in the following passage, where Woolf makes it clear that she is *not* committed to the "essentialist" view that men are innately more violent or domineering than women.

> Inevitably we [women] look on society, so kind to you, so harsh to us, as an ill-fitting form that distorts the truth, deforms the mind; fetters the will. Inevitably we look upon societies as conspiracies that sink the private brother, whom many of us have reason to respect, and inflate in his stead a monstrous male. . . . (TG 105)[29]

So there is no reason to think that Woolf would disapprove of Baier for supporting individual male students. And while Woolf might have had reservations about the academic degrees and positions from which Baier's resources flowed, she was realistic enough to recognize their instrumental value. She might have thought that the crucial question was the extent to which Baier could be trusted with these potential corrupters.

Similar points can be made about the equally revisionary vow of chastity—a vow not of bodily but of mental chastity: "By chastity is meant that when you have made enough to live on by your profession you must refuse to sell your brain for the sake of money . . ." (TG 80). Here again, the qualification "when you have made enough to live on" shows that the author is anything but naive. This is clear from her discussion of Mrs. Oliphant, whom the author says "sold her very admirable brain, prostituted her culture and enslaved her intellectual liberty in order that she might earn her living and educate her children" (TG 91–92). The discussion continues:

> Inevitably, considering the damage that poverty inflicts upon the mind and body, the necessity that is laid upon those who have children to see that they are fed and clothed, nursed and educated, we have to applaud [Mrs. Oliphant's] choice and admire her courage. But if we applaud the choice and admire the courage of those who do what she did, we can spare ourselves the trouble of addressing our appeal to them, for they will be no more be able to protect disinterested culture and intellectual liberty than she was. (TG 92)

The point is powerful: it is bad faith to ask the daughters of educated men to sign manifestos supporting culture and intellectual liberty while refusing to help them secure for themselves the economic resources necessary for exercising their own intellectual liberty.

Woolf's own intellectual liberty was very much an issue. For until she and Leonard Woolf founded Hogarth Press, she had to rely on others to publish her work. And publishers then tended to be men, many of whom seem to have been threatened by (at least some of) her work. Some, indeed, might have been threatened in a personal way: imagine her having to ask her first publisher, her abusive half-brother Gerald Duckworth, to publish her account of the sexual liberties his brother George took with her.[30] The purchase of Hogarth Press must have played for Woolf something like the role played by tenure in the service of Baier's intellectual chastity. For Baier says in her presidential address, "I myself meekly did the philosophy that men had initially instructed me to do, and rewarded me for doing, until I safely had tenure."[31] Important and complicated issues of trust lurk here. Can *men* trust such women? Can *women* trust such women—or trust *themselves*— not to become so enamoured of male approval that they are unwilling, by the time they win tenure, to risk or flout such approval in order to protect their intellectual chastity?

Woolf knew that she was psychologically vulnerable to the views of her predominantly male critics, which may explain her refusal to lecture to male audiences. Perhaps she did not trust herself not to be seduced by the more immediate and therefore more tempting prospect of male applause: writing may have provided her with the distance required to protect her intellectual chastity—a kind of "intellectual chastity belt."[32] It does not follow from this that Woolf would disapprove of Baier's willingness to lecture to audiences that are predominantly (if not exclusively) male. Woolf might think this acceptable to the extent that Baier is justified in trusting herself not to be seduced.

Woolf's realistic assessment of the dangers of intellectual seduction helps to explain the importance she attaches to the refusal to be separated from "derision." Woolf is not much worried that men will fail "to provide [women] for many centuries to come . . . with what [she claims] is so essential for sanity, and so invaluable in preventing the great modern sins of vanity, egotism, and megalomania—that is to say ridicule, censure and contempt" (TG 82). What worries her is that women may be tempted to sacrifice their intellectual chastity in order to escape such ridicule, censure, and contempt. Hence she enjoins women to "hold that obscurity and censure are preferable, for psychological reasons, to fame and praise" (TG 80).

There was much derision in male (and some female) reviews of *Three Guineas*, and there is still much derision in male (and some female) reviews of feminist books today. A case in point is Colin McGinn's joint review (in the *New Republic*) of Baier's *Moral Prejudices* and Virginia Held's *Feminist Morality*. In response to Held's proposal that we take mothering rather than contractual relations as our moral paradigms, McGinn asks contemptuously, "Should I be able to discipline people who don't do as I tell them? Am I expected to buy everybody Christmas presents?"[33] Perhaps that's how McGinn thinks of mothers—as sources of discipline and Christmas presents.

McGinn also reported that Baier had seriously proposed in her book that universities attempt to accommodate the demands of women's reproductive clocks by allowing women to postpone tenure decisions until the age of fifty. The *Chronicle of Higher Education* trusted him on this, and called the unsuspecting Baier, who knew nothing of McGinn's review. When they asked her why in the offending sentence she had said "fifty," she replied that she supposed it was because that was after menopause, thus reinforcing in their view McGinn's claim that she seriously endorsed this proposal, which they then reported. The *Chronicle* might simply have read the paragraph on which McGinn's claim was based. For the alleged proposal appears, followed by a question mark, in parentheses, in a sentence which concludes with objections to the proposal and is followed by Baier's own serious proposal!

> Other ways [to address the problem], involving not just pregnancy and parental leave but different expectations as to when women will get into full professional stride (tenure decisions delayed at the candidates' request until age 50?), would be bound to raise reasonable complaints of exploitation of the untenured and of unfairness to men. Still, we need to come up with new measures. One possibility, perhaps the best solution, would be to make all tenure decisions rest on evaluation only of what the candidate selects as say, her or his four best articles.[34]

Like many reviewers of *Three Guineas*, McGinn simply failed to acknowledge Baier's patent use of irony. G. M. Young, one of Woolf's reviewers, suggested that she claims that Permanent Secretaries in the Civil Service "rectify the imperfections of the examination system by selecting their Private Secretaries from the families of friends."[35] Young's suggestion is preposterous in light of the *Three Guineas'* sustained attack on patriarchal ties. Here is the relevant passage from Woolf:

> . . . we shall agree at the outset that the professions are very queer things. It by no means follows that a clever man gets to the top or that a stupid man stays at the bottom. This rising and falling is by no means a cut-and-dried clear-cut rational process, we shall both agree. After all, as we both have reason to know, Judges are fathers; and Permanent Secretaries have sons. Judges require marshals; Permanent Secretaries, private secretaries. What is more natural than that a nephew should be a marshal or the son of an old school friend a private secretary? To have such perquisites in their gift is as much the due of the public servant as a cigar now and then or a cast-off dress here and there are the perquisites of a private servant. But the giving of such perquisites, the exercise of such influence, queers the professions. Success is easier for some, harder for others, however equal the brain power may be, so that some rise unexpectedly; some fall unexpectedly; some remain strangely stationary; with the result that the professions are queered. Often indeed it is to the public advantage that [they] are queered. Since nobody, from the Master of Trinity downwards (bating presumably a few Head Mistresses), believes in the infallibility of examiners, a certain degree of elasticity is to the public advantage; since the impersonal is fallible, it is well that it should be supplemented by the personal. Happily for us all, therefore, we may conclude . . . boards and divisions transmit human sympathies, and reflect human antipathies with the result that the imperfections of the examination system are rectified; the public interest is served; and the ties of blood and friendship are recognized. (TG 49–50)

Any doubts about Woolf's irony should be put to rest by the remainder of the passage and the characteristically sarcastic footnote appended to it. After noting that examination results do not indicate the sex of the examinee— an obvious imperfection, insofar as a woman's sex may offend those in the Church and elsewhere with whom she is supposed to work—Woolf inserts a footnote with the following quote from the Archbishops' Report on the Ministry of Women (1936):

But we maintain that the ministration of women . . . will tend to produce a lowering of the spiritual tone of Christian worship. . . . It is a
tribute to the quality of Christian womanhood that it is possible to make
this statement; but it would appear to be a simple matter of fact that
in the thoughts and desires of that sex the natural is more easily made
subordinate to the supernatural, the carnal to the spiritual than is the
case with men; and that the ministrations of a male priesthood do not
normally arouse that side of female human nature which should be
quiescent during the times of adoration of Almighty God. We believe,
on the other hand, that it would be impossible for male members of
the average Anglican congregation to be present at a service at which
a woman ministered without becoming unduly conscious of her sex.

Woolf concludes her note with the following remark: "In the opinion of the
Commissioners, therefore, Christian women are more spiritually minded
than Christian men—a remarkable, but no doubt adequate, reason for excluding them from the priesthood" (TG 161).

Neither Young nor McGinn strikes me as sufficiently credible to raise
the interesting and important issues involved in trusting more credible reviewers—reviewers one might, through repeated convergence of one's judgment with theirs, come to regard as "other selves" of a sort.[36] Since these
issues are at the heart of my concern, I want to pause briefly to examine a
recent review of a feminist work by a reviewer whose judgment I myself have
often trusted—that is, Ronald Dworkin's review of Catherine MacKinnon's
Only Words. Dworkin is widely perceived as one of MacKinnon's most sympathetic male reviewers, and rightly so. He shines in comparison with Carlin Romano, who began his review by asking his readers to perform various
thought experiments involving the rape of Catherine MacKinnon.[37] And
unlike Richard Posner, who represents *Only Words* as a "verbal torrent that
appeals, much like pornography itself . . . to elemental passions . . . rather
than to rational intellect," Dworkin allows that MacKinnon offers arguments for her position—arguments that Dworkin then subjects to serious
examination.[38] But in spite of his generally respectful tone, which commands
our trust, Dworkin seems to misrepresent and trivialize one of MacKinnon's
most important points.

The point is explained clearly by Rae Langton, so I can (as I must) be
brief.[39] One of MacKinnon's central concerns is to ensure that women are

not "silenced" by pornography. She is concerned, for example, that the acceptance of the rape myths that she takes to be encouraged by pornography not bring it about that men fail to understand and accept what women mean when they say "no." This aspect of MacKinnon's argument is obscured by Dworkin's account of her "silencing argument." Dworkin says:

> [This argument] is premised on an unacceptable proposition; that the right to free speech includes a right to circumstances that encourage one to speak, and a right that others grasp and respect what one means to say. These are obviously not rights that any society can recognize or enforce. Creationists, flat-earthers, and bigots, for example, are ridiculed in many parts of America now; that ridicule undoubtedly dampens the enthusiasm many of them having for speaking out and limits the attention others pay to what they say. Many political and constitutional theorists, it is true, insist that if freedom of speech is to have any value, it must include some right to the opportunity to speak. . . . But it goes far beyond that to insist that freedom of speech includes not only the opportunity to speak in public but a guarantee of a sympathetic or even competent understanding of what one says.[40]

Obviously we cannot guarantee a sympathetic or competent understanding of the views of creationists, flat-earthers, or feminists. But there is an important difference between attempting to guarantee that men understand and respect what women mean when they seek to reject unwanted sexual advances, and attempting to guarantee that people understand and respect what flat-earthers mean when they express *their* views. To assimilate the former to the latter is to trivialize one of MacKinnon's central claims.

I do not mean to suggest that Dworkin willfully misrepresents MacKinnon's views. For the argument of *Only Words* is often obscured by rhetoric that is clearly intended to shock and provoke.[41] Nor do I mean to endorse MacKinnon's views or expect you to trust *my* account of them. I am simply asking that you not ridicule and denounce the book without having read it. For Dworkin's review, while not itself derisive, seems to have fueled considerable "derision" on the part of his admirers, who feel entitled on the basis of his review to treat the book in a far less respectful—and far less knowledgeable—manner than that in which Dworkin himself treats it.

Obviously none of us can read everything, and we must often rely on reviewers we *trust*, if only in deciding what is and is not worth our while to read. But there is an important difference between deciding on the basis of reviews not to bother reading a book, and deciding on the basis of reviews to ridicule and denounce in one's own confident voice a book one has never read. For we all know that even intellectually honest and sympathetic reviewers sometimes misinterpret the books they review. It is wise—especially where there is reason to think that a reviewer's biases may intrude—to reserve a modicum of distrust even for a reviewer whom one has come, through similarity of judgment, to regard as a kind of "other self."[42] This point applies to feminist reviews of other feminist works as well—especially to uncritical reviews. For there are clear and present dangers in thinking it "unsisterly" to criticize one another's views.

This brings me to the fourth traditional teacher of women, namely, "freedom from unreal loyalties." This is Woolf's label for the "lack of rights and privileges" that secures women's alleged freedom from loyalty to "old schools, old colleges, old churches, old ceremonies, old countries" (TG 95–96).[43] The author clearly intends to contrast these and other forms of unreal loyalty (like "sex pride") with the principles to which she claims men and women should be similarly devoted—liberty and equality, principles defended no less by suffragists than by anti-fascists. These principles are the proper objects of loyalty, the "real loyalties," with which the "unreal loyalties" of sex, country, church, and school sometimes interfere.

Women's alleged freedom from these unreal loyalties is explained in a passage where the author expresses lack of trust in her own ability to understand what she calls the "instinct" to fight:

> The outsider must leave [her brother] free to deal with this instinct by himself, because liberty of opinion must be respected, especially when it is based upon an instinct which is as foreign to her as centuries of tradition and education can make it. This is a fundamental and instinctive distinction upon which indifference may be based. But *the outsider will make it her duty not merely to base her indifference upon instinct, but upon reason.* When he says, as history proves that he has said, and may say again, "I am fighting to protect our country" and thus seeks to arouse patriotic emotion, she will ask herself, "What does 'our country' mean to me an outsider?" (TG 107)

After describing the outsider who is considering all the rights and privileges her country has withheld from her, the author suggests that she may remove any lingering patriotic sentiment by comparing English history and art (etc.) with French history and art (etc.); and French history and art with German; and German with Greek, and so on.[44] The point seems to be that English history and art have not been significantly kinder to women than have French and German (or any other) history and art; and that lack of rights and liberties is just that, whether one is deprived by English, French, or German patriarchs.

It was Woolf's attempt to link the cause of women at home with the cause of fascism abroad that rendered *Three Guineas* so controversial when it was published and ultimately—according to Quentin Bell—spoiled its argument.[45] Many people, men and women alike, regarded her "feminism" as anachronistic in light of women's suffrage and the admission of women to universities and the professions; and pacifism was no longer fashionable in the late 1930s. But this link is essential to her argument, and it makes good sense in light of her claim that our real loyalties should be to the common causes of liberty, equality, and peace. Her point might have been clearer and more persuasive to her compatriots had she emphasized her example of the German women who took their *real* loyalty to liberty and equality to require them to reject *unreal* loyalty to their country, and perhaps even to their own husbands and brothers.

Woolf's primary target is blind patriotism, to which she might, following Aristotle, add blind friendship. It is not obvious, as E. M. Forster suggests, that we should prefer betraying our country to betraying our friends: betraying our country may be preferable if we have true character-friends, but the decision should ultimately rest on where justice and the other objects of our real loyalties lie.[46] I have argued elsewhere that this is the point of Aristotle's commitment to an "ethocentric"—as distinct from an "egocentric"—conception of friendship.[47]

I have coined the term "ethocentric" from the Greek word *ethos*, which refers roughly to a person's character. I mean by an "ethocentric" conception of friendship a character-based conception in which love of your friend is based primarily on the *content* of her character and not on any of the contingent relationships in which she happens to stand to you, though these contingent relationships may serve as conditions for your *appreciation* of that content. You are to love her *not*—as on the egocentric conception—

simply because she is *your* sister, *your* classmate, *your* teammate or compatriot, all characteristics she has in virtue of her relation to *you*. For such love is easily co-opted by ethnocentric and other "unreal loyalties." You should instead love your friend primarily on account of her virtuous character, which may belong to her independently of her relation to you.[48] The "ethocentric" conception is thus intended to counter "ethnocentric" and other "unreal loyalties."

It is important to be clear just what is meant here. Although commentators often stress the similarity in character of Aristotelian character-friends, it is the *content* of your friend's character, and *not its similarity to your own*, that does the justificatory work. This is clear from the case where there is similarity in the absence of virtue. The fact that your friend's vicious character is similar to your own does nothing to justify your love for him. So it is not an attachment to similarity as such that runs Aristotle's argument. The role played by similarity is largely a function of pragmatic and epistemological constraints. For the very beliefs and values that explain and justify your approval of certain character traits in *yourself* will *also* explain and justify your approval of the same traits in *others*. If you value justice as such, and strive to cultivate it in yourself, you will inevitably tend to value others who resemble you in this respect.[49]

But there are complications here associated both with human fallibility and with the contested nature of the objects of our real loyalties—complications that help to explain why it is reasonable for virtuous agents and those who think of themselves as such to cultivate a certain sort of distrust of their "first" and "second" selves. These complications, moreover, serve to recommend certain sorts of *dissimilarity* among "other selves," since disagreements with those we respect, unlike disagreements with those we fail to respect, may help us to detect and correct our own errors.[50]

We are all familiar with cases in which we respect what might be called "formal" features of a person's character, while rejecting some of the "substantive" ethical views which are fundamentally important to him. I might, for example, respect one of my colleagues as someone who strives to be honest both with himself and with others, as someone who is willing to listen to those who disagree with him and to modify his own views in light of such discussion, and as someone who is sincerely concerned about how to improve the position of African-Americans in our society; at the same time, I can disagree with his "substantive" views about how exactly to remedy racial inequality. Perhaps he is firmly committed not only to ends but also to means that are color-blind, a policy I view as hopelessly naïve. My attitude toward this colleague will differ significantly from my attitude toward a former segregationist whose newfound attachment to color-blindness strikes me as a convenient cover for his real agenda of preserving white privilege. My respect for my colleague's "formal" virtues may allow me to regard him, in spite of our disagreement about color-blindness, as a kind of "other self" (or at least a close approximation). And my disagreement with him may serve either to help me clarify my objections to color-blind policies or to convince me that my objections are misguided.

I have been recommending a certain sort of distrust of one's "second" selves as a sensible response to the dilemma posed by the way in which attempts to correct our own fallible and contested conceptions of virtue may be stymied by the fact that there is an important sense in which we can turn for assistance only to those whom we respect and trust. And I have been suggesting that such distrust is ultimately a form of self-distrust. It is an important mechanism of the sort of self-examination to which Socrates devoted his life. Socrates is an important example for many reasons. His paradoxes serve to remind us not only of the difficulty of separating the moral from the epistemological aspects of trust but also of the role played, in the cultivation of trust, by the sort of distrust I have been recommending. For Socrates' constant scrutiny of his own and others' views no doubt contributed to the confidence with which he held to his belief that it is better to suffer than to commit injustice—even if suffering leads to death. Socrates also serves to remind us of the dangers posed by those who trust too easily in the views of their "first" and "second" selves: a little less self-trust on the part of his accusers and judges, and Socrates might have been acquitted.

This point was of primary concern to Woolf, who was troubled by the ways in which power and privilege contribute to trust of one's own and other selves. For it is in many ways psychologically easier not only for dominant but also for nondominant individuals to accept dominant views. (Think, for example, of "expert" witnesses called before juries; the more prestigious their institutions, the better.) Unfortunately—and this seems to have been the point of Woolf's recommendation that women remain outsiders—the ease of achieving self-*trust* is often directly proportional to the importance of self-*distrust*. A corollary of this—also unfortunate if outsiders are sometimes better placed than insiders to appreciate certain truths—is that the importance of self-trust is often inversely proportional to the ease of achieving it.[51]

I am reminded here of one of Baier's recent experiences. After dedicating *Moral Prejudices* to her "women students—past, present and future," she received a note from a distinguished male philosopher objecting to her dedication on the ground that she had somehow discriminated against her male students. Baier was quite shaken by this, so much so that she began to question *herself*. She approached with serious concern one of the men currently writing his dissertation with her, to ask whether he had been hurt or offended by the dedication, to which he replied "of course not." I have little doubt that he meant what he said, and that he appreciated what Baier's dedication might mean to her women students qua members of a class to whom philosophical works are so rarely dedicated—that is, the class of women philosophers as such. It is in any case instructive to compare the ease with which Baier was brought to question herself with the confidence with which I suspect her colleague fired off his letter.

I doubt that he paused to think how rarely philosophical works are dedicated to women as philosophers, rather than to women as beloved wives and daughters. I doubt that he paused to ask himself how many male philosophers had never dedicated a single book to a woman philosopher as such; or whether it might not be at least as acceptable for Baier to dedicate her book collectively to her women students as it is for a male philosopher to dedicate his books seriatim to a collection of male teachers, students, and colleagues, with the occasional wife or daughter thrown in for good measure. Why do I doubt that he paused to ask himself these questions? Because charity seems to me to forbid allowing that he would have sent the letter had he paused to ask them.

One of the points often made in the currently flourishing literature on trust is that trusting another involves the disposition to interpret him charitably, often in ways that go beyond the available evidence. If I trust my spouse, I will tend with little or no evidence to prefer more to less innocent interpretations of his behavior. The corollary—again frequently cited— is that distrusting another bears a similar relation to interpreting him uncharitably: if I distrust my spouse, I may fail to consider innocent explanations of his behavior even where they seem, given the available evidence, to be the best explanations. But it is rarely noted that similar points can be made about *self*-interpretation. If I trust myself, I will interpret myself charitably, often in ways that discount or go beyond the available evidence: I will, for example, tend not to question either my behavior or the attitudes on which it rests. If, on the other hand, I distrust myself, I will be less inclined to interpret myself charitably and more inclined to question my behavior and the attitudes on which it rests. Too much distrust of self, of course, can have inhibiting and even paralyzing effects. Whether or not this is a good thing will depend on what is being inhibited. Similarly, too much trust of self may lead us to do things we would not do if we stopped to question ourselves, and the value of self-trust will depend once again on what it is we are about to do.

Excessive charity in the interpretation of one's "first" and "second" selves is one of the mechanisms of the sort of self-deception that enables us to maintain positive self-images in the face of our own moral failings.[52] This point applies no less to the interpretation of our moral theories than to the interpretation of our behavior. If I fire off a note to Baier, criticizing her dedication on the ground that it conflicts with my gender-neutral ideals, my "first" and "second" selves should be questioning those ideals as well as the action of firing off the letter. And the same goes for my "second" self if he fires off such a letter; his "first" and "second" selves (*my* "first" self included!) should be questioning his ideals as well as his actions.

This last example nicely illustrates the difficulty of separating the cognitive from the motivational aspects of our wills. But much work remains to be done on this issue, and I cannot undertake it here. I have failed, no doubt, in what Woolf called the "first duty of a lecturer—to hand you after an hour's discourse a nugget of pure truth to wrap up in your notebooks and keep on the mantelpiece for ever."[53] I hope, however, that my admittedly incomplete argument carries conviction on at least one point: I hope that even those of you who have come to regard Baier as a kind of "other self" will agree that we should question her assumption that you cannot have as a "second" self someone you distrust.

NOTES

I dedicate this paper to the memory of Tamara Horowitz, who helped to organize the conference for which it was originally written. The conference, "Different Voices," was held at the University of Pittsburgh in October of 1995 to honor Annette Baier on the occasion of her retirement, and I have benefited significantly from the comments and questions of members of that and other audiences (at the University of California at San Diego, the University of Wisconsin, Cornell University, Williams College, and the New Zealand Division of the Australasian Society of Philosophy). I am especially grateful for comments from Donald Ainslie, David Brink, Eric Brown, Myles Burnyeat, Jackie Goldsby, Paula Gottlieb, Molly Hite, Paul Hoffman, Joyce Jenkins, Karen Jones, Rob Shaver, Alan Sidelle, Gisela Striker, and Iakovos Vasiliou. I also thank the Andrew W. Mellon Foundation for supporting my fellowship at the Center for Advanced Study in the Behavioral Sciences at Stanford, where I researched and drafted this paper. But I am most indebted, for daily advice and occasionally brilliant suggestions, to Tom Berry.

1. Annette Baier, "Trust and Antitrust," *Ethics* 96 (1986): 231–60: reprinted in Baier's *Moral Prejudices* (Cambridge, MA: Harvard University Press, 1994), 95–129. The passage cited appears on p. 97 of the reprinted version. For Aristotle's references to the friend as "another self," see *Nicomachean Ethics* 1166a31–32; 1170b5–6; *Eudemian Ethics* 1245a34–35; and *Magna Moralia* 1213a12–13.

2. Aristotle uses '*pistis*' and its cognates in roughly the same range of moral and epistemological contexts in which we use 'trust' and its cognates (which are in fact often used as translations of '*pistis*'): he speaks, for example, of how we *pisteuein* our senses, speakers, and arguments; of the time it takes for the *pistis* characteristic of friendship to develop; and of how tyrants win the *pistis* of the people.

3. See, in addition to "Trust and Antitrust," the other papers on trust collected in *Moral Prejudices*. For trust as reliance on the goodwill of another, see p. 99; for the addition of competence, see p. 132.

4. Aristotle contrasts character-friendships both with friendships based on the pleasures the friends receive from one another and with friendships based on the advantages they receive from one another. And he seems to think that it is primarily— perhaps only—in character-friendship that friends can love one another, not for the pleasures or advantages they provide for one another, but rather *for themselves*. See especially *Nicomachean Ethics* VIII.3–5. See also John Cooper, "Friendship and the Good in Aristotle," *Philosophical Review* 86 (1977): 290–315; reprinted in Cooper, *Reason and Emotion* (Princeton: Princeton University Press, 1999).

5. For the connection between practical wisdom and virtue, see *Nicomachean Ethics* VI.12–13.

6. On this sort of deference to the "authority" of others, see Karen Jones, "Second-Hand Moral Knowledge," *Journal of Philosophy* 96 (1999): 55–78. Aristotle clearly thinks that friends assist one another in living virtuously. See 1159b2–7, where he says, "[virtue friends] neither request base things <of one another> nor assist in such things, but even, so to speak, prevent them. For it is characteristic of

good people neither to go wrong themselves nor to let their friends do so" (my translation).

7. See John Cooper, "Political Animals and Civic Friendship," in *Aristoteles' Politik*, ed. Günther Patzig (Göttingen: Vandenhoeck und Ruprecht, 1990): 221–41; reprinted in Cooper, *Reason and Emotion*.

8. See my "Impersonal Friends," *Monist* 74 (1991): 3–29.

9. Baier says on p. 12 of *Moral Prejudices* that self-trust is a "dubious or limit case of trust." She discusses self-trust briefly on p. 179, where she stresses (in ways relevant to the arguments I give) the dangers of self-trust on the part of those in positions of power.

10. See Annette Baier, "How to Get to Know One's Own Mind: Some Simple Ways," in *Philosophy in Mind: The Place of Philosophy in the Study of Mind*, ed. M. Micheal and J. O'Leary-Hawthorne (Dordrecht: Kluwer Academic Publishers, 1994), 65–82. See especially pp. 74–75 on "conspiracies of mutually aided self-deception."

11. Consider also Virginia Woolf's discussion of Shakespeare's hypothetical sister, Judith, in chapter 3 of *A Room of One's Own* (New York: Harcourt, Brace and World, 1927).

12. See Amartya Sen, *Commodities and Capabilities* (New Delhi: Oxford University Press, 1999), Appendix B. Sen has referred (in discussion) to a similar study conducted ten years later, in which the widows' assessments had become less positive, not as a result of changes in their actual medical condition but as a result of education leading to changes in the accepted standards of female health. I suspect that similar points hold with respect to differences, both between men and women and between members of different socioeconomic classes, in levels of satisfaction with educational achievements: I suspect that women (or members of lower socioeconomic classes) who express greater satisfaction with low levels of achievement than do similarly educated men (or similarly educated members of higher socioeconomic classes) may, as their educational opportunities and expectations increase, become less satisfied with such low levels of achievement.

13. I refer to *Plato's* Socrates simply to acknowledge that there is a question about how the views of Plato's character map onto those of the historical Socrates. For some discussion of this question, see chapter 2 of Gregory Vlastos, *Socrates: Ironist and Moral Philosopher* (Ithaca, NY: Cornell University Press, 1991). It is also worth noting here—because I want to keep the parallel with intellectual virtue in play—that Gregory Vlastos, who spent a lifetime revising his views about Socrates, is a notable (and not, I think, coincidental) example of an intellectually honest author who welcomed disagreement and criticism of his views, even by his own students (whom he repaid in kind). See, for example, his warm exchanges in the *Times Literary Supplement* with his "intellectual friend" and former student Terence Irwin,

when Vlastos reviewed Irwin's first book, *Plato's Moral Theory* (Oxford: Oxford University Press, 1977). Vlastos's review appeared in the issue of February 28, 1978; Irwin's reply appeared in the issue of March 1, 1978, followed by more letters back and forth (all in 1978) on April 8, April 18, May 23, May 31, June 30, July 12, and September 3. Such "intellectual friendships" provide useful models for character-friendships insofar as they serve to undermine the tendency to require too much substantive ethical agreement among character-friends. I return briefly, toward the end of this paper, to the distinction between "formal" and "substantive" aspects of character-friendship.

14. These reciprocal attitudes are a function of the character-friends' common view that at least part of the *point* of their friendship is to promote one another's good, which they take to consist largely (if not exclusively) in living virtuously. This view, which may seem foreign to us, is easier to comprehend if we think of the way in which "philosophical" (or "artistic" or "athletic") friends might take it to be part of the point of their respective friendships to promote one another's good, which for them consists largely (if not exclusively) in philosophical (or artistic or athletic) accomplishment. This renders it intelligible that the friends should desire uninhibited criticism (or competition of the relevant sort) from one another. Virginia Woolf, for example, not only desired and expected, but also feared and sometimes wondered if she would receive, honest criticism from her husband Leonard. See *The Diary of Virginia Woolf*, ed. Anne Olivier Bell (assisted by Andrew McNeillie), 5 vols. (New York: Harcourt Brace Jovanovich, 1980–), 17 July 1931 (vol. 4); 4 and 5 November 1936 (vol. 5).

15. See, for example, Plato's *Gorgias* 458a–b.

16. It is important to my subsequent argument that it is not simply Crito's *beliefs* that are appropriate objects of distrust. To the extent that these beliefs (such as his belief that he should help Socrates escape) stem from inappropriate concerns (such as concern for his own reputation) or are subject to motivated distortions, distrust of his *beliefs* cannot easily be separated from distrust of his *character*. I shall return to this point shortly.

17. "Getting in Touch with Our Own Feelings," *Topoi* 6 (1987): 89–97; the quote is from p. 92.

18. Baier, *Moral Prejudices*, 132.

19. Aristotle too, though less explicit on this point, may (as John McDowell has suggested) fail to draw a sharp distinction between cognitive and motivational states. This would be one way to explain why Aristotle says that one cannot have practical wisdom without moral virtue, or moral virtue without practical wisdom. See John McDowell, "Some Issues in Aristotle's Moral Psychology," in *Ethics*, ed. Stephen Everson (Cambridge: Cambridge University Press, 1998) ; and "Virtue and Reason," *The Monist* 62 (1979): 331–50; both reprinted in John McDowell, *Mind,*

Value, and Reality (Cambridge, MA: Harvard University Press, 1998). I believe that this reading of Aristotle deserves to be taken more seriously than it has been, and I take some first steps in that direction in my "Locomotive Soul: The Parts of Soul in Aristotle's Scientific Works," *Oxford Studies in Ancient Philosophy* 22 (2002): 141–200.

20. Susan Glaspell, "A Jury of Her Peers" (London: Ernest Benn Limited, 1927). The stageplay, "Trifles," has been reprinted in *Plays, by Susan Glaspell*, ed. C. W. E. Bigsby (Cambridge: Cambridge University Press, 1987).

21. Because of the ways in which Woolf's logical acumen was challenged by other reviewers (see notes 26 and 32 below), it is worth quoting more fully from this unsigned review, published in the *Times Literary Supplement* on 4 June 1938. Extracts of this review are reprinted in *Virginia Woolf: The Critical Heritage*, ed. R. Majumdar and A. McLaurin (London: Routledge, 1975), 400–401.

> Mrs. Woolf in her novels makes masterly use of the reflecting mind's haziness and inconsequence to build up, out of images, a brilliant picture; and admiring readers, stimulated by this poetic process, are sometimes misled into supposing that it constitutes her chief artistic equipment. It is in her criticism, whether of books or institutions, that the keen edge of *her other tool* becomes apparent; and that other tool is *precision, consequence, logic, directed by an irony that is sharp but never inhuman.* Mrs Woolf seldom writes a pamphlet, but she is the most brilliant pamphleteer in all of England. (Emphasis mine)

22. Quentin Bell, *Virginia Woolf: A Biography* (New York: Harcourt Brace Jovanovich, 1972), 2:205.

23. Joan Russell Noble, ed., *Recollections of Virginia Woolf by Her Contemporaries* (New York: William Morrow and Company, 1972), 195. *Three Guineas* has continued to provoke hostility in ways that suggest its message still strikes at the core of cherished values. See, for example, Theodore Dalrymple's "Blame it on Bloomsbury," in the *The Guardian*, August 17, 2002. Dalrymple says of *Three Guineas*, "never were the personal and the political worse confounded."

24. Virginia Woolf, *Three Guineas* (London: Hogarth Press, 1938; New York: Harcourt Brace Jovanovich, 1938), 11; 85. Here and throughout I follow the pagination of the Harcourt paperback edition, indicated as follows: TG 11; 85.

25. Baier's 1990 presidential address to the Eastern Division of the American Philosophical Association, entitled "A Naturalist View of Persons," is published in *The Proceedings and Addresses of the American Philosophical Association* 65 (1991): 5–17; reprinted in the paperback edition of *Moral Prejudices* (Cambridge, MA: Harvard University Press, 1995), 313–26. The Carus lectures, delivered in 1995, have been published as *The Commons of the Mind* (Chicago and LaSalle, IL: Open Court, 1997).

26. See Nigel Nicolson's introduction to vol. 5 of *The Letters of Virginia Woolf: The Sickle Side of the Moon* (New York: Harcourt Brace Jovanovich, 1979), xvi:

Her refusal of titular honors one can understand; but proudly to turn down the Clark lectures, when she was the first woman to be invited to give them, only weakened the cause of women in general, and contrasts with her natural eagerness to win literary recognition, to accept, for example, the award of the Femina prize for *To The Lighthouse.* Applause for a serious lecture delivered in a college hall is not different in kind from applause for a book in the *Times Literary Supplement,* but she persuaded herself that it was, perhaps rationalising her dislike of lecturing, or because it would have been inappropriate for the audience to boo.

Nicolson's introduction also contains a condescending and unsympathetic account of Woolf's "feminism," which he thought "anachronistic." His recent book in the Penguin Lives Series is marred by similar condescension. He misses the point, I think, of many of Woolf's complaints, as evidenced by his reference to "school-*girls*" in the following passage:

> In later life Virginia would sometimes complain that she was denied the educa-
> tion that was given automatically to boys, but her protests were not consistent
> nor wholly justified. Once, in middle age, she wrote to Vita Sackville-West, who
> had reproached her for her lack of "jolly vulgarity," that she had had no chance
> to acquire it. "Think how I was brought up! No school; mooning alone among
> my father's books; never any chance to pick up all that goes on in schools—
> throwing balls; ragging; slang; vulgarities; scenes; jealousies!" But would she
> have become a different, more rounded person if she had experienced this all in
> company with *schoolgirls* instead of with her siblings? (Nigel Nicolson, *Virginia
> Woolf* [New York: Viking Penguin, 2000], 9, emphasis mine)

Woolf was clearly referring to the sort of education that *boys* were in fact given, not to the sort of education that girls *would have been given* had they been sent to school. For more on Nicolson's criticisms, see note 32 below.

27. Joyce Jenkins has noted (in private correspondence) the sharp contrast between the alleged epistemological advantages of poverty so-defined and the epistemological disadvantages of what we might call the "ordinary poverty" of the Indian women mentioned above and discussed at length by Sen. (See note 12.) Jenkins objects that the example of the Indian women provides reason to be wary of the "traditional teachers"—or at least of poverty as a reliable teacher. I agree, and think that Woolf herself clearly shares this concern, both in *A Room of One's Own* and in *Three Guineas.* But this concern seems to me compatible with her insistence that even ordinary poverty may have its epistemological advantages, in the sense that it renders its subjects better able (than economically more privileged subjects) to appreciate certain realities. Woolf seems to me to be a kind of "standpoint theorist," in the sense explained by Nancy C. M. Hartsock in "The Feminist Standpoint," in *Discovering*

Reality: Feminist Perspectives in Epistemology, Metaphysics, Methodology, and Philosophy of Science, ed. Sandra Harding and Merrill B. Hintikka (Dordrecht, Holland: D. Reidel). I should note, however, that I think that Hartsock and others err in casting standpoint theory in terms of the *possibility* of appreciating certain realities rather than *facility* in appreciating certain realities: it is significant and worth worrying about if certain social positions—such as those associated with class or gender—simply make it more difficult (even if not impossible) to appreciate certain realities.

28. For this point, and for much more general inspiration, I am indebted to Tom Berry.

29. Woolf had good relationships with her full brothers, Thoby and Adrian Stephen, especially Thoby, for whom her novel *Jacob's Room* was a kind of eulogy. She also came to have close relationships with several of Thoby's friends, especially Lytton Strachey and Leonard Woolf. Her relationships with her half-brothers George and Gerald Duckworth were rather different.

30. Recounted in the posthumously published memoirs collected in Virginia Woolf, *Moments of Being* (New York: Harcourt Brace Jovanovich, 1976).

31. Baier, "A Naturalist View of Persons," n. 26.

32. This would undermine Nigel Nicolson's objection, quoted in note 26 above. But Nicolson is an unsympathetic editor who is in my view far less successful than Woolf is in living up to his professed standards of consistency. Consider the following passage, again from his introduction to vol. 5 of Woolf's letters.

> It is worth investigating why Virginia took up the cause of women so heatedly. There is no doubting the strength of her feeling, *but nothing in her own life, nor in the lives of her close friends explains it*, which makes her protest unselfish and all the more impressive. *It was true that she and Vanessa had not been sent to Universities, as both her brothers were*, but Vanessa went to art school and she was taught Greek and Latin professionally. . . . Among her friends, only Ethel Smyth considered that her career had been thwarted by male dominance, and Virginia thought her wailing embarrassingly strident. *Virginia liked men, and since her childhood had no upsetting relationship with any of them*. . . . [What she had written] *had all welled up from her childhood—the horrid masculinity of Leslie, George, and Gerald which had humiliated her and weakened her sexual nature*. . . . (xv–xviii; emphasis mine)

Concerning *Three Guineas*, Nicolson says (in the midst of the very passage just quoted):

> [Virginia] was an imaginative, emotional writer, and in *Three Guineas* attempted to use *for the first time* the apparatus of logic, scholarship, and politics, and the scope and shape of it were not suited to her particular cast of mind. (xvii–xviii; emphasis mine)

Perhaps Nicolson was simply too dim to recognize the appearance of logic, scholarship, and politics in her earlier works, particularly her essays. For the inconsistencies italicized in the first quotation suggest that he was no logical whiz. Perhaps, however, his claim that "nothing in her life nor in the lives of her close friends explains" the strength of Woolf's commitment to the cause of women is based partly on his apparent view that the "nasty erotic fumblings" of one's adult step-brothers are not all that upsetting, provided they stop short of rape. See Nicolson, *Virginia Woolf,* 12–13.

It is also worth noting, in connection with Nicolson's reference to Woolf's view of Ethel Smyth, Woolf's own letter to Smyth of 8 June 1933, printed in this very volume edited by Nicolson himself: Woolf recommended that Smyth contain her "strident wailing" not (as Nicolson suggests) because it was *unjustified,* but rather for *strategic* reasons:

> But my dear Ethel *your case is that there are a thousand others.* Leave your own case out of it; theirs will be far stronger. Enough, I only say this because— well, I didn't write 'A room [of one's own'] without considerable feeling even you will admit; I'm not cool on the subject. And I forced myself to keep my own figure fictitious; legendary. If I had said, Look here am I uneducated, be-
> cause my brothers used all the family funds which is the fact—Well, they'd have said; she has an axe to grind; and no one would have taken me seriously, though I agree I should have had many more of the wrong kind of reader; who will read you and go away and rejoice in the personalities . . . because they prove once more how vain, how personal, so they will say, rubbing their hands with glee, women always are.

All this leaves me wondering whether Nicolson really appreciated the material he was editing.

33. *The New Republic,* October 22, 1994.

34. Baier, *Moral Prejudices,* 298. For the *Chronicle's* reference to this passage, see the "In-Box" on p. A22 of *The Chronicle of Higher Education,* September 28, 1994. For Baier's letter, pointing out their mistake, see p. B4 of the November 9, 1994 issue.

35. See G. M. Young. "Women in the Modern World: Mrs. Virginia Woolf's Survey," *The Sunday Times* (London, England) June 19, 1938. Such failure to recognize irony is not limited to male reviewers; see Q. D. Leavis's review of *Three Guineas* in the September 1938 issue of *Scrutiny,* pp. 203–14; reprinted in Majumdar and McLaurin, *Virginia Woolf: The Critical Heritage,* 409–19.

36. The term "convergence" may mislead if it is taken to suggest that one always finds the reviewer's judgment in accordance with one's own prior judgment: being persuaded out of one's own prior view into the reviewer's view counts here as a form of convergence, and there is no reason to assume that a reviewer whom one legitimately regards as a "second self" would not sometimes, if given the opportunity,

be persuaded out of his prior views into one's own. In-principle reciprocity is important here. It is just that our relationships with reviewers are in fact rarely reciprocal in the requisite way.

37. Carlin Romano, "Between the Motion and the Act," *The Nation*, November 15, 1993. Romano's misreading of MacKinnon's views, which suggests falsely that she draws no distinction between the imagination or depiction of rape and real physical rape, is echoed in Dalrymple's misreading of *Three Guineas*. In the article cited in note 23, Dalrymple says:

> [Woolf's] inability to distinguish metaphor from literal truth is unremitting. Discussing the struggle for female emancipation, she says: "It is true that the combatants did not inflict flesh wounds; chivalry forbad; but you will agree that a battle that wastes time is as deadly as a battle that wastes blood." As deadly? Over and over she lets her rage blind her.

But it seems to me that it is *Dalrymple* who fails to distinguish (Woolf's) metaphor from the literal truth that he blindly—or perhaps willfully—misreads into the sentence he quotes.

38. See Richard Posner, "Obsession," in *The New Republic*, October 18, 1993. It is worth noting that *Three Guineas* too was charged by reviewers with trading in *emotion* rather than *argument*. See, for example, the review by Q. D. Leavis cited in note 35. This raises important questions about the relation between argument and emotion, questions about which Woolf herself had views and questions related to those (touched on above) about the alleged distinction between the cognitive and motivational aspects of our wills. Unfortunately, I cannot deal adequately with either set of questions here.

39. Rae Langton, "Speech Acts and Unspeakable Acts," *Philosophy and Public Affairs* 22 (1993): 293–330.

40. Ronald Dworkin, "Women and Pornography," *The New York Review of Books*, October 21, 1993, p. 38.

41. One of my undergraduate students at Pittsburgh once made the very perceptive remark that the argument of *Only Words* would be clear to someone—and perhaps *only* to someone—who had read MacKinnon's more academic articles. We need to keep in mind both the intended audience of *Only Words* and the various factors that might have led MacKinnon to adopt so different a method of presentation of what is clearly, as my student saw, the argument of her more academic works. Perhaps it was frustration with the repeated failure of people to be moved by her arguments when they were presented in the academic mode.

42. See TG 95, where Woolf recommends that the daughters of educated women, in order to become acquainted with the facts of politics, "read at least three different papers, compare at least three different versions of the same fact, and come

to [their] own conclusion[s]." Woolf herself often read papers with widely different points of view.

43. One can of course question the extent to which women have in fact been free from unreal loyalties. For example, consider the white mothers who opposed the desegregation of schools not because it involved bussing their own children away but because it involved bussing children of color in.

44. The passage continues:

> When all these comparisons have been faithfully made by the use of *reason*, the outsider will find herself in possession of very good reasons for her indifference. She will find that she has no good reason to ask her brother to fight on her behalf to protect "our country". "'Our country,'" she will say, "throughout the greater part of its history has treated me as a slave; it has denied me education or any share in its possessions. 'Our' country ceases to be mine if I marry a foreigner. 'Our' country denies me the means of protecting myself, forces me to pay others a very large sum annually to protect me, and is so little able, even so, to protect me that Air Raid precautions are written on the wall. Therefore if you insist upon fighting to protect me, or 'our' country, let it be understood, soberly and rationally between us, that you are fighting to gratify a sex instinct which I cannot share; to procure benefits which I have not shared and probably will not share; but not to gratify my instincts or to protect myself or my country. For," the outsider will say, "in fact, as a woman, I have no country. As a woman I want no country. As a woman my country is the whole world." (TG 108–9)

One is reminded here of the ancient skeptical strategy in which consideration of equally balanced arguments on opposing sides is supposed to lead to suspension of judgment. The conclusion, however, is reminiscent of the cosmopolitanism of ancient cynics, who claimed Socratic (and so arguably a kind of skeptical) pedigree for their views.

45. "What really seemed wrong with the book . . . was the attempt to involve a discussion of women's rights with the far more agonising and immediate question of what we were to do in order to meet the ever-growing menace of war." See Quentin Bell, *Virginia Woolf*, 2:205.

46. See E. M. Forster, "What I Believe," in *Two Cheers for Democracy* (New York: Harcourt Brace, 1951): "I hate the idea of causes, and if I had to choose between betraying my country and betraying my friend, I hope I should have the guts to betray my country."

47. See my "Impersonal Friends."

48. Donald Ainslie has questioned (in private correspondence) the extent to which the content of my friend's character really is independent of the various relationships in which she stands to others (including me). His idea is presumably

that my friend's character is partly shaped by the sorts of people to whom she is re-lated (myself included) and the sorts of relationships in which she stands to them. But this point—about *sorts* of people and *sorts* of relationships—is not something I mean to deny. My point is rather about *particular* instances of the relevant *sorts* of people and the relevant *sorts* of relationships. My friend, even had she never known me, might nevertheless have been similarly enough related to similar enough others for her to have had, in spite of my absence, the same basic character that she in fact has thanks in part to her actual relationship to me. So my point does not require us to disparage the *actual* contributions we make to the *actual* characters of our friends.

49. If you fail to admire those who resemble you in this respect, this suggests that you do not value justice *as such*. It may suggest that you are egocentrically at-tached to your *own* justice—that you desire, arguably incoherently, that *your* justice exceed the justice of *others*. But this raises a question about your commitment to jus-tice as such. For further discussion of the notion of "moral competition" among vir-tuous agents—a notion that is often but I think wrongly attributed to Aristotle—see my "Self-Love and Authoritative Virtue: Prolegomenon to a Kantian Reading of *Eudemian Ethics* viii 3," in *Aristotle, Kant, and the Stoics: Rethinking Happiness and Duty*, ed. Stephen Engstrom and Jennifer Whiting (Cambridge: Cambridge Univer-sity Press, 1996), 162–99.

50. See Baier, "How to Get to Know One's Own Mind," 75.

51. Think, for example, of the difficulty even a scientist with impressive cre-dentials might have in trusting her own judgment where it conflicts with that of the majority of recognized experts in her field.

52. For more on this point, see the discussion of what I call "ethical selection" in my "Impersonal Friends."

53. Woolf, *A Room of One's Own*, 3.

Because of their frequency, references in the notes to Descartes, Hume, Kant, and Annette Baier have been omitted.

JOYCE JENKINS
is associate professor of philosophy at the University of Manitoba, Winnipeg.

JENNIFER WHITING
is Chancellor Jackman Professor of Philosophy at the University of Toronto.

CHRISTOPHER WILLIAMS
is associate professor of philosophy at the University of Nevada, Reno.
